Crying with Cockroaches

Argentina to New York with two horses

marianne du toit

Published by Liendi Publishing
Molyneaux House
Bride Street
Dublin 8
Ireland

Copyright @ Marianne Du Toit 2007
2nd Edition, first published November 2006

www.tatachallenge.com

The moral right of the author has been asserted

Designed and typeset by Carla Benedetti at Designetc.
Printed by GraphyCems Ltd., Spain
Unless otherwise credited, all photographs from the author's collection.
No 1 Gaf Du Toit; No 5 Magadalena Trigo; No 11 Sheila Misdorp; No 70 Melania Iglesias;
No 101, 103, 115 Joy S MillerUpton; No 102 Mary Muldoon; No 106 & 107 Louisa Emerick;
No 108 Terry Toole; No 110 Lou Ann Coleman; No 115 Andy Webb; No 117 Turlough O'Sullivan

A catalogue record for this book is available from the British Library.

ISBN 13 978-0-9553714-0-0
ISBN 10 0-9553714-0-6

*To my mom and dad
who gave me wings,
and to my horses
for helping me to fly*

ACKNOWLEDGEMENTS

I would like to thank my parents Gaf and Rea, my brothers Stefan, Neil and Francois and Jeanette for their unconditional love and support when I needed it most. It meant everything to me. I am grateful to Turlough for his true friendship, the laughter and his continuous encouragement. Special gratitude goes to Cornet, my cousin and friend, who rooted for me non-stop. I count myself lucky for having Antoinette in my life, my best friend in South Africa, who proved to be a constant source of positive energy during this adventure. I can not even begin to thank Deirdre who travelled every kilometre with me in spirit and without whom this journey would have been nearly impossible. Fiona, friend and confidante, who, typical of her sparkling and joyful personality, encouraged me enormously from the very beginning and whom I knew was very proud of me. I am indebted to Dave, friend of many years, who taught me so much about life and living. His optimism and consistent friendship carried me through the good and bad times. Tracy, who kept my spirits up, had faith in me and who helped wherever she could. Tony, for his wisdom and good vibes, always reminding me of the magical side of life. Caroline for her warm support and my dear friend Jean Larmurier for his numerous hand-written letters that I picked up at different embassies in Latin America. Mrs Kilmartin, whose regular prayers to Saint Christopher no doubt kept me safe. I am also thankful to Nicola who did the Spanish translations during my journey with great panache and goodwill.

Heartfelt thanks as well to each and every person who believed in me and who gave support in every which way. Each gesture was noted and very much appreciated. For the purposes of this book I was forced to be selective about the stories I was going to include. It was impossible to name each single individual whose assistance and kindness hugely contributed to the TATA Challenge. You know who you are. Thank you so much.

I am very lucky to have had the know-how and literary expertise of Brian Kilmartin, Turlough O'Sullivan, Sheila Misdorp, Tim Carey, Denis O'Callaghan, Dave Kilmartin, Fiona McGrath and Cathy Cooney who so unselfishly assisted me with the editing of my book. Their input and suggestions were invaluable. I can not thank them enough.

My sponsors played a major role in this challenge. Without their generosity my travels would have remained just a dream. I am very grateful for the contributions of two Irish philanthropists who wish to remain anonymous. A big thank you also to DHL (specifically Vicky La Touche-Price), Dell, IBEC, RehabCare, Conn's Cameras, Dairygold, One on One Productions, The Irish Times, Scant Design, Aughinish Alumina, Bausch & Lomb, Royal Liver Assurance, CRH, Townlink Construction, Lazcar International, Musgrave Limited, Lola Mora, Herbalwise, Horseheaven, Chanelle Veterinary Group, Zero One, Lady Chryss O'Reilly, Deirdre and Sean Keane, Cadburys, Pennys, ABN-AMRO, Baxter Healthcare S.A., Kayfoam Woolfson, Compaq, Aisling Foundation, Dulux Paints Ireland, Ronny Turner Clinic, Arup Consulting Engineers, BIM Irish Sea Fisheries Board, Connaught Electronics, Easons, Barclays, Nestle, Guinness Ireland, Transitions Optical, PJ Carroll, Horgans Delicatessen Supplies, United Drugs, Coyle Hamilton, Jurys Doyle Hotel Group, Miguel Reznicek, Los Sargentos, Juan Rafael Lizano, Luis Frances, Alfredo Fernandez, Cordova family, Sarka and Osvaldo, Virginia Thoroughbred Association, L. Trice Gravette IV, Ellie Shapiro, Kathleen Crompton, Mary & Dante, Gone Away Farm, Ginger Brown and family, Joel and Diane Johnson, Chantilly Turf Farms, Doroty H. Klashburn, Todd and Maria Merritt, Betsy J. Healey, Mary Ann Stiffler, Robert Hunker, Alltell, Outfitters Supply, Sam Quick, the Holland family and the Leaches.

Lastly I would like to express sincere thanks to Carla Benedetti who did such a wonderful job with the design of my book, Mr Albert Reynolds for organising my participation in the New York St. Patrick's Day parade and An Taoiseach Bertie Ahern for launching my book.

CONTENTS

Prologue

They saw it long before I did. Mise had a slight tremble and Tusa's ears were erect. I looked around to see the cause of their edginess but saw nothing. We were on a spacious stretch of grass, on the side of a busy road, 45 kilometres from Jesús Maria. Tusa was attached to the saddle by a brand new leading rope. About fifteen yards to the left were railway tracks. My eyes followed the line northwards and then I spotted it too. It made little noise but it became bigger and longer as it curved towards us. Our first train.

These were early days and I was still getting to know the horses. What will make them jump? What will startle them? What are they comfortable with? I looked at the train approaching faster now and thought it wise to move away further from the tracks and more towards the road. I patted Mise on the neck and spoke to her in a soothing voice.

"Okay, okay, take it easy. It's only a train."

By the time the train was directly opposite us, we were a safe distance away. Or so I thought. The carriages kept on rumbling past, they must have seemed like prehistoric reptiles on the attack to the horses. Without warning Tusa bolted and took off. The rope did not break and Mise followed awkwardly in hot pursuit. I was caught completely off-guard and clung on to her for dear life as they charged towards the main road. I managed to grab on to the reins but could not bring Mise to a stop. Tusa was stronger and his fear and brute force kept dragging us along. I feared the worst.

At one point I almost became detached from what was happening. I could see the three of us, out of control, heading straight into danger, but there was nothing I could do. I was aware of traffic and trucks on the road and I felt hopeless. *Oh God, is this how we will meet our end? We have not even conquered Argentina yet. There is still so much to see and do.* What happened next was a blur. All I could hear was the sound of hooves on tarmac, hooting, the screeching of brakes and then the silence.

The smell of burned tyres filled my nostrils. The truck came to a halt, not more than four yards away from where Tusa had been forced to stop by a fence on the other side of the road. I had difficulty catching my breath. My body trembled and I felt weak. I looked at the truck driver and he stared back at me, wide-eyed. Nobody spoke. Nobody moved. We just stood there, breathless. You could feel the relief hanging in the air. Mise snorted and sighed. I was too shocked to cry. A range of emotions swept through me but I could not give any of them a name. The truck roared away. Cars passed, motorists waved but I had no strength, even to lift my arm. My eyes were transfixed by the long black marks on the paved road.

Oh My God! This is crazy. How could I ever have thought I was up for a journey like this? What have I let myself in for?

1. INTRODUCTION

"Those who say it can not be done should not interfere with the person doing it"
— Chinese Proverb

This is my story. My hope is that it will entertain and inspire. Some might say this is a tall order – not even the best written books always get that crucial combination right. But I said 'hope' and even if it entertains one and inspires another, then I will be happy. If reading my book makes you chuckle to yourself at times or stirs something in you – maybe a craving for adventure or a feeling that you want to follow your dream, a desire to change things about your life or simply to be a better person and to be kind to the world. If that is what you get when reading this book, then I have achieved my goal.

I had to be true to myself when I wrote about a journey that took me across two continents on the back of a horse. For more than eighteen months, my most frequent companions were two loyal friends who neighed and broke wind at regular intervals. Nobody or nothing annoyed me more than these two could but nobody or nothing managed to make me smile in the way they did.

Being competent in all things equestrian, I soon realised, was not the most important prerequisite for a journey like this.

I remember how, before I left, one of my sponsors who loved horses and rode regularly said, "You must be an amazing horsewoman to do this."

If only she had known how inexperienced and afraid I was. I soon found out that to do a trip of this magnitude, travelling in solitude most of the time, having to manage and control two horses for eight, nine, ten hours a day, finding places to sleep and things to eat, dealing with strangers who speak foreign tongues – being an amazing horsewoman was not what would enable me to do this. One had to have other qualities. Time was going to tell if I had the perseverance and determination to see things through. Humour and a touch of madness was going to help a great deal too.

Some might argue that I had stars in my eyes before I commenced a journey of this scale. My response was 'ignorance is bliss'. Had I known how difficult this journey was going to be, I would never have attempted it. Thank God, I did not have a clue. This trip was the most important thing I have ever undertaken. It showed me that I am capable of a lot. It showed me that I could do so much more than what I had thought possible. It also showed me that nearly anything is possible. I say 'nearly' because I do believe that not everything is possible. It sounds good on paper but reality is different. I am not saying that to deprive anyone of hope. All I want to get across is that I truly feel that most things within reason – yes, I know that is quite subjective – can be accomplished. But sometimes it takes more than want, desire, determination or will. I think it has to do with luck but others told me that is not so.

Oprah Winfrey, the well known American talk-show host says there is no such thing as being lucky.

As she puts it, "There is only preparation, meeting the moment of opportunity." I agree to some extent but I do believe that luck plays some part as well. I do not necessarily conclude that everybody creates her own luck. I think it is more mystical than that. Luck to me is something that happens when you are in the right place at the right time. I was lucky that people believed in me. I was lucky that people were willing to be generous, enabling me to undertake this journey. I was lucky that most people reckoned I was not totally insane to have wanted to do this.

I worked hard, I organised, I planned. But luck was on my side too.

2. PLANNING AND HOPING

"But you can't even ride a horse"
      — Gaf Du Toit

There is a time for everything.

A time to weep and a time to laugh, a time to mourn and a time to dance, a time to keep and a time to throw away...

Even though I had, for many years, harboured the dream to undertake a long journey across foreign lands, I was waiting for the right time to make this dream a reality. I had to feel right about where I was, how I saw my future, where I thought I fitted into this crazy, compelling, exciting and often frustrating world. Others might argue that journeys of this sort are undertaken exactly for the opposite reasons – the wannabe adventurer is confused and has no clue about his or her purpose and place in the world. They want to go off to 'find' themselves. Maybe I should rephrase – the timing for me was right because I felt, more than ever, a pressing need to explore, to dare, to experience. The itch to go out there and do something different overwhelmed any other desire or ambition I had. So truthfully, I did not have my life sussed out, nor did I know what the future held. But for me the timing was perfect, perfect to seek new horizons, get out of my rut, saddle up and follow my heart. It was right because, to me, it felt right.

This did not mean of course that just because the time was right everything would fall into place and that there would be no difficulties and headaches. No, it simply meant that I could better deal with all those hiccups and challenges because the conviction was there that this was now the right time to shake loose and push myself that extra bit. My utter conviction that I simply *had* to see this through gave me the determination to proceed with my planning, despite the fears and doubts of those around me and the silent nagging inside me that this was lunatic stuff.

It was clear to me that my journey had to be on horseback. I had already done a three month cycling trip through Europe in 1991 and fancied the idea of a horse for company this time around. I never thought I would need two. Another major question hanging over my head was where exactly I was going to undertake these travels. In the frame were Africa, Europe and North America. It did not take me long to decide that for a girl travelling alone, Africa would be just that bit too dangerous. Europe I considered too tame and unexciting for horseback travels so that left North America.

The idea of going from East to West Coast appealed to me but it was reading *Tschiffely's Ride* that made up my mind for me.

Aimé Tschiffely, whose name is inextricably linked to long distance horse riding, was from an old Swiss family. He was educated in Berne and later taught in Buenos Aires. Some people claim he used his vacations to explore the *pampas* on horseback, others say that he had no prior equestrian knowledge to fall back on before his burning adventurous spirit eventually spurred him on to undertake his famous 10,000 mile journey in 1925 with his much loved native Argentine horses, Mancha and Gato.

At least I had possibly one thing in common with Tschiffely, relative inexperience in equine matters.

With rugged determination the trio traversed the *pampas*, scaled the Bolivian Andes, struggled through Peruvian sands, swam crocodile infested rivers in Colombia and fought their way through the jungles of Panama. They crossed Central America through countries devastated by years of war to reach the United States and perhaps, for horses, the greatest danger of all – tarmac roads and speeding traffic, for which reason journey's end was Washington DC more than two years later.

The book had me mesmerised. It was as if I was meant to read it. As if I was meant to attempt to follow his footsteps. But the book also terrified me. This is not what I had planned. I imagined travelling for three to six months on horseback, not two years! I could not ignore though the story of incredible equine endurance and it was as if a power greater than myself urged me to go for it. My relief was profound once I had my mind made up. I was thrilled. Thrilled and scared. Not only would I be riding through the United States, but I would also get the chance to wander through South and Central America for the first time. Even though the magnitude of what I was planning threatened to choke me at times, it felt good to be able to know what continents we would be exploring at least.

In May, 2001, I spotted a reading of my Libran star-sign in a magazine;

There is such a far-away look in your eyes, no-one seems to be able to reach you. You are pondering journeys, adventures and other fish to fry. It is fun doing the contemplation. But it is when you try and put your thoughts into action that reality strikes. If you want to take off in any sense then you are really going to have to get your act together.

It was so true. Initially my discipline did not match my enthusiasm. My head was full of ideas about what I wanted to do but fear of the unknown prevented me from putting tangible expression to my desires. I felt safe in the notion that I *knew* I wanted to do something unique. I was reluctant though to share my dream with others. I had no doubt that making my plans public, even to a few close friends, would force me to go ahead. It was a terrifying thought. But after months of toying with the idea, I finally took the plunge and let a small number of people into the secret. Their responses were different but they all had the same theme – "we will support you, no matter what".

I swore them to secrecy. These were the infant stages of a large undertaking and I needed to protect what I was planning until things were more secure and definite.

Dave, a friend I have known for many years, laughed.

"You have nothing to worry about. Do you really think somebody on hearing about your plans would jump up and say, 'This is it. I'm going to travel across two continents on horseback'."

I was serious though and made it clear that nobody else was to be informed just yet.

"You can never be too careful," I emphasised.

It turned out that my 'paranoia' was justified. A few weeks before I set off to Buenos Aires, a girl in a health shop in Dublin, informed me of her two friends who "are planning to do Tschiffely's Ride". My heart stopped for a moment. She did not notice and continued.

"Yes, and they hope to talk to Gordon Roddick" [he attempted Tschiffely's ride but did not succeed].

I heaved a sigh of relief. Been there, done that. I had already met him. I forced a smile.

"Great. I wish them luck."

I was clearly well ahead of these two girls in my planning. I wondered if they would proceed once they found out somebody else was attempting the same adventure. I felt sorry for them, but only momentarily. At that point, I had already put in too much time and energy to hand my dream over to somebody else.

I was thinking big and knew my planned journey would attract attention. I had no doubt that others would benefit from the exposure. I also knew from the start that I wanted to support and increase awareness for a specific cause. Therapeutic riding was mentioned and soon I decided it fitted in quite well with my expedition.

Therapeutic riding gives an opportunity to an individual with special needs (physical or mental) to experience the benefits of horse riding. The horse's synchronised and repetitive movements are very similar to the human gait, improving the rider's balance, body symmetry, muscle tone, and head and neck control. There are also cognitive and emotional benefits. But the real reward of this highly effective therapeutic treatment is witnessing the look on a child's face, sitting astride a horse, beaming and confident at doing something 'normal' and challenging, discovering abilities and strengths they never knew they had.

In June 2001, I made the following 'to do' list:

Write to potential patrons
Identify and write to some companies requesting sponsorship, especially equipment
Decide on fundraising ideas and start organising
Start planning the route

I needed a catchy name for my project. I asked everybody I knew to come up with something but, secretly still felt I should be the one to choose the title. After many funny and some not so funny attempts at different abbreviations, I eventually decided on TATA. It stood for Travels Across The Americas. But 'tata' can also mean 'goodbye' and 'ta' means 'thank you'. I thought it most appropriate. I wanted to say thank you for a full life and for opportunities that came my way, thank you for being in a position to be able to undertake such extraordinary travels. And the other meaning of 'tata' was inevitable. To leave, one had to say goodbye.

Naming the horses was another headache for a while. I wanted something different so when the Irish words, Mise (pronounced Misha, meaning 'me') and Tusa (meaning 'you') were mentioned, it sounded right immediately.

I was advised that I definitely needed patrons. "People need to know that your journey is supported by people in the spotlight," was the general feeling. I could think of many names but it was important to choose ones that would fit in with what I was doing. Individuals who had an understanding of what I was planning to do. Above all I needed genuine support.

Gordon Roddick, Financial Director of the Body Shop and husband of Anita Roddick, founder of the same company, was the first person I asked. Endless emails were sent between his PA and me before I finally managed to meet him face to face at their offices in London. Gordon wanted to emulate Tschiffely's ride in 1974 but after a couple of months on the road, one of his horses had an accident and had to be put down. Anita and their three young daughters were back in England and for reasons of his own he decided not to continue with the journey.

Gordon decided to help me with contacts rather than substantial sponsorship. We met up in London. I was nervous. I had heard he was a very nice man and that was true. He has doubts though about my travelling alone. He relayed stories of how he was under threat of attack in some places and how dangerous the route was. He tried his utmost to convince me to take somebody along but soon gave up.

"You're a stubborn girl. I can see you won't change your mind."

It was clear that he also had doubts as to whether I would ever set foot in Argentina with two horses.

"A lot of people have come to see me. Everybody wants to do Tschiffely's ride."

I did not feel the need to convince him of my determination to see this through. Time would tell.

Gordon gave me a letter of support but I thought it sounded negative. He mentioned how he had tried to persuade me not to travel alone. I asked for another, more uplifting few words. I was happy with his next offering;

It was not hard to catch the glint of determination in Marianne's eye and I assessed that it was probably a sign of sure success in her quest. I am happy to give her my support for this venture and I can understand her drive and determination to do such a journey. I attempted it myself for the very same reasons.

In Dublin, a friend told me about Caroline Casey, an Irish woman my age, who was visually impaired but nevertheless travelled on an elephant through India, covering 1,000 miles.

On a bright Tuesday afternoon I took the train to her house. We shared a bottle of red wine while Caroline read my letter from Gordon, her nose only a few inches away from the paper in her hand. It was not long since she had returned from her trip so she could share in the energy and excitement bursting out of me for my own expedition.

"I would be honoured to be a patron of your project," she said with a wide grin.

Not long after I went to see her, she handed me a book that Mark Shand (brother of Camilla Parker Bowles) asked her to pass on to me after she had told him about my plans. *No Guns Big Smile* was written by James Greenwood after he had travelled 4,000 kilometres on horseback from Argentina to Peru in 1989. I wanted him to be a patron too and so I took the train from London to Wales where he lived.

A friendly face with at least a four-day stubble picked me up from the station. We drove to his farm in the middle of nowhere and chatted over pasta and wine. I was hoping James would give me some tips on what equipment to use but he told me nothing. Even though he was pleasant and jovial, he appeared cagey about what he knew and I was disappointed to leave with virtually no practical, much-needed advice from him. He had a positive demeanour though and reassured me that I would be just fine travelling through Latin America, a girl alone.

A work colleague mentioned the name Tracy Piggott. I had never heard of her but soon found out that not only was she a talented television presenter, mainly involved with horse racing, but also the daughter of one of the world's most famous jockeys, Lester Piggott.

I got hold of her number and left one message after another. After weeks of chasing, I managed to meet her for a quick coffee in the Radisson Hotel, near Dublin. She was easygoing and chatty and seemed delighted to have been asked to be patron of TATA. I was excited.

"This is it," I said to myself. *"Things are beginning to happen."*
Dave's email to me summed it up;

I'm delighted that your meeting with Tracy was so uplifting – such meetings are as important as any promise of cash. They keep your motivation, interest and passion high. They deepen the belief that you have what it takes. Once you keep going at the rate you are, the rest will fall into place.

Last but surely not least, was my fifth patron. I was unsure how somebody from the business world in Ireland would respond to news of what I was trying to attempt. I hoped Turlough O'Sullivan (Director General of the Irish Business and Employers Confederation) did not notice my sweaty palms when we shook hands in his office. He was known for his excellence when it came to letter writing and I reckoned it was a good start when he complimented me on mine to Gordon Roddick.

"I'm impressed with the letter. It's very well written and clear that you wrote from your heart."

The highlight of our meeting was his genuine enthusiasm for what I wanted to achieve. He vowed unconditional support and assistance and, since then, has never failed me once.

Fitness was another issue I could not ignore. I did yoga and skipped regularly in my apartment but needed more that that. I was clear in my mind that I had to get horse-fit. Not only that but I also had to get comfortable and acquainted with horses again.

I had not ridden in ages apart from a few spells at a couple of riding centres where all you had to do was mount an already tacked-up horse. My experience in South Africa, having been brought up on a farm amongst horses, was really the same. One of the helpers would get the horses ready and my brothers and I would go for a somewhat out-of-control gallop. At this point I would usually jump off. Back at the stables we would hand the horses back, having very little opportunity to learn the basics of horsemanship and horse maintenance. Up to the time that I had started to plan my journey, I had never in my life even lifted the foot of a horse.

I had to face the truth, even though I could not admit it to anyone. I was green when it came to equestrian skills. Those with an expert eye would probably have described me as a novice. The idea of a trail ride was alien to me. I could not remember ever having spent more than an hour on the back of a horse. Make no mistake, I adored horses but I was also secretly terrified of them – all that muscle, huge nostrils and powerful legs. I feared them but also could not get enough of them.

But I was a master at bluffing. I had no difficulty getting on a horse, no matter how spirited. Those watching were oblivious to the sickly feeling of trepidation and downright fear that took over my whole being whenever I got on a horse. I mentally prepared myself to meet the ground in uncomfortable and hurtful fashion while desperately trying to nonchalantly apply the basic few things I had in my head about horse riding.

During my journey across the Americas I soon came to realise though how much there is to be said for 'common sense'. I was fortunate to have had a fair dose of that. 'Common sense' was my saviour many a time. It was my guide when knowledge failed me. It showed me the way like the moonlight would on a very dark night. It proved to me that I had to trust my instincts and that it was okay to do that. The natural connection I felt with my horses was part of that instinct. Even though I lacked the experience, I intuitively knew what I needed to do to ensure their comfort.

A contact in Dublin mentioned a place where she rode regularly and indicated that they might let me use one of their horses a few days a week. I made arrangements to go and see them and, on a rainy Saturday morning, arrived at a very posh establishment on the outskirts of the city. A jockey turned trainer, half my height, took me to the stables where he introduced me to one of their most reliable hunters. He passed me the bridle and reins.

"Can you tack her up for your ride?" he said.

He watched me with an eagle-eye while I studied the piece of leather equipment in my hand.

"I need to use the bathroom," I said after an uncomfortable silence.

I said a silent prayer. *'Please God, let the horse be saddled up when I get back.'*

But it was not to be.

I tried first to get the bit in her mouth, then tried to figure out what to do with the breast plate. My awkward fumbling made the jockey step in.

"It doesn't look like you've ever done this before," he said before taking the equipment out of my hand.

I blushed and did not know what to say. In a patronising tone he continued to tutor me on the correct way of saddling up. We led the hunter outside and I got on. We came to a field.

"Take her around," he said.

I put the horse in a gallop immediately and tried to show off my equestrian abilities. I struggled somewhat to bring her to a halt and nearly ran the man over in the process.

Over coffee the jockey looked me square in the eye.

"I don't think you're ready to come riding here, just yet. I suggest you go for riding lessons first."

I looked at him sheepishly. "I'm not *that* incompetent," I said.

He shook his head. "I don't have the time and patience to show you the basics. You have confidence on the horse alright, but you need to learn a lot more."

I left with my tail between my legs. I was devastated and the impact of the jockey's words hung like a dark cloud over my head.

'*Feckit,*' I thought. '*I'm screwed.*'

It was a tricky situation. I could not go for riding lessons in Ireland; imagine the response once the publicity about my trip commenced. I could see the headlines already.

'*Woman attempting 10,000 mile journey on horseback goes for riding lessons.*'

My head spun. Even going to the UK was too close for comfort. I considered France for a moment. But not speaking French that would have been too challenging.

I was rattled by the verdict of the jockey but not enough to let him or my equine incompetence deter me from doing this journey. I thought that as long as I did not succumb on the road, I would be okay. I could cope with discomfort, disasters and even mockery. I would learn with each passing day. I would enter at the deep end but I would swim. Boy, would I swim!

I had my mind made up. Being an amateur horsewoman was not going to stop me undertaking the most important challenge of my life.

'*It can't be that difficult,*' I told myself over and over again.

In December 2001, Deirdre, my good friend in Dublin and her husband Sean handed me an extremely generous gift – an airplane ticket to South Africa for the last time to see my family, four months before I left for Buenos Aires. They instinctively knew how important this last contact was and I did not know how to properly express my gratitude.

Deirdre's incredible and selfless help before and during my travels was invaluable. She was so much part of this adventure and shared in every joy and setback along the way. The hundreds of emails between us were a testament to that. She was always there for me, no matter what.

I still have the going-away card she gave me, two days before I left Ireland.

What can I say? I can't believe the time has actually come for you to head off on your great and very exciting venture. I'm going to miss you so much. Thanks for letting me be part of the planning of your project. I have no doubt you will enjoy every moment and in lots of ways I envy your courage and energy. However, by the time the eighteen months is up, I hope to have lost my sensible side and be more carefree! I'm so happy for you. Only one good thing about your departure... my productivity at work will get back to normal once again! Have a fantastic time. Dee.

While at home, I had my very first radio interview with a South African radio station. It was in fact my first one ever. Feeling apprehensive I did not sleep much the night before. In case I drew a blank I had two sheets of paper covered with lines about my journey, my mission and my fears. I remember mentioning vampire bats in South America.

A friend commented afterwards, "You sounded out of breath."

I pulled a face. "Well, at least the listeners did not detect my heart beating in my chest."

With time I became more and more at ease with media matters, but being in the spotlight and the centre of attention never sat easily with me. I wanted to do things. I wanted to make things happen. It was never important to have my name or face 'out there' while doing that. Getting recognition was not what I was after. Making the difference was what mattered. But for this undertaking I needed media exposure and I was going to have to get used to it. It was a means to an end.

I had heard stories of how my dad in his younger days had jumped out of a second story hotel room into a pool to impress my mom and friends. So having been a bit of a dare-devil all his life, my dad was very proud when he learned of my plans. But he had his concerns, especially relating to my equestrian skills.

"But you can't really ride," he said with the utmost sincerity.

The worry on his face was clear. But he could see I had my mind made up. I treasure a note he wrote before I left for Argentina. He told me that he would think about me often, would miss me a lot but would also pray for me.

"Remember, you will never be really alone."

I often reminded myself of his true words, gaining strength from the power they had.

Francois, my youngest brother, had his doubts too. We climbed a hilltop behind the house at my father's farm.

"There are bad people in this world," my brother warned. "Why don't you take somebody with you?"

Being a natural horseman and always seeking adventure Francois would have loved to go, but his wife and three kids most likely did not share his enthusiasm. It was Francois that whispered to my family, "I think she has more guts than brains."

Neil, a brother two years older than me and true to his sensible nature seemed puzzled with my undertaking. I could not figure out what he made of it. And protective older brother Stefan was as direct as ever.

"I'm not sure if you'll be able to do this. It sounds a bit far-fetched to me."

My mom, always the nurturer and supporter, acted brave whenever we discussed my upcoming journey. I knew she was afraid but not once did she try to dissuade me.

One morning she said, "I had so many dreams about your trip last night. What type of hat will you be wearing?"

I hugged her. "That should be the least of your worries, mom."

I wished I could ease her fears. The only way to do that was to pretend that nothing was a big deal. When she asked where I would find lodging, food and how I would stay warm, I always had a ready answer. I'm not sure if she always believed me but she did a good job pretending.

Francois turned out to be the one who gave me my 'horse confidence' back. I spent a morning with him and patiently he went through all the aspects of saddling up a horse, handling feet and generally being at ease around them.

"Never hit a horse on the neck," he said. "That part of his anatomy should only be associated with pats and affection."

We took his frisky Arabian into a ring. The horse was already fired up and my heart was beating very fast. I felt like doing a runner.

But surprisingly all went well and when Francois said, "You're a much better rider than I thought," I punched the air with exhilaration.

That was all I needed to know. I felt so much more confident that I had proved to be a better rider than everyone had thought. Not fantastic I know, but not too bad either.

Back in Ireland, my biggest worry was finding sufficient sponsorship. In retrospect, I spent too much time chasing companies to sponsor me with certain much-needed products. But the reason I kept on chasing was straightforward; the more I got for free, the more cash would be left over at the end to go towards my aim of supporting therapeutic riding. I had the same thinking during my trip. I never stopped bargaining to get things cheap or 'on the house' and whenever I had to pay for accommodation, I chose the cheapest option. Friends would encourage me to 'spoil' myself after a difficult stretch and even though I was sometimes tempted to treat myself to a bit of luxury, I always ended up booking into the five to ten dollars a night room.

End of January 2002, three and a half months before leaving Ireland for Buenos Aires, I took a rather impulsive flight to Dubai. My aim: To track down the powerful Maktoum family to ask for financial assistance. I thought it was a sign of good things to come when on the way there I got upgraded to first class in Paris.

Renowned for their participation in and passion for horse endurance activities, I decided that the Maktoums and I had much in common. My task was easier said than done however. Not only are they jetsetters, spending lots of time in exotic places around the world other than Dubai, they are also well-protected. After five days of waiting in a low-grade hotel room, eating unexciting overcooked supermarket food, bored mindless by the one and only news-based English station on television, and many phone calls later, I finally headed for government offices not far from the commercial centre. It turned out one of the Maktoum men was Minister for Defence.

But I was a tiny insignificant fish in a very large ocean and despite my enthusiasm and round-the clock smiles I could not even grab the attention of his personal assistant. The red tape and bureaucracy one had to get past just to get a letter delivered to one of these powerful men was unbelievable. The guards at the entrance gates, dressed in traditional Muslim attire, tried to make up for my lack of success by offering strong espressos and syrupy cakes as they saw me walking past the barriers, rather deflated. Short on cash I returned to Ireland a day later.

The quest for sponsorship and financial aid continued. It took at least ten emails and numerous phone calls to the United Kingdom before I secured a first-aid kit for myself. I needed a tent, walking shoes, sunglasses, thermal under- and outerwear and other camping equipment. I walked from one outdoor shop to another and all I received were a series of rejections.

For many frustrating weeks I attempted to get a company in Ireland to provide me with a phone and service, free of charge. After an agonising wait and too many empty promises I finally gave up. I ended up purchasing a phone in Argentina and managed to use it as far as Salta in the northern part of the country. I went without telecommunications for the next eighteen months until I got to the USA. It took only a ten minute explanation to the manager of Alltell, a mobile phone company in Georgia, for me to become the happy owner of a brand new phone. Unlimited talking time within the States was thrown in. It made a tremendous difference.

Being a girl that does the 'clean, tone and moisturise' routine religiously every night, I knew I had to get a company to sponsor me with cosmetic products. Regrettably I failed and only later in my journey did I receive some tubes of high factor sun block from RoC.

I also imagined that Red Bull with their advertising emphasis on endurance and 'giving you wings' might be keen to 'sign on' but ultimately all I got from them were twenty-four cans of high energy drinks. I did not complain. It kept me going through the crazy times.

On the 8th of March I wrote on a piece of paper;

I have less than 2 months left before I leave the shores of the Emerald Isle for Buenos Aires. It is a blue day for me today. I received four reject letters for sponsorship and I can feel the disappointment in my gut.

However, there were many 'yeses' to come. DELL generously provided me with a laptop and my most significant sponsorship came from DHL Ireland. I still maintain that my journey would have been ten times the struggle without their involvement.

I was also extremely grateful to the Irish companies that donated towards the TATA Challenge. I have no doubt that they were bombarded regularly for sponsorship for different causes, yet they felt they wanted to support my adventure. And then there were the true philanthropists, entrepreneurs who had made millions and who helped me without expecting publicity, recognition or tax relief.

I always maintained that I did not expect individuals to give just because they had money. I was adamant they did not have a duty to help just because they were rich. Giving comes from the heart and I made sure never to make anybody feel obliged to assist financially. There were a few rejections from people I had hoped would assist but then again, doors opened in places where I never thought they would.

Dealing with negative people was another 'chore' I could have done without. Those encounters were draining and a waste of energy, yet I found myself in the beginning, time and time again, explaining and reassuring. Funnily enough, the majority of my close friends never expressed any pessimism. The doom and gloom came from strangers who had just heard what I was planning or acquaintances, who felt they had a licence to bombard me with their negativity. Later, I learned just to walk away. It was so important for my sanity and self-belief that I surrounded myself with people for whom the cup was half-full.

While looking for sponsorship from an equestrian shop I stumbled across a book by Ann Hyland on the endurance horse. Inside was a piece called, 'Buenos Aires to New York' – an account of Tschiffely's ride. Most of what I read was old news but it was the last few lines that gave me sleepless nights for a while;

Many long-distance treks, some races of prodigious length, have been achieved since Tschiffely's ride, but none has captured the imagination of so many nations, none lived as a legend, and no one I warrant has voluntarily undergone so many hazards, discomforts, and privations. Indeed with the constant South and Central America unrest today it would take an even more intrepid voyager to clear the hassle of paperwork, visas and permits, and inter-country vaccinations for the horses. Some things are easier, but danger there still is, particularly as half of those eleven countries live in a state of perpetual ferment.

My focus thankfully shifted when I read Ann's views on endurance horses. She mentioned the Arabian breed whom she believed truly meets the claims of excellence attributed to it. She then continued to sing the praises of the Criollo (pronounced criojo) horse which proved worth their weight in gold. According to Tschiffely these were the toughest horses alive, conditioned and bred for hundreds of years by the laws of nature. Since it reproduced mainly in the wild, the Criollo developed into an extremely hardy horse. Hunted by Indians and wild animals they learned to survive the extreme heat and cold, subsist with little water, and live of the dry grasses of the area.

In my limited experience and certainly after some thousand kilometres on the road, I realised this trip would have been too arduous for an Arabian horse. This is largely because of their digestive systems. My Criollo horses had to make do with a different diet almost on a daily basis and only once did Tusa have a sore tummy. I do not think that the Arabian would have had such a tough, accommodating and resilient gut. I believe this is what sets the Criollo apart. They are small but yet dynamic. They are more than the sum of their endurance abilities; they are also tractable, intelligent, willing and sensible. Like many others who have had the privilege of getting to know the Criollo intimately, I came to believe they were the perfect package.

My friend Eoin persuaded me to get a few self-defence classes under my belt. The instructor came out to the apartment, armed with a knife, stick and toy gun. He put me in different attack scenarios and I had to wriggle out of them, using the movements he showed me. It was a rough session and when my arms and legs developed purple-blue bruising by the second class, I did not arrange for another one.

In between working for a salary, fundraising, begging, getting fit and trying to stay sane, I also enrolled in Spanish classes. My busy schedule allowed me to attend about four out of twenty so instead I acquired 'teach yourself' Spanish CD's to listen to at night. Neither gave me even a basic level of proficiency.

Fiona, one of my best friends in Ireland, agreed to assume the official role of TATA Project Manager. With her journalist background, she was well qualified when it came to writing profile pieces for my website, responding to interested parties or assisting me in begging for stuff. We are so similar in character and like me, she also believes there is always light at the end of the tunnel, always a solution to any problem. I loved her uplifting emails throughout my travels, also sharing with me her own journey – that into motherhood.

Another friend offered to organise the logistics of the trip and I asked him to prepare a summary of every country I planned to go through. I needed to know what the requirements were, weather conditions, basic geography and very importantly, any health and safety issues I should familiarise myself with. It was a huge task but as it turned out, never came to fruition. My friend's dad fell seriously ill and I ended up leaving Ireland with hardly any information about the countries that lay ahead. It was clear that I was going to have to ad-lib and plan as we went along.

Seeing that I was soon going to spend most of my time with two horses, I arranged with a farrier to give me a rundown on shoeing these animals. Pepsi, a mare, was a saint and stood very still while it took me about half an hour to nail one shoe on. Despite only a few hours of training, my back and upper legs felt as if a bus had driven over them as I stiffly tried to get out of bed the following morning. I came to respect all good farriers for a skill that looks much easier than it is.

There were funny moments too. I remember a fundraising gig that left me with less than 50 euro profit after paying the band and the rent for the venue.

All the planning and anticipation of my forthcoming journey brought not only excitement but regrettably also some sadness. The hectic days prior to my leaving Ireland also saw the passing of Josephine, a dear friend to me and many others.

Jo was part of TATA from the word go and believed in me from the very beginning. The day after I had told her about my plans, she sent me an email;

> I had difficulty sleeping last night and I could not stop thinking about your trip. You make it sound like going shopping, just much more exciting!

It was not *me* and my project, but *we*.

Many a time she would say, "how are we for money, what are we going to do to get you more sponsorship, what will we do to get in touch with so and so?"

We worked for the same company and I still have visions of her coming into my office with a twinkle in her eyes, doing a little jig while holding out a cheque that had just came in. The negative responses had to be blacklisted immediately. "We'll never shop there!"

Two weeks before Jo left this world I rang her in hospital. She was heavily sedated and I struggled to have a conversation with her. She kept on asking about my trip. She needed to feel comfortable that things were happening.

"I want you to do me a favour," she whispered. "I want you to put up a wooden cross for me when you come to a beautiful place during your travels. Some place where you can see for miles and miles over mountains and valleys."

I had a lump in my throat. I felt like saying don't be silly, there is no need for crosses or discussions like this. I wanted to believe and I wanted her to believe that she was going to pull through. But there was such finality in her voice and I felt I had no choice but to tell her I would do as she asked.

Jo's presence was tangible every day and every mile as the horses and I traversed foreign lands. I spoke of her often and felt touched by the emotional responses of strangers. Tears were shared and glasses raised regularly in celebration of a very special woman.

Nothing about my trip and what I had planned was written in stone. I had to give an idea to people about what I anticipated and where I intended to go but these were subject to constant change. I said from the start that I would have liked to finish the trip in eighteen months. I only gave this time-frame because I had to. My mother would have had even more sleepless nights had I not set a date and my sponsors needed to know there would be a planned end to this 'lunatic' journey. That was it. I knew that most likely it would take longer, but two years just sounded so long. I relied heavily on the advice of locals and as a consequence, my plans changed all the time.

My best friend Antoinette in South Africa sent me a long letter a month before my departure. One part in particular stuck with me;

And you know what Marianne, I know that the way Peter and I lived in the jungles of Sumatra and Borneo will not be a patch on the ruggedness of the terrains you will have to pass through, but at the end of your journey we will have something in common. You would have learnt so much about everything around you but more so about yourself. How far you can push yourself, how much you can endure, how many times you fall only to pick yourself up again... And that is the part that you will never be able to put into words for others to understand. Because no-one can understand what you go through on a journey where you have grown as a person, where you have gone through so many internal journeys and where discovering yourself is what it is about.

*"We don't receive wisdom – we must discover it for ourselves
after a journey that no one can take for us or spare us"*
                                        — *Marcel Proust*

It would be wrong to say that I arrived at Buenos Aires airport with stars in my eyes. It was more like a steel grip around my throat. Also, it did not help that there was nobody to meet me. I managed to sleep well throughout the fourteen hour journey from Frankfurt but my appetite was gone. For me that is not a good sign. Feelings of apprehension filled me and I was relieved to be distracted by an Argentine businessman sitting next to me. He gave me a run-down on the situation in the country, politics and polo. When he heard me mention the name Zavaletta, he became animated.

"Aah, one of the polo players. They are considered the aristocracy in Argentina."

Before I could respond, he continued. "They are not well liked. The men who don't have much money marry women who do, or otherwise a model."

I smiled.

I knew very little of my host family except for the fact that Clemente Zavaletta was indeed a polo player and a contact through Gordon Roddick. I started corresponding with Clemente almost three months before my departure from Ireland. He assured me of his assistance with paperwork, vaccinations, finding the horses and whatever else I might need. My requirements for the horses were very specific. In an email to him I wrote;

I need two Criollos for my trip. Temperament is of course very important and if I could get two horses which are used to being handled, it would help a lot. It would be good if they were used to their feet being picked up and if they were not nervous when you go behind them or touch their hind quarters. It would also help if they were not the kicking type! I do like horses with character and who have a bit of fire in them but I would not like the trip to be a constant struggle with two difficult horses. The tamer and easier they are, the less hassle I will have, especially as one horse will take turns to be led (on a rope) behind the other horse. My friend said I should add that I would like them to be pretty. It's probably a female thing.

The plan was that Zavaletta would start looking for suitable Criollos. Once I arrived, I would go and view the ones he deemed worthy and make my choice. It was serious business. I had to choose two equine companions to walk with me every day of every week for probably eighteen months or more, until we reached our goal. They had to be special.

There is something quite reassuring, walking into a sea of people at Arrivals, spotting a familiar smiling face, obviously delighted that you have arrived safely. Even if it is a stranger picking you up, just seeing your name on a board and knowing someone is there for you is very comforting and welcoming. So needless to say, to set foot on Argentine soil with no, "Welcome to my country! How was your flight?"– made me feel somewhat deflated. My knowledge of Spanish extended to *"hola"* and *"por favor"*. I needed more than that. My body language was pathetic enough for an Argentine man to take me momentarily under his wing. His mobile phone was as foreign to me as the language he was speaking and he dialled the number of my hosts.

Sunday morning 8 a.m. was not a good time to ring the Zavaletta household. The man of the house was grumpy.

"I did not know you were going to be staying here," he said with a sleepy voice.

Somewhat embarrassed I replied, "I spoke to your wife or daughter two days ago to give my flight details. Gordon said that I could stay with you. I told him I will pay."

I could hear a whispering voice in the background and Clemente mumbled. "Take a taxi and come here."

It turned out to be almost an hour journey, south-east, towards Pilar.

"Que lindo" (how pretty), the taxi driver whistled through his teeth as we stopped at the security gate to enter La Emilia, the villa of the Zavalettas.

A man in his forties, with a dark tan and serious face stood at the top of the driveway. He looked momentarily shocked at the sight of my luggage. I could almost hear him think, *'You want to take that on a horse?'* Amelia, Clemente's effervescent wife made up for his luke-warm reception and literally welcomed me with open arms.

She was a pretty, petite woman with long blonde hair that looked as if it had not been cut since she was twelve. She was warm and glamorous and even more famous than her polo playing husband.

She was one of the *Las Trillizas de Oro* (the Golden Triplets) and she and her two sisters performed as back-up singers for Latino heartthrob Julio Iglesias for a few years. Even if nobody had told me this I would have gathered this information rather rapidly just by moseying through the house. Everywhere you turned there were pictures of the couple in their heyday.

I felt quite lonely that evening. Thoughts of the magnitude of my journey seemed overwhelming as I sat outside smoking a cigarette and throwing a ball for the resident Labrador.

A timely email from Dave, my friend in Ireland, lifted the spirits;

Mar,

As I sit down to let my thoughts roam through my hands to finally find their expression on this electronic page, the magnitude of the adventure and challenge that will be all yours comes immediately to mind. Envy, fear, excitement, awe and just plain 'fair fucks to you' are some thoughts and feelings that I have towards you in unison with your adventure. For you and the adventure are now one, you will live through it and it through you. Reflect on it, detach from it yet remain forever immersed in it. Always break that adventure up into small victories, victories not over the adventure but with it. Remember always why you chose it as your partner. And finally remember your horses – each in harmony representing and inspiring you and your adventure.

I was in a strange mood, waking up the next morning in a strange bed in strange surroundings. I stared at the ceiling for a long time. *'So this is it,'* I thought. *'I am in Argentina and soon I will be covering ground on the back of a horse.'* I found the idea quite incredible and my heart was thumping faster. There was so much that still needed to be done. *'Am I in the right place with the right people? Will Clemente and his family, my only contacts in the whole of Latin America, prove to be encouraging, positive, helpful? What if I can't find good horses? What if they are too expensive? What if I run out of money? What if I can't cope with the horses? What if we're in an accident? What if I simply can't hack it?'*

A call for breakfast broke my anxious thoughts and the sweet biscuits and coffee soothed my mind for a while. I was still hungry afterwards and wondered how I would last until lunch.

For the next week or so my life merged with that of the Zavaletta family. Church with Amelia and the girls was a peaceful experience even though I could not understand a word apart from *"Cristo"* and *"Dios"*. I helped the girls with their homework and offered to assist the mature and confident 14-year old Sonya with her *'controlling genes means controlling life'* debate for school. I acted as chaperone when her 19-year-old sister wanted to go clubbing in Buenos Aires and even had my first veterinary experience when I pulled out a piece of cloth that got stuck in the Labrador's backside.

Clemente, it seemed, had done nothing about finding potential suitable horses and blamed the stormy weather since my arrival for the lack of action. I refrained from mentioning our correspondence where he had committed to explore options while I was still in Ireland. I kept on thinking, '*I don't mind getting a bit wet to go and look at a few horses.*' But he was adamant.

"The roads are muddy and inaccessible and we must wait until the rains have stopped."

Clemente was not a man who smiled easily. I sensed that he could be moody and difficult. All I could do was wait. One would have thought that this waiting time would have given ample opportunity to improve my Spanish. Sadly, this was not the case. Everyone in the Zavaletta family had good English and I could not be bothered to attempt conversation in a foreign language amidst everything else that was on my mind. My sporadic attendance at the *Institito de Cervantes* back in Dublin showed and I could hear the lecturer's words echoing: "*Señorita* Marianne, you have a fine accent and pronunciation, probably better than most students in the class, but you know the least."

I brought CDs and a phrasebook along to perfect my Spanish once 'on the road'. The phrasebook especially was ideal. It had translations for almost every possible scenario. I would be able to say anything from 'My gums hurt', to 'Turn the TV off' to 'I'd rather not'. I would be able to discuss music, social issues, bull fighting, gay travellers and typical dishes. Attached to the hip, that little phrasebook would soon become my best friend. Even better than that, it would only be too happy to help out, never asking for anything in return.

During this time with the Zavalettas I got to befriend a national obsession, *dulce de leche,* a gooey sticky paste somewhere between toffee and condensed milk. As an ice cream flavour, dessert filling or spread on bread, it was impossible to escape it. It was literally everywhere. The Argentines claim their version is the best, made as it is from the purest fresh milk from cows grazing the *pampas.*

I loved the sumptuously rich taste and silky-smooth texture and found a finger dipped in a jar of *dulce de leche* to be the perfect solution for my sweet cravings. Not to mention its ability to counteract the bitter aftertaste of *yerba mate,* a type of tea which is grown mostly in South America and considered an institution in Argentina.

This bitter green tea is obtained by adding hot water to leaves held in a seasoned gourd. This gourd, or *mate* container, is then passed to each participant in a circle, who drains it through a metal straw called a *bombilla,* before refilling it with hot water for the next person.

I quickly came to understand that drinking *mate* was not only a social ritual but an important part of everyday life for Argentines. I found it endearing and reassuring that such a decorous ritual, a convivial part of these people's lives, had so much to do with intimacy and friendship between them. The fact that Argentines were so open and willing to share their *mate,* also with strangers, said more to me about their warmth and spirit than any other act of hospitality.

I have to be honest though that this practice, slurping from the same *bombilla*, left me squeamish at times, especially if the sharer before me turned out to have mostly rotten teeth and foul breath. Some people, especially women, simply refuse to share the same *bombilla* and had it not been for my desire to please, I probably would have said in some cases, *"No gracias,"* as well.

Throughout my journey I had a typical *mate* bag made from suede attached to the saddle. Inside were a flask, gourd, *bombilla* and *yerba mate*. Apart from its thirst quenching properties and caffeine-like effect, I found the mere fact that I was engaging in a ritual so dear to Argentines was something the local people appreciated very much. The bonding that the sharing of a *mate* could create between people was powerful and not to be underestimated.

It was six days before I got to see a Criollo for the first time. Clemente had finally made contact with José, the Secretary of the Criollo Association and it was arranged that the three of us would go out the following day. José looked like a pin-up *gaucho*, wearing traditional horseman clothes. His outfit consisted of *bombachas* (trousers of enormous width) and a crisp white shirt, completed with a cheeky red scarf around his proud Argentine neck. They say that the best business in Argentina is to buy an Argentine for what he's worth and then sell him for what he thinks he is worth. José would have bargained a good deal for himself.

"Do you speak Spanish?" he asked in his native tongue.

I shook my head left to right. He gave Clemente the eye and looked at me again. I could almost hear his thoughts.

'You foolish girl. You want to take a horse across my country and you don't even speak the language. You are in for some surprises.'

It did not bother me much that not another word was spoken to me by either man until we reached the farm more than an hour later.

There were five horses to pick from. They were all bundled into a dusty *corral* and, unceremoniously, I mounted the first one. The saddle and reins on the horse were typically *gaucho*, made from raw, hard leather and had an uncomfortable feel. The stirrups were too short but I said nothing. The horse was quiet in demeanour but had a funny trot.

'At least he might be able to amuse me during our long journey,' I thought with a smile.

José introduced the next horse with *"mucho espiritu"*. He had spirit and energy, for sure, but I found him difficult to handle and could not imagine him on the side of a busy road. I had my eye on a white horse whose pretty face I liked. He seemed calm enough until we started galloping. His head jerked up and down and I feared that he was going to knock me out. I prepared myself mentally for meeting the ground very soon and clung on awkwardly. He came to a snorting halt in front of Clemente who shook his head disapprovingly.

Another white horse was saddled up by one of the helpers.

After our spin, I announced with feigned confidence, "He seems to have some personality but at least is not as wild as the last one."

I received no reply.

Once I had dismounted, Clemente said, "The real test will be when I take him for a ride."

I had to suppress a snort myself. In true show-off fashion, Zavaletta grabbed the horse by the mane, jumped and swung his leg over without touching the stirrups.

"Not bad for a 45-year old, is it?" he smirked.

'Not bad if you were approaching seventy,' I felt like saying.

Clemente took the opportunity to show off in full glory. He galloped at top speed and stopped abruptly so many times I feared for the horse's mental wellbeing.

When he rejoined the bemused group he announced, "This one is good. Very good."

I asked if I could try the first quiet one again.

Clemente stepped in and said, "Well, you put on the reins and saddle this time."

'Fuck,' I thought. *'This is not good. The reins have so many different bits of leather and the saddle is tied up in the western way. I did not have a clue.'*

I tried anyway but must have looked thoroughly confused. The horse gritted his teeth and I struggled to get the bridle into his mouth.

'Damn it!' I felt a right fool. All eyes were on me.

Clemente approached irritably, almost shoved me to one side and finished off the job in a macho way. I felt like shouting, *'If only you would show me once, I would know the next time.'* But I kept silent as I chewed on my lower lip. *'Please God, let this moment pass.'*

After another ride round the *corral,* I asked Clemente what he thought of the quiet one and the white one. He answered without hesitation.

"If I was doing your journey, I would have taken these two horses with me."

He spoke with such conviction that I did not dare argue. I wish I had.

José ushered us into the house to talk business over some *mate. 'I wish we could just leave,'* I thought. I was not overly keen on any of the horses. *'But what will I do if I don't choose a horse today? Clemente does not seem to have anything else lined up and I would not know where to start looking for other horses. I don't want to anger him. But why* am I afraid of him? Why don't I just speak up? Well, he is a horse expert and a good polo-player, he must know what he's talking about. But why do I feel uneasy?'

José towered over me, "The horses cost 500 dollars each."

Clemente nodded his head in approval.

'It's less than what I imagined they would be,' I thought.

"Bueno," came my reluctant reply.

Clemente discussed final details with José and we left. 'Soon I will be the official owner of two horses.' The thought filled me with elation. But also with trepidation. Something like a sixth sense told me not to call my horses by their names just yet. I had this nagging feeling they would not be there for the long haul. So, initially I referred to them only as 'brown horse' and 'white horse'.

"When are you planning to start your journey?" Clemente asked on the way.

"I would like to spend a week or so with the horses before I do," I said.

His reply was formal.

"You have two choices. Stay at La Emilia, rent a car and go back and forth to the stables or stay in a room at the stables which belong to Orasio, my brother-in-law."

I agreed to the second option. I needed space away from people where I could think, plan and reflect.

Back at the house, Clemente walked over to me in the kitchen and said, "I am surprised that you are not as prepared as I thought you would have been."

"What? What do you mean?" I asked. "I needed to get the horses and now that I have them, I will sort out the equipment, the insurance..."

He interrupted me, "You have no papers ready or anything."

"But how could I start organising the papers before I have the horses?"

He was relentless, "You are not ready to go yet."

Sure there was merit in what he said. But I did not need to hear it in this way. I was desperate for support and enthusiastic help. It felt like Clemente resented me for wanting to do this journey. He did not seem to be a happy man. Maybe the idea of my journey made him nostalgic for the adventurous life he once led. I did not know. Or maybe my being a woman, wanting to undertake what might be considered by many as a male pursuit, did not sit easily with him. His negative attitude was puzzling.

The phone rang and, after taking the call, Zavaletta came back to continue his tirade. I was close to tears. "I am not claiming to be the top horsewoman in the world, Clemente, but I feel you have been unduly critical."

"You could not even do up the girth on the saddle."

"I have never even seen a saddle like that! How could you expect me to tie it up in a way that is completely foreign to me?" My voice was getting very edgy.

"You needed to spend more time on a horse before you came over."

I sighed. Whether I was a competent horsewoman or not was not the issue. I was going to do this journey no matter what. So Clemente was right, I did not have a notion. It was not that he said it, but how he said it that bothered me. I so wanted to feel good about this massive undertaking. I was open to learn and ready for somebody to teach me. But Clemente was not going to be the man for the job. I was going to become competent and get experience the hard way. Maybe that was the best way.

I was crying now.

"I know that I am not prepared in the most perfect way, Clemente, but this is the way things are now. I can't turn back time. I will make the best of where I am and what I have and can only look to the future."

Clemente retracted his harsh words slightly and said, "I am only thinking that you should spend more than a week with the horses because you will be very sore and stiff."

He continued, "Initially I did the favour for Gordon to help but now I do it for you and I feel responsible for your well-being."

"It's not your fault," I said emotionally. "I just feel a bit vulnerable and I find it upsetting that you don't have much confidence in me. I don't want to let anybody down."

I felt silly for the tears but perhaps I needed to get all the pent-up emotions of the last ten months out of my system. My heavy heart lifted slightly. I felt better. Nothing like a good cry.

Things stayed very much in limbo for another week. Before the deal with the horses could go through, they had to undergo anaemia tests. These tests, a prerequisite for crossing borders, refer to equine infectious anaemia (EIA) — a persistent virus initially causing fever, anaemia, body oedema and lethargy. Only months later would I realise just how important a test this was.

Instead of hanging around at La Emilia, I chose to spend the weekend in Buenos Aires, a handsome cosmopolitan city of wide boulevards, pavement café's and elegant apartments. A city of modern construction and dynamic activity mingled with old traditions and charming corners. I was fascinated by the atmosphere and the individual personality of each of its neighbourhoods. The city with its eleven million inhabitants was bustling and exciting. It took my thoughts away from horses, fears and bad feelings.

I strolled the streets of San Telmo on the Sunday, browsing absent-mindedly through the cramped antiques market, camera in hand, when, *bang!* I bumped into a man nearly flattening him.

"Aah, a woman who loves the camera," he exclaimed in a distinctly Italian accent, rubbing his crushed chest and grinning.

Before I could apologise, he continued, "Photography is a drug. Are you a Pisces?"

"Actually, well..."

"No, no, quiet. You're a Libra. Every woman who ever made an impact in my life, was a Libra."

I did not know if he was trying to be ironic or funny.

"Let me tell you," he proceeded enthusiastically in a mixture of broken English and Spanish, "you are intelligent, you feel pain of the heart more strongly than most people and you are harmonious."

His name was Iller, a photographer, who knew Buenos Aires better than most Porteños (local inhabitants). He was busy working on a photo-book about the tango. Over coffee he showed me some of his pictures. They were moody and good. And all of a sudden from knowing not a single soul in this city I had a new friend who would show me the fascinating world of the tango. A dance of bittersweet melancholia, only gringos, it is said, dance it for fun. In a way it is sex by other means.

Later we shared a Lucky Strike over pasta and red wine. Iller was curious about my life and deliberately speaking very slowly so he could understand me, I told him why I was in Argentina. His face lit up when he finally understood what I was saying. He was genuinely surprised.

"It's remarkable. You must be careful."

I nodded and he continued, "This journey will change your life forever."

We discovered that we both love the rain and our favourite part of the film, *The Piano,* was where she plays *"The heart asks pleasure first"* on the beach. He told me a story of when he was in Ireland, visiting Connemara with his wife.

"It was misty and drizzling. We stood on a hilltop overlooking a beautiful place. I felt alive and happy. My wife said, 'let's go home'. I took my head in my hands and wept. We separated shortly after."

I told him about Jo, my friend that died. I felt happy to cry.

Jo's passing was a blow to me. When my grandmother died I was seventeen. I struggled with that too. In fact, I struggle with the whole idea of death. The finality of it. The conclusiveness. That sense of helplessness – there is nothing one can do to bring the person back. You just have to accept it.

Dessert consisted of little espressos and biscuits at El Café Tortoni, one of the oldest establishments in Buenos Aires. From where we were sitting I could hear the haunting and heart-rending tango melodies from one of the backrooms. I could have sat there forever. Horses, my travels, strange people and potential hardship seemed a thousand miles away.

The following day, I spoke to the Irish Ambassador in Buenos Aires. She knew about my plans and invited me for dinner the following Monday.

It was a strange thing – the more often I looked at my map and the route I intended to take, the shorter the distances seemed to become. When I watched those thin lines curving from one village to the other, one town to the next, I tried to convince myself that nowhere is too far, no distance too great. The map became my house, my saviour, my trust. Looking at it gave me strength and confidence.

'With my map on our side, we could conquer the world.'

I made mental pictures of trotting across the border out of Argentina, convinced that in no time we would reach Bolivia. As long as the horses stayed healthy, we would cover ground and make progress.

I had it all sussed out – Monday we will arrive here, Tuesday we will trot from here to there, Wednesday will take us to this village, Thursday we will do easily 50 kilometres, Friday and Saturday will be rest days. I especially liked to work out time-frames. It provided me with a goal and something to focus on and work towards.

I thought, 'I could do an average of 40 kilometres a day. If we travel for five days, non-stop, that means covering 200 kilometres in a week. Then we would have two days for resting. "That's marvellous – we can do 800 kilometres in a month!'

Yeah, it all sounded wonderful. In theory. But, in reality, very little worked out as I had planned in those early days. But planning and scheming kept me going and took my worried mind away from what was ahead. When doing my calculations, I tried not to think of having nowhere to stay as we ventured into foreign territory. That was the least of my worries.

At the local saddlers' shop in Pilar, nobody in the shop could advise me about the saddlebags. They catered mostly for polo players, so a long distance horse traveller with different needs was obviously quite alien to them. I noticed a lot of sniggering and talking behind hands. I did not know much more myself and thought I would be able to rely on the hard-sellers in the shop.

Had I known how important a purchase this was, no doubt I would have spent much more time finding the right type for my trek. Keeping the saddlebags and all they entailed balanced and secured on the horses for the duration of my trip, proved to be the greatest challenge that faced me. It was ironic that something perceptively so small could be such an issue on the trip. Not the every-day riding, not getting used to the horses, not worries about my safety, not the hunger or cold. No. None of that was as much of a challenge as those damn saddlebags which seemed to have a personal vendetta against me.

Around the dinner table that evening Clemente said, "I have received the results from the anaemia tests. My brother-in-law has a company dealing with export of horses and he'll organise those papers for you. You owe me 400 dollars."

I was taken aback. This was much more than I had anticipated. I bit my tongue and did not argue. Surely he is doing everything in my best interest.

"Yes Clemente. I will organise to get the money sent from Ireland."

He looked very pleased. Still grumpy, but pleased.

I had a lump in my throat when I said goodbye to Amelia. I was picked up by a young lad who took me to the stables where my two new horses were waiting for me in a *corral* – the sides were open but at least had a roof over it to protect them from the rain. They were jumpy and the brown one pulled his ears back when I approached. Not knowing if they were planning to kick or bite I kept a safe distance.

Later, I went over again to bribe their affection with lots of brushing and loving pats. They appeared to like it and both seemed calmer. I practiced putting on head-collars and bridles. It was a bit of a struggle but I managed. What was more difficult was to stop the white horse jumping at everything when I took them round the yard for a ride. He seemed to have an abnormal fear of anything resembling red, yellow or blue.

At least he was not colour-blind.

My room was a dirty little space with two bunk-beds, one of them covered in polo horse-gear. The shower did not work. The room was chilly and I was glad of the extra blanket Amelia had thrown in. I felt quite lonely where I sat in a dilapidated chair, looking at all the stuff I was planning to take along. It was far too much but I did not know what to leave out.

I remembered Gordon Roddick's words, "Travel light. The only way you will finish a journey like this is if you travel light."

I have never been good at travelling with only the minimal, always worried that I might need this or that. This occasion was no exception. Actually, I did not fare too badly on the personal belongings front, although I imagined that jodhpurs in three different colours was a bit excessive. I had lots of horse-gear with me and Chanelle, the veterinary group in Ireland, made sure that I was not short of anything. It was difficult to know what was needed and what could be left behind. I felt so out of my depth. Things were moving closer to what I wanted but the idea still scared the hell out of me. I wanted to be on the road, I wanted to cover ground, I wanted to meet people and become best friends with my horses.

I also wanted to go home. My new living quarters depressed me. Even more depressing was the fact that I could not make conversation with Marco, the farm worker who picked me up, and his friendly wife who also lived on the premises. The only one who seemed to understand me was their ten-month old baby who did not need speech. My contorted facial expressions and saying 'ga ga ga' proved to be enough for us to communicate for a while.

The day after I arrived, I thought it wise to take the horses for another spin. '*At least I should ensure they could trot together and that both were okay with being on the leading rope.*' This turned out to be my second and last practice run before actually undertaking my first official day of the trip two weeks later.

Perhaps that sounds foolhardy but there was some method in my madness and I shall explain. I did not want to know how difficult it would be to travel for hours on end, mile after mile, day after day on horseback. I thought that if I found out before starting my journey, the reality of what my days would possibly be like, I might have been discouraged or doubtful whether I would be able to make it or not.

I did not really want to know if the horses were able to work together. I did not want to know how easily they spooked. I decided the best option for *me* would be to learn and gain experience as we went along. I knew I was a survivor and I believed that when things went wrong, they simply had to get better again. It was blind faith that kept me from practising with the horses before we set off. But it also kept me going. I was too afraid to find out that maybe I could not do it.

In hindsight, I wished I had paid more attention to fitness – specifically for horse riding. No amount of skipping and yoga could have prepared me for the toll that constant riding takes on every fibre of one's body.

I was in better spirits that morning when after having some muesli, I stepped into the bright sun. The horses, standing quietly in their *corral*, looked rather content and happy and obviously had no idea what I was planning for them for the next eighteen months.

'*Boys, you don't know what you are in for,*' I felt like saying.

I saddled up the brown horse. When I was satisfied that everything was in place, I stepped into the stirrup. Just as I had put my full weight on it, I lost my balance and slumped pathetically with the saddle to the ground. It was not done up tight enough. Embarrassed, I looked around to see if anyone had noticed. The girth had to be done up the western way – no buckles but only a strip of material that had to be tied up using a specific technique. I called Marco who showed me how to do it, patiently and with great expertise.

'*Oh Marco, come with me!*' I wanted to yell. I took a deep breath. '*I'll be fine.*' Another sigh. '*I will have to be fine. I'll get there. I have to stay positive and remember that silver lining. This was just the beginning.*'

On the second day hanging out with my new equine friends, my fingers were still awkward with the girth and with the saddle coming off twice when I tried to mount up. Just as I was ready to take the brown horse on the leading rope, it started to rain. So while sitting on the white horse, I tried to put on my rain poncho. My hands were shaking and I waited for the horses to get a fright at the sight of this black plastic thing and take off. I panicked when my head got stuck and for a moment thought how comic it would be if they started running with a headless rider on top. Mercifully, they both stood very still.

Our ride was progressing smoothly until we had to pass a stationary truck on one side of the road and large industrial pipes on the other. The white horse refused to move forward. She might have felt trapped. I pleaded and dug in my heels but had no success. One of the workers on the road took pity on me, came towards us and led the horses through with me still in the saddle.

I felt ten years old again, with daddy leading me around the yard on our pony.

I got fed up rather rapidly with the horses being afraid of everything, the dampness and my clumsiness trying to manage the two of them, so I headed back to the stables.

'Hmm,' I thought, 'it's more complicated than I imagined having a second horse in tow.'

I remembered my dad's words. "Do you know how to lead a horse when riding another?"

I looked him straight in the eye and said "Well no...no, I don't."

He was almost sympathetic when he asked, "And what will you do when the second horse won't come?"

My answer was quick, "I'll just make him come!"

My dad was realistic when we had this conversation. Me? I still had lots of hope and enthusiasm. Nobody was going to deter me.

To strengthen my confidence, I left the brown horse behind at the stables and took off into the fields in a gallop with the other one. After I had done a good few lengths at full speed across the field, I saw Marco charging towards us on his own horse, arms waving in the air.

"You can not ride there! You must go somewhere else to practise with your horse," he shouted in Spanish.

Well, actually, I did not understand a word but his frantic limb movements explained enough. It turned out I was digging up the earth on sacred polo ground. Tail between legs, white horse and I made our way back. The thrill of our gallop was gone. Later over tea and cake with Marco and his wife, he tried to apologise for his strong reaction. It seemed I was not the only one terrified of a Zavaletta.

Later, a photographer from the paper, La Nacion arrived. My first interview in Argentina. I should have been excited but I was not. I felt lost, lonely and scared. I was beginning to have doubts about my trip. Was I too ambitious, too naïve, too optimistic? I said a silent prayer for a good outcome. I had to grit my teeth and march on. There was no going back now.

Dinner a few days later at the Irish Ambassador's residence was a highlight. Everything was so civilised and orderly. I was flattered to be the guest of honour for the night. Paula Slattery, the Ambassador, had paid close attention to the guest list and made sure that everybody around the table had something in common. She particularly thought one couple might be very good for me to meet, given our mutual interests. The woman had Irish roots and they both loved horse riding. Ciro was a small Bolivian man with an intense personality and quickly took to me.

"There is a reason that we had to meet tonight," he said, leaning towards me over his lamb cutlets. "I can feel you will have a guardian angel on your way."

I told them about Jo. Maria, who was twice his size, was a formidable woman with an even stronger personality. She cut him short many times and it was obvious she tolerated no nonsense from her husband. Not after twenty-five years anyway. After dinner we retired to the drawing room with liqueurs and studied the South American map in detail. I was amazed at all the enthusiasm and goodwill.

I stayed at Hotel Dora that night and at breakfast the following morning, the Egyptian manager who had been living in Argentina for twenty years approached me.

"Somebody told me you are planning an idiotic journey on two horses. Is that true?"

He scrutinised me from head to toe. He looked horrified when he realised I was serious, and continued.

"People are desperate in this country and will kill for anything. You will not make it past the Province of Buenos Aires."

I was not in the mood for negative talk. I found it rather draining so I cut him short.

"I'll be careful."

As I headed for the main door he had the last word. "I definitely think you should not go."

Ciro was keen for me to meet the rest of his family and I ended up spending the following two days at his house. His children were very likable and engaging. Ciro was well-off having made his fortune through the beef trade with the Middle East. From just looking around his home it was obvious to see he had no problem spending vast amounts of money on, among other things, a large number of religious artefacts.

On one occasion Ciro asked, "Do you want to touch her?"

Standing solemnly in the corner of the living room was an almost life-size statue of the Virgin Mary.

I declined.

"Ciro, she has not the same meaning for me. It would be like touching a pillar or a pavement," I replied, unaware at that stage that he had converted to Roman Catholicism only two years before.

He had determination in his voice when he said, "God wants you to do this journey. He is going to protect you. When you are finished you will be a Catholic."

I forced a smile. He meant well.

Although Ciro admired what I wanted to do he was also concerned. He was the type that needed answers and everything in place before he would act.

"Have you got a boat organised that will take you from Ecuador to Panama?" Ciro asked numerous times.

When I indicated that I did not, he became animated. He explained that I needed to know now, while I was still in Buenos Aires, whether it would be possible or not. I told him that I operate differently, that I do not look too far into the future, that I will take every day as it comes.

"Ecuador is about eight months of riding away," I said to him. "I have to get through many other countries first. Why would I want to burden myself now with what might or might not happen, so far into the future?"

He was adamant though that I needed to know if a boat service was available to take the horses across. I told him that if there was going to be a problem I did not want to know about it now.

"I can only do what is in front of me at any given time, Ciro," I said.

Throughout my journey I found this way of thinking worked for me. I was at my happiest when I was just thinking about the stretch of road under the horses' hooves at that very moment. I believed that what was ahead would look after itself when the time came.

Margarita Perkins, a dignified woman of seventy-two with erect posture and piercing blue eyes agreed to accompany Ciro, his daughter and I to check out the horses. She was a real character, a strong woman in her own right, and I imagined that only the brave or foolhardy would try to mess with her. She was quite well-known in the horse world around Argentina. She met us in her interesting and antique-filled house wearing a flamboyant cowboy hat. She looked the part.

Ciro looked at me, winked and said, "You are very lucky to have this woman helping you. She is one of the best."

Miss Perkins interjected in good humour, "You have always been biased Ciro. Now let's get going."

At the stables it felt rather intimidating to get on a horse under the watchful eye of Margarita, the great horsewoman. She was not critical though and had a nice way about her. However, she noticed immediately how I held the reins and said, "Criollos have a different sensitivity in their mouths. Turn your hand around with your palm showing upwards and it will be better for you and the horse."

It did not feel comfortable but I did it anyway. I made a mental note to perfect this grip.

That evening I got the chance to nurture my soul with the soothing tones of Rostropovich, the world famous cellist at the Teatro Colón. This theatre has entertained Porteños since 1908 and is also the second largest performing arts theatre in the southern hemisphere. It had all the trimmings of a great old opera house but from outside it looked almost sombre. Inside, the grand staircases added to the interior of this elegant hall with tiers of balconies and velvet draped private boxes. As I glanced at the old chandeliers, centred in the cavernous upper reaches of the hall, I was surprised at the number of young people around. Wearing jeans and causal dress, they were squeezed on to the standing-gallery, straining their necks to catch a glimpse.

It was an unusual sight, this enthusiastic attendance at a cultural event that would bore most teenagers. So I wondered why these young Argentines were so keen to spend an evening at the opera. The more I thought about it, the clearer it became that the music must have served as a distraction, a soothing outlet to forget life's hardships and relax. To lose oneself in music is like meditation or painting – the mind is focused on the good energy and in that moment, nothing else matters.

Negativity was in overdrive in Argentina at that time. The country had been in turmoil, politically and economically, and I understood how going to the opera and being embraced by the magnificent sounds could help people to escape from their problems – even though it was only for a short while.

In 2002, Argentina experienced an economic collapse of immense proportions. By September, more than half of the country's population was living below the poverty line. Argentina captured the world's attention with a massive social upheaval in late December that ushered in and out five presidents in less than two weeks. The crisis had been building for years.

The massive demonstrations that erupted in December 2001 were commonly referred to as *cacerolazos*, or protests in which demonstrators banged on empty pots and pans symbolising their inability to purchase the basic necessities of life. In Buenos Aires, the *cacerolazos* usually occurred every Friday when thousands of demonstrators descended on the historic Plaza de Mayo, the site of the presidential palace and the national congress. Smaller, but very militant protests were also organised against the banks. The middle class in particular was furious with the banks, as the Government had frozen long-term savings accounts, many of which were in dollars. Starting in the middle of 2002, the Government promised to repay the deposits – which totalled nearly 20 billion US dollars – in eighteen monthly installments. Payments would be made in the national currency, which meant they would be devalued by at least forty percent. It is small wonder that many middle class demonstrators, sometimes in suits, smashed bank windows and spray painted slogans such as 'thieves', 'traitors' and 'looters' on bank walls.

During the four years that Argentina had been in economic recession, an alternative barter economy emerged. It was estimated that over two and a half million people were participating in local exchanges called *nodos*. People took their products or commodities to the exchanges – fruit, vegetables, chickens, jams and clothing – where they got credit slips which could be used to pick up products they needed in return. One local textile manufacturer who was on the verge of bankruptcy called together his workers and told them that since he could no longer pay many of their salaries, he would instead hand over blankets produced in the factory which the workers could either sell or exchange for other commodities.

While I was in Argentina, the *piqueteros* (unemployed workers, also called pickets, who block major highways demanding jobs and causing disruption), the *cacerolazos* and the popular assemblies were driving the political process. Setting aside rosy and totally unrealistic economic projections by government officials, virtually no one saw an early end to the deep economic crisis, meaning that social and political instability would prevail for some time to come. As one political commentator stated, "the only certainty in Argentina is that the future is uncertain."

Amidst these uncertain times, Argentina also experienced a wave of kidnappings and armed assaults. They had thrown its people into panic as the imploding economy forced the poor to steal and the rich to seek bullet proof protection. I heard stories from people who had been ambushed in their own homes with demands for money and jewellery. When Ciro and I planned to travel out of Buenos Aires for a day, we used his battered old vehicle and not the comfortable Mercedes gathering dust in the garage. Ciro explained.

"If the robbers around town see us driving a fancy car, they will follow us and know where we live. We can't take that chance."

I also heard of private schools telling pupils to 'dress down' and vary their routes to school.

Some might wonder as to whether all this uncertainty and turmoil made me more fearful about my trip. After all, a girl alone on two horses could be an easy target. If the truth be told, I did not allow myself to be consumed by the fear and worry of so many Argentines. I had great sympathy for the plight of those who struggled but, in ways, I also felt very much removed from it all. My mind was in another place. I was careful, but I still walked the streets. Most days I carried a video camera and was never hassled. I continued to enjoy the pulse of this intoxicating city.

Opera in the majestic Colon Theatre was impressive and most enjoyable. This was followed by a dinner, consisting mostly of kidneys (which I could not stomach) around eleven that evening.

I struggled with the Argentine eating habits. During my journey it was not unusual to be served an enormous T-bone steak an hour before midnight by my generous hosts. My vegetarianism of seven years had to play second fiddle. I would have starved if I did not go back to my carnivorous ways. Many times a juicy chunk of meat with some white bread was all I would be given for my dinner after a long day's ride. Sink or Swim. Chew or choke.

My kidney dinner at Ciro's house was disturbed by a phone-call from Zavaletta. He probably thought I was avoiding him and sounded irritable. He might not have liked the fact that I had found new friends who were keen to help and that I was planning to move my horses from where they currently were.

Zavaletta quickly brought up the subject of money and said, "You still owe me 400 dollars for those anaemia papers and the exportation documents and 800 dollars for your accommodation."

I nearly fell off the chair.

"Can you just repeat that amount, Clemente?" I managed to mutter.

The line went dead. I went back to the dinner table and told the others about the phone call. They were shocked.

"You only spent about fifteen days with them," Ciro said accurately. "What is he *thinking*? It looks as if he's trying to make money out of you."

'*My sentiments exactly,*' I thought.

I pushed my plate of kidneys to the side. My appetite was gone.

I excused myself from the table and said, "I will ring him tomorrow and get all the details."

I had a fitful night.

Ciro had bought me a chain on a silver cross.

"Wearing it will protect you," he said solemnly.

He was adamant that it had to be blessed by the local priest. He brought me over to Father Sombrioso, an 87-year-old Irishman with a look of mischief in his eyes. I liked him immediately. Ciro introduced me to the priest and kept on saying 'Brother' to the man.

"I am Father," Sombrioso would correct him gently.

"I am so sorry Brother," replied Ciro.

He did this about four times. I could feel a fit of giggles coming on and I think Father Sombrioso did too. Ciro suggested that the priest held the cross in one hand, my hand in the other and said the Lord's Prayer. During the prayer, I opened my eyes.

Ciro's mouth moved to the words but without a sound. His face was peaceful but intense. I had a peek at Father Sombrioso and quickly shut my eyes when he stared back at me. I opened them again as he was going through the passages "... and lead them not into temptation... " with a crooked smile on his face.

My last night at the stables, I had dinner with Marcus and his wife. It did me good. They were simple people but so sincere. Despite our language difficulties we had a great laugh. They had meagre belongings and were obviously poor but their serenity and goodwill dominated everything else. Discreetly I tried to hand Marcus money for his help with the horses.

"No señorita, por favor."

He was mortified by the gesture and handed it straight back to me. I insisted that he took it. I wished I had more to give.

The next morning, two young men arrived to transport the horses to Ciro's farm called San Diego, 150 kilometres north-west from Buenos Aires. I was eternally grateful to Ciro for this offer and the opportunity to take the horses somewhere else.

They were likeable lads and the four-hour trip (we got lost on the way) was one of the best social experiences of my journey. They had hardly any English and ditto for my Spanish but that did not stop them from teasing me from the moment we got into the van.

Mathias, who was studying to be a vet, was very charming. His friend, tubby and ordinary, made up for his lack of physical appeal by being extraordinarily funny. I sat between the two of them and the banter and laughs did not stop for the duration of the trip. I took out my video camera and had mock interviews with them. I did not understand most of it, but the bits I did had me in stitches.

At one stage, the tubby friend looked over to Mathias who was driving and said, *"Pienso que te gusta la chica?"* (I think you like the girl).

Mathias grinned and blushed. The feeling was mutual. It was nice to have had that buzz even though I knew it would not lead anywhere and, as it turned out, he had a girlfriend anyway.

On the way to San Diego we stopped off in the town of Lujan. I had one more important thing to do. The Museum of Transport was also the home now of Mancha and Gato, whose eerily life-like bodies had been stuffed and preserved in a glass box there. These were the two world-renowned equines of unparalleled endurance that made it possible for Tschiffely to have his adventure across the Americas. I had a lump in my throat when I saw them. It felt like I knew them.

"Hello," I whispered.

Their lifeless eyes stared into the distance. They were uglier than I imagined, I was sure they must have been more handsome when alive. I looked at them and something stirred in me. It was almost spiritual. The thought that I, too, would soon be breathing the same air and touching the same ground as they did eighty years ago, was overwhelming.

I took one last look and said out loud, "Wish us luck."

The bright sun outside brought me back to reality.

At San Diego, one of the oldest and best preserved *estancias* (a large estate) built by Irish immigrants, Maria had laid out a scrumptious spread for lunch in the spacious back garden. The front lawn was enormous too and I was told how in days gone by it was used as a polo ground for families spending a sophisticated Sunday afternoon together.

Sitting outside underneath the trees was pure bliss. I had more peace in my heart, although I felt a tight grip around my throat every time I allowed myself to think of what was ahead. But I knew I was in a better place now. Wine and conversation flowed in equal measure and were it not for my looming journey I could have sat there forever soaking up the atmosphere. Ciro asked me about my 'final moments' with Zavaletta and I relayed the story.

Ciro said, "Can you show me the invoice that Clemente gave you for the export of the horses and anaemia papers?"

Ciro looked at the invoice and did a double-take, showed it to his daughter Magdalena and said, "This invoice says 400 pesos and not dollars. The dollar sign in Argentina means peso, the local currency. If it was in dollars it would have had US before the dollar sign. These papers should not have cost you more than about one hundred dollars."

I felt sick. I had paid four times that.

All I could find was an almost unreadable faxed copy of the anaemia results and no export documents. I was so stupid. I never looked at the papers when Clemente handed them to me. For 400 dollars, all I had to show was a poor copy of an anaemia result which did not even have the names of the horses on it. Later that day, I made a much needed phone call.

"Clemente, I would like you to give me a *receipt* for the 400 dollars that I paid you."

He replied, "Why? Don't you trust me?"

His words sounded ironic. "No, it's not that. It's just that I have to justify my expenses and this is a substantial amount."

I could imagine him shifting uncomfortably. "Ring me on Monday, I can't do anything now."

Before he hung up, I managed to say, "Oh yes, and what about my export papers? I can't see those in the envelope."

I got no answer.

The day after I arrived at San Diego with my horses, Juan and Baby, friends of

Magdalena, came over for the day and we all went riding together. The white horse was temperamental and difficult. Juan also tried him out and gave his verdict afterwards.

"The white horse is good with a fiery character but he is not suited for the trip you have in mind. I predict accidents and struggle."

I trusted Juan implicitly. How I wished he had been there when I had searched for suitable Criollos.

I was very lucky how events turned out. Ciro made contact with a guy called Dr. Tapia, the manager on Monetta's farm where they have a number of Criollos. He agreed to a straight swap with the white horse. And that's where I found my Tusa. He was on a rope, tied to a tree and while we were standing around, he blew through his nose and scraped the ground with his hoof. It was as if he wanted me to pick him. He looked like he had life in him and a trot around the ring confirmed this for me. Juan looked pure *gaucho* when he took him for a spin and I envied his ease and confidence on Tusa's back. They looked like one.

The deal was done and my departure date was looming. I made the decision to leave on the 15th of June, five days away. Physically I was not prepared. On the mental front? Well, I would not even go there. I knew I just had to get on with things. *'It will all gel together once we're on the road.'* It became a mantra in my head.

Eight days before my journey officially commenced I received the mail below from Dave;

Mar,

I'm sure you are getting a few tingles down the spine with the thoughts of heading off on your wonderful adventure soon. I have been thinking about it a lot and am genuinely very excited for you. I am glad that your early days are well sorted out with very definite destinations targeted. This will give you a chance to really get into the swing of the trip and get used to the horses. How are you getting on with them? How are they getting on with you! I was thinking of a snag list but on second thoughts there is no real need – I'm sure you have thought of everything. Just make sure you save your diaries on floppy disk and get them sent home. Always prepare food wise – have emergency reserves (especially when you get into more remote areas) – use high carbs and plenty of protein. Are you ok for money as you progress along? Have you a way of sorting this out? Other than that there is not much else but always put yourself first – look after yourself. All I will say Mar is make sure you enjoy every moment, take each day as a new one. My thoughts are with you as you embark on this great trip. Remember 'fear stops action, action cures fear'.

Ps: Just off the phone to my mam and the first thing she asked me was how you were getting on. Had to remind her I was her son! She is saying a Novena for you!

1. The 'apprentenship' begins. My brother and me on our farm in South Africa.
2. San Diego, Argentina. Our first day – soon everything would be on the ground.
3. Ciro Trigo and Margarita Perkins.

4. Mathias and friend who transported my horses from the polo stables near Pilar to San Diego.
5. In front of the house on the farm of Ciro and Maria Trigo.

6. José escorts me out of Tucumán, past *piqueteros* demanding money from motorists.
7. Santiago (left) and Florencia with his parents at El Datil.
8. Music with Daniel Paz, his wife Veronica (right) and sister-in-law.

9. Accommodation starts to get basic in Yuto, 120 kilometres north of Salta.
10. My *Movitrack* expedition with Jacinta (far left) and Orlaith (far right).

I sent him a reply a couple of days later;

Dave,

Thanks for your correspondence with all the sincere good wishes and advice. It is a really good feeling to know that you are behind me and excited on my behalf. I am dying to hit the road and find a bit of solitude and time on my own. You ask about money. I will be carrying some cash (dollars and pesos) in my money belt but will try to pay for most things with the credit card where possible. I've had a lot of expenses so far – many unexpected. Tusa is now a brown horse full of character. I swapped him for the white horse, which was totally unsuitable.

That Monday I tried to make contact with Clemente again but could not get hold of him. Over the next few weeks, I tried at least six more times. Once I actually managed to speak to him but he was making a lot of excuses.

"I am tired of *mañana, mañana* Clemente," I said.

He hung up. Whenever I rang after that, he did the same. Weeks later I was staying with a family in Cordoba and the man of the house sent him a lawyer's letter, demanding that he pay me what I was owed, immediately. We are still waiting for his reply!

It was sometime in July when I made a last and final attempt to get in touch with Clemente Zavaletta. I sent him an email with the subject: Urgent Request.

He never bothered to answer this plea either. I knew I had to move on from this negative experience. I had learned an expensive and hurtful lesson but chasing him was draining my energy. The wheel always turns. What goes around comes around.

The day before I officially took off with the horses, Magdalena and I left the city of Buenos Aires behind and travelled down to San Diego for final preparations. Thanks to Ciro and Maria, I had a number of contacts in my little black book of people to call on. Ciro had spoken to them all and they were happy to receive me. The hope was that *they* in turn, would get in touch with others to provide havens on my way as we ventured north. At the start, this idea worked quite well but as my journey progressed the chain was often broken. Still, it was reassuring to know, especially in the beginning, that somebody would be looking out for me.

"Life is either a daring adventure or nothing"
— *Helen Keller*

On the day of my departure, the morning was spent with Magdalena who helped me pack. She was meticulous and knew what she was doing. She was ruthless too.

"The skipping rope has to go. The horses' leading rope will serve that purpose."

The following items were allowed into my saddle-bags:

1 pair of jodhpurs

Small bag of cosmetics

Spanish phrasebook, dictionary and tuition CDs

Walkman and Dictaphone

A pair of flip-flops

2 pairs of socks

3 pairs of knickers and 1 sports bra

2 t-shirts and 2 long sweatshirts

1 pair of jeans and a black top *(for social occasions)*

A medical aid kit for myself

Veterinary supplies – *(I could take only about a fifth of what I arrived with in Buenos Aires)*

Windbreaker

Flask in brown suede bag containing gourd, *bombilla* and *yerba tea*

Irish tin whistle

Map of Argentina

Horse documents *(dodgy anaemia papers)*

Letter from Irish Ambassador in Argentina, *(requesting assistance should I need it on the way)*

Hoof pick

Brush for horses *(I went without)*

One spare horse-shoe

Hammer

Horse-shoe nails

Torch

White soap *(to wash horses, myself and clothes)*

Toilet paper

We proceeded to load the horses with the saddlebags containing my meagre belongings but soon realised that both Magdalena and I were equally green and neither were exactly sure how to do it. A leisurely lunch followed. I did not taste the food and my palms were sweaty. Everybody around the table was making small talk and I sat there with a heavy heart. They did not sense my anxiety and thumping chest. I felt like screaming, *'Do you know what I am about to start today? Do you have any understanding? Think of me! Pray for me!'* I tried to force myself away from melodramatic thoughts and was scared. It was winter outside.

After lunch we all moved to the front of the house to take pictures. The longed-for moment had arrived. A doomed sense of unreality swept over me but only for a split second. There were too many practicalities to deal with. I sat on Tusa and the original brown horse carried the pack. Three dogs were sniffing around us and one tried to urinate against Tusa's leg. I noticed the pack was a bit lopsided and made a mental note to fix it once the flashing of camera bulbs had ceased. But I never got the chance because the next moment, the packhorse jumped (why, I never found out) and started to run down the garden like an animal possessed. Tusa, on whom I was sitting, acting in typically equine fashion, did not think to assess the situation first but instead just gave a bolt himself and followed at high speed after the packhorse. The chase finally came to a (temporary) halt at the bottom of the garden.

With heaving chest and shaky hands I looked back at the startled family in the front of the house and, after having caught my breath, shouted, "Where is the video camera *now* Magdalena?"

My heart was in my throat but for some reason, I also felt like laughing my head off. I leaned over towards the packhorse which was just about arms reach away from Tusa. I decided not to get off, worried my red poncho would be unnerving. But he jerked up his head and set off again, this time kicking and bucking as if a cheetah was on his back.

At this stage, my carefully packed horse had managed to get all the belongings that were on his back round his belly. The more he kicked the more frightened he got and the more desperate he became to shake it all off. While trying to control a bolting Tusa, desperately clinging to clutches of mane, reins and muscled horse-neck, I witnessed first my tripod being kicked to pieces and then my saddle bags being ripped apart, their contents strewn all over the lawn. I could not watch it any more and cast my eyes away, still trying to get to grips with an over-excited eight hundred kilogram chunk of powerful animal underneath me.

I could not remember whether it was me who managed to bring Tusa to a halt or if he just stopped himself but, needless to say, the relief was profound. We found a disgruntled packhorse next to the house, looking like he could fly off again at any moment. A frail-looking leather rope was hanging loosely around his trembling body.

Ciro sighed heavily and looked at me with a scolding eye.

"Why did you make a joke out of it? If you did not laugh, the horse would not have run away again? What are you going to do now? You will have to get these saddlebags fixed and where will you do this? It is going to be very expensive to get them back from Buenos Aires. What will you do?"

I silently wished he would just disappear. The heavy air was slightly diluted when my hosts from the neighbouring farm arrived to check on my progress, or serious lack of it.

For my own sanity and to prove to myself that I had what it took, I insisted that I would ride the 12 kilometres to their farm. The family took my battered belongings and, after quick goodbyes, I made my way to the little dirt road. Ciro, still very serious, had already mounted his horse and waited to join me for a few miles. My pack-horse (minus the pack) was not co-operating and I was struggling.

Ciro saying every now and then, "Can't you make your horses walk faster?" was not helping.

But it was not long before his frustration got the better of him, and after about a mile, he announced he was turning back.

But his departure actually made things worse. The packhorse did not like the fact that one of the horses was going home and he attempted the same. I was holding the leading rope in my right hand and, with all the pulling back I was losing more and more skin from my palms with each passing minute. It burned like hell. Horses play off each other and when Mr Packhorse started to act the giddy goat, Tusa followed suit. We were twisting and turning every twenty yards and a few times I lost the leading rope. What's more, at every opportunity the packhorse would annoyingly turn around towards San Diego, causing me to charge past him with Tusa and grab hold of him. In a very short space of time he had become the horse equivalent of a problem child. Once, when I attached the leading rope on to the saddle, he pulled back so violently it snapped in two. Two of the buckles on the back of the saddle were also torn off.

My patience was wearing thin. It was near five and the sun was starting to disappear rather rapidly. There was another ten kilometres ahead of me. But one thing I knew – there was no turning back. Setting up camp in the darkness of night in the middle of nowhere was a much more likely prospect at that particular point. Only one problem though – I had no tent.

Our progress was more like one step forward three steps back and it was not long before I realised the writing was on the wall. There was a farm gate opposite where we were but the big rusty lock on it was not the most inviting. There was nothing and nobody else. I was not going back so the packhorse got hobbled (the hobbles are similar to a pair of handcuffs and are tied or buckled around the pasterns or cannon bones of the front legs of a horse) and left on the side of the road.

Although the hobble is a tool that dates back centuries and was used in horse cultures around the world, it is not commonly in use by today's more recreationally oriented horse owners. The historical use of hobbles with a trained or 'broke' horse was, and remains, primarily to slow him from wandering too far too quickly. It has most definitely not outlived its usefulness in modern times.

Hobbling is not a practice I am in favour of. Neither would I impose it on my horse on a regular basis but this was an emergency. The need to continue for my own sanity, self-esteem and pride, was crucial. We were on a little farm road and no car had passed in the last hour and a half so at least I was quite sure that Packhorse would not meet his end under the wheels of some automobile. At this stage I was so fed up with this mule for a horse, I did not care if he was robbed that night. In fact, that would have done me a favour. But being a sentimental girl, of course there was a pang of guilt when I was mounting Tusa, only to see our hobbled companion staring at us with wide eyes as we headed northwards. There were no neighs from either horse as we set off again. I looked back only twice.

Time was of the essence and for the next hour we galloped. Soon we were on a bigger dirt road. It was dark and, as the road was under construction, quite a few trucks passed us with blinding lights. It was my first time ever in the dark on horseback and I found it quite eerie. Tusa was awesome though. He only spooked slightly when we passed road signs which gave off a whitish luminosity in the dark. I talked to him constantly, re-assuring him (and myself) that all would be fine and that we would be there in no time. I had a little handwritten map and needed to stop every now and then to check, under the light of the moon, to see if we were still on the right track. We were not. The turn that we took, half a mile back, brought us to a locked gate. I could see a farmhouse in the distance and as luck had it, somebody arrived in a pickup truck just as I was contemplating our next step. I shouted in a bad mix of English and Spanish and the next moment the vehicle came our way. It was a young boy, around fourteen years of age with not a word of English.

"Your Papa," was our only line of communication and, with a knowing nod he made his way towards the house again.

A few moments later, Papa arrived. His English was about two notches above that of his son but he managed to understand that I was heading to a particular farm and from his five fingers up in the air I gathered I still had that distance in kilometres to do. They good-heartedly offered to drive in front of me and I could follow on Tusa. The pace was hectic. Tusa was hot and I was frozen in the winter evening chill. I was terrified of us stumbling in the dark, Tusa stepping into a hole or running into something. After a while, the party came to a stop and the farmer and I swapped places. Man and horse arrived on the farm about an hour after me.

I was exhausted but not sweating as much as poor Tusa who seemed as if he had all life drained out of him. But I felt exhilarated too. I did my first day's journey and I was in another place. Sure, we did not do many kilometres (with thousands more to go) and I had travelled really with only one horse, no pack. But still it was the furthest I had ever gone on the back of a horse.

I was on a high even though my spirits were temporarily dampened when I received a phone call from a not-so-happy Ciro. He must have been worried sick when he saw my horse on the side of the road and probably feared the worst. He ranted on about my irresponsibility and stupidity. I was worn-out and listened with 'half an ear'. I was just so relieved to be home. My hosts were wonderful and my bed soft and cosy.

I needed an honest assessment of the packhorse's ability to be part of the TATA trio. After the previous day's performance, I had serious doubts. The next day Mercedes, my host, offered to ride Packhorse back from where he had been left behind. Her face said it all when they arrived on the farm.

Out of breath, she said, "I think he is untamed and more *burro* (donkey) than fancy Criollo. His walk and trot are so uncomfortable."

I nodded in agreement and said, "Yeah, this is the second dodo I've bought. I should have listened to my intuition when I went to pick the horses."

It was going to be a long journey.

I was not sure how to proceed. I had one good horse and one bad one. I was pretty convinced that the packhorse would have to stay behind. But that left me with only one horse. It was like starting all over again. I had to make up my mind and I did it rather rapidly. I was going to proceed with only Tusa until I found another suitable Criollo on the way. I just could not hang around any longer, also I did not want to be a burden on people any more. I needed to show myself and everybody that I could do this. With one or two horses – it did not matter so much at this stage. Or that was what I thought. The first dilemma was my belongings. I had to put everything into one bag that fitted behind the saddle.

But it also meant leaving behind a lot of things I needed. Even though I lightened the pack greatly, it was still a substantial weight.

That evening I went out to the packhorse again. I put my arm around him affectionately but he jerked up his head and hit me on the chin. The bloody taste on my tongue was like an omen. Later I went to bid farewell to him where he was standing alone, his stocky body etched against the falling sun. I had a lump in my throat and my eyes filled with tears when I thought of what might have been and hoped that he would be okay. I stretched out my hand in a sympathetic gesture, but with cold eyes he turned his back on me and pulled back his ears. Already I was less sad. It was time to move on.

Josefina, an eight-year-old cousin of the family asked a lot of questions and gave recommendations: "Don't think too much about your journey and the future – just enjoy every day and everything!"

I received another timely email from Dave in Ireland;

I have no doubts that you are making the right decision about the horse as he probably would have proved difficult over time. Time and resources well spent now will yield results later, so it is best to be patient now, although I know by you, you are itching badly to get 'ar an mbothar' (meaning 'on the road' in Irish). Listen as much as you can to people who know the area, take it on board and then make your own decision in as pragmatic a way as possible. It is important you get off to the right start as this will give you confidence and greater belief for the rest of the journey. Listen to your heart and spirit.
Be safe, happy and confident.

A chilly morning greeted me and I was reluctant to leave the warmth of the house. There was frost on the grass and my fingers were numb when I saddled up Tusa. I was seen off with good wishes and friendly hugs which I did not want to end. I felt quite lost as I put Tusa into a trot, going down the driveway towards the main dirt road. The horses called for each other. I whistled to block out their neighing. Tusa was not in co-operating mode. Every time we passed the entrance to a farm he tried to go in. There were bags and bits hanging from every side of the saddle and I felt uncomfortable on his back. He sensed my vulnerability and kept on taking chances. When I used a soft rope as a punishment crop to spur him on, dramatic antics followed in the shape of jumps and jolts. I could not seem to get him into a lively walk and we trotted a lot. This was not great for the pack and it kept on slipping to the side. Soon we were covered in dust from a few vehicles that had passed. The only positive thing at this point was that Tusa did not fear automobiles and seemed undisturbed by the hooting trucks. I had to get off four times to adjust the pack.

Every day we proceeded in more or less the same fashion. Tusa continued to be a challenge. He kept on pulling to the left and the strain on my right arm, trying to keep him on the straight was exhausting. I was definitely not the boss yet.

'It will come in time,' I told myself, 'It will come in time.' Tusa annoyed me badly but I knew it had to get better. The glass had to be kept half-full.

Our pace was too fast. It meant we covered ground rapidly but I knew maintaining that speed was foolish. Tusa would not cope in the long run. I had no rhythm or sense of being in control and just kept my eyes on the horizon. The air was chilly most days and my face numb and cold. The landscape was dreary and did not provide much visual stimulation. It was dry. It was winter. We passed lots of farmland and open spaces and the road was straight and unexciting. Our contacts on the way were sincere and generous and everybody wanted to be a part of the journey in some way. It was not unusual to find representatives of the local newspaper or television waiting at my destination regardless of the town where we arrived.

There were always some riding days which were worse than others and I remember one distinctly when nothing went smoothly. Early in the day I lost my leading rope and had to turn back to find it lying in the long grass a few hundred yards back. There is nothing as demoralising as having to backtrack on horseback – even if it is only a hundred yards. The pack behind the saddle went lopsided constantly. Irritation was building up inside me from having to get off, fix it and mount again, just to repeat exactly the same a short distance on. I kept on swapping my belongings between the bags to get it balanced. My rain poncho, which was tied up behind the saddle on top of the saddle-bag, fell off numerous times. On one occasion I did not notice. I just heard a noise from behind and when I looked back, saw a man getting off his tractor.

He walked over and said, "I think this belongs to you," and handed me the poncho.

"Can you please help me to tie it up properly," I pleaded.

He was more successful. Men are so much better at making knots and doing little manoeuvres with bits of rope. I also got the idea they loved to show off this talent. I exploited it thoroughly throughout my journey.

I was greeted by two truck drivers who were chatting on the side of the road. They were intrigued to hear about my plans.

One of them commented, "Your horse seems a bit small."

I replied, *"Si señor*. He is small but powerful."

They laughed and waved me off with *"mucha suerte"* (lots of good luck).

Tusa's walk was painstakingly slow and the only way I felt that we were getting ahead was when we trotted. This was difficult with the pack though. My camera weighed down too much on the left side so I held the bag in one hand and used the other for holding the reins. My palms were facing upwards. I still had about 10 kilometres to do to reach my next destination and got a brain-wave. *'I could leave the pack somewhere on the way and simply pick it up with my host later.'* I spotted a gate at the entrance to a farm. It was locked but to the left of it were numerous shrubs and bushes.

'Perfect,' I thought.

I took everything from Tusa's back and hid it underneath the foliage. My spirit felt much lighter as I mounted a happy-looking horse and we made our way down the main road again.

In the town of Rojas, it was Paul, a farmer with Irish blood, who helped me a great deal. We were soon friends. We got on so well, you would have thought we had known each other for years. In his spare time he played polo and was naturally interested in my Zavaletta story. A good gossip and a laugh was all I needed after all the frustration. Paul was perfect for that.

He was also one of the most decent people I met on my way. He helped me without hesitation and never expected anything in return. There was no hidden agenda. What you saw was what you got. I knew that he liked my company but not once did he act in a way that made me feel uncomfortable. He was the perfect gentleman. One day we were having lunch when his large, loud neighbour joined us.

"I love the Irish people," the boisterous man bellowed for everybody to hear.

He took every opportunity to show off his English. "How many points do you give men in Argentina?" he asked with a straight face.

"In which way?" I asked, pretending to take him seriously.

He replied, "Start with physical looks and sexual performance."

Paul blushed. I shook my head and laughed. "Well, I find most men here so physically unappealing that sadly I never had the chance to find out about the other bit."

He looked shocked so I quickly added, "Only joking. The men here are very nice but I did not come to Argentina to find a boyfriend. Although I'm sure that you Latino men would be sensational in all aspects of love and passion."

He looked like an oversized peacock on hearing my words and pushed out his chest. I was waiting for the ruffling of feathers next. He had more questions though.

"Would you date a black man?"

'Strange question,' I thought but answered it nevertheless.

"Yes, if we were on the same wavelength. I think it is about connecting with somebody and not their skin colour."

He looked at me with a sceptical expression and said, "Your answer has just eliminated you from having a relationship with Paul and a thousand hectares."

We all laughed.

My body was in agony from the very beginning and after a few days on the road it continued to ache. Every part of me was sore and I wondered if I would ever recover. I was hungry a lot of the time too. The flimsy insubstantial breakfasts consisting mostly of a few sweet biscuits and a hot drink only, left me craving for food all day.

One morning the host of the house I was staying in came into my room and said, "What do you want for breakfast?"

Aah, life was sweet. I had visions of scrambled eggs, hot toast and fried tomato but before I could answer, she said, "Tea or coffee?"

This was not a good way to start the day and it was not long before I was losing weight. Many a day it would not be until the evening before I would have something decent in my stomach again. Given the ungodly hours of the night that Argentines had their dinner, it meant that fourteen hours could pass between breakfast and my next meal. Water and a few crackers or snacks had to fill the gap most of the time. Later I learned to ask my hosts to take me over to a local shop to buy stock for the next day's ride. Space was limited though and I could only take a few extra bits every time. Liquid always got preference. Hunger can be dealt with but thirst and dehydration were much worse as I was to find out.

Food was the least of my worries. What was more troublesome was that I knew that travelling with one horse was not going to work. It bothered me that the pack was too heavy on Tusa and he struggled, even though we were not travelling long distances. *'Maybe his difficult behaviour is just his way of protesting,'* I thought. But what was I to do? Up to this point no one could assist me in finding a good second Criollo in the vicinity and the only suggestion had come from Dr. Tapia who felt I would get the right horse in Cordoba, a city to the north, in the interior of Argentina. *'Is this where I would find the perfect companion for Tusa? Would a journey there be worth my while?'*

Clarity and the answer to my questions came much sooner than I thought. An unexpected phone call from Florencia, a contact in Cordoba, changed the course of events significantly.

She was ecstatic when we spoke. "When will you be in Cordoba? We are waiting for you!"

I replied, "It might still be a little while. I must get another horse first."

She shrieked over the phone, "Come now! You'll find all the good Criollos here. Don't waste any more time."

Her enthusiasm was infectious and something inside told me to go for it.

"Thanks Florencia. I'll think about it and will let you know tomorrow," I replied.

My mind was already half made up.

The decision to head north to find the missing link in the travelling trio, turned out to be the most important of my whole journey. What I found there was my saving grace. It was meant to be. It was with reason that the first two horses I bought were unsuitable. It was meant to be for the packhorse to act the complete *burro* on our first day's ride. It was meant to be that I was put in touch with Florencia. Fate would have it this way.

Once I had made up my mind to get myself and Tusa to Cordoba, I took transport back to Mercedes and Jorge's farm where I had left most of my belongings. They were not home and I was met by Tommy, their 82-year-old uncle. I arrived quite late and it seemed that I would need a bed for the night. Tommy's wife was not there either.

We sat in front of the fire and he said, "I would invite you to stay for the night but I don't want the neighbours to talk." I had to suppress a smile.

He continued, "But what the hell. My wife trusts me."

Meanwhile, Ciro was sorting out important business for me. He got in touch with José from whom I had bought the two original horses and, after lengthy conversations and explanations, it was agreed that the packhorse could be returned to José's farm. I was told that I would get only 400 dollars back.

I said to Ciro, "But I am not giving him back a horse, minus the tail."

Ciro suggested I accepted the offer and run.

The city of Cordoba, a large and densely populated urban area, is located in the foothills of the Sierra Chica Mountains on the Suquía River. Florencia and her husband Santiago had organised for Tusa to stay at El Galpon, the polo club in Cordoba.

Eduardo, the resident polo teacher received us warmly. His father was also there to give a helping hand. I liked him instantly. He was flamboyant and loved to chat. He also reeked of alcohol. Arriving at the house of the Castellanos felt like coming home. Florencia had good English and Santiago had none. No, to be fair, he had about two words.

In all sincerity, he asked me in Spanish, "Do you think my English accent is more American or more British?" I liked his sense of humour.

Tongue in cheek he would proclaim regularly in mock Hitler-fashion, "Now we speak only Spanish."

Florencia whispered in my ear at one stage, "I think my husband is a little envious of us laughing and talking in English."

She translated whenever she could. I decided to spend more time studying my Spanish phrasebook. I knew the further north we were going to travel the less likely we were to encounter people who spoke English. I had to start making an effort.

The first few days with the Castellanos flew like the wind. I was constantly introduced to family, friends and acquaintances.

Florencia's mom kept on hugging me and said excitedly, "I luuuv to speak the English."

Radio and television interviews happened in abundance. I had a forty-five minute interview with a radio station in South Africa and local television stations in Cordoba got wind of my story. Florencia was the translator and 'out of her skin' to be part of a live interview.

"I can't believe we'll be on television," she kept on saying with a nervous grin.

I soon found out that if you do not speak the lingo, just smile a lot and say "si, claro" (yes, sure).

Before the two presenters even talked about my journey, one of them asked, "How do you like the Argentine men? I am sure you will say we are the best."

Without waiting for my answer, he roared with laughter. Throughout the interview, the two of them competed to come up with the best one-liner and the quirkiest comment. I laughed and blushed throughout the interview. Nothing else was really required.

Another station came out to the stables to get some footage of girl and horse together. On the question, "are you afraid," I had my standard answer ready and said, "Yo no tengo miedo pero tengo cuidado" (I am not afraid, but I am careful). It sounded like a broken record after a while but it was actually the truth.

The unstable political situation continued in Argentina and Santiago was unfortunate to be caught up in the turmoil one day. He was driving with Miekie his friend through town when they found themselves in the midst of a melee of angry strikers. They were attacked. Somebody smashed the side window of the car and punched Santiago in the face. There was no provocation and I felt so sorry for him. Santiago was one of the most serene, fun-loving and gentle people I had ever met. The violence in Argentina did not seem to discriminate.

On my fourth day in Cordoba, Miekie picked me up. We were going to spend the day looking for a Criollo. At the first farm the horses were a skinny English mix and had bad hooves.

"Not suitable," came my quick verdict.

Down the road we visited a *gaucho* who had one black horse which was, apparently, half-Criollo. His tail was cut, it looked like a rat had tried to chew it off.

I said to Miekie, "The one thing I won't have is a horse with a cut tail."

I found the practice horrendous. A horse had a tail for a reason and the ones with these stumps constantly had to battle with flies and insects. I heard they were cut for aesthetic reasons. I could not think of anything more hideous-looking. I especially loved the Criollo tails – they were long, thick and lush and it was as if they wore these beautiful appendages with pride.

Miekie and I drove to Tortoral, which was supposedly the true *gaucho* part in the province of Cordoba. Here we encountered rough and ready cowboys living off the land. Everybody knew Miekie.

"Hola doctor, hola profesor," came the greetings from all directions.

We were entering a little dirt road and Miekie said, "In these parts, some *gauchos* take some land, set up house and then refuse to move. When the owner or police come to investigate they are threatened with violence."

He was still talking when we heard *bang!* Miekie slammed on the brakes. I did not know whether to duck or run.

"We've been ambushed," I whispered under my breath.

Miekie seemed undisturbed even when a man came through the trees in our direction, a large shotgun pointing at us.

"*Amigo,* it's me," shouted Miekie.

The *gaucho* gave us a toothless smile. *"Professor, que tal?"* He explained that he did not recognise the car. I looked at him and his gun warily while Miekie introduced us.

"She's looking for a good Criollo," Miekie said.

The armed *gaucho's* face lit up.

"Follow me, *amigos.*" We were brought to a little settlement just around the corner.

"Also illegally obtained," Miekie mumbled in my ear. There were about seven horses in a *corral,* sheepskins hanging like Christmas decorations from the trees and chickens everywhere. We were met by an unshaven *gaucho* with dirty scarf and leather chaps. Sweat was dripping from his forehead. He was busy in the back, shoeing a horse. The place was tranquil and quiet.

"I have one very good Criollo to show you," he said while chewing with bulging cheeks. This 'very good' horse turned out to have a cut tail too and badly cracked hooves.

The *gaucho* said, "This one will be especially good for a long distance."

Miekie and I looked at each other and I simply said. "Lovely horse but no, he's not right for my journey."

Back in town everybody seemed keen to sell a horse but none could come up with the goods. We drove back to Cordoba in Miekie's car with the broken window. A freezing wind blew through the plastic sheets we taped around the frame. Miekie gave me an encouraging smile.

"You will find your Criollo. This was just the first day."

"I know," I shouted over the noise of the whistling wind, trying to sound more upbeat than I felt.

Florencia met us at the door when we returned. "Did you find your horse?" she asked with a glint in her eye.

I shook my head.

"Don't be discouraged yet," she said. "Eduardo called and he thinks there is a Criollo at the Polo Club. He wants you to go there tomorrow."

"Even if you are on the right track, you will get run over if you just sit there"
— *Will Rogers*

I woke up in the morning with a strange knot in my stomach. It was not nervousness. No, I was excited. It was as if an invisible force was urging me on to get to the stables as quickly as possible. When I got there, a mare was already saddled up in traditional tack. She wore her black fringe long and it covered her eyes. Her look was mysterious. She gave an impatient snort and had attitude as she moved around restlessly, ears perked up. Mounting, I trembled slightly but it faded as soon as we got going. She had a bouncy walk and her head swung from left to right. She was out to impress. It looked comical from where I was sitting and I relaxed into the saddle.

Back at the stables, Eduardo waited with a knowing look on his face.

"What do you think?" he asked.

My happy grin gave it away.

"She's wonderful. She is absolutely wonderful. This is it Eduardo. This is my Mise."

I kept shaking my head in disbelief at my good fortune.

Eduardo said, "Don't come near me when I negotiate with her owner. I will get you a good price."

I paid 350 dollars for Mise. She was worth a million.

The next day, I sent an email to friends;

I'm in Cordoba at the moment, where I stay with very nice people. Found my second horse (a she) and I am delighted. She was right under my nose at the polo club. A real Criollo with nice spirit, good hooves and legs and a fast walk (very important). She leads perfectly as well, trotting alongside the other horse. The anaemia tests will be finished tomorrow and I hope to leave soon. The weather is really cold and wet at the moment so keep your fingers crossed for a bit of sun and blue skies. I've done quite a few interviews here. Argentina is in a state of economic crisis and any non-depressing news is very popular. I still don't like the publicity but it is good from the perspective that people will know about me and I am not a complete stranger on two horses when I travel through the country. So from a safety point of view, it is probably beneficial.

Thanks for not forgetting me.

A reply from Dave followed shortly. It reminded me that life went on while I was planning to spend my days experiencing the world from the back of a horse. His words were testimony that some things would always stay the same. I found comfort in that.

I'm delighted that you have now got the two horses you are going to use over the course of your adventure. It is also amazing to see the route – so many towns and so many experiences to be had. I think the publicity will be good for your safety overall and will possibly provide contacts along the way. Life here is quiet enough – I think I'm still recovering from the weekend in Barcelona. I've just heard there are going to be two permanent jobs in another college which is a bit of a pain as I wouldn't like to leave where I am. We're having a surprise party for my mam at the end of this month – her 70th. Mello has a marquee which will be erected in the back garden and we'll get kegs. I'll have one of those nice glasses of Guinness for you. If you get a chance, drop her a short note via me. Keep on trekking on and on and on… Give Tusa a kick in the arse for me!
Ciao bella

Florencia was celebrating her birthday on the day I found Mise and the double-bash suited perfectly. The house was festive when I got there and there were enough cakes and pastries to feed an army. The conversation turned quickly to my journey and everybody had an opinion and good advice to throw in.

One of the female guests, making big eyes, said, "You must look out for a bug called *vinchuca*. You will find them in the poor houses in South and Central America. They will give you *chagas* disease."

I nodded and she continued.

"They live in the grass on the inside of the thatched houses. In the middle of the night they fall on to their victim. Their bites are small and can look like a spider's but the consequences are dire."

I shivered. She was not finished yet.

"These insects infect the blood and if it's not fatal, recovery is very difficult. I know of somebody dying from a bite like that ten years after she was bitten."

I asked, "Will insect repellent help to keep them away?"

She replied with a serious face, "Nothing but God will help you."

'Well, that's that then,' I thought. 'I had better start praying.'

I had a vision of myself, kneeling on a sheepskin, '…and dear God, when I enter those poorer dwellings, please protect me from the falling bugs. I promise to be good if you do. I don't mind the mosquitoes and the spiders. Just not those blood sucking bugs.'

Eduardo suggested that I leave on a sunny day.

He explained, "It is too depressing to pack up, say goodbye to friends and set off with two horses on a miserable rainy day. It's not a good way to start."

My departure happened sooner than expected. It was inevitable. Just as the weather had to improve and the head cold that had hung around for days would pass, so the time to say *adios* had to come. But is there ever a right time to leave? There are always things you feel you should have done, conversations you should have had and places you should have seen. While so much lay ahead, sightseeing was probably the least important in this case. Throughout my journey, I never felt like a tourist and I hardly ever visited any must-see spots on my way. It suited me like that. I had other things on my mind.

When I got to the stables on the morning of my departure as the sun rays were already warming the earth, I discovered that it was not just Eduardo that would be accompanying me out of the city but also his girlfriend and her sister.

It was a slow start as preparing one *mate* after another got preference over getting the horses ready. I was anxious to leave early. It was 50 kilometres to Jesús Maria. I had calculated at least eight hours of riding for the day with maybe two half hour stops.

While mounting Mise I was clumsy and managed to twist one of my fingers.

"What's wrong?" Eduardo shouted over his shoulder.

I forced a smile. "Nothing." The pain was intense.

Eduardo led us through back roads and, before I knew it, he was urging his horse to go through a small area where rubbish had been dumped. I was annoyed. *'I'll be damned if the horses stepped on to broken glass or an open tin,'* I thought.

"Is there not another way?" I asked.

He waved me on. "Go for it."

He just did not get it. He would be riding not more than ten miles that day and, that night, his horse would be cosily tucked into a stable. If his horse sustained any injuries during the day he would be left to rest and recuperate until he got better. I did not have that luxury. My horses were my only means of transport and getting them injured was most definitely not part of the plan. I held my breath as we made it through the rubble. Later we passed a few shops and ended up going on the footpath. Tusa had to answer a call of nature and as we passed a butchery he lifted his tail. The owner came out, shaking his head furiously.

"*Perdon señor,*" I said with a friendly wave.

His face softened. "*Suerte señorita.*"

"I think he saw you on the news," said Eduardo.

People kept on hooting and shouting good luck and Eduardo did not want to miss the opportunity to fill in curious bystanders about the nature of my mission.

"She is going as far as New York," he said almost with fatherly pride.

We reached the outskirts of Cordoba around noon. I was happy to say goodbye. It was time to be on my own. Eduardo and the two sisters were on the edge of the highway on their horses and looked on as we trotted away. Tusa led with difficulty and pulled back all the time. I pretended not to notice. I could not bear the thought of the others seeing me struggle. At this stage it was still all about appearances. It did not matter what happened behind closed doors. I could deal with most things on my own, but in front of others I had to keep up the facade.

"Everything is under control," I muttered to myself.

It was not. Five kilometres down the road, Tusa spooked and jumped. The leading rope caught my leg and I was pulled off Mise's back. I fell flat on the ground. Mise also got a fright but thankfully did not step on me. I was not hurt but suffered more from a bruised ego – especially when I spotted a group of young people a distance away, amazed by the spectacle.

I walked the next kilometre on foot until the shakes in my legs had ceased. When I got on Tusa again he continued his antics, lowering his head constantly in the hope of grabbing some grass. Mise trotted like a crab. I could feel the aggravation inside me building up. This was no fun. I would be damned if we would have riding like this every day. I bit on my teeth, sighed and visualised better days.

I arrived on the outskirts of Jesús Maria, very weary. It was almost dark, it was cold and I had the shakes. I made my way to the petrol station, the pre-arranged 'meeting spot'. I was trembling from hunger too and grabbed a few crackers from the saddlebags and finished off a coke. I had not eaten all day. It was pitch dark when my hosts, who were friends of the Castellanos in Cordoba, pulled up.

"It's still another two miles to our house," Sebastian said as he got out of his vehicle.

"Really?" I said with a deep sigh. My body was in agony.

The girls stepped in. "We'll take the horses. You go with Sebastian."

I felt like hugging them. "Thank you, thank you," was all I said and made a beeline for the car before they changed their minds.

By the time the girls arrived at the house, I had already taken a shower. I was worn-out and could not stop looking over at my bed. My finger from the morning's injury was throbbing and a vet friend of my hosts, Fabiane, had a look. She applied a cream and then strapped it with a piece of metal and bandage so I could not bend it.

I looked at her and said, "It will be interesting to see how I cope tomorrow with only nine fingers. If today is anything to go by, then the future looks bleak."

I told her how I fell off Mise and then about the train incident, the three of us nearly getting flattened under the wheels of a truck. She gave me a reassuring hug. "You're doing great," she said. "Things will get better for you every day."

Later, Fabiane and I checked on the horses. To avoid them having sore muscles in the morning Fabiane administered *buta*, an anti-inflammatory, orally with water in a syringe.

'Soon I will have to do this myself,' I thought. *'There's not going to be a Fabiane on every corner.'*

Dinner, consisting of king-sized chunks of barbequed meat, was served around 11 p.m. that evening. I was so tired, I could hardly swallow.

Sebastian, who is a farrier, looked at the horses' feet the next morning. "These horses are badly shod," he said with authority.

Next thing he had his chaps on and with tool in hand, proceeded to take Mise's shoes off. The shoeing of the horses turned into a social event with everybody watching and it was lunchtime before I managed to get on the road again. We had only 24 kilometres ahead of us, most of it on dirt road.

It was funny how the mind worked. Suddenly it was no big deal to do more than 20 kilometres on horseback. Initially I thought I would collapse if I had to do more than five, and indeed felt like it after our first day. The day before I had done more than fifty and now I considered our next stretch as if it was merely a jog in the park: *'Only* 24 kilometres ahead of us!'

While I saddled up, somebody asked, "How much did you pay for your saddle?"

"About 300 dollars," I replied.

Knowing looks were exchanged around the circle of friends. "What?" I said. "Did I pay too much?"

"You did. You shouldn't have paid more than half of that."

I spared them the details of Zavaletta.

Carlos, host at our next stop, met us with an armful of *alfalfa*. Their house was humble and devoid of luxury. But their hospitality, together with Silvi's peach pie and Carlos' advice on Criollos was fit for a king.

Carlos said, "You can do about 50 kilometres a day but remember to change the horses halfway (packhorse becomes riding horse and vice versa), so they don't get bored."

'At last somebody is thinking about the psyche of a horse as well,' I thought.

He continued, "I suggest you start using a whistle or sound that's the same every time so that they will come towards you when they hear it."

I said, "Like when I take food to them you mean? A bit like Pavlov and his dog?"

He paused a moment. "Exactly."

The next day at 12:30 p.m., we took an hour's break. We had already done 30 kilometres and I was pleased with our progress.

"Good," I said to myself and the horses. "This means we'll be able to do an average of 15 kilometres in one and a half hours. That is 45 kilometres in four and a half hours."

I neglected to add that it would mean trotting all day, an unrealistic idea to say the least.

Deep down I knew we would not be able to continue at that pace. I still found the constant riding uncomfortable and was not accustomed yet to the gait of the horses. I did not know what to do with myself when we trotted and did a half-hearted English-style lift out of the saddle. I had never been tutored to ride like that and had to rely on my gut feeling. Soon my knees were in excruciating pain and I had to stop every hundred yards or so to give them a rub. During our breaks, I unsaddled the horses completely. I had an apple and raisins for the hunger pangs. People watched us curiously from a distance but no-one talked to me.

Further down the road, I encountered two men standing next to their broken down car. I stopped to chat. One of them kept on touching my arm.

I said, *"Tengo que irme"* (I have to go) and left.

I was proud of the few Spanish phrases I knew to get me out of trouble. When I stopped at a garage for refreshments on the outskirts of the town, the men were there too and approached me again.

I had an uneasy feeling and said assertively, *"todo bien"* (everything is okay).

They looked a bit offended.

"We only wanted to see if you needed a phone," one responded.

I felt silly for having been overly cautious.

We were welcomed by the Bechara family as if we were doing something very special. Despite my aches and pains I revelled in the cheers and hand-clapping from Pinki and her three children as we trotted into town. Before I could get my feet out of the stirrups a microphone was pushed in my face and Juan Carlos, Pinki's husband, was translating my story to the local press. The kids bulldozed each other out of the way to get to stand as close as possible to me in the hope that they too would be on television that evening. Mise and Tusa stood very still for the camera. Mise looked bored though and gave one long yawn after another. She had an air of 'been there, done that' about her.

We had another few miles to do to get to La Feria del Ganado where a sandy *corral* awaited the horses. They could hardly contain themselves while I saddled them down.

"Why do they move around so much?" Juan Carlos asked.

"You'll see in a moment," I laughed.

I was still taking off the bridle and reins when Mise went down on her knees and, with one smooth movement she was on her side, wriggling in the sand. She was struggling to roll on to the other side and looked comical with all four legs kicking in the air. Some horses with high withers find it difficult to roll over and usually have to get up and down again. Like most other horses, mine loved to roll. Mostly they did it for pleasure, grooming, to relieve discomfort or to rest. During the journey they always tried to roll after being untacked. This was to ease the irritation of moisture on skin by drying the sweat with dirt. I was told that the dirt acts as an extra layer of protection against biting insects. It made sense – I noticed I was bitten least when at my dirtiest.

When we got back into the pickup truck, I felt happy and content. I said a silent prayer.

'Please God, give us a safe place like this every night.'

At the house the kids followed me everywhere. They were still on a high from having what they considered an unusual visitor and they watched my every move. Pinki ran me a hot bubble bath and had to 'shoo' the kids out of the bathroom.

"Give our guest a chance to wash in peace."

They left dragging their feet.

When I made an appearance again after a lengthy much needed soak, I was presented with roses and a little welcome card. Each child stepped forward for a hug and I cautioned them not to come too close.

"I still have a bit of my Cordoba cold left," I said, coughing and patting my chest when it seemed they did not understand.

The next day over breakfast, Juan Carlos asked, "So what do you think about while riding?"

I sneezed and said, "Nothing really at this stage. I'm too busy managing the horses and trying to get them into a comfortable rhythm so my every thought is occupied with surviving from one mile to the other."

Juan Carlos said, "I will take you to the chemist. You seem to be still unwell. Stay another day."

One day became four when my head-cold turned into a nasty chest infection. I felt miserable and low. I missed home. I also missed my mom and I so much wanted her to be around. I felt teary-eyed but managed not to cry. I was well pampered though. My meals were served in bed and reading material was brought to me to kill the boredom. I kept on studying my maps and planning the next stretch. When I became concerned about the unknown ahead, I reminded myself of Josefina, the eight-year-old's words.

"Enjoy every day, don't think too much about the future."

My backside was particularly sensitive despite the fact that I had a comfortable saddle with a cushy sheepskin. I feared saddle-sores so I asked Pinki to look out for cycling shorts in town. I remembered my youngest brother's words clearly.

"Wear padded cycling shorts under your riding trousers. In fact, wear two."

Female vanity won over comfort but I did take some of his advice and got one pair of shorts. I had a pang of self-consciousness when I mounted Mise with an enlarged, albeit well protected rear-end. It worked a treat.

Juan Carlos worried about my getting into the saddle again and expressed his concern. "The next stretch is very remote and there are only salt lakes. I think it will be too difficult and very tough for you and the horses."

"I know what you mean," I said. "But I feel I want to rough it a bit as well. I need to be able to take the good and the bad."

"True," he replied. "But this is different. Between San José and Totoralejos there are 80 kilometres of nothing. No food or water for you and the horses. No place to stay. It's winter and you are still not well. It's too cold to camp out. It's not safe either."

"What do you suggest?" I asked.

He said, "Let me take you through that part at least."

I knew his suggestion made sense. It was a bit of a Catch 22 for me. I so badly wanted to ride but I needed to be sensible too. I did not want to jeopardise our journey by being foolish so early on. The horses were my main concern. I reluctantly agreed to Juan Carlos' offer.

It was when we picked up the horses that I was to witness cock-fighting for the first time. There were two cocks battling it out in a small, make-shift steel ring, their heads bobbing up and down as a couple of young men sat around, drinking beer and laughing. Music blared in the background. I felt sick and wanted to leave immediately. On the way I asked Juan Carlos about it.

"It is illegal but nobody pays attention," he said.

Day 35. A massive Argentine flag, blowing blue and white in the wind greeted us on arrival in the town of Frias. Our host, a man known locally as Dr. Gringo, had a jovial look on his face when he met us. It was evening and with a line-up of 4 x 4 pickup trucks behind us, we made our way to the farm where the horses would be staying. I was leading Mise (we jogged) and Tusa followed behind with the stream of lights from the vehicles illuminating the way. It was an exciting moment. It felt like I was on the set of a blockbuster movie. The air was soft and breezy.

That evening I wrote in my diary;

I studied the road very carefully as we drove through the remote and isolated Salinas. I made the right decision. The horses' welfare and happiness are my main concern. I can't put them through too much at this stage. They are not fit yet and this kind of hardship can break them totally. I will only be able to ride with them into New York City if I am careful. I have to assess every situation and every road with much caution. I also hope to get more experienced as time moves on – to know what I can put them through and when to be vigilant.

Gringo's family was half-Arabic and their diet fully so. I was the only one who disguised the raw minced meat that evening with salt, pepper and olive oil. If I thought it would not offend, I would have blocked my nose while swallowing the uncooked dish on my plate.

Gringo who had a permanent twinkle in his eye, said, "While you travel through my country I want you to look for a humble Argentine. If you find one, I want you to ring me."

"Sure," I said tongue in cheek.

"But that's not all," he continued. "When you travel through your next country and you find a Bolivian who smiles, I want you to ring me too."

Gringo was very impressed with what I was doing and treated me like a son of whom he could be very proud. I was not allowed to chit-chat with the ladies and had to participate in the more manly pursuits that he was interested in. After breakfast the following morning, he left the dining table and appeared with two hefty guns. He handed one to me.

"Let's go. We're going to do some shooting."

Puzzled, I said, "What type of shooting?"

"Just wait and see," he said with a mischievous look.

I had a flashback from my youth of my brother trying to shoot birds with his airgun. I would follow him in secret, he would aim and just as he was about to pull the trigger, I would cough, sneeze or laugh. Sometimes I threw stones. It worked until he pointed the gun at me, threatening to get me if he did not get a bird. I never knew whether it was a real warning or a bluff, but usually I left him alone at that point. I would walk back to the house with my hands on my ears.

Gringo's plans for shooting left me uncomfortable and I tried to find an excuse not to go. I was too slow though and before I knew it we were in the pickup. We went off the main road on dirt paths and, through the trees I spotted a big pond, almost like a dam. Gringo was excited – he did not know the place existed. He walked purposefully towards the water. On the way he got his gun ready and before he even came to a complete standstill he fired a shot. Hundreds of birds scattered out of the trees.

Feathers flew in all directions and I could see a few doves tumbling to the ground. I was horrified.

"My God!" I shouted. "You're shooting with a shotgun. That's not fair. You're giving those birds no chance."

Gringo hardly listened and re-loaded his gun. He handed it to me. "Shoot. Shoot those stupid birds."

My legs were wobbly and my hands shook. "No, I don't want to use that gun. It proves nothing to shoot a bird like that."

"Oh go on. We don't have another gun. Just point and shoot."

I closed my eyes when I pulled the trigger. I missed the tree completely and only managed to chase all the birds away that had settled in between the leaves again.

"Did you do that on purpose?" Gringo asked.

"Of course not."

It was half a lie.

After the massacre Gringo picked up his trophy-birds. I had no doubt what would be on the dinner-menu that evening. A dove was on the ground half alive, twisting and squirming. I noticed his little heart, beating up and down in his chest. He tried to get away from us.

Gringo said, "Grab that bird."

"No way," I said.

Without hesitation Gringo stepped forward, picked up the helpless bird and broke his legs as if they were match-sticks. I was on the verge of throwing up.

"That's terrible Gringo. You have to kill him humanely. He's suffering."

He looked at me. "You women are too soft."

We left the once-tranquil area behind, used cartridges scattered on the ground, terrified birds everywhere and Gringo's empty Marlboro packet floating on the water. On the way back, Gringo asked if I wanted to drive his fancy Cherokee. I only said yes to escape the writhing birds at my feet. I was disgusted. I looked at him in the rear-view mirror. He could tell from my eyes that I was not smiling.

"I am going to call this place Lake Marianne," he said from the backseat. "I am so happy because there are many birds and I only found it today because you were here."

I did not answer.

Gringo showed his softer side later and provided me with a whip, called a *fusta*, for the horses. He even painted the Argentine flag on it. I found the mere presence of a *fusta* kept the horses in line. I hardly ever used it, but they knew it was there.

Gringo said, "People of the world are good. Everybody is helping you because God wants you to be safe."

He rang his uncle in Salta and asked if I could be treated to a trip on the *Tren de las Nubes* (Train to the Clouds), a famous tourist train that travels through beautiful landscape up to 13,800 feet above sea level.

"It's an exhilarating ride," Gringo said, "a ride with views that will make you feel as if the train was flying. The train winds through the high mountains, rumbling through small towns where time seems to stand still. It is one of the world's greatest railroad experiences," he enthused.

He told his uncle about my trip and said, "She can't do more than 50 kilometres a day, because she's a woman."

He was a funny man and when I looked beyond that morning's shooting expedition, I could not help but like him.

At one point he said, "You know, doves mate for life. I am the same. I will perish the day my wife dies."

"So why do you shoot the doves if you know they mate for life?" I asked.

"I don't know," he said.

An email he sent a few weeks later, never ceased to make me smile;

Hi, darling !! when are you in this moment ?
Arrived to Salta? Mister Jorge Vidal Casas wose friendly , hospitalary whit you ? I hope all your things are well, fine, and your heart continous whit power , bleeding for conquist the way of Mayas and happy for can make this, your work, your job , the litle and great motiv of the life – Tell as please , answer to me, in who site are you in this time, ? Are you well ? I can reed in your tatachallenge taht all the people is hospitalary whit you , and love you very much – ? Is taht true ? I belive . I send for you blesings and love – Go, Go ..!! *En vuelos raudales hacia conquistas infinitas* !! Un abrazo- Elias (Gringo) and Silvia.

Later, Gringo's politician brother and the Mayor of the town came over to the house. They made a few calls to arrange places for me and the horses to stay en route to Tucumán. It would take me five days of riding to cover the 220 kilometres.

My kidneys ached and gave me a lot of grief the day we were supposed to face the road again. I ignored the dull, constant pain and put on my half-chaps. Fernando did not like *mate* but offered me my own cup. He and his vet friend kept on saying *"muy lindo"* (very nice), referring to my journey.

They could not get their heads around the craziness of my trip. *"Una chica. Solita. Con dos caballos"* (A girl. Alone. With two horses).

It was the 'alone' part that intrigued them most.

They fancied Mise and reckoned she was the better horse.

"She'll take you all the way."

Poor Tusa stood with head hanging, as though he knew he could not win such praise. He drew back his ears to get some attention but was ignored by the men. I noticed though and patted his neck. I was very fond of both my horses. I loved Tusa, but Mise was my heart's delight. She was the one who would give me hope when all seemed bleak. Every day she would work so hard to please. Often I thought to myself, *'How can I ever give up when she is putting up such a courageous effort.'*

On the morning we left Frias the men helped me saddle up. It took a while to get the saddle bags balanced and it troubled me that I did not know what to do to make it better. I had a suspicion that a complete system change was necessary.

The weather was very pleasant when we finally set off. A mild breeze blew beneath the blue skies – close to a perfect day. The side of the road was far from perfect though. Pebbles were strewn everywhere and the horses stumbled over spiky shrubs and thorny bushes. I discovered a small dirt road to the right and had a full two kilometres to enjoy the luxury of the smooth, sandy surface. Mise was trotting very fast and I suspected she caught sight of a farm which she thought would be our next port of call.

During the day's ride Tusa sporadically broke into bursts of energetic trotting, pushing to be head to head with Mise. This was not the best move. Cars came from the front and left us with almost no room to manoeuvre. There was little margin for error. If one of the horses spooked and jumped to the side of the road we would all be history. The constant rubbing from the saddle-bags against my leg when Tusa came too close, started to test my temper.

Sylvie's *milanesa* (meat similar to schnitzel) roll proved to be an excellent snack. During my journey she was one of the few people who took the initiative and made me a sandwich or something small to eat on the road. People did not realise the difference that made in a day's ride. It was the small things that had the most effect.

The road stretched out before us in a long line. As far as I could see there was not a curve or bend. On the side were lots of bushes and burnt grass. We did not arrive in Lavalle before five that afternoon and I was given a basic room for the night. While I hosed the horses down, a car stopped and Nestor, the Mayor from Frias, and a friend got out.

"We are just checking that you're okay *señorita*." They looked at my host. "Make sure you feed the lady well. She is going to New York."

Nestor patted my back and put a fatherly hand on my shoulder.

I managed to buy *alfalfa* and maize for the horses and groomed them extensively while they chewed and basked in the late-afternoon sun. It was already dark when I rode Mise bare-back to the farm where she and Tusa would be staying. Tusa followed us without a leading rope. The caretaker assured me that the stallion next door would pose no threat.

"I'm not so sure about that," I said. "Mise is an attractive (I nearly added 'and willing') lady."

I gave the stallion a warning finger when I left.

The house where I had pizza that evening was poor with hardly any furniture visible. They brought in a television from the bedroom especially for me and dessert was acquired from the next-door neighbour. Sandra, the woman of the house, chatted incessantly. You would swear I had perfect Spanish but she did not notice I was quiet.

My sleeping bag got used for the first time that evening. The air was fresh and chilly.

The stretch between Lavalle and San Pedro was one I would rather forget. The tarmac was hot and rough and traffic was heavy so we had to go off the road. It was horrendous. Every open space was covered by a thin, black, sharp-edged thorn that stuck to everything. And stick it did – to my trousers, the horses' legs and bellies, my poncho, the saddle-blankets – anything that had the potential for sticking on to. It was misery. To add to the frustration I had to chase after Mise. Twice. The leading rope had come loose and she simply turned around and started walking back towards Lavalle. I silently prayed for patience. The lack of this noble virtue was still in short supply.

Soon the vegetation turned to vicious-looking thorn plants and small stones covered every inch of riding space. When I reached for water out of a small bag, I touched an empty space. The bag had fallen off.

"Fuck it," I said out loud.

Back-tracking. The last thing I wanted to do. I cursed under my breath as we made it back through the prickly plants and long grass. I had to try and think when the bag was last there. It could have been anywhere. I was making mental pictures when I spotted a piece of green material on the ground.

"Hallelujah!" I was less uptight for the remainder of the day's ride.

I signalled with a long outstretched arm for every car and truck that approached to go across to the other side – given that there was no oncoming traffic. Most of them complied and waved. Five kilometres from town a policeman stopped us. He told me he was ordered to look out for me. I asked him if he would take my saddlebags and poncho to San Pedro, anything to make the pack lighter and give the horses some respite.

My next host was a lady called Alba Garay, the Mayor of the town. She had not a word of English and a young boy of about fourteen was summoned to act as translator. He looked under pressure though and stuttered his way through his limited knowledge of English. It was 4 p.m. before I had my first snack of the day.

The rest of the afternoon was spent pulling out thorns.

Monica, Alba's daughter, offered to wash my clothes. She was warm and friendly and made a real effort to speak very slowly in Spanish. She took me around the dusty town to buy corn for the horses. She smiled gratefully when I handed her an ice cold drink. We sipped the sweet liquid under a lowering sun while the horses ate. A number of young boys watched curiously from a distance. The clown in the group made the odd chirpy remark but suddenly became dumb and shy when challenged by Monica.

That evening she sat on the edge of my bed and said, "I wish you could stay another day but I realise you have a programme to follow."

I was tired enough to stay longer but it was not time for a rest day yet. I told Monica that I had to press on. The road ahead was long.

A crowd gathered when I went to collect the horses in the morning. It was a beautiful day – overcast but not too warm. The young translator informed me that he and his family were going to Tucumán (a city which I hoped to reach in about three days).

I grabbed the opportunity. "Can you please take my *alforjas* (saddlebags) with you to the next town and drop them off?"

He was happy to help.

It seemed as if half the town followed as we made our way to a colourful, bright yellow church where I wanted to take a few pictures. Somebody mentioned 'interview' and, before I knew it, I was ushered into a basic, small studio-room behind the church. My young translator did his best but I feared the message that went out was quite removed from the real deal. I managed to answer a few of the questions without his help.

Just as I was about to mount Mise, somebody shouted from the crowd, "There is another radio station that wants to speak to you."

I shook my head. "I'm sorry, it's already late. We must go now."

Everybody waved as we trotted through the dusty town. The houses we passed were plain and unpainted, with sheets of flat roofs made from corrugated iron. They reminded me of the shanty towns in South Africa. Music was blaring and everywhere there were dogs, chickens and people standing around chatting.

"Ciao Marianne," came shouts from all directions.

Obviously everybody had a radio in town.

Just as we reached the outskirts, Tusa's leg got tangled up in the leading rope. I panicked for a moment but managed to keep him calm. He snorted and pranced around with his leg in the air, but at least did not try to break free. Two men came to our rescue and released his leg.

Lamadrid was 40 kilometres away.

We rode the first stretch on the tarmac and the young translator and his family who had my bags, drove past and then stopped to chat. They offered me some *mate* as well as religious cards from two elderly gentlemen whose picture I took earlier in town.

I took a picture of a small settlement later and a boy on the side of the road suggested that I take a small dirt road that ran parallel to the main one. He was still talking to me when three men with hunting guns appeared from the bushes, as if from nowhere. They were not too friendly and looked at me suspiciously. I returned the look but decided not to hang around. I slowly lowered the camera into my money-belt, pulled the reins to the left and put Mise into a fast trot. I did not look back.

I followed the small dirt road for a while but soon it got too thorny and bushy and I had to go on the tar road once more.

We passed through Taco Ralo. There were only a few poor mud huts and nothing else. Outside Lamadrid some young people with orange dyed hair and strange faces stood in the middle of the road with banners. They were *piqueteros* and tried to stop the cars and trucks. I passed with a simple *"hola"*.

At a petrol station a couple approached me to have their picture taken with the horses. An older woman, who, I found out later was the mother of my next contact, was waiting there as well. With her was a sweet young girl of about three. I asked the woman to lift up the girl and put her in front of me. It was another two miles to the house and the girl did not object. The heat of the sun and the motion of Mise's swinging walk must have made her drowsy and soon she was fast asleep in my arms.

At the railway near the house, I tied up the horses. My hosts offered dry bread and coffee which I devoured hungrily. A young boy came along to take the horses to their *corral* and I walked with him to where another family lived on a tiny plot of land. There were three stables. The whole family watched while I organised the horses. I settled them in for the night and administered *buta* without much effort. I was invited for cakes and *mate*, which I found sickly sweet. Up to now, I had been drinking *mate amargo* (bitter) but was warned that the further north you go in Argentina the sweeter it becomes.

Something else that changed as our journey advanced was people's knowledge of English. It became more and more difficult to communicate. Dinner that evening passed in silence. I ate only vegetables and salad and I used the little girl as a bit of a distraction. I made my excuses early. The 'I have to write my diary' phrase came in very useful throughout my travels.

The next morning I walked through the quiet streets of Lamadrid long before sunrise to collect the horses. It was calm and tranquil. I loved this time of the day – the quiet before the madness. It also meant fewer preying eyes.

Back at the house an hour later, the woman of the house was up and offered me coffee. When nothing else was forthcoming, I proceeded to pack. By now a few curious spectators had gathered around. Everybody stared but nobody was interested in giving a helping hand.

Once on the road, Mise was in joyous mood and tried her best to get in front of Tusa. This was troublesome, given she was on the leading rope. Two friendly policemen stopped.

"Are you going to Simoca by any chance?" I asked eagerly.

I thought one of them said yes and proceeded to take off the saddlebags. I was wrong – I misunderstood and they were not going there at all. I hid my disappointment and loaded Mise up again. The word got around fast because, a short while later, two more policemen came over. They shook my hand and had many questions.

One said, "You should ride on the right side of the road. It's safer."

The other one added, "And don't travel at night."

I shook their friendly hands once more. *"Si señores. Y muchas gracias."*

The rest of the day passed in boring fashion. Although I found small secondary roads occasionally, there were too many little stones. Bushes were everywhere and I found nowhere comfortable to stop for a rest. We encountered a few dodgy characters and unfriendly young men standing on the side of the road. Also, more 'human roadblocks' in the form of *piqueteros* – we ignored them and Tusa trotted through nonchalantly.

I was grateful for the change of scenery later. We crossed rivers and bridges and the landscape opened up more. It was still overcast but cooler than the day before. Our only pit-stop for the day was next to a modest hut. I shared some of the corn I was carrying with the resident donkey. A woman with horse and carriage drove past.

"How far to Simoca, *señora*?" I shouted behind her.

She looked back at us. *"Cerquita. Muy cerquita"* (Close, very close).

It was not.

The road unfurled dauntingly in an unbroken line to the horizon and it seemed Simoca was just an illusion. My back and shoulders ached and I stretched as much as possible while sitting on Tusa. We passed many mud huts with lots of scrawny dogs and dusty pigs. The latter wore wooden sticks around their necks so they could not get through the wired fences. When I first spotted some at a distance, I thought they were some new breed of pigs with horns. Most people I passed only looked on suspiciously or stared. Even the kids seemed apathetic – no white toothpaste smiles like you would get in Africa. No enthusiasm. No joy. My waves and *holas* were met by silence. The odd child would raise a shy hand but most of them showed no emotion. I must have been a strange sight indeed.

It was almost dark when we entered Simoca. I could feel the strain of the 50 kilometres in every part of my body. Obscured by high walls and gates, I found the house of Felix Mote, the Mayor and my next contact, quite easily. I tied up the horses and according to custom, clapped my hands to get somebody's attention from inside. Just as the maid came out of the house, high pitched squealing erupted from behind us. I looked around and saw a sow being taken off a truck, leaving her distressed piglets behind. Two men held her high up in the air on a scale and then dropped her down where she landed on the cement with a painful thud. It was a slaughterhouse. I shivered and felt sick. Mise was agitated too and looked disturbed. Throughout the trip she proved to be very sensitive to other creatures and she was always the one to react emotionally to any dead animals we encountered on the road.

Felix's brother, Miguel, came out after a while. His English extended to 'yes' and 'no'. He had an amiable, open manner and said in Spanish, "I did not know that you were staying here. My brother Felix is in Buenos Aires and did not tell me anything about you."

Before I could reply, he said, "But that is no problem. You're very welcome in my house."

Miguel was in his late thirties and cared for his mother who suffered from Alzheimer's. He had gentle eyes. We took the horses to their farm outside town. Back at the house I fell asleep in a chair while he threw together something to eat. Later he went out and returned with chocolate for me to take on the road the next day. That evening I spoke to Pancho. He had fluent English. He was expecting me to arrive in Tucumán the next day. Like a true gentleman, Miguel gave up his room for the night. I was asleep before my head hit the pillow.

Rising from my slumbers the next morning is best described as a shock awakening. I heard the alarm go off at 7am. The bed-side table was out of arms' reach so I stumbled out of bed and tried to locate the switch. In the process, I touched the metal part below the bulb. It was a mistake. A powerful shock shot through my hands, up my arms and through my entire body and I was flung to the other side of the room. I screamed in agony as the shocks continued to vibrate through me. Miguel rushed into the room.

"*Que pasa!*" (What happened), he shouted.

I had uncontrollable shakes and could not answer him. I pointed to the lampshade. Miguel grabbed me around the shoulders.

"*Dios mio, Dios mio*" (my God, my God).

He sounded devastated. He kept on rubbing my arm and held me tight. He cried when he saw my tears. I did not know if I should feel sorrier for him or myself. He put me back into bed and I heard him on the telephone. Ten minutes later the local doctor entered my room. I only half-felt the needle sting on my bottom. Shortly after, a woman that I did not know came into the room. She brushed my face gently with her hand. *'Is she an angel come to take me away,'* I wondered in a blurry daze. But I was not dying and she was only a masseuse. I was asleep when she left and did not wake up until lunchtime.

The relief was visible on Miguel's face when he looked around the door to see a smiling woman in bed. I had three portions of the lasagne dish he prepared. Later we went for a spin around town in his open jeep. To make up for my accident and the guilt he felt, he insisted that I have more than one ice-cream.

On the way, Miguel said, "I am going with you tomorrow on horseback to Tucumán."

"There is no need," I said. "Thanks, but I'll be fine."

He insisted, "I want to go with you to make sure you are okay. I am worried about you."

"It's 50 kilometres," I said. "You will be so sore afterwards."

But he was adamant. "I don't care. I will feel better if I go with you. Also, I could visit my girlfriend who lives in town."

We left the next morning later than planned. I insisted that Miguel put a sheepskin on the flimsy English saddle he was planning to use. Everything moved a bit too slow for my liking. I was riding in the front and kept on looking back to see if Miguel was all right. We crossed a river and 13 kilometres from Simoca we stopped on the side of the road for *mate* and tasty pastries he had bought earlier. I heard a click-click sound when we got going again. I did not have much experience but I was sure where that sound came from. I told Miguel to check his horses' feet. He got off and checked only the right back foot.

"Everything is fine," he answered. But the sound continued.

"Stop," I said.

I got off Tusa and lifted his horse's back left foot. The shoe was hanging from two loose nails. Miguel got a tool from a nearby house but would not let me assist him. I guess one accident was enough for him. After a clumsy attempt he finally got the shoe off. Most of the nails remained though.

"You won't be able to ride your horse like that Miguel," I said.

He agreed. The relief on his face was visible. He decided to leave the horse there, go back to Simoca and get a trailer. We said our goodbyes and I continued towards Tucumán, a city at an altitude of 1,476 feet above sea level, sitting on the slopes of the Aconquija Mountains, the eastern-most mountain range before the large Chaco-Pampean flats.

Under the blazing sun, we passed sugarcane fields and wide open spaces. A range of mountains in the distance framed my view.

Young boys passed on bicycles. *"Hola señorita."*

They were in the mood for chatting. The area was quite deserted and I only greeted them in passing. I did not want to linger and take unnecessary risks.

I was expecting to meet Pancho, a 72-year-old ex-paediatrician with silver-white hair on arrival in San Felipe, outside Tucumán. However, not only was Pancho there but also the local press and a *gaucho* on his white Peruvian Paso horse. They were soon joined by a large group of curious onlookers. We had covered the 50 kilometres in good time but it was tough on the horses.

After the interview, the Peruvian Paso with his natural and smooth four-beat footfall gait, led the way to a tidy settlement nearby. We were met by José, an Indian looking man with shiny long black hair and the whitest smile I had seen in a long time. He liked saying *"no drama"* (no problem) and acted as if it was the greatest privilege to be of assistance in some way. I knew the horses would be fine with him.

Once in Pancho's pickup truck, I realised how worn-out I was.

Pancho looked at me, rubbed my hand and said, "You are very brave."

I felt a bit sorry for myself. The planned four-day rest happened at the perfect time.

Pancho and his family were well-known in Tucumán. His father used to be Governor of the province and his mother worked tirelessly all her life for children with tuberculosis. After I had my shower in the house he showed me pictures on the walls and told me the stories behind the faces. I listened with half an ear though – I was starving and all I could think of was food. His wife was in their mountain retreat and I did not plan to invade another woman's kitchen, so his invitation to grab a bite somewhere was met with genuine enthusiasm.

"Do you want to have pasta or shall we have something to eat in the park, which is very nice," he asked.

"I don't mind. Really, I don't. Anything would be great," I enthused.

Pancho steered towards an open area in the middle of the city surrounded by mature trees. He parked the car underneath one of the trees and through the dim light I spotted a little café some twenty yards away. We did not bother to get out though – food and drink were brought to the car on trays that attached to the windows. It reminded me of my favourite childhood Friday afternoon treat when my parents brought my brothers and I to the milkshake drive-in.

This time, however, I was with a man who could have been my grandfather that I had met only a few hours ago. What's more, we were sitting in close proximity in an isolated park that was far too dark for my liking. The gin and tonics arrived. Pancho lit a cigarette, and stretched out his arm to his right. I could feel his hand on my shoulder.

He said, "I'm enchanted. This is wonderful. I'm enchanted."

11. Planning my route with Richard and Caroline Leach.
12. Colourful mountains not far from Humahuaca, northern Argentina.

13. Salt lakes in Argentina.
14. Juan the ultimate *gaucho*, and also my guide for one day.

15. Rodeo Argentine style. Regrettably they used spurs on the horses.
16. Carlos and friends organising a system to tie up my pack.

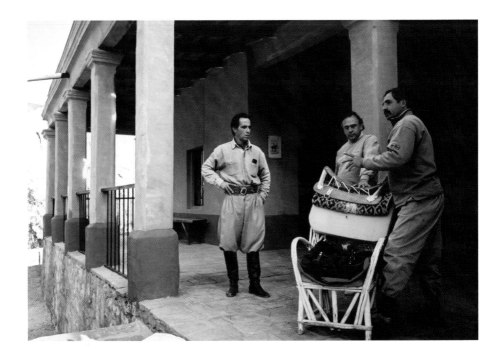

17. Close to the Bolivian border.
18. Our last stop in Argentina with the Gendarmeria.

I looked at him and shifted to get his arm away from me.

"Don't be so uptight," he said in a flirting tone. "Nobody will know."

"You have a wife whom I've met in Cordoba," I said. "I liked her a lot. And anyway, I am not interested in whatever you have in mind."

He could see I was not comfortable but took his time to remove his arm. It seemed his appetite for food had gone and still feeling hungry, I finished off his cheese and tomato sandwich as well. I tried to talk about trivial things and hoped he would not try to push his luck again. I was annoyed that he put me in such an awkward position.

Back at the house I checked my emails. There were thirty-eight messages in my inbox. I went to bed satisfied that I was still being remembered. But I had a fitful night. Dreams, vague and with no name, made it impossible to switch off. I was awake for much of the night. I missed my family. I missed home.

I was on the front-page of one of the leading Sunday newspapers the next day. The headline read, *'British Photographer Intends To Cross The Continent On Horseback.'* Obviously my explanation that the Republic of Ireland was separate from the United Kingdom had not been understood.

Pancho's wife, Josefina, introduced me to her two close friends. Over decadent cakes one of them talked about her controlling husband and her worries about her children.

I said, "Stop having expectations for them because that way you won't be disappointed and they won't feel the pressure of what you want for them."

They were intrigued to hear about my life in Ireland and how everything fell into place. I told them how my travels fourteen years previously had taken me on a ferry to Ireland. Having little money I hitched everywhere. A visit became a long-term stay. I carried a South African passport though and it took years of uncertainty and drifting before I finally became legal. I progressed from doing bar and restaurant work, playing the piano and temping for different companies to finally having a full-time position with pension, the lot. They laughed when I said I think fear of having a mortgage and a husband made me undertake this trip.

"Anything to escape the routine of life," I said.

I realised the irony of my statement afterwards. Saddling up and going through more or less the same motions every day was as close to routine that one could get.

Sarita said, "Don't feel guilty for having been so lucky."

I smiled to myself. *Was it luck? Or maybe I was just a good planner?*

Josefina, who led a privileged life, had strong views about some of her fellow Argentines. She told me of the poor people in the city who are lazy and only want to sit around, drinking *mate*.

"They are dirty," she continued. "They are not ecologically minded and have no conscience or understanding of preserving the environment."

She pointed out how a poor Argentine in the country is so much more decent, clean and civil with a different code of ethics than their city counterparts. Sarita also told me how she advertised for people to work on her lemon farm for a few months.

She said, "Forty percent quit after two weeks. They are just not interested in work."

I did not get to see much of the city of Tucumán. Instead, mornings were spent with Josefina at her tennis club, followed by a massage at home from a lady she used regularly. It was just what I needed. A nap was next on the agenda and afterwards catching up on emails. In the evenings the house would be bustling with friends and family coming and going. The juicy *empanadas* (a pastry pocket filled with a spicy or sweet filling) were rich and filling and enjoyed by everybody without exception.

On the third day, Josefina's friends took me to see Tafi del Valle, a village 6500 feet above see level, 107 kilometres from Tucumán. Nestled in a magnificent valley and enclosed by summits, I was bedazzled by the many twists and turns on the way there. Often suffering from motion sickness, I indicated how grateful I was for being allowed to sit in the front. As we curved higher and higher on the narrow tarmac, the subtropical wilderness on both sides made way for drier, yet still spectacular forest-like vegetation.

The sun shone when we reached the village but soon it turned foggy and cold. I was shown around and it was not hard to miss all the development and new houses sprouting up everywhere. I was told how Tafi used to be owned by four families, one of them the Zavalettas. Apparently the land was divided and sold later. We passed an entrance to a cheese farm with a Zavaletta sign in front. It was a unanimous decision not to purchase anything from there.

A visit to the Rotary Club was organised by Pancho. I was asked the hows, whys and whats about my journey but disappointingly nobody offered any forward addresses or contacts as I had been told they would. I was hoping especially to have assistance during what I believed would be a two-week stretch from Salta to the Bolivian border.

I will always remember my time in Tucumán fondly but when the time came to leave again, I felt ready.

Josefina presented me with a silver owl bookmarker and said, "I hope you won't forget us. We will pray for you everyday."

A few days later, I received an email from her daughter;

Dear Marianne

we miss you a lot. My frend, Jesus, called me by phone, from Arequipa, Peru. If you want to stop your trip, you can´t do it, because all Peru are wait for you. Jesus want to know you, when you arrive to Peru. Jesus toll me he has a lot contac of people they have hors. The T.V. are waiting too. My mather hoppe the best for you, she think of you every time. Marianne, te recordamos siempre, segui adelante, todo lo mejor desde aqui,

Anita Critto y Flia.

José and his brother accompanied us on their horses around the city. I explained to José about my aching shins and feet and his response came quick.

"Your stirrups are too short." He adjusted them straight away.

The outskirts of Tucumán were horribly dirty with paper, plastic bottles and scrap metal everywhere. We also encountered kids on the road stopping trucks for money. They would not let the trucks pass until they were handed something.

A man on the side sang, "It's a long way to California."

I waved and smiled.

Before José and his brother turned back he took off his woolly beret and handed it to me. When I got off Mise to say goodbye he showed me a message that he had written on the raw side of the sheepskin. I knew how much he would have liked to do something like this and his full embrace was comforting and strong.

Not long after, I was stopped by a man who asked for my photograph. It felt strange that somebody would want that from me but I was happy to oblige. He was not satisfied though and half an hour later, arrived with his son. Unceremoniously he plonked the boy on top of Mise and took a picture. He was not finished – next he stopped a man on his bicycle and asked if he would take a picture of him with me and the horses.

It was a slow exodus. The man who sang arrived and we exchanged a few words. He left just to return a short while later with snacks and something to drink. I was truly grateful. For as long as we trotted along the main road, people waved and gave me the thumbs up. I made a mental note not to stop again. Vipos, our next destination was more than 50 kilometres away and I could still see the outlines of Tucumán behind me.

But my best intentions came to nothing. A German woman and a man brought their pickup to a halt in front of us and we were forced to stop.

"I travelled 1000 kilometres on horseback but did not have the sponsors to continue," she said.

I did not know what to say. Further down the road, another man on a bicycle tried to start a conversation but I pretended not to speak Spanish and continued. That's when I heard shouts to our right, coming from across a field. I turned my head and saw a little girl running and yelling excitedly.

'Oh no,' I thought. 'I can't stop again.'

I ignored her and put Mise into a trot. But the yelping continued and I did not have the heart to keep going. Out of breath, she reached us and handed me a little card. It said, "Bienvenido, Dios esta contigo" (Welcome, God be with you). Her name was Gabriela and for some reason she made a lasting impression on me. She asked me to write my name on her hand. I thought of her often and have a picture in my mind of her sweet, open face.

After that we stopped very little on the way. I did not want to reach the farm of Daniel Paz in darkness. The road was windy with long stretches up and down hills which I did not mind. It was a refreshing change after the monotony of unexciting tarmac between Frias and Tucumán.

Daniel met me on his horse when we reached the dirt road leading to his farm. I asked him for advice about Tusa constantly pulling back, but he did not have an answer for me. My body ached severely when we reached the house and if somebody had offered to carry me inside I would not have objected. I shuffled to the house aware of every pain in every limb. Veronica, the lady of the house, treated me to a hot bath filled with lemon oil. Soothing music filled the house. I soaked for about an hour and then took a nap.

Dinner was at Daniel's brother's house, which was on the same property. It was a cosy set-up with the two houses, corrals and stables. The solidness of the Andes in the distance complemented the picturesque setting. Daniel was one of four brothers who formed a folk music band called Los Paz and the evening progressed in a joyous mood of deep baritone voices, vino tinto and tasty food.

Until Daniel asked, "Who is Jo to whom you refer to on your website?"

I had a lump in my throat when I explained. Suddenly, the tiredness, my aching body, worries and the alcohol caught up with me. Seeing the two couples so much in love put me in more of a melancholic mood. I felt so far removed from everything that was dear to me. People continued to live their lives meaningfully and here was I, merely a bum on a horse. Talking about Jo brought back many memories and when I looked at Veronica, her eyes were also shining with tears. We raised our glasses and drank to Jo.

We all agreed that we have to live for today.

Daniel spoke the truth when he said, "There are two types of people in this world – those who are directed by their hearts and those who are directed by their minds."

"Salud," we said in a choir. We sipped our wine in silence.

The next morning, outside, I found only half of the crop given to me by Gringo. The other part had been chewed to bits by one of the dogs. The groomsman made me another one with some inscription about my journey that I did not understand. Daniel put the part mutilated crop on a woodblock and asked me to scribble down something for him to keep as a memory. He also gave me another bulky sheepskin to put on top of the one that I already had. I looked the real *gaucho* lass but it made me sit much higher and my legs were stretched too wide.

The ride to El Tala was tiring. Tusa was in a lazy mood and the new crop soon got some light use. Between the roads were wide open grass fields and at least the surfaces were fine to ride on. Just outside Vipos, a man stopped.

"Why don't you join us for lunch," he enquired.

"Thank you," I said, "but we still have about eight hours of riding left and we need to keep going."

Next he walked over to his car and appeared with a video-camera and microphone.

"I work with a local TV station," he said while extending the legs on the tripod.

I had no chance even to argue and there and then on the busy side of the road he did a mini-interview with his son filming.

My aching feet and shins were better that day but I had a rash on my backside. It was rather sensitive. Later I found a quiet spot, dropped my trousers and rubbed cortisone cream on the sore parts. The cooling sensation gave temporary relief.

Tusa continued to challenge me and kept doing what he did best – pulling to the left. The strain on my arm was intense and I struggled until the wearisome trio arrived at El Tala around six that evening. The name of the farm was El Datil and it was the same house where Lola Mora, a famous Argentine sculptress had lived some years before.

I had a visitor the next morning. Augustin, a representative from the Criollo Association in the North, came to see me.

He settled into a chair on the veranda. "I am surprised that the Association did not give you my name."

I was tempted to say, "Well, maybe they thought I would never get here on horseback."

"Your saddle blankets are wrong," he said. "Also, I think your gelding is in some pain. You must rest for a few days."

"Yes, that was my plan and I also want to get a vet out to check on the horses," I said.

He talked about himself a lot and showed me his belt buckle with his name engraved.

Abruptly he left and appeared some time later with a saddle-cloth he had bought.

"You have to look out constantly for poisonous grass on the way," he said with a serious face.

'Nobody mentioned that to me,' I thought as I nodded my head. I had no clue how one looked out for poisonous grass. In a negative tone he continued to outline all the dangers I might encounter going into Bolivia. I got the feeling he was trying to put me off. I only gave the odd, appropriate nod and left him to finish his monologue.

I was glad for the saddle cloth he got me but also felt happy to see him leave.

One thing I did pay attention to was his advice to try and not do more than 30 kilometres a day. I knew this was the ideal but sometimes things did not work out exactly like that.

Despite having arrived virtually without any contacts in Argentina two months before, I now had a chain of people who were willing to help. Most days, riding through Argentina I had somebody waiting for me at the end of a day's ride. It meant I had to do the distance from point A to B, whether it was thirty, forty or fifty kilometres, even though I might have preferred to do less. Sometimes I felt dancing to somebody else's tune inhibited my freedom. In a strange way people's goodwill and generosity was almost confining. I thought I had left my nine-to-five job behind. But I knew this was no time to be selfish. Ultimately people's goodwill was the glue that bound my journey together. I had no doubt though that it would be different in Bolivia. I knew nobody and it would be up to me to decide how much ground we would cover every day.

I felt odd the following day. Alone on the farm, I had the Sunday blues. Santiago and Flor who came from Cordoba especially to see me, had gone back the night before. And the owners of El Datil, relations of Santiago, had to go to Tucumán for a day. I felt isolated and very far from home. I stretched and meditated for a while and felt lighter afterwards. Mise strolled over to me when I walked to their *corral*.

'She is such a darling,' I thought.

A worker and his son led them to *avena* (oat) fields and Tusa seemed to have forgotten his pains when he saw all the food. He was quite obsessed with eating and I soon found that whenever he needed to be distracted, anything edible did the trick.

I had to make a decision about him though. But I was also terrified to make the wrong one.

"This might be your last chance to change him for another suitable horse," Santiago said before they left.

"True," I said, "but maybe he is pulling back so much on the leading rope because he has pain somewhere. And maybe he is going left all the time, because he is uncomfortable."

I dreaded the idea of leaving him behind. He was a problem but I could not desert him just like that. I thought of Mise too – surely she would miss him. And who's to say that the next horse would be good. It can be hit and miss. The vet was coming out the next day and I decided to rely on his expertise.

For the rest of the day the wind blew forcibly outside. I sat in front of the fire and read National Geographic magazines. Ester, the maid, put chicken and sweet potatoes on the coals. I waited for Daniel, who was bringing my saddlebags, to arrive for lunch. When he had not turned up by 3 p.m., I decided to eat. Sitting alone at the big table, I craved a glass of wine or two. There was not a sound in the house.

The vet was convinced that the anti-inflammatory injections would sort Tusa out. He advised me to wait another couple of days. When he left, I took a *remise* (taxi) to the police station in the middle of nowhere, next to a national road. There was only one policeman present, one desk and one picture on the wall. He offered me the one and only chair in the room. The taxi driver asked him to stop a bus that went into the city. I was going to spend the day in Tucumán, catching up on correspondence. Five minutes later we heard the roar of a bus engine. The policeman rushed out, waved his arms and brought it to a halt. I entered the bus full of merry German tourists, fell asleep and woke up when the bus stopped.

The driver walked over to me and said, "You have to get off. We are not going into the city."

I had hardly set foot on the pavement when another car stopped and picked me up. The driver dropped me off in front of an internet café.

Ten hours later, I made my way back to El Datil again. I felt fatigued after staring at a screen all day but could not fall asleep on the bus. I looked out of the window into the black of the night, deep in thought. I was proud of the progress I had made in different ways. I was now much more comfortable around the horses. I did not feel like fainting whenever one (or both) of them got a fright and I had found my 'spot' in the saddle. I had a few more words and expressions in my Spanish repertoire and generally I was much more at ease with things. It was a good feeling. But I was conscious too that my world remained small compared to what was happening 'out there'. Uncharacteristically, I thought little about affairs of the world. It was not as if I did not care. My vision needed to be blinkered to survive. My focus had to be here and now.

I did wonder if friends and family would be the same on my return home. All our lives were moving on, mine on the back of a horse, theirs in the world they had carved out for themselves. I had to remain optimistic that we did not journey in separate directions.

It felt strange to be on a bus on the same route I had done two days before on horseback – sweating, agonising and cursing.

Tusa was a live wire when we finally set off from El Datil again. He broke into a fast trot the moment we got off the dirt road. In the village, a dusty wind blew through the isolated streets. Two kilometres on, I was dismayed to hear the dreaded 'click click' sound and on inspection found that his back foot only had half a shoe left. I cursed at myself for not having had them shod during our previous stop. I thought about it but was so preoccupied with everything else that I forgot to check their shoes again before we left. We backtracked and I led the horses to a farm nearby. One of the workers offered to help, but Tusa did not trust him and would not stand still. The man grabbed a rope and tried to put it around Tusa's legs.

"Don't do that," I said. "I will lift up his leg."

The man was not comfortable with me holding the foot and insisted on putting the rope around. The moment it was tightened around Tusa's legs, he started to panic and kick.

"Take it off immediately," I shouted.

It is a miracle the man did not get a kick on the head while he tried to do it. We finally managed to get the half-shoe off. I had a spare shoe but did not trust either one of us putting it on. This part of my travels was still alien to me and I feared the idea of having to take off a shoe, never mind nailing one on. My half day spent with the farrier in Dublin did not give me the confidence I needed. I lacked experience. I hoped that this would come with time.

The road was not great for the rest of the journey to Rosario De La Frontera and with Tusa wearing only three shoes, I did not want to go on the tarmac. On the side of the road there was little room and we went through ploughed fields for most of the way. Soon the horses were perspiring. It was hot and I ran out of water. It was early evening before I had something wet or dry and the tea and sweet breads offered by my hosts tasted like champagne and caviar. Bernard and Nora were very affable and I felt at home immediately.

The next day, a farrier and his men arrived early morning. We decided to shoe all the feet on the horses. They worked fast and charged me only a third of what I paid in Jesús Maria. When they were done, they painted the hooves with burnt motor oil, apparently to keep them lubricated.

During the shoeing, they discovered an open sore on the back of Tusa's left hind foot, just above the hoof. I realised that it must have been an old sore that re-opened the day before when the rough *gaucho* tried to put the rope around his legs. I regretted having allowed him to do it. We called out the vet. He cleaned the wound and applied antibiotic cream. His advice was not to ride for a few days. I was itching to go though and decided to transport Tusa to Jujuy and to carry on with only Mise. The farrier's helper thoughtfully offered his trailer for free.

Bernard talked a lot about the situation in Argentina. The problems affected them too and the future was not very optimistic. I was surprised to hear that a set of horse-shoes costing three pesos in December had tripled in price by the following May. Everywhere people's standard of living took a dip and the only option was to adjust. For most, leaving was not even a possibility – savings were lost and the peso was worth very little.

After lunch a woman came out to do a radio interview in the house. Bernard seemed pleased to translate. Later, my hosts' son Bob, a frog farmer, took me to the Hotel Termas. Built on a hillside, the hotel has some of the finest hot springs in the world and arguably the widest variety. The massage I had there was a highlight. If I could have taken the masseur or even just his hands with me, I would have.

It was a bit of a struggle to get Tusa into the trailer the next morning. I scolded the man when he tried to hit him.

"You shouldn't hit a horse to get him into a trailer or a box," I said. "He should not fear it. You have to get his trust and he will follow you in eventually."

He looked at me as if I had two heads.

Mise watched the spectacle curiously. When the pickup and trailer finally took off, she called for Tusa.

Bernard and I stood next to her and said simultaneously, "Aah, how sweet."

Suddenly, without warning, Mise started running behind the trailer. When she got to the bottom of the garden, she gave one jump over the cattle grid and continued to chase the vehicle. Bernard clasped his head in his hands. I shouted and ran after her. When I got to the main road, I could not see her anywhere. The pickup and trailer were out of sight too and I suspected the driver did not notice Mise behind him. I paced the streets while Bernard and Nora followed in their car. I was frantic and had visions of somebody taking her and hiding her until the search was over. I got in the car when I ran out of steam. After a half an hour search I spotted her tied up to a tree surrounded by a group of men. I kept on hugging her for the rest of the day.

Mise started limping on the way to Metán. I had an idea what caused it. On our way I had spotted a secluded resting spot just off the road and urged her into a trot uphill. It was probably too steep and she must have pulled a muscle somewhere. I led her for the rest of the way and it was in complete darkness when we reached our destination. A vet came out the following morning and rubbed some cream on to Mise's right leg. Later I established that he actually treated the wrong side. At one point I even thought her limping was psychosomatic. She seemed to forget her pain when something caught her intention. The ears would be erect, head swinging and she would be very alert and no limp in sight... until the fuss was over and she got in to 'hop-along Cassidy' mode again.

I received an email from an ex-boyfriend with whom I was still on very good terms. He shared the news with me that he was seeing somebody and it was serious. I was happy for him but also felt a pang of sadness. I was doing what I had dreamt of for a long time. I was meeting interesting people, experiencing and seeing the world in a unique way. I had the freedom to go where I wanted and I was responsible for only myself and two horses. But I also missed the intimacy and closeness of someone special.

Not all the time though. When we were on the road, I was so engaged with making it to the end of the day that I hardly ever had time to think about the 'heavy stuff'. Going through parts where there was nothing and nobody did not leave me lonely or wanting. I felt most content during those times and I embraced the silence and the isolation. I knew it was a luxury and a privilege to be part of that. But it was when I rested for a few days with a family who had ordinary lives that I missed that normality most. It reminded me of everything I did not have and I struggled sometimes to see myself as somebody doing something extraordinary. People fussed and praised when they learned what I was doing. I could never understand that. It would take me many months before I could see myself as something more than just a bum on a horse.

A letter from Magdalena with whom I spent a few days in Metán, warmed my heart tremendously;

Dear Marianne,

It was so difficult to say goodbye, I kept my eyes on you as you were leaving and my husband said, 'not cry, not cry' and I laughed because I realised he noticed my sadness. I just wanted to tell you how much I've learnt from you during this couple of days you were here. I admire your challenge but I mostly admire you as a woman. I'm sure that with your example you keep dreams of many people alive because great hopes and dreams come from great people like you. And believe me 'the world needs your talents'. I really wish you the best for this trip. I hope people can understand how little it costs to give a thought, to try and make your heart happy today, just giving you a hand, one bit of kindness or a tender smile as you go on your daily way. I spent two lovely days with you and I will never forget it – you were so nice to me and you were always happy as well. I must say about that: 'A cheerful heart and a smiling face can put sunshine in every house' and you put sunshine in mine. Kisses.
Magdalena.

"Every day you may make progress. Every step may be fruitful.
Yet there will stretch out before you an ever-lengthening,
ever-ascending, ever-improving path. You know you will never get
to the end of the journey. But this, so far from discouraging, only
adds to the joy and glory of the climb"
— Sir Winston Churchill

Our next important port of call was Los Lapachos – a vast and beautiful *estancia* that had been part of the Leach family for three generations. It had always been a sugar cane farm. Historically, the Leach family owned various properties known collectively as Leach's Argentine Estates which quoted on the London Stock Exchange in earlier days. Eventually, however, the company was dissolved and the properties divided up amongst the families of the original brothers. Richard and Caroline were the current owners.

Caroline told me, "Even when I got married in 1964, we still drank from the irrigation channel which had to be filtered and boiled. We also had a kerosene fridge and a light motor which ran on diesel and had to be started by turning a huge fly-wheel every evening. I recall doing this while heavily pregnant. The last one to bed pressed a button to stop it at night."

I was impressed. In less than forty years they now had smooth paved roads, an airport ten minutes away, direct TV and internet.

The farm was spectacular. I stayed in one of the guest rooms. The main house had high ceilings, wooden floors and dark brown wooden shutters. It was cool and airy and it felt like I had arrived somewhere exotic. Tea and scones were served on the wide veranda of the house with the dogs dozing lazily at our feet. The garden was sprinkled with the pink and white lapacho trees that inspired the name Los Lapachos. Caroline and I later went to see the resident *gaucho* to enquire about Mise's leg.

"The people are strange here," Caroline said. "You ask them to go and find out about something, they leave but then never come back to report."

That evening, Richard suggested that I take another route to Bolivia.

"The road through Humahuaca is dry, hilly and full of stones," he said.

He proposed another way which was more tropical and less cold at night. I had enough time to plan our onward journey to the Bolivian border. Los Lapachos was somewhere we would rest for at least a week as Mise's leg needed to get better. I also had to organise contacts for the next stretch and psychologically I had to prepare for a very different country. Ciro had warned me on the phone.

"You will be shocked when you enter Bolivia. Everything is different. It will be much more difficult for you. It will also be much more dangerous."

At first glimpse, the city of Salta, almost an hour's drive from Los Lapachos, was not exactly what I had imagined. It was very big and not as quaint as I had pictured in my mind. Nicknamed in Spanish as *Salta la Linda* (Salta the Beautiful), it is visited by a great many tourists because of its colonial architecture, the Cathedral, and the Plaza 9 de Julio park. During the war of independence from Spain the city became a strategic commercial and military point between Peru and the Argentinean cities. Between 1816 and 1821 the city was governed by local military leader General Martín Miguel de Güemes, who defended the city and surrounding area from Spanish forces coming from further north.

Caroline dropped me off on the plaza and I spent the day like a lazy tourist. I had a cheese and chicken *empanada* and then two more were washed down with a light Salta beer. I bought a packet of Marlboro Lights and sat in the sun, watching the world go by. I was not finished until I had a *cortado* (espresso), complemented by a bitter-sweet biscuit.

Going home in the car with us was Caroline's daughter-in-law, Gabriela.

"You are very brave," she said sincerely. "The situation in Argentina is very unsafe."

"Other people have said the same to me," I replied. "But I haven't seen any of it. I've had only good experiences so far."

I had two more weeks of travelling through my first South American country but it was getting suitable contacts and not my safety that I was more worried about. The unknown in Bolivia and what was ahead filled me with some fear. But there was also excitement and an adrenalin rush.

Two girls from Ireland travelled 28 hours in a bus from Brazil to meet up with me in Salta for a few days. We had never met before. They were bubbly and full of enthusiasm. Together we decided to do the *Tren de las Nubes* aka *Movitrack*. It was a company that followed more or less the same route as the train but one travelled with six or eight others and a guide in a converted 4 x 4. Everything was more flexible which better suited the three of us.

I found it weird to be away from Mise and Tusa. I was glad for the distraction and good company but I was not used to being a tourist. I thought of all the things I still needed to do before we could start trotting again.

I made a mental list:

1. Fix buckle on leading rope
2. Get a crop
3. Leather strap for tying tent and poncho on back of saddle
4. Get a better system for the saddle-bags
5. Check and see if export papers needed to go into Bolivia
6. Get contacts for the first five days
7. Give up smoking

The girls explored the mountains while I met with Ernesto Day, a well-known and much loved folk singer. He introduced me to his friends, Maria-Ines and Manolo who ran a bookshop. They heard about my ordeal with Zavaletta and were appalled. Manolo handed me two bottles of wine.

"It's in compensation for that negative experience," he said.

Maria-Ines joined in. "I would have killed you if you were my daughter undertaking this trip."

We went through my future route while Ernesto chain smoked. After a while he got up.

"I have a headache," he declared. "I am not used to speaking so much English."

They also suggested the tropical way.

"You'll find the route through Humahuaca very difficult. It's isolated and there won't be much food for the horses."

At least I was clear now where I would enter Bolivia. Ernesto took me to the Bolivian Consulate. They provided me with maps and distances between the major towns. I tried to ignore the column that dealt with altitudes. I preferred not to know the hardships that were to follow, just yet.

I was ready for bed when my two Irish friends returned from their Flora and Fauna expedition and suggested we go out for the night. I had nothing to wear. Jacinta loaned me a floral dress and sandals. They fitted well and I felt quite womanly. I only had a sports bra with me and got to try Orlaith's lacy black one. My underarms were not a pretty sight so I also had to borrow her disposable razor. I was still bleeding from the cuts when we headed for our taxi.

The Güemes restaurant was quite formal and had little atmosphere. The folk music was very loud and a man with a microphone talked non-stop. He went around the tables and encouraged people to sing along to the tunes. When he got to our table, he enthusiastically introduced us.

"*Las Trillizas de Oro!*" (The Golden Triplets).

It did not matter to him that Jacinta was the only blonde in the group. He surely would have been amused if he knew how well acquainted I was with one of the real "*Trillizas*".

We ended up in a bar which was packed and immediately got pounced on by a photographer. We bought some of his work.

When he heard that we were going into the mountains the next day, he said, "I'll get you some coca for the high altitudes."

He told us most men there chewed coca leaves, mostly to suppress appetite and to have more energy. That of course explained their bulging cheeks and bad breath, emitting a bitter alkaloid odour. However to say 'chewing' is a bit of a misnomer. The coca would be bundled up, inserted between cheek and gum, forming a pouch. This would be sucked until the flavour had gone. It both looked and smelt disgusting. I spotted some men going around with a little container and white powder. '*Aha, Cocaine,*' I thought. It turned out to be simply sodium bicarbonate, which was believed to extract the full flavour and strength from the coca leaves. I also saw some of them licking what looked like a type of black soap – it was a mixture of sodium bicarbonate and ash. I found it equally repulsive. I could not stand the smell of the coca leaves and felt nauseous every time they came too close to my face. However, I found the coca tea much more palatable. I swore by its effectiveness for altitude sickness, especially later in the high Bolivian mountains.

There is a traditional mystique to coca-leaf chewing. It was once a restricted privilege of Inca royalty before becoming common practice among indigenous people in the Andes. It seemed useful as a treatment for gastrointestinal ailments and motion sickness, as a fast-acting antidepressant, as well as a substitute stimulant for coffee. It was accepted that in leaf form coca does not produce toxicity or dependence although Bolivians have no illusions that a good portion of their coca crop is being converted into cocaine.

We danced the night away to traditional music and arrived back at Maria Toffoli's B & B at 5 a.m.

The alarm went off forty-five minutes later for our *Movitrack* expedition. Following the same route as the famous train we ascended into the mountains, fast asleep. We were soon woken though by the persistent streaks of sunlight on our faces. Not long after we stopped for an early brunch. The train passed while we stretched our legs, excited tourists waving frantically at us.

Richard Leach picked us up three days later outside Jujuy. He had invited my friends to stay for the night at Los Lapachos. On the way, Richard broke bad news.

"Tusa is injured. He was bitten by Mise."

I had no idea how bad it was until I saw the wound. It looked as if he had been attacked by a vicious animal or bird. The wound was at least four inches long and very raw.

"How could that have happened?" one of the girls asked.

I shook my head. "I don't know. Maybe Mise was in heat and Tusa annoyed her."

It did not look good and I envisaged more delays. The wound had to get better first and the hair had to grow back before he could carry anything. I felt frustrated at the unnecessary hold-up.

I was sad to see the girls getting ready to leave for Buenos Aires. We were back in Salta for one more night and, while they packed, we discussed my different options with regard to the horses. They could sense my reluctance to hang around for much longer.

"Maybe I can send on my belongings and ride only Mise with Tusa on the leading rope," I suggested. "Or maybe I should put Tusa in a truck and pick him up at the border. But where would he stay? How would I know he's being looked after?"

They could offer little advice. They cared, but did not know what was possible and what was not. Neither did I really. I spoke to Caroline that evening on the phone.

"I'll get a vet out in the morning," she said. "He'll give us a good prognosis. You can stay here for as long as you want."

Her words were like a soothing balm for a worried mind.

It was a frustrating twelve days, waiting for Tusa's back to heal. I also found that I had much less energy by just sitting around. Doing nothing was wearing me out. I signed up for Spanish classes in Salta but my head was in other places so I stopped after the second one. What was more important during this wait was meeting the right contacts in the Gendarmeria – the Argentine army that protects the borders. With Maria-Ines, who orchestrated the meeting, I found myself in an office with Victor, the *Comandante Principal*. Over strong espressos he expressed his enthusiasm and willingness to help.

"You have done the worst part in Argentina," he said. "From here to the border will be much less dangerous."

He suggested a back-up jeep following me all the way to the Aguas Blancas border. I thanked him.

"That's very sweet of you but I would be happy just to have places to stay along the way and maybe at times somebody could take my bags to the next destination."

He was happy to assist.

When we were leaving he turned to me and said, "Do you have permission from your mother and father to travel like this?"

I laughed and Maria-Ines said, "She is over twenty-one you know."

Lunch at her house was delicious – especially the vegetable soup – made by the ambitious house-help who told me she wanted to be a lawyer. Maria-Ines then took me to the offices of El Tribuno for an interview. On the way back, a haggard, frail-looking man wanted a lift when we stopped at a traffic light.

Maria-Ines shook her head and said to me, "These days it's too much of a risk to pick up somebody like that. If we were in an accident I would have to pay the same as if he was blond and blue-eyed."

I was surprised at her comment. In what way was I really different from the frail, haggard man? I could not help but wonder if she had not known me, would she have stopped to pick me up?

After another four days in Salta I felt like I needed the peace and tranquillity of Los Lapachos. I also missed the horses. The man who sold the tickets at the Terminal Central said that the bus did not stop where I needed to get off.

"And they wouldn't, even if you asked," he said miserably.

'Sod them,' I thought and continued to walk up-hill out of the city with a copy of the latest TATA article under my arm. It took a while before somebody responded to my thumb in the air. An Indian-looking man stopped and said he was going to Güemes. I showed him the article but I did not think he understood it was actually me in the picture.

A bit down the road he stopped on the side and said, "I have to wait here for a while for somebody who owes me money."

I thought nothing of it and nodded my head.

"Are you married?" he asked.

"Si señor," I said without hesitation.

This was by far the safest answer in these Latin American countries.

I was looking out of the window when I felt a tug on my sleeve. I turned my head and saw the man taking out a few notes from his wallet. He offered them to me and pointed to his groin area. I had no doubt about the nature of his suggestion. I shook my head in disgust but I was not afraid.

"No señor, that won't happen," I said strongly and reached for the door-handle.

Once I was outside, he started the engine unperturbed and drove off. I made a 'crazy' gesture with my hands to my head which I hoped he would see in his back-mirror. I was lucky that nothing more serious happened. I decided not to tell anybody about it.

Ten minutes later another car stopped. I reckoned that any man travelling eighty kilometres to attend the first birthday party of a niece, had to be decent. He dropped me off at the entrance of Los Lapachos.

I was happy to be with the horses again but the sight of Tusa's wound healing very slowly did not put me in a good frame of mind.

Somebody who did see the article in the *El Tribuno* was a man called *Ingeniero* Roberto Osvaldo Tschiffely. He sent me an email on the 18th of August telling me that he was a direct descendant of Aimé Tschiffely. He wished me luck with my undertaking and indicated that he would like for us to meet up once I got closer to the Bolivian border. I received his correspondence at a busy time and unfortunately never responded. Once I was in Bolivia I had nobody to help me translate a letter into Spanish and by the time I did, I had completely forgotten about his email.

Such was the nature of my journey. At times things got done, other times they did not. It was not for lack of trying or because I was disinterested. I was simply surviving every day, trying to do as best I could.

Before the horses and I could point our heads in a northerly direction again I had to re-think my equipment and in particular the state of the saddlebags. Back in Salta I was introduced to Guillermo, a friend of Maria-Ines and Manolo. He was a real Don Juan but posed no threat. He wore traditional Salta *gaucho* riding clothes but spoke zero English. He took me to his house on top of a hill outside town. Sheepskins were in abundance on every potential seating area. Guillermo softened a piece of leather and tied it around the top of my saddlebag to make it hang shorter on the sides. We sat outside and he talked about himself but mostly his interest was in my journey.

"Few people understand what you are doing," he said.

I realised that much by now but I only smiled and said I guess it was rather unusual, a girl travelling alone with two horses.

"It's not only that," he continued, "people are asking *why*."

He said it in a way as if he was posing the question to me, expecting an answer. I shrugged my shoulders and took a sip from the cup in front of me.

"Who knows," I said, staring past him into the distance. "Who knows."

I hoped that he did not think I was snubbing his curiosity. Truthfully I was not exactly clear in my own head why I was there. I decided that the answer would present itself with time. But also it might never come. Did it really matter why? Guillermo did not press for more answers.

Later we made our way to an equestrian shop. Guillermo had a clear picture of what I should get and I let him have the floor. He enjoyed being the centre of attention and I was happy for his help. I bought a saddle frame made from metal, wood and raw leather. The idea was to tie the saddle frame to the packhorse using a girth and the saddlebags would go on top.

"This might be the best system for the saddlebags I've had so far," I said, pleased.

Guillermo grinned from ear to ear. We could not find a decent machete anywhere. That evening, Manolo suggested that I wear *gaucho* clothes including the wide *bombachas*.

"Those tight jodhpurs are too inviting for South American men," he said.

The following day I was picked up by friends of Guillermo to visit a farm outside Salta that he managed. The road that led to the farm and into the mountains was built by hand between 1935 and 1950. The house and setting were impressive and a little church on the grounds added to the uniqueness of the place. Mountains in red and pink surrounded the farm and complemented the colour of the house which was painted in the same shade. The spacious porch was cool and inviting with a wooden bench, two rustic chairs and simple wooden trunks with strands of long grass inside. An Indian woman prepared *mate* but I asked for coffee. While we were sipping our hot drinks Guillermo mentioned that although the woman spoke Spanish, it was almost in a different dialect.

He laughed, "*We* don't always understand what she says. You might have a problem with that in Bolivia."

They asked about my route and mentioned how beautiful the road is from Aguas Blancas (the last town before the Bolivian border) to Tarija in Bolivia. They mentioned more places of interest I might encounter on the way. No one referred to danger.

When we said our goodbyes, Guillermo brought something from behind his back. A machete! It was a thoughtful gift.

We left with the sun setting over a mountain that loomed like a giant bear over the farm. It stretched high up into the sky surrounded by the chilled early evening air.

A friend of the Leaches, Sheila Misdorp, a university lecturer, journalist and teacher invited me to talk to one of her classes of students of English in the city of Salta. This was the second time I had met Sheila and this time I found her to be less concerned about the safety of my journey. She was Zimbabwean, had had a challenging life and told me how they had been attacked on their farm in the Chimurenga war in 1976. Her husband was shot in the leg. A few months later they left Africa as virtual refugees for the Paraguayan jungle.

"I spent almost a year there with my husband and two kids, living in a microbus in the most basic conditions in the hinterland of Paraguay," she said without self-pity.

They moved to Salta in 1978 where twenty-three years later, her marriage broke up under difficult circumstances. She is a tough woman and a survivor. I also found her to be one of the most reliable people I know. When Sheila said she would do something she put words into action. There was no hesitation or compromise and I admired her for that.

The students in her class were all interested in and positive about my trip.

One young woman, Karina, said, "I am ashamed that I haven't done something out of the ordinary like this."

They dished out their cards and urged me to call should I need any help.

Later that afternoon I was still on a high from all the good vibes when Maria-Ines and I entered the Gendarmeria compound for the final meeting.

Everything was organised. I was assigned my own 'officer' who would oversee the logistics of my ride between Salta and the Bolivian border. Before we left, I was asked to pose for a photograph with three Gauchos de Güemes (named after Martín Güemes, one of the major figures in the Argentine struggle for independence against Spain). Dressed in their traditional clothing, their spurs sounded like a chorus of jingle bells. Their elf hats looked hilarious and I bit my lip trying not to laugh.

Maria-Ines gave me a long embrace when we said goodbye.

"Be very careful and don't hesitate to turn back if things get bad or dangerous."

We both had tears in our eyes. She departed with wise words for me.

"Make sure to always approach women first when you enter a village or town."

I promised her I would.

At Los Lapachos good news awaited me. Tusa's back had healed miraculously and I had no doubt that it was due to the loving hands of Caroline who cared for him every day. Well, that and her brilliant idea to regularly put a fresh aloe vera leaf directly on the wound. The rawness had gone completely and hair covered most of the sore. I was delighted. I could almost hear the call of the road again. I felt good and confident about my trip now. Richard and I studied my map and he made suggestions for stops and stay-overs. Caroline thought that I should join them the following day for an excursion to the north-east of the province for the first presentation of the full bible translated into *Wichi*, the indigenous language in that area.

"Leave on Tuesday. That way you can use Monday to get ready and you can come with us to Mision Chaqueña."

I thanked the gods for their compassion and understanding.

Sunday morning we had an early start and drove up to the Anglican mission 200 kilometres north of Los Lapachos in an area known as the Saltanian Chaco. This is a vast low-lying plain some 900 kilometres in breadth. In the east some areas are known as the 'Impenetrable' or 'Green Hell'. South America's highest temperatures exceeding 45°C are recorded here and we certainly got a taste of this when the thermometer hit 40°C – and it was not even spring yet. The Chaco is one of the main centres of indigenous population in Argentina and is home to two of the largest minorities, the *Toba* and the *Wichi* Indians.

By the time we arrived at the mud church, its corrugated iron roof bristling with heat, it was packed with *Wichi* from far and near, accompanied by delegations from England and Finland. There was no room inside but we took in the proceedings from the windows and got a real taste of how tough life must be for the residents. I was struck by the number of babies – most of them plump – happily nestling in cloth slings on their very young mothers' hips.

After the three hour church service, *locro* was served, a hot, thick soup based on maize, pumpkin and pigs' trotters. It had been prepared in half drums on open fires in the dry, dusty semi-desert. We had a bit of a commotion when one of the houses was set on fire by a missionary's child playing with matches on a highly inflammable mattress. Some dashed to the rescue with buckets of water while Sheila latched on to the bucket of sand used for one of the 'long drops', a deep hole in the ground used as a toilet. The room was gutted, with the polystyrene excuse of a ceiling suffering most. I photographed the culprit in a flood of tears after receiving a cuff about the head from her Argentine missionary mum.

Another missionary lady from England who heard about my travels, came over excitedly.

"We met Gordon Roddick and his friend in 1974. They and the horses stayed with us at La Paz Mission."

It seemed that Gordon's wife, Anita, was uneasy about his safety and secretly organised somebody to travel with him. Apparently, she told Gordon that the man was a photographer and interested in doing a picture-book of his journey.

'*It's a small world,*' I thought to myself.

Up to now, there had been very few encounters with insects on my way. The Chaco was hot and humid though and mosquitoes and midges were drawn to me. I got bitten everywhere and made the mistake of scratching constantly. Two days later the bites turned black and blue. The sores were obviously infected and looked septic.

The day before my departure Anthony Leach took me to Perico, a small town not far from their farm, for last minute shopping. We could not find a suitable waterbag for the horses and ended up having one made. The tailor, a man with a mop of unruly black hair, sat behind an old fashioned sewing machine in a hot little blue room. On the wall behind him hung numerous football posters, a picture of a blonde girl with breasts exposed, an oversized watch and the smiling face of Che Guevara (the

Argentine-born Marxist revolutionary and Cuban guerrilla leader). I bought a pair of cheap canvas shoes, batteries for my torch and toothpaste. I also purchased ample repellent and bite-soothing creams. I was ready to go.

Richard and Caroline made contact with people they knew on the way and I was more or less sorted between them and the Gendarmeria, up to the Bolivian border. I felt a flutter of apprehension at the thought of being on the road again after three weeks. Bolivia, which was once a country hundreds of miles away, was approaching fast and the excitement was building up inside me.

By the time I was ready to leave the following morning Chito the *gaucho* had already saddled up Mise and Tusa.

'Great way to start,' I thought. 'I could get used to this.'

Chito felt honoured to be the person to guide me through the small farm roads that would eventually bring me to the main road. We had an animated chat on the way and understood each other completely.

"*Tiene muy buen español*" (you have good Spanish), he praised me.

I was surprised at the level of proficiency I exhibited. When I was relaxed and not under pressure, the words would flow from me. I was very pleased.

"I can see you love your horses," he commented riding alongside me.

Chito was over fifty but had the physique of a very fit man half his age.

"It's because I ride everyday," he said.

"So there's hope for me," I joked.

A truck rattled past and Mise jumped wildly. We both laughed.

"She'll have to get used to traffic again," I said.

I knew it would take a few days to get them relaxed and less anxious after their spell of rest. In a way it was like starting out all over again.

At the main road I thanked Chito, handed him some pesos and he turned back. He was hardly out of sight when the leading rope got tangled in Tusa's shoe. It was badly stuck and I had to wave cars down to stop. Everybody stared but nobody offered to help. Finally a truck came to a halt and the men managed to get the rope out.

We just got going again when a bright orange bag came blowing in our direction. I tried to distract the horses, but Mise's eyes were transfixed by the alien thing which continued to flap in our direction. She gave a massive jump when it got too close. Tusa stayed calm and fortunately I kept my position in the saddle.

The side of the road consisted mostly of flat short grass. It made for good riding. My machete got baptised when we passed sugarcane fields and the horses could not get enough of it. An old man with a horse and cart passed but he seemed to be in a world of his own and did not even notice us. We stopped often. After 15 kilometres we took a break at a police checkpoint. They offered me water and the horses were hosed down. The day was a scorcher.

My room at the Gendarmeria quarters was the most basic I'd had so far. There was no linen and no pillow. I asked for the latter but either they did not understand, did not care or did not have a spare one. A fan dangling from the ceiling whirred noisily overhead and with my tent propped under my head, I tried to take a nap. Next door the music was on full blast and after twenty minutes I got up to take a shower. I had already taken care of the horses and Tusa was walking around with an aloe vera leaf taped to his back. I did not want to take any chances.

A man who had promised to take me to town to buy food never showed up. I sat alone in my room washing down a couple of biscuits with apple flavoured tea. My mosquito-bitten foot was very sore and swollen. It was obvious that I had a bad allergic reaction to the bites. I had to force myself not to scratch.

A knock on my door announced that dinner would be served. I could not face the fatty bits floating in the *locro* soup and only had a piece of bread. I hoped for better nutrition the next day.

Breakfast was black coffee with small dry bread crusts. It was 8 a.m. and already exceedingly hot.

One of the men advised, "You can take a short-cut over the little wooden bridge."

He pointed to a stream to our left. The 'bridge' turned out to be two fragile-looking planks put together across the water. I shook my head in amazement. I would not cross that on foot let alone encourage the horses to do so.

The surface on the side of the road was horrible and it was impossible to steer the horses away from all the little stones and pebbles. Tusa pulled back a lot but Mise made up for his mule-like behaviour and acted like a star. She only stopped when nature forced her to do so.

We encountered yet more *piqueteros* outside San Pedro. The road was completely blocked and around 150 people were sitting around. Some of them had erected make-shift tents. A few men whistled when we approached. I had no intention of stopping. I put Mise into a light trot and lifted my arm in a friendly wave.

"Hola, hola, buen dia," I said with a smile.

I even got a few in return.

We manoeuvred our way through the crowds with not much difficulty. After the second roadblock, I made sure that I was a safe distance away before I stopped to drink some water. I was even brave enough to take a picture.

We were about halfway when the heat forced us to stop. I spotted a dirt road leading to something that looked like a farm in the distance and took it. I was greeted warmly by a man called Luis. He invited me into the 'house' – a dilapidated building with only two rooms in habitable condition. A man with grey hair, no shirt and glasses sat at a table, writing something on white sheets of paper. Sweat was dripping from his face and back. He looked up only briefly when we passed. It was lunchtime and Luis dished up flavoursome pasta. I noticed he had no chicken on his plate and left mine for him. The room was hot and stuffy and flies stuck to everything. He made his own lemonade for us using near-fermented lemons, lukewarm water and sugar. Warm wind and dust storms were raging outside. When it calmed down, we checked on the horses and Luis used my machete to clean their coats.

"Get rid of the white sponge," he advised. "They are for polo ponies and will make your horses sweat too much."

I had noticed Mise's hair becoming thinner in certain parts of her back and decided to take his advice.

Back in the dark blue room he showed me his anti-poison kit for snake bites – a yellow rubber tube to extract the poison, a sharp blade for the incision and a rope that goes around the arm.

"This is what you must get for yourself," he said. "You will encounter many snakes on your way."

I was just going to say 'okay' when he got up and opened the cupboard behind him. He turned towards me with a large shotgun in his hands.

"This is what you need," he said with a grin.

He rubbed the long barrel affectionately with a cloth. It felt quite surreal sitting with a strange man I had only met an hour ago, discussing different plans of action should I get attacked and him caressing a lethal gun, arms-length away from me.

But I was not afraid. He was adamant that I purchased a pistol. He then proceeded to give a detailed imaginary scenario of me in a room somewhere, hearing a suspicious knock and answering the door with the gun behind my back, James Bond style.

"People will think twice about whether they should harm you or steal from you when you have a gun," he concluded.

He was right of course but I was not ready for one yet. My dad's take on it was, "Carry a gun if you are prepared to shoot. If not, you'll get the bullet."

It was a grey area for me and I still had to make up my mind.

After nearly three and a half hours, I reluctantly got up. The wind, heat and dust were still there but it was less intense. We had about 18 kilometres more in front of us.

In Fraile Pintado, I received directions to the wrong house. A woman came out when she heard her dogs bark frantically. I asked her if this was where Cora lived. With a sour expression, she replied,

"Que quiere con Cora?" (What do you want with Cora?).

I found out later it was Cora's sister and apparently a family feud was brewing. Cora turned out to be the opposite of her sibling. She held and rubbed my hand and had a helper ready to take care of the horses. I was very dehydrated and finished a litre of water and half a litre of coke in less time than it took the man to take the saddle off

Mise. Fresh from a shower and wearing Cora's bathrobe, I crashed out on my bed. A soft breeze blew on my face through the netting in front of the windows. I half-woke later when I heard the engine of a vehicle. The next morning I saw my bags outside the door. The Gendarmeria was doing a good job.

Day 75. On the way to Rio Zora we were pestered by midges and if we stopped for a break it was even worse. The horses became agitated and the only solution was to keep going. We crossed a few very long bridges. The horses were doing fine until a boy on his bicycle, carrying a noisy plastic bag, crept up behind us. I did not hear him until he was on top of us but Tusa did and all of a sudden he charged forward at great speed. I got a terrible fright and gave the boy a right scolding look.

Not far from Rio Zora, I heard hooting and when I turned my head around, saw Richard Leach and his daughter. We had a picnic right next to the road. Tea had never tasted so good. Richard gave me 'pour on' – an insect repellent used on cows that I could try on the horses and a clip for the leading rope. They left me with a stock of biscuits and apples. I was sorry to see them go.

We arrived at our Gendarmeria stop, the fifth last before the Bolivian border, early afternoon and I was just in time for lunch. The horses were taken from me for saddling down. Over a cigarette after our meal, the young men chatted and relaxed a bit more. We played card games and they laughed at my mock outrage when somebody tried to cheat. When it got milder outside we took the horses to the river for a thorough wash-down. I loved the feeling of pebbles and mud seeping through my bare toes.

Back at 'base' I administered all that was needed. Each horse got an aloe vera leaf on their backs – they say prevention is better than cure. I also gave them little white *buta* pills for muscle relaxation and rubbed antibiotic cream on a sore on Tusa's leg. The 'pour on' covered the length of their backs and behind their ears.

I had a shower under a thin trickle of water after I had attacked all things flying and crawling in my room. A nap was compulsory and I felt refreshed and full of energy on waking. My request to go downtown to buy wine was met by loud cheers. I bought six litres of good Argentina *vino* and walked around the village in search of fresh vegetables. A disabled boy with black hair and no front teeth walked towards me and shook my hand. He kept on doing so until the lady in the shop gently pulled him away. On the bus back, one of the army told the bus-driver about my travels. He could not hide his surprise and kept on staring at me in his rear-view mirror. I was more concerned about the bus crashing than all the attention.

The evening was very enjoyable. We played more cards, ate and watched bad TV. They persuaded me to try cold red wine with coca leaves. It was palatable but more than a glass would have knocked me out.

I was woken at 5 a.m. the next morning by the sounds of Abba's "*Dancing queen*". After black tea and fresh bread I hurried outside to get ready. A group of army guys were observing my daily ritual but I got no assistance. I do not think it was ignorance though – they most likely thought I was in control and that I would not welcome help or interference. They may also have found a woman travelling independently like that a bit intimidating.

Mise shivered a lot on the way to Yuto and I wondered whether the '*pour on*' had burned her skin. She also had an uncomfortable trot with bursts of sudden acceleration. A lot of trucks roared past. One driver flashed his lights and stared open-mouthed.

We did the 32 kilometres in good time. We did not stop too often – I rather wanted to arrive early and give Mise and Tusa an opportunity for a good rest. In Yuto, the horses had lots of space to roam next to a big dam. The grandmother at the humble house where I stayed was small and wrinkly and looked about a hundred years old. Everybody was very friendly and my comfort was their priority. I shared a room with the grandmother and her husband. The room had one light bulb hanging from the ceiling and a large picture of Jesus. There was a hole in the wall to let in the light. The bathroom outside, measuring 1.25m^2 to be exact, had muddy floors and unpainted concrete walls. Its contents consisted of a toilet bowl, a little wooden bench, a chair and a bucket with lukewarm water. A big bottle of shower gel dominated the little space. It took some Houdini manoeuvring to pull on my jeans without the legs touching the wet surface.

After a long nap I went to check on the horses. When I got back I noticed a bed had been moved into the storeroom for me. Dinner consisted of black coffee and dry bread in front of the television. The grandmother took a branch from a tree to discipline the naughty children. I showed an article about my travels to one of the girls but she was more interested in her 'soap' on the box. The dog got kicked when he tried to cuddle up on the carpet. I went into my room to write my diary and to nurture my multiplying insect bites. After I had killed a lethal-looking spider on the wall I put out the light to deter the insects. I read by torch light for a while.

I woke up twice during the night to put cream on my itching sores. When I got up at 5:30 a.m. the old man was outside cleaning the yard. He shuffled around, his back in a permanent bend. I declined an offer of coffee and managed to leave an hour later. It was a pleasant overcast day with a cool breeze. A short while into our journey I developed a splitting headache and made a mental note never to say no to coffee in the morning again. We managed to cover 23 kilometres in three hours.

I saw the YPF petrol station in the distance and a *gaucho* waving frantically. He walked towards us. He was dressed in cow-skin trousers, had no teeth and his cheeks bulged with coca leaves. He grabbed me and smacked a kiss on my cheek.

Juan was the worker on the farm where I was staying that night and had an order from his boss to meet me there. I passed him a packet of cigarettes and a lighter while downing a long overdue coffee. He got on his horse and we headed for Colonia Santa Rosa. He was very impressed with my travels. He told me what excellent companions he thought horses and dogs were. I could not agree more.

On the way, we stopped at a very poor house consisting of only one room. Juan was proud to show me where he lived. His two kids came out and he insisted they kiss the *señorita* hello. He gave water to the horses and took off Mise's reins and bit affectionately. I had told him on the way that Tusa's leg between the fetlock and the heel was still a bit sore and quickly he brought out a remedy. It was animal fat that looked like it had been soaked in blood. He looked comical when the red paste stuck to his moustache after lighting a cigarette. I gave his kids lollipops and biscuits. Juan then cut off a piece of sponge for me to put underneath the saddle.

"It's better than *mandil*," (a sponge with velvet cover, selling for fifty dollars in Salta) he said.

He was delighted when I told him it was perfect. I feared another coca-smelling kiss on my cheek but was glad when he only shook my hand vigorously.

We arrived at Pepe and Helena's farm, receiving many warm welcome kisses and hugs. Pepe said, "Treat this house like your own and stay as long as you wish."

With one eye I tried to watch the U.S Open Tennis Championships on television over a hearty lunch. I had not been watching any of the major tournaments the year before, mostly due to a hectic schedule, and the players were strange to me. My hosts much preferred talking and I soon gave up on the tennis. Everybody was very impressed with my level of Spanish and convinced I understood everything. I did not feel the need to change that perception. I gave them a copy of the *La Nacion* article I had been carrying with me since Buenos Aires. They showed it proudly to everybody that came into the house.

The daughter said, "I am tired, just thinking about your trip."

I got the impression that the Indians were considered very much lower class and they were referred to as *Negros*. One of the men asked me where I stayed the night before.

He replied, "Well tonight you'll sleep in a room with no mosquitoes and where we don't sell fruit."

Juan the *gaucho* offered to show me a short-cut to Oran which, I calculated, was 28 kilometres away. He reckoned his route would be half of that. The next day was a lazy Sunday and I took my time to groom the horses. Geramine, a little Indian girl with a pretty scarf around her head kept on saying, *"Hola señora Marianne."* She was very sweet, followed me around and asked a lot of questions. I taught her a few English words and told her she must learn more.

Lunch was a drawn-out affair and just before dessert we all went out to look at Juan who stood outside, dressed to kill. He had a different pair of leather trousers on – this cow was black, brown and white. His thoughtfully composed attire was complemented by a little rag of a scarf around a thin and weather-beaten brown neck. A rifle at his side finished the ensemble.

He had saddled up Tusa already and said to me, "No rush *señorita*, Oran is just round the corner."

We did not leave until 2:30 p.m., riding through the village first, then taking back-roads on dusty pathways between the bushes. We came to a high sand precipice and were forced to stop. Juan tried to level the surface with his machete but gave up after a while – it would have taken him all day to get it flat enough for us to get down. He directed us to another road that led through a shallow river. Juan got off his horse to inspect what was ahead. He took off his shoes, rolled up his trousers and, with milk-white wiry legs, braved the waters. He broke off a branch from a tree and, Crocodile Dundee-style, licked his finger and then raised it in the air to see which way the wind was blowing. He stuck the branch into the sand to mark where he had entered the water.

There was no need for this. The river was not full and there was a big rock where he had gone in. I had to suppress a giggle as I watched in amusement. He returned after a while and motioned for me to follow him. Once in the water, Tusa had the urge for a drink and got down on his knees. I felt as if we were sinking into the sand and were about to fall over and I jumped off clumsily. My shoes, socks and chaps got completely soaked.

The forest in front of us soon became a jungle and I continuously had to duck to avoid the long thin trees and thorny branches lashing my face. After a while it became less dense but the surface now was hard dried mud and uneven. I was becoming worried about the horses' legs and feet and feared they might twist an ankle. It was not long before we were surrounded by jungle again.

It was now almost impenetrable and Juan used his machete to open up the way. Large leather shields protected his legs – these were attached to the side of the horse and covered most of his lower-body. I had none and felt every bang against me. When it became impossible to ride we led the horses. Soon we were covered in bits that fell from plants and trees.

Juan mumbled a lot and I did not know if he was angry with me or just talking to himself. He walked very fast, lashing out at the denseness with his machete and did not look back to see if I was behind him. The horses were fantastic. Tusa followed behind my every step and neither of them spooked once. It was impossible to see the sky through the thick jungle trees and I gathered that there was not much daylight left. I could not imagine having to share my tent with Juan that night.

It was 6:30 p.m. when we emerged into open space. We were surrounded by sugarcane fields. Juan teased me about fretting.

"The Gendarmeria is only five kilometres or less away," he said with confidence.

He peered up into the sun to decide which way we should go. I noticed the distance and space that stretched out in front of us. Darkness was looming and I felt less sure than he did. The horses were worn out and I found it difficult to get them to move at reasonable speed. When darkness set in completely, I got off and walked with them.

Juan lingered in the back and, by now, communications between us had ceased completely. I could not see any signs of life, even a blinking light, anywhere. At last we reached a crossroads. It was almost 9 p.m. Juan suggested we continued straight on but I insisted that we wait for somebody to pass to ask for directions. It was not long before a truck, working on the roads, drove in our direction. The pleasant young man noticed my distress.

He broke the devastating news, "The Gendarmeria is still 20 kilometres away."

He pointed in the opposite direction to Juan's recommended route. His solution was that we make our way to a police checkpoint, about 5 kilometres from where we were.

There was no moon to guide us in the pitch-dark night and I could hardly see my hand in front of my face. Juan was still sulking and continued to drag behind. When another truck passed, the horses got a fright and broke away from me. I shouted after them in the dark. I had no clue where they were but, thank God, they were frightened too and stopped. I stumbled across them about two hundred yards up the road.

At the police checkpoint they were given water and tied up in a space with enough grass for the night. I spotted Juan in the distance, walking slowly with a flashlight but he did not come over to me.

I got a lift to the Gendarmeria and with concerned faces everybody bombarded me with questions. I thought I had arrived at a deluxe hotel. I had a spacious room and a cool-box with drinks and ice awaited me. Someone came around and asked what I would like for breakfast. I was almost caught in the nude when I took a shower in the communal bathrooms but I was so exhausted I could not have cared less. I thought of Juan my *gaucho*-guide just before I fell asleep. I felt bad that we had got lost and that he had 'lost face'. He was so excited about helping me. Nobody could have guessed it would all go so wrong.

Jorge, a First Lieutenant at the camp was assigned as my personal helper. He had a nice way about him and his English was good. I was very interested in the activities of the Gendarmeria and he told me hair-raising stories of drug-seizures at the border. The pictures gave the full story. Narcotics were smuggled in from across the Bolivian border in every possible way – cars, clothes, shoes, spare parts, batteries, shampoo bottles and then, of course, in more intimate places.

He said, "Our guys are very good and they are usually right about suspects."

I found it all fascinating and had many questions. He told me that coca from which cocaine is made, is the main product in Bolivia and more profitable than bananas. Somebody also told me that the Bolivian government turns a blind eye to this because they profit so well.

I stayed for two nights at the camp in Oran and could not have asked for more friendly help. Jorge tried his best to bargain for things I needed in town and was disgusted when one man would give no discount on horse-food.

I needed a few pens and he said to the girl behind the counter, "This woman is famous."

She handed them over for free.

Embarrassed I smiled and said, "You should have been my agent from the beginning."

My left hand looked quite sore from all the insect bites and the scratching I was still happily engaging in. Jorge arranged for the resident doctor to give me an injection in my bottom. It burned like hell for three minutes and I thought that one side was about to go numb.

Somebody else advised me how to tie the saddle-bags which were still not functioning as they should. After the advice I felt better about the pack and found everything more manageable. No request was too much and without fuss I had my machete and Swiss Army knife professionally sharpened. They put a fatty substance on the blades and rubbed a lubricant into the leather part of the machete. Jorge showed me the ammunition room – it was covered with guns from wall to wall. I asked him his opinion about my taking a pistol.

"I can't give you an answer," he said honestly. "There are pros and cons but personally I think I wouldn't take one."

The morning that I left the horses got shod. I was not sure how clued-up the farrier was but at least he did not cut too much away on the soles of the horse's feet. Some farriers get completely carried away and can cause the horse a lot of harm. Mise was tense and I rubbed some lavender aromatherapy oil on the tip of her nose. It seemed to calm her down a bit. Jorge came into the room as I was packing my bags. He looked at the sheepskin and read the message from José in Tucumán on the inside with great interest.

"Mmm," he chuckled, "I think this *gaucho* liked you."

I could feel myself blush. "What does it say?"

Jorge smiled, took out a pen and paper and translated the words which I read once I was on my own again.

I wish you all the best in this crazy journey you have undertaken and I hope luck is by your side throughout. I hope you enjoy it and know that I admire your courage in making this journey alone, and I nearly forgot to say that I think you are lovely. You know I envy you because your journey was always my dream and I never managed to make my dream come true. So for as long as your journey continues, know that from my corner of the world I will be with you in spirit and each time I think of you I will wish the best for you...

Your friend always

José de Tucumán

While reading the message I was reminded once again just how lucky I was. But I felt a sense of guilt too that it was me and not José, who was without doubt ten times the horseman that I was, who got the opportunity for this unique, life-changing undertaking. I thought about that mystical element in life where our paths seem to move in a particular direction, often without our force or will. It just happens. I was no more special than José because I got the chance for this incredible adventure. I was just lucky. So lucky that people believed in me, so lucky that I got help. José had big dreams too but his circumstances had been different. Had he been dealt different cards I am convinced he would have been conquering the world from the back of a horse as well.

The Gendarmeria base, called 28 de Junio, was the second last stop before the border. When we trotted out of Oran, I encountered a few men on the side of the road who made lip-smacking sounds as we went past them. I did what local women do and just ignored them.

There were a few bridges on the way and when a long one loomed in front of us, I steered the horses towards the half-dry river. It was a mistake. The rocks were much bigger than I thought and we struggled through to the other end at a snail's pace. A pit-stop at the entrance of a farm was indeed just that – after ten minutes the midges got so annoying that we had to go. We continued on the side of the road. After a while, for some reason I looked down at my money-belt. The zip was open. My heart missed a beat and I put my hand slowly inside, fearing the worst. My little camera was gone. I felt sick. Knowing I could not continue without searching for it, and with heavy heart, we turned around.

We backtracked for two kilometres and when I found it by a gate where we had rested for a while, I jumped with joy and took a picture there and then to remember the moment.

The man at the Gendarmeria said *"tranquilo"* (take it easy) a lot and showed me to my room.

One guy asked, *"Viaje sola? Solita, solita solita?"* (Are you travelling alone? Alone, alone, alone?).

I could feel the irritation building up inside me. This was the most frequent question asked and it started to get on my nerves. I developed a standard response.

"No solita. Con dos caballos" (Not alone. With two horses).

A few saw the funny side of it.

I did not have much to do and later walked to the checkpoint to look on as the Bolivians' bags were searched. Everybody on the bus had to get off and queue. The mosquitoes were relentless and kept on eating me alive, despite the fact that I was covered in insect repellent. Later Schumaaister, the chief in charge, knocked on my door and introduced me to the chef who wanted to take my dinner order.

My diary read;

So, at the moment I am sitting on my bed with two ceiling fans competing and making a lot of noise. I am eating raisins and almonds and waiting for my dinner. I can't wait to go to sleep.

I dined alone but had a feast of a dinner, a plate full of veggies, another one filled with meat and sweet potato, another container with cut tomatoes and fresh French bread. I could not finish it all and hid some tomatoes and bread for the road for the next day. I left the meat at the side of the bungalow for a hungry dog I saw sneaking around.

The vegetation on the way to Aguas Blancas was green and lush. There were banana plantations everywhere with workers dotting the fields. There were many little settlements of poor people and the kids were excited and shouted when we passed. I responded to all the waves and *holas* but did not stop. I felt on top of the world and my spirits were high. The excitement reached a climax when I saw a sign for Aguas Blancas – 10 kilometres. I kept on smiling and patting Mise's neck. We were 10, 000 metres away from Bolivia! A woman with one shoe on and the other one in her hand walked in our direction. I asked her if she could take a picture of me and the horses next to the sign. She shook her head.

"No puedo." (I can't).

A man came out of his house on the side of the road and I made the same request. He took the camera and walked a few yards back. He lifted the camera to his face. I laughed.

"No, it's the other way around."

He looked confused and held the camera arms distance away from his squinting eye. It was still upside down. A young boy intervened and the picture was finally taken.

The town of Aguas Blancas was located to the right of the Gendarmeria base, nestled deep in a valley. I was given something to eat and had the company of a young man in uniform. He was a bit in my face however, speaking very fast and stating the obvious.

"It's a long, long road that you are riding," he sighed. "It's difficult, very difficult."

I was not in the mood and replied in *staccato* mode. He sensed my lack of enthusiasm to engage and left me alone.

Eduardo, my assigned 'right-hand' man, suggested later we go to the border and sort out my papers and entry. The contrast between the two borders was obvious. On the Bolivian side there was no electricity and the man used a candle to inspect my passport. The officials made a point of excluding me from the conversation and, with reluctance, took my extended hand when I was introduced.

The town of Bermejo was chaotic and hectic. People and children occupied every space and dogs were stretched out on the warm streets, oblivious to the dangers of automobiles. Our first stop was the 'export' offices. The man said he needed a letter from the Gendarmeria that he would stamp and Eduardo and I returned to base on the Argentine side to get this done. He typed up the letter and made photocopies of my horse papers – proof of ownership and anaemia results from when they stayed at Los Lapachos. On returning to the offices, there was another man on duty. He went through the documentation with a fine tooth comb. A lengthy phone call to his superior followed. Afterwards, he took it upon himself to explain my route in detail – twice.

He was not shy with advice either. "Stay on the roads and don't travel at night."

Eduardo and I sighed when I finally got the necessary stamp and removed ourselves quickly. However, the bureaucracy was not over yet and we had to visit another 'official' who had to make a call to the border control, informing them of my non-requirement for an entry Visa into Bolivia.

Eduardo's friend, shook my hand warmly and said, *"La gente de Bolivia son muy bueno, pero siempre ten cuidado"* (The people in Bolivia are very nice but always be careful).

On Friday the 6th of September, two and a half months since my journey started, I woke at 6 a.m. with loud music in my ears. I got up and started to pack. I looked out of the window and noticed there was not a breeze – it was going to be a hot day. I could not swallow the dry toast and drink the sickly sweet cappuccino fast enough. Outside, the men studied my every move while I got the horses ready. This was the first time since leaving Los Lapachos that one of the horses would have to carry the saddlebags again. We had been spoilt by the Gendarmeria.

I struggled to get them to sit comfortably on Tusa but a volunteer stepped forward.

19. Three curious Indian women approaching shyly for a chat.
20. 'No man's land' – the fascinating Bolivian *altiplano*.

21. A wheelbarrow for entertainment and transport.
22. A church in the making in Lamadrid.

23. The German cyclists and I in the tiny village of Tola Polca.
24. A moment for reflection in La Merced.

25. Traditionally clothed women in Tarija.
26. Dorota and Marx in Camargo.

I was dubious about his attempts and wondered what the stability would be like once we started to trot. Pictures were taken and last *mates* gulped down. I could not *wait* to get going – I was entering another country on horseback!

Argentina was good to me. The acts of hospitality and friendly embraces received everywhere we went, were extraordinary. Every day I was so thankful for the offers of endless help and gestures of goodwill. It strengthened my confidence and I knew that this good start to my journey would set me up to be able to cope with what lay ahead.

Eduardo said, "I will meet you at the border point."

I waved, "See you in about twenty-five minutes."

But it was not meant to be. We had hardly covered fifty yards when Mise broke into a trot and immediately I felt a strong pull on the leading rope. Fearing the worst, I looked to my right. Bloody hell. The usual routine. Kicking, jumping, bucking. Belongings scattered. Tusa head down with a guilty look. I felt like laughing and crying all at once. Everybody kept their respectful distance and, after a while, Eduardo came over and picked me up. Someone else took the horses back to base.

I needed a new *alforja* and a better system to tie up the saddlebags. On Gendarmeria time and money, three young men accompanied me back to Oran in one of the army vehicles. In the shop I struggled to explain in Spanish exactly what I needed and felt like banging my head in frustration when nobody understood. Jorge was away and there was nobody else with sufficient English to translate. Finally after a lot of sighs, head-shaking and sign language, they got the message. I was told to come back later that afternoon. They would fix and strengthen my bags and the man would make me a leather strap, combined with nylon rope, to secure all my belongings on the packhorse. I had to believe that it would work. It was very quiet that evening at the Aguas Blancas base and I could not spot Eduardo or any other familiar face. I went to bed without dinner but slept soundly. My heart was happy although not without the occasional excitable flutter. I was full of hope for the future.

7. BOLIVIA BECKONS

*"All you need in this life is ignorance
and confidence, then success is sure"*
— *Mark Twain*

A spider harassed me throughout the night and by 4:30 a.m. I was wide awake. The sight of an overcast day outside put me in joyous mood and I minded less about the red bumps on my stomach. After sweet, weak coffee and a couple of pieces of dry bread, I was ready to take on another country. The bags sat secure on Tusa and I felt good. Eduardo was at the border point to help and nobody mentioned that I had overstayed my three month limit in Argentina. A crowd of Bolivians had gathered and, without exception, everyone looked on with great curiosity. Roars of laughter erupted when I said that one of my horses was called Tusa. Apparently, one of the boys standing around went by the same name.

I was glad I did not have to go into the town of Bermejo, putting our noses instead in the opposite direction on a road that led through the mountains. I was in great spirits. For me, the adventure had started. I was now on my own. Nobody was waiting for me ahead. Nobody knew where I would be that night. It was just me and the horses in a big, wide world. We called the shots and could go at the pace that we wanted. We could stop when we felt like it and for as long as we desired. We could go slow and enjoy the scenery or up the pace. We could dream and contemplate. We could do five kilometres or fifty. It was for us to decide. I had no qualms about not knowing where we would put our heads down that night. The gods had been with me throughout Argentina. I had blind faith that we would have the same luck in Bolivia.

Mise and Tusa must have felt the good vibes and positive energy for they had a zest and pride in their step. On the way, I was greeted by friendly waves and smiling faces from women on the side of the road. My thoughts went back to my host in Frias who warned me about sulky-looking Bolivians.

'*Eat your hat, Gringo,*' I thought with satisfaction.

I reflected on my own capacity, and indeed everyone's, to stereotype others. Seeing the innocent smiles from the local people reminded me to always keep an open mind. It was important on this journey that people accepted me at face value. The least I could do was to do the same for them.

The scenery was spectacular. It was lush and tropical and, all along the way I spotted little settlements nestled among the mountains and dense vegetation. Mothers would call their children to come out of the houses when they heard the clip-clop of hooves on the tarmac and the beaming grins of the young ones gave me a great boost. I knew these were early days, but what a magnificent and reassuring start.

The Rio Bermejo far down below, which curved alongside the road, looked beautiful and seriously inviting. What I had not bargained for were the massive rocks and stones we had to cross before we got there. Mise drank eagerly but Tusa declined. He stuck up his nose so I splashed the water on his sweaty legs. By the time we got back to the road the three of us were in need of something cool again.

We did another 12 kilometres when I spotted a little house close to the road. Three girls gave the horses water and, when we left, one pushed a packet of biscuits into my hand. They were obviously very poor but their generosity knew no bounds. It was a very sociable day's ride. A man on his bicycle followed me for a while and chatted animatedly. Later two young girls walked with us and one of them warned me of the *perros* (dogs) ahead. Another man who worked the fields came over to talk to me. He shook my hand and I told him where I was heading. His teeth were rotten from the coca leaves.

When we arrived at a truckers' stop, I knew that was where I wanted to stay for the night. Ariel, who ran the basic establishment with his sister, was very helpful and gave the horses water and maize. I got the opportunity to pitch my tent for the first time with five young curious faces watching my every move. I had something to eat and surrounded by the kids I sat on the ground and picked the horse hairs from my poncho. The next thing I knew the horses were gone. They had been happily eating their corn (untied) and then all of a sudden disappeared. I ran with the kids through the sugarcane fields but there was no sign of them. I was sure that they could not have gone far in the short time. Ariel came running at top speed past us and appeared ten minutes later on Mise's back with Tusa on a rope.

The kids were all chewed up by the mosquitoes and I introduced them to repellent for the first time. They were intrigued and loved it.

"Don't scratch your bites," I said in an authoritative tone.

I felt pure contentment that evening having my dinner in the open with soft music in the background. I looked out on the road where the odd truck still roared past. The horses munched on something and chickens scratched around them. '*One can truly be happy with the simple things,*' I thought. I felt so much at peace. Two women sat on the side of the road, waiting for a bus. They had been there for hours. Ariel invited them over later and we all had black coffee and home made pita-like dry bread. Their bus came along and they did not manage to stop it in time.

They shrugged their shoulders. "We'll get the next one."

They were still outside when I was ready for my slumbers two hours later. Just as

I was ready to crawl into my tent Ariel suggested that I sleep in his brother's room.

"It will be more comfortable and less cold," he said with a convincing nod.

He made up the bed specially for me and even folded back the sheets. The room had pictures of a muscular Van Damme, a poster of a blonde with big fake breasts, another romantic scene of a couple strolling on a beach, the Virgin Mary and Jesus. I felt safe in such diverse and distinguished company. Ariel gave me their only lantern and used candles for themselves. My windbreaker and some rolled-up carpet served as a pillow.

The next morning I had to beg Ariel to take money for his hospitality. I shoved some pesos into his hand as he finally relented.

I loved going on dirt road. It meant one worry less as I knew it would be a while before the horses needed shoes again. I rode Tusa and Mise came along unattached. Sometimes she would linger at the back but the moment we were round a bend out of sight she would panic and quickly catch up with us. The road was quiet apart from the odd bus blowing dust in our faces and disturbing the peace. There were very few houses and settlements. In contrast to the day before, the people we encountered seemed less friendly and most of them just stared. During our first break I hungrily devoured Ariel's bread and had a *mate*. The horses welcomed the rest too and rolled around. Mise's back still seemed to be sensitive from the *'pour on'* that had burnt the skin.

A man came walking up the road in our direction. "How far to Mamore *señor*?" I asked.

He told me it was far. Very far.

"*Cuantos kilometros?*" I feared his answer.

He scratched his head. "*De aqui hasta Mamore.... sesenta.*"

60 kilometres! I could not believe it. Ariel's father obviously got it wrong. I cut our break short and saddled up. I did not know if I was going to find a place for us before nightfall. I was slightly apprehensive but a glimpse of a spectacular view was more important than my apprehension and I did not hesitate to stop for a picture. I wanted the composition to be just right and got off Mise to position myself. Just as I was about to press the shutter, Tusa jumped and took off. I was not surprised when Mise followed. The reason for Tusa's fright was a tiny 'landslide' – bits of earth had tumbled down from the cliff on our right. It was hardly noticeable but you could count on Tusa to react. I did not panic though. To the left was a steep precipice which led to a river below. On the right hand side the cliff towered up into the sky.

I calmly proceeded to take my snap and then continued to stroll down the road. There was not a sound and I relished the tranquillity. It was not long before I heard the soft clop of hooves and saw my two friends come back in my direction. A time to chase and a time to be chased.

The gods were on my side when, at 4 p.m., we entered a tiny village consisting of four houses, a little school, a soccer field and a church. It was perfect. A pretty young girl passed on permission from the headmistress to pitch my tent in front of the church. It was as safe a spot as one could have wished for. The nearby river was an ideal bath for the three of us and just as I was about to take off my clothes, I heard a cough in the bushes. A young boy working the fields discreetly made his presence known.

Everybody watched with great interest while I pitched my tent. An old woman dressed in typical Bolivian attire came over to chat. She wore long trousers, a pink skirt and a patterned blue jumper that reached her knees. Her jet-black plaited hair reached below her waist and a traditional bowler hat completed the picture. She had not a single tooth in her head but that did not stop her from talking without taking a breath. The two *empanadas* that she handed me were still warm. She must have sensed how hungry I was.

When darkness fell I tied Tusa up. The horses had become very fond of each other and I had all the faith in the world that Mise would go nowhere without her pal. It was not long before Tusa got tangled in the rope and broke free. Fortunately I got hold of him before he and Mise could even contemplate roaming. Later in my tent the toothless woman sat herself down outside and continued her conversation through the netting. It did not bother her one bit that I had very little to say.

"Put all your belongings in the church," she suggested after a while.

The kids eagerly helped to carry the saddle and bags over. One girl asked what I used the crop for.

"Sometimes for the horses," I said, "But also for bad men."

The girls giggled shyly.

I walked across the road in search of more food. With difficulty I could make out the shapes of two boys sitting on a porch table in complete darkness. They pointed at where their mother was and I disturbed her just as she was squatting down at the side of the house. I apologised and turned around quickly. I was sceptical about the hygiene of the *empanadas* she offered but hunger got the better of me. A skinny dog gave me a grateful look when I threw him the last one.

I felt content when I climbed into my tent under a soft glow of moonlight. There were no lights on in the village. It was very quiet. It was chilly though and I put on a second layer of clothing. I pulled my poncho from underneath me and threw it over the sleeping bag. The saddle-blankets, alas smelling of horses and sweat, served as a mattress and helped mask the dampness from the earth beneath.

I had a cold and restless night and the rooster's crow an hour before the sun came up did not help matters much. I overslept and when I finally emerged from my tent it was already 7 a.m. and hot. Mise and Tusa lay on the ground an arms-length from the front of the tent.

The old woman brought me three eggs for the road but I gave them back to her.

"They will break on the way *señora*. Thank you but they will be wasted."

She returned ten minutes later – they were hardboiled and she handed me a little bag with salt. I gobbled down two pieces of stale bread with *mate* and continued to organise the horses.

I led them for the first few kilometres, adjusted the saddle on Mise and got on again. The next ten kilometres were tough as we climbed higher and higher. At one point the road became very narrow and I held my breath as trucks passed us far too close for comfort. I deliberately cast my eyes away from the impressive precipices on our left. I had to fix the pack on Tusa a few times. It was hard work. When we got to the top I dismounted and led them all the way down. They were not very energetic and my pace was faster than theirs. I tied the rope around my waist so as not to have to pull them using my arms, but the rope tightened around my stomach and I could not breathe. I told myself to chill. There was no reason for the haste so I slowed down.

The sun was shining and the high cliffs and trees surrounding us cast long, streaky shadows across the road. There was only the sound of the horses' hooves and the odd snort. I did not even hear the birds.

In the late afternoon having passed numerous road works, a very short man with a peculiar build stopped his pickup and came over to shake my hand.

"Good luck, *señorita*," he said. "May God look after you and protect you from illness."

I was surprised by the unexpected warmth and sincerity and felt like I had just been personally blessed by a divine spirit. My tummy even ceased rumbling for a while.

We arrived in La Mamora, a non-event of a town halfway between Tarija (capital city and also the state department) and the border earlier than expected. Looking across the river, it was possible to see Argentina. There was not much to the town apart from narrow streets full of small make-shift stalls selling fruit, household materials, cigarettes and cold drinks. An interesting circular church was under construction with windows that would open to the mountains on all sides.

At one of the stalls I approached a friendly-looking woman who offered that I stay in the church or at her house.

"There is no grass for the horses," she informed me. "But you can buy corn here."

The yard at the back of the woman's house sloped steeply downwards. She pointed to where I could leave the horses.

"It's very steep, *señora*," I observed. "The horses won't be able to lie down."

I thanked her and decided to move on. Just then I spotted the most pathetic, scrawny little dog, almost obscured by the dust he was lying in. His fragile body looked lifeless and was covered in sores. He did not seem to have the strength even to look up at us.

"*Que terrible,*" I said to the woman. "You'll have to kill him mercifully. He's suffering too much."

She did not even look embarrassed about having a dog in that condition.

After more searching and waiting, I ended up in the local priest's house, two hours later. Each horse was tied to a tree outside.

In my room, one bare bulb hung from the ceiling. There was a table, a mattress with sagging springs, flimsy curtains and no carpet. Padre Juan was very obliging but I wondered why he appeared slightly jittery. I had not washed my hair in a week and when I discovered there was no water, I sat down on my bed and gobbled up the last of my crackers. I felt run-down and a throbbing in-grown toenail and tight sore muscles added to my misery. My dusty face felt marginally cleaner after wiping it four times with toner and cotton wool. I heard dogs whine and could not stop thinking about the skinny one I had seen earlier. I found out that the bathroom door locked from the outside and made sure I finished whatever business I had inside rather rapidly.

Later that evening I was well looked after by Padre Juan. Pancakes with a meat filling were served and they were so tasty, I did not even mind the long strand of black hair decorating the hot, spicy tomato sauce. A little Indian boy and his father stayed in the room next door. Once in my bed, I gave a few exaggerated coughs to silence the boy's chirpy chatter. It worked, only to be replaced a short while later by the father's deep, guttural snoring. I sighed and put the pillow over my head.

The following day we were on our way to La Merced when disaster struck, only four days after the last incident with a lopsided pack. I had been thinking how well things were going. It was a little reminder: never to get too comfortable. My saddlebags, tent and everything else flew in all directions on the tarmac. I exhausted my repertoire of both soothing and cursing words to calm Tusa down. The saddle frame hung from his belly, he had broken skin on his legs and blood was dripping from his thigh. He gave an undignified snort.

There were houses on both sides of the road and I begged the roadside gapers to help me remove my belongings before a bus or truck came along. We were going uphill and somebody speeding from the other side could easily have crushed everything I had. Only the women lent a hand. I washed Tusa's wounds. The cuts were not deep and needed only antiseptic cream. My biggest concern was the broken strap that was used to keep the whole pack together. A man, who watched the whole spectacle from the comfort of his chair without batting an eye-lid, dragged himself over. His help was not the most imaginative but at least he came up with a temporary solution to keep the pack secure.

Later on the road I stopped an elderly man. I could not help but notice his cracked feet filled with dirt and red earth. He was walking into town with his family. He had an open, friendly face and the serenity of somebody who had lived a thousand years. He borrowed a knife and expertly cut into the leather to give it more grip. He also exhibited some skill when it came to tying it all up. Like a wise old guru, he patiently showed me how to do it. I was convinced that his ingenuity and craftsmanship came from many years of hardship and survival. He relied on no-one but himself.

In a way, I was in a similar position. All that mattered was to get through every day. Ultimately I had only me to count on. The idea of having no immediate fall-back or tangible support could be an unnerving thought but, in my case, it made me feel stronger. Everyday I learnt I was capable of so much more than I thought. Sure the tears would still come easily and there were moments of self-pity when things got tough, but emotionally and physically I found myself in a much better place with each passing day. It was like nature rewarding me for living through some of the hardships.

The surroundings changed on the way to La Merced. The mountains were further away but still gigantic and impressive. I noticed that the river down below was almost dry. We passed a small village with mud houses blending in so well they were almost unrecognisable between the dry, brown mountains. I stopped and asked a woman for water. Her answer was a brisk no. I was taken aback and slightly annoyed. My departure was as rapid as her answer. If I had known it would have been another two hours before I had something wet to my lips, I would have been pushier, or as a last resort, tried the tear-in-the-eye approach.

Our next break was memorable in a painful way. I nearly put the blade of my pen-knife through my thumb when I tried to fix Mise's reins, which she had stepped on earlier. It hurt like hell but seeing that there was nobody to show sympathy, I bit my lip and squeezed my hand until the bleeding stopped. When I got ready to leave, Tusa came over when he heard the cracking of paper, thinking it was food. He thrust himself against Mise who in turn pushed against me. I shouted in agony when she stepped on my foot.

La Merced was an interesting village. Built on a slope, most houses consisted of three or four levels. One had the feeling of climbing up and down all the time. A church took centre-stage, sitting on a large square in the middle of the village. A few hundred yards at the bottom of the valley, was a large, wide river, consisting more of oversized rocks than flowing water.

I had arrived early and managed a luxurious nap. It was cut short when I heard a girl shouting, *"Los caballos, los caballos!"*

We caught Mise and Tusa on the main road. They were covered in little black thorns and Tusa had blood above his right hoof and on his legs. It seemed he led the escape attempt and then got caught in wires and thorns. The corn stalks and bits of sugarcane obviously did not fill them up and they must have gone in search of better food. I could not be angry at them. I spent the next hour using my machete to get rid of the thorns. They did not move and enjoyed all the attention and grooming. A man looked at their shoes and did a bit of hammering and pinching.

"They won't need new shoes until you are in Tarija," he said.

The people in the village were completely self-sufficient and rabbit farming for fur was one of their enterprises. The rabbits were kept in tiny cages and they breathed heavily from the heat and cramped conditions.

One of the kids showed me her homework and how well she could write.

"What are the names of your children?" she asked.

I did not know how to explain to a ten-year-old that at the ripe old age of thirty-two, I did not have any. For them it is not unusual if a girl has a baby at thirteen or fourteen years of age. Only those who get an opportunity for education and broader thinking can break this cycle.

Mateo, my host, invited me to join the monthly communal meeting in the church that evening. The financial situation of the village was on the agenda. Everybody talked very quietly and in an orderly manner. There was no cutting in or interrupting. They even chuckled at the odd joke. The women were more assertive and gave most input. They sat erect on unforgiving wooden benches and the clik-clik of knitting needles almost gave a rhythm to the proceedings. Nobody seemed bothered by the occasional squeaks and laughter from a few playful children and a baby in the middle of the room.

From what I gathered, the village was operating at a deficit and heads were put together to brainstorm ways of generating more cash. My Spanish was still not great and as a result some of the ideas went right over my head. Tired from the day's ride and the uncomfortable seating, I slipped away to my room before the meeting was over.

Mateo was pessimistic about my travels as we sat talking around the breakfast table the following morning.

"It's dangerous in South America. They'll rob all your bags in Peru."

I shrugged my shoulders. I knew he was concerned but what could I say? His wife, keeping herself busy with their three children, kept quiet and I wondered what she was thinking. Did she silently applaud me for my courage or did she think I was foolish?

I tasted an appetizing traditional dish called *malal*, made from beans, corn and meat, which is then wrapped in a corn leaf and baked. Mateo gave me one for the road and also a jar of honey – their own.

"This will last you until La Paz," he said with pride.

The mountains surrounding us on the way to Padcaya were rainbow layers of browns, greens, greys and blues. It was a beautiful morning. Later, the valleys turned brown and dry and looked like something out of a cowboy film, I could just imagine a line of *Apaches* appearing on the horizon.

Tusa was acting up again and the constant strain on the leading rope was noticeable. But I found a magic trick by chance. If I called out or talked to him in a certain voice, preferably high pitched with lots of variation in my tone, he became much more compliant and obedient. I do not know why it worked, I was just so happy that the trotting had become smoother.

Ten kilometres from Padcaya I found a shady spot next to a little school which stood between two tiny houses. A young boy took down the Bolivian flag just as we arrived. I unsaddled the horses but they were jaded and stood motionless while I had my *malal* lunch. Two kids peeked at us self-consciously from a distance. They covered their faces and laughed when I took a picture.

Two men passed. One on a horse – a rare sight in these parts – and the other one walked behind a number of donkeys. The little boys came over later and looked on as I saddled up. Rather pleased at the opportunity to show off in front of my small audience, I assembled the saddle and saddlebags with exaggerated speed and efficiency. I winked at the boys when I was done. They still did not say a word but waved goodbye as I was mounting Mise. I put my foot in the stirrup and too late realised the girth was too slack. Losing my balance I tumbled down as the saddle slid to the ground. I landed flat on the tarmac on my side. The boys stood wide-eyed and speechless, their faces showing their amusement. I looked at them sheepishly and slowly got up. I said nothing either and walked over to where they were standing at a safe distance, clutching each other's hand. I handed them one boliviano each. They understood our unspoken agreement – nobody would talk about what they had just witnessed. With a few *"gracias señora"* they hopped away, happy with the treasures in their fists.

When I arrived in the town of Padcaya, I waited for three hours in the square until somebody from the municipality showed me somewhere to keep the horses and my room for the night. I had spent all day on the road and felt worn out. Somebody gave me three oranges which I wolfed down. A pushy woman brought over a letter from friends of hers, written in English.

"Can you translate?" she asked, with heavily made-up eyes.

At first glance I thought she had connections in higher places when I saw the names at the bottom of the letter – Tony and Cherie. But as it transpired, this couple lived in the USA and both had already celebrated their 70th birthday. I translated sentence by sentence and where I was not sure, I improvised and made something up. She was satisfied and began to enquire about my journey. Shocked, she could not believe that I actually wanted to travel alone. Her husband was more understanding.

"Sometimes I go fishing on my own," he said. "Everyone thinks I'm nuts."

I told him that I had empathy with his need to get away from everyone sometimes. *'Especially from your wife,'* I nearly added.

The horses were put in an area where there was some grass to eat. There was also a ten-foot rubbish hole which was empty. I asked a girl from the school next door to help me find something to block it off from the horses. We made it pretty secure but I did not sleep well. The thought of the horses in the dark near such a dangerous dungeon gave me the jitters.

It rained during the night – the first downpour in months and the air the following morning felt crisp and clean. I left with the horses at the same time that the rubbish van went through town. They made a lot of noise and the horses were skittish. A man came running after us.

"You're going in the wrong direction," he shouted.

I stopped and used the opportunity to do up the saddle bags once more. I was starting to learn something, never set off if in doubt about the bags' stability. If you are doubtful when saddling up, you can be sure that very soon everything will start to slip.

The road to Tarija rolled away in a straight line in a series of very gradual ups-and-downs which made it hard-going on the horses. I found this frustrating and slow. At least when you go downhill through the mountains the scenery is exciting and every bend brings a surprise. Here the road was plain boring. The heavens opened up unexpectedly and I struggled to get my poncho out from behind the saddle and over my head. Just as I sat back into the saddle again the rain stopped. Breakfast was an hour later on the side of the road. I heard a giggle coming through the trees behind me and, shortly after, a woman appeared. She had an enchanting smile and was dressed in the traditional clothing. She left to collect fire-wood and on her return asked for my surname.

We had 53 kilometres to do and I urged the horses on until 1 p.m. The mountains on the side were covered in white cloud, spilling over the edges like candyfloss. The vegetation was still dry and brown. Thorn trees and cactuses dotted the landscape. There was nothing for the horses to munch on and during our break I gave them a bit of *avena*. A man on his bicycle swished past us twice. He put me in alert mode as we were slightly off the road and out of sight. But when I saw him a short while later pedalling uphill in the distance, I knew his curiosity was harmless.

Vito met me on the outskirts of Tarija. His Bono sunglasses gave him a cool look which belied his sixty years. I followed him through two roundabouts to the Army base. Before we got there, two men in uniform approached me. I did not know who they were and continued to go after Vito. They ran after me frantically and tried to explain that they were sent to help me. A group of army men was standing at the entrance to the camp when we arrived. I had to squeeze through the control barrier and one of my saddle-bags got ripped. Colonel Lopez seemed delighted to have us as his guests. Over coffee and pastries he vowed to help me on my way through the *altiplano* (high plain, mostly in Bolivia) with food for the horses.

An army lad came over and I went cross-country with him through shallow rivers and mud to get to where Mise and Tusa would be staying. Mise was in heat so I put her in a separate *corral* from Tusa. For Mise's protection I asked that the stallion be kept away from her. Adding to our trio was certainly not on the agenda.

Vito lived alone in a spacious double storey house a few blocks away from the town centre. I learned that his wife had died a few years earlier in tragic circumstances. He told me the story.

"She went off to visit friends or that's what I thought." He cleared his throat.

"Next thing, I got a phone-call from a hospital to say that my wife was in trouble. It turned out she was secretly having plastic surgery."

He shook his head as if he still could not believe it.

"She died under anaesthetic."

I felt so sorry for him. He seemed such a jovial man and I imagined it being hard living alone like that.

Tarija, a delightful small and clean city, its principal plaza full of palms and flowers and surrounded by small pavement cafés, is also the place where some of the best Bolivian wines are produced.

I planned to stay there for at least a week.

The horses needed new shoes and I had to organise a number of things before we could tackle the infamous *altiplano*. Sleep was also high on my priority list.

It took me more than three days to answer the thirty-four emails that awaited me. I was grateful for the continuous support and interest but it was an exhausting task. Great was my delight when I spotted a piano in the house. Every day I tinkled those ivories as if I was performing on stage and at that moment I could forget about everything. It was the only time I could ever really switch off. I needed it badly. I also had a very appreciative audience and Vito did not hide his joy at hearing the soothing sounds that filled the empty corners in the house.

"Music is very important," he said with emotion. "It brings out the sentimental side in people."

When Vito told his daughter-in-law about the nature of my mission, she laughed out loud in disbelief. His son regularly brought up the hardships I was bound to encounter in the high mountains.

"The *altiplano* is a different world," he sighed. "There is nothing. Absolutely nothing. There is almost nowhere for tourists to stay. I don't know where you will even find food."

The mere thought seemed to cause him tremendous agony. If only he knew what was going on in *my* head. The thought of the mysterious *altiplano*, the unknown and the possible dangers, filled me with dread. The numerous warnings from people spun like a merry-go-round in my head. But part of me tried to imagine that it would be okay. My heart said that I was meant to be there, I was meant to do this. The other part of me protested in exclamation marks. I did not know what I would possibly have to face. I was not ready to die yet. I could not imagine my horses perishing. Was I getting in too deep? Should I have had a backup team? Should I have stayed home? There was only one way to find out – keep on going, hoping and believing. The unknown was always going to be part of this journey. A journey into new lands and into the self.

Throughout my trip, I was worried about how my skin would be affected. I was out in the elements every day and feared that I would have crocodile skin by the time we trotted into New York City.

I had not shaved in weeks and the thought of silky legs and a facial spurred me into action when I saw a 'beauty salon' sign. I could not wait to be pampered. Sadly, they did not have a clue. The girl used tiny little strips of wax that came out of a filthy pot and ripped the hair off my legs. I could see myself being there for hours.

"Stop," I said. "Can you please do my underarms instead?"

It was worse. The wax was too hot and she neglected to hold the skin tight when she pulled. I waved my hand.

"Gracias señora, pero no."

I also declined the facial. The woman in the front, who I assumed was the manager, apologised and kissed me on the cheek. It was bizarre and I would have laughed had I not felt so utterly disappointed.

That afternoon, over tea and bread, I waxed my legs at Carmen's house. She was the sister of Vito, a lecturer in architecture and a very interesting woman. I liked her style and we took to each other instantly. Her French husband died when she was thirty-two. She had three small children at the time and never remarried. As I did my waxing, we chatted about everything. I told her that the idea of a live-in relationship put me off but living apart really appealed to me.

"Familiarity breeds contempt," I said.

She chuckled. "I think what you want is not a husband but a lover."

She could have been right.

Carmen told me how things had changed in Bolivia. "Generally for the worse," she said.

"Before, there was a lot of respect for gardeners, hat and shoe makers and tradesmen. They have lost that status for some reason. The old man in charge of the plaza would regularly keep the kids in line and give them a clip on the ear if he deemed it necessary." She shook her head. "That doesn't happen anymore. What could have gone wrong?"

I laughed when she told me about driving in Bolivia.

"Before it was even worse, when you were stopped by a policeman you told him that *he* was wrong before he could even get a word in."

Vito had organised an interview for the following day. My Spanish was still poor and Denise acted as translator. That Monday I adorned the front page of one of the newspapers. I found it useful to carry these articles with me, especially when communications were troublesome and where I found it difficult to explain my mission to those I met along the way. It also gave me respite from the endless questions and time to myself while curious faces hovered over the battered pages, taking in every word.

We had not had much contact with Colonel Lopez and Vito was worried that he would not be able to keep his word and help me through the *altiplano*. His initial offer was to get his men to deliver food for the horses in different spots. We went to Lopez's office that afternoon. I did not understand much and let Vito do the talking. He was very assertive.

"I want you to sort out what you promised," he said strongly.

Lopez assured us of immediate action.

Vito began referring to me as *"una amazona"* when talking about my trip. At the time I did not know the meaning of the word but when I found out, I liked the sound of it, meaning 'horsewoman' – it brought up images of a tough and self-sufficient girl, yet not too masculine.

It turned out the horses were losing weight while resting. I was not vigilant enough and hoped that the helper at the stables would pay attention to my request.

"Please feed the horses twice a day," I clearly instructed.

He was not interested though and it transpired later that he wanted money upfront for his help.

I wrote in my diary;

You simply can't trust anyone to care for your animals. Here I truly thought I had help and support from Colonel Lopez and his men and that everybody was committed to do their best. But they could not care less really. I feel bad that the horses had to go hungry. This is an important resting period for them before the next very demanding stretch through the *altiplano*.

I gave the boy at the stables the cash I intended to hand over when we left. I also informed him that I would now come out twice a day to feed the horses myself.

Carmen lent me a pair of sandals to wear to lunch at the Argentine consulate. Amongst the guests were a psychiatrist and an Arabian-looking man with very deliberate, slow movements that reminded me of a sloth, a South American mammal with the same characteristics.

The psychiatrist had an interesting theory.

"There is a link between suicide and corruption," he announced.

We all looked puzzled and he continued.

"Look at Finland. They have a high suicide rate but you would find very little corruption there. Contrast that with Bolivia where cheating and doing things under the counter are common practice and the suicide rate is very low."

We all thought about it for a moment. It sounded right but common sense told me there would be other factors too that needed to be considered. Nobody argued with him though.

During lunch we made arrangements for a 'piano night' at the consul's house. Herman was a keen pianist and when he realised we had a common interest, plans were made for an entertaining evening.

After lunch, Vito and I met again with Colonel Lopez to check on progress and see what preparations had been made. He was singing a different tune now.

"We don't have the vehicles to transport the food but might be able to organise one of the buses to drop off the bags," he said shamelessly. "It will be as far as Camargo only and it must be at your own expense."

Vito exploded and told him very clearly what he thought of him and his broken promises. I listened quietly and even though they spoke fast I could see by his response that it was not going to happen. We left with a fuming Vito at my side.

The next morning I cycled to the horses. The dirt road was stony and bumpy and little blisters had formed on my fingers by the time I reached the stables. The next day I took the bus. Another time Carmen lent me her jeep and Chiquito, her Alsatian, made sure he was included. Driving in Bolivia was no joke. Drivers had their own rules and most journeys were a nightmare.

At the same time, I had to keep Chiquito's panting mouth, heavy with dog-breath, away from my face.

I was looking forward to the piano night although I preferred to play for myself and not in front of others. As it turned out, the piano, an old-fashioned one with candles and copper holders on either side, was in a separate room away from where everybody sat. That suited me just fine. I lit the candles and the room was all of a sudden cosy and inviting. Some of the guests, most likely getting nostalgic at the sounds of "*Don't cry for me Argentina*" and "*Those were the days*", drifted in and out of the room, showing their appreciation.

Later in the living room, one of the guests mentioned Tschiffely and what he had accomplished.

He said, "Tiefie had a dog throughout his journey."

I found his pronunciation hilarious but refrained from laughing.

"No," I corrected him. "He only had a dog on the first day and, after a kick from one of the horses, it had to be left behind."

I did not know which version of *Tschiffely's Ride* he had read but the book I devoured had him travelling alone. At one stage a little Indian boy joined him for some months. The know-all did not budge though and insisted that he was right.

"You shouldn't do more than 15 kilometres a day," he proposed.

I smiled. "If I had three years, I would consider that."

He got up to get us more wine.

"Oh, and don't forget to take a gun with you that makes a lot of noise. You can fire from your tent to scare them away."

I did not get the chance to ask who 'them' were.

Carmen suggested that I took plastic Irish flags with me to give to people on my way.

"A lot of the Indians will be suspicious of you," she said. "It will break the ice to give them something from your country."

We walked through the market to buy orange, white and green sheets of plastic. We also needed tiny wooden sticks. These were taken to a dress-maker who promised to have them cut, pasted and ready the following day.

I had to make other arrangements when it became clear that more help would not be coming from the army. With Carmen, who bargained on my behalf, we bought large quantities of *avena* and maize. We put a mixture of these into separate bags. My next stop was the bus station and the woman in charge agreed that the food-bags could be sent, free of charge, on a *flota* (bus).

"Where do you want the bags dropped off?" she asked.

I had already looked at my map and calculated distances and gave her the names of seven obscure little towns and villages on the way. Because of the isolation and long distances, I knew there would be days where no food-bag would be waiting for us. There was nothing I could do about that. The bus driver would leave another six bags in Potosí, a city with the highest altitude in Latin America – 13,400 feet above sea level, from where I would arrange with another *flota* to have them dropped off en-route to La Paz, the capital of Bolivia. Had I known it would take us forty days to get from Tarija to La Paz, I would have squeezed in a few more bags.

I cannot say that anything dramatic spurred me into buying a weapon. It was most probably the accumulation of people's comments about my safety. I did not want to be foolish and find myself in a situation thinking 'I wish I had protection'.' This was merely a precaution, something to scare 'them' away.

So, the day before I left Tarija, I bought a .22 pistol for 165 dollars as well as twenty bolivianos worth of ammunition. It was rather a conservative purchase compared to Tschiffely who not only had a .45 Smith & Wesson with him but also carried a 12-gauge repeating shotgun, a Winchester .44 and a .45 long six-shooter. He clearly expected more trouble than I did.

The man in the shop took a copy of my passport and told me to come back two hours later. All I needed to become the owner of this small but clearly lethal little weapon was to get clearance from the police.

When I returned to the shop the man said, "You seem to have no criminal record."

He took my money and handed me the gun. Had it not been for the weight, you would have sworn it was a toy. It fitted perfectly into my moneybag.

There was no need for a demonstration from him. I was used to guns. On the farm where I grew up they were a common sight and we regularly did target shooting. Never overly fond of guns, I tolerated them. From a young age we were made aware of the devastating impact such a weapon could have.

"You have to have respect for it," Dad reminded us often.

The stretch ahead was going to be lonely and isolated. Knowing that I had a little bit more than a machete and my wits to rely on, made me feel more secure.

"Energy and persistence conquer all things"
— *Benjamin Franklin*

Day 102. Vito took me to the stables the day of my departure from Tarija. I cried when we said our goodbyes. My tears reflected my sorrow at departing but also my absolute fear and trepidation at what was coming. I was worried about the unknown ahead and did not know if I would make it. Vito had tears in his eyes too.

He hugged me.

"If you need anything, contact me. I am well connected."

Just as I turned on to the main road with the horses, Vito pulled up again.

"Come and live with me if you get fed up with your journey," he said through the window.

I waved and smiled.

"Thanks Vito. I'll remember that."

A short bit up the road, I stopped to tie up the saddle-bags again. But I did not notice that the leading rope that Tusa was on had manoeuvred its way in between Mise's legs. I mounted Mise and when we moved forward, the rope tightened up towards her thighs. She reacted like an untamed horse in a rodeo ring. With no warning, she ran on to the road, leaping and bucking. Tusa tried his best to dodge her vicious hooves and I tried my best to stay in the saddle. Cars came to a screeching halt within inches of us. I roared for help but people either ran away or stared wide-eyed. Nothing I did would make Mise come to a stop. Because of her kicking, Tusa kept pulling back and the rope continued to tighten and hurt her. We zigzagged manically through the streets and over pavements. My hysterical shouts continued and I struggled to hold on. I looked at the ground and contemplated jumping off. But the pace was fast and I knew I was bound to hurt myself. After what felt like an eternity, Mise came to a halt under a tree. We were all out of breath. Two men came over cautiously. I was shaking and burst into tears from shock. Arms reached out to help me to the ground. A young boy approached me.

"Su sombrero," he said. He handed me my hat.

Mise had a large superficial wound on her inner thigh. The skin had come off and left a red, sore-looking ring of flesh. She kicked lightly in my direction when I bent down to take a closer look. She would not let me go near it. It took a few minutes to compose myself and, after a few deep breaths, we tackled the road again. Mise was now very worked-up and jumped at everything – a hole in the ground, oil spillages, a white stationary car, a cyclist leaning on his bike, a discarded jumper, flags creating shadows on the road, even a bridge.

'Oh God,' I thought to myself. 'What has she learned? We've been travelling and crossing endless bridges for three months and still she jumped at something she knew so well.'

Cars, buses and people filled the streets as we tried to get out of the city. There were markets everywhere. The intoxicating buzz and constant action made me think of the madness one might find in New Delhi. On the outskirts, I stopped at a tiny shack of a stall. A woman came out and I asked for a Coke. She poured the liquid into a plastic bag, put a straw in and gave it a knot. She handed it to me while I sat on Mise. Down the road I passed a man who was idling on the pavement.

"Can you please throw this in the bin for me?" I asked.

In a friendly manner, he reached out to take the empty plastic bag from me and without hesitation dropped it on the ground. My first instinct was amazement. I did not comment but wondered how you teach people to take pride in their environment and where they live? Later, I gave it more thought, it was not that simple.

Although I tried to lead by example throughout my journey, hoping that it would rub off in some small way, I was somewhat naïve or even short-sighted about the dynamics in a lot of the countries I passed through. When getting through every day and surviving were your main concerns, then why would you bother about keeping your town, street or house tidy and clean? In a way it *was* simple, it just was not a priority. Not when heavier things weighed on your mind. Not when you were planning and scheming where to get the next plate of food for your children from. Not when life was a daily struggle.

The sign for Potosí, more than 400 kilometres away, led us on to a dirt road and soon we started to climb. Tusa pulled back a lot. Mise sensed when the leading rope was about to tighten and broke into a spontaneous trot. Tusa had no choice but to up his speed as well. It was late afternoon when we entered Tucumilla. I led the horses to a muddy dam to quench their thirst. Mise kicked the water with her front leg. A little Indian boy stood on the bank observing us.

"Why is she doing that?" he asked.

He took me to where he believed the horse food had been dropped off a couple of days before. I knocked on the door. A man opened and without a word, handed me the bag. I asked him where we could stay for the night. He looked up into the distance and pointed to two aerials high up on a mountain.

"There," he said.

I grabbed the food and walked on. The little boy approached us again. He led us to another house.

"I think you can stay here," he said.

A man with a donkey came to greet me.

"I have to ask my wife first," he replied to my request.

He returned shortly.

"I'm sorry," he said. "We have visitors already."

The little boy ran to his house further down the hill and reappeared rapidly, out of breath.

"My father says you can come to us."

At the house the dad approached me in a reserved manner. His wife followed shyly behind. He asked me a few questions and then announced formally.

"Yes, you can stay."

I put the kids to work and they carried the saddle-bags and the rest of my belongings to the porch. The horses hungrily devoured their food. I walked with the children to the river and let them lead the horses. They loved the responsibility and argued about who should take the rope on the prettiest horse.

A girl sat on her haunches washing clothes. I borrowed a plastic bucket from her and washed the horses down. Back at the house, I sat on a chair in the sun and wrote my diaries. The boys craned their necks to see what I was writing. They moved away to play but reappeared in a flash when they heard the rustling of papers. I gave them a handful of sweets each. Before darkness fell, I took the horses uphill where there seemed to be more grass. On the way, Mise attempted to steal the pigs' food. I tried to put honey on her thigh wound but she got restless and would not let me go near it.

I sat outside until the sun had lowered its face completely behind a mountain. The village of about thirty inhabitants was quiet and serene. I looked for the man of the house.

"Where can I put my belongings?" I asked. This was code for 'Where will I sleep?'

He told me to bring the saddle and bags inside. Four beds lined the walls of the large, yet very humble cement-floor room. It was candlelit as there was no electricity. The space also served as their kitchen and family gathering room. I imagined this would be my spot for the night and began to prepare my bed. I threw the saddle-blankets on the floor and covered it with my rain poncho.

The man looked and me and said, "Don't you have a bed?"

I said no and hoped he did not see the tent. We were high up and I knew it would be a cold night. He directed me to a room, attached to the building. He brought in a chair, plonked himself down and showered me with questions about my journey. I showed him the article from Tarija. Shortly after that he brought in a bowl of food. It consisted of rice and about two peas. He had his dinner with me in the room. We chewed in silence.

The rest of the family joined us later and spread themselves out on my bed. They looked at my maps and followed my every move as I dug in and out of my saddlebags, trying to look occupied.

They were kind but I was so keen for some rest and finally hinted with a long yawn, "Aah, the people in Argentina go to bed very late. *A mi, no me gusta*" (I don't like it).

They got the message and soon I had the room to myself. I took my torch and went outside in the darkness, a roll of toilet paper in hand. A dog barked frantically. I did what I had to do and rapidly moved back into my room. I had no candle to read by and was soon fast asleep. The pistol was tucked under my pillow. Just in case.

A bowl with sweet milk and rice was on the breakfast menu and I made sure to eat every last morsel.

As soon as we left the village we started going uphill and it was not long before we were all out of breath. Mise had very little energy and I put the saddle on Tusa. He was even worse and Mise seemed a bit out of place having to be on the leading rope. I changed them back again. There was no traffic on the road and I let Tusa run free. Mise was struggling as we climbed higher and higher and I got off to walk with her.

Within ten minutes I was fighting a blinding altitude-induced headache. The air was so thin I could only manage shallow gulps from my chest. Mise's walk was painstakingly slow and Tusa trailed behind at a distance. Every now and then he recognised that we were out of sight and came running towards us, fearful of being left behind. He stopped a few times to turn back to Tucumilla but Mise and I simply continued. Eventually he would come trotting towards us again. A few times he neighed when he wanted to urinate. He did it so that we would stop and wait for him.

Although the sun was shining under blue skies it got chillier the higher we went. I passed the two antennas that the man pointed out the day before as a place to stay.

'*What a ludicrous suggestion,*' I thought to myself.

The spot was four hours away from Tucumilla with no sign of life or movement.

We encountered only one woman on the way. She looked at the ground when I smiled at her. At 1 p.m. we reached the highest point of the day's ride. In the distance, down in the valley at the end of the winding road, I could see Iscayachi, a little village, 11,200 feet above sea level.

The 27th of September was a memorable day when we travelled the 33 kilometres from Iscayachi to our next destination. It was also my 33rd birthday. I had no breakfast and bought two bananas and two bits of bread.

"Pobres caballitos" (poor little horses), the friendly woman in the shop clicked her tongue in sympathy.

The pack sat very high on Tusa. There was a bag of left-over food on top of the saddlebags and it took Tusa only one short trot before it all fell off. I left the food behind. After four kilometres Mise started to drag her feet. We passed a few houses with drunken men sitting outside. They indicated for me to stop. I ignored them and unsaddled the horses later in what I thought was a secluded spot, protected from the chilly wind. Just as I was about to nibble on something a group of kids came running down the hill. They stopped in their tracks when they saw us. They were excruciatingly shy and hid behind each other. I urged them to come close and handed them each a few crackers.

"No gracias?" I asked.

Demurely, they chorused, *"gracias señora."*

I gave them a big smile. *"De nada"* (You are welcome).

They watched while I ate. When I asked their names I got different responses and a lot of giggles. The girls clung to each other. I managed to persuade a few of them to take a ride on Tusa and soon I had led most of them around. Their shy enthusiasm was infectious. They whispered behind their hands when they spoke to each other.

I was imitating them and asked in a hushed tone, "Why do you talk like this?"

We all laughed and there were even more giggles when I took a picture of their feet. They all looked alike, dry, rough toes peeked out from their hard, uncomfortable-looking rubber sandals.

The road continued to slope upwards. We were surrounded by valleys, cactuses and dry vegetation. There was no sign of water. I spotted a few men on bicycles in the distance and got my pistol ready. I held it tight in my pocket, my finger on the trigger. I moved to the other side of the road when we got closer to them. They were leaning on their bikes. I gave them a friendly, yet assertive *hola*. I got a friendly greeting in return. I relaxed, they were harmless. I approached a woman when we entered a tiny village.

"Would you have water for my horses, please *señora*," I asked in Spanish.

She indicated that I would find some further down the road. She was right. What she did not say was that the water came in the form of a filthy dirty pond. Nevertheless, the horses drank eagerly and Mise kicked the black, muddy water all over her legs. My green saddlebags looked like leopard skins when we left.

We passed a few men standing next to a truck. I could hear them discussing me, the journey and the horses. News obviously travelled fast – even in this isolated, godforsaken *altiplano*. The scenery was breathtakingly beautiful and wherever you fixed your eye, you saw precipices, valleys and endless open spaces. The enormity of the silent expanse seemed to act as a reinforcement of my own smallness in this world. The narrow little road curved round and round and every bend brought with it the anticipation and promise of something special.

The village of El Puente was my next planned stop but by 4:30 p.m. that day we were still struggling through the mountains. We eventually arrived at a small settlement consisting of four houses and I was told that 25 kilometres straight on would bring us to our desired destination. I had it all wrong and it seemed that Vito and I had miscalculated the distances. I asked Reynalda, a woman in her early twenties if I could stay there for the night.

She had an amiable way about her and said, *"Todo tranquilo"* (no problem) and led me to her grandfather's house.

They were poor but proud and tidy. Without fuss she cleaned out the one and only room with water and a brush. The room had concrete flooring and in the corner stood bags of potatoes, a wheelbarrow, a few baskets and a table. Colourful streamers hung from the ceiling. I gathered it had been somebody's birthday recently.

'How appropriate for me to stay there,' I thought, and smiled to myself.

There was no running water and Reynalda brought a bucket and cleaned the outside toilet. It was one of those where you stand up – male or female. I've never liked them. They are messy and the little hole always seems a mile away. You usually end up with urine splattered all over your shoes or trousers.

The dirty pond where we let the horses drink turned out to be the same spot where everybody's water came from. We collected dry maize leaves. It was barren country and there was nothing else for them to eat. I filled my arms with the bundle of leaves and later discovered a large number of bites on my arm. A spider must have had his home in there. Reynalda dabbed vinegar on the swollen, red spots.

It was my favourite part of the day. The late afternoon brought with it a particular tranquility. I sat on a stone wall outside my room and prepared a cheese and tomato sandwich as the day slowly came to a halt. Just then Reynalda's little sister came running towards me. In a distressed voice she shouted from the top of her lungs.

"The horses have run away! The horses have run away!"

I jumped up, kicking over the flask of hot water and sprinted towards the road. My speed was handicapped by my blue cotton house-slippers. I spotted Reynalda in the distance chasing the horses at a frenzied pace. I could just about make out Mise and Tusa, trotting southwards. I roared at them and teasingly they stopped for a moment before continuing their exodus. It looked like Mise was the instigator. I came to a point where I could either follow the road or take a shortcut through the mountain to the winding road downhill. I took the latter option but paid dearly. I half-jumped, half-slid down the slope and got caught in prickly plants and cactuses. I could see the horses far down in the valley, persevering, chasing bends. A fierce wind blew. I was not wearing a bra and must have looked comical, cupping my breasts in my hands as I upped the pace. At the bottom of the hill there were two houses and, as I approached, a woman and child came out on a bicycle to help in our hot pursuit of the horses.

I kept running until I managed to flag down a truck.

Jumping inside the cabin, I pleaded, "Please *señor*. Please take me fast in front of the horses. We need to block them off."

The woman and her son on the bicycle did what I intended and we found the party down the road under a few trees. I half-heartedly scolded Mise. It was almost dark when I mounted her. She had only her halter on.

"You can ride Tusa," I said to Reynalda, but she could not make him move.

"Hold on to his mane and give me the leading rope," I said.

I took the rope in my hand and pulled Tusa along with Reynalda on top. Mise's bony back cut into me as we went uphill. A gentle breeze was blowing; I felt I was in the middle of a real adventure. It was dark when we finally reached the top of the mountain, save for the blinding lights of a few trucks approaching from both directions. The leading rope slipped from my hand a couple of times. The road was very narrow. On the right were high rocks and on the other side a drop of about fifteen yards. It took some manoeuvring to get the trucks to pass *and* keep the horses calm – especially with no reins. If one decided to bolt and take off we would have been in serious trouble. Reynalda seemed afraid on Tusa with nothing to hold on to but his mane. She did very well. She also seemed in much better form than me when we finally reached Puesto Grande three hours later. I promised myself never to trust the horses again to roam free. Before retiring I drank cold camomile tea from a plastic cup complete with crunchy bits, which, I later realised, must have been insects that had fallen into the liquid.

Reynalda's little sister woke me at 6 a.m. the following morning. I dragged myself from the warmth of my sleeping bag. My muscles ached and I discovered a few sores on my backside from the previous day's escapade. The horses needed vitamins and it was my mission for the day to get transport back to Tarija to buy a large quota. Reynalda's family also asked me to bring them back four chickens and a kilo of coca leaves.

I sat outside on a dry cactus trunk for three hours before getting a lift in the cabin of a truck. I considered myself lucky as most hitchers had to go in the back. The trucks in Bolivia serve the same purpose as buses. Fares are charged and, like the buses, they stopped wherever somebody wanted to get on. I had no seat and sat with my legs outstretched on the drivers' bed, my back against the side of his seat. Later I took off my shoes and socks. The only sound in the cabin was that of the driver spitting out chewed coca leaves through the window. A young boy stood in the front, facing the others in the cabin. For the duration of the journey he had his hands over his private parts. The drive was nerve-racking. Every time we went round one of the many hairpin bends, I could swear we were about to tumble down the mountain. Considering the number of crosses on the road, indicating deaths where buses had gone down, it was not an unreasonable fear.

It took the truck three and a half hours to get to Tarija from Puesto Grande. The same route took me and the horses three days. In Tarija I also arranged, as before, for a bus driver to deposit more bags of horse food in villages for collection on the next leg of my route. This time it would be for the 220 kilometre stretch between Camargo and Potosí, destinations with respective altitudes of 7,900 and 13,400 feet above sea level.

Back at Puesto Grande I had my first attempt at administering an injection to the horses. The villagers circled around us keen to witness the event. I was squeamish, shaking nervously as the needle sunk into Tusa's neck. But fortunately, he was so absorbed in his food that he did not even flinch. Chuckles rippled through the crowd. Mise though, could not be bribed so easily and would not stand still. I tried to nose-tie her but she became even more agitated and broke away. People scattered when she came too close. I thought I would surprise her and casually stab her hindquarters but it did not work. She knew exactly what I was up to. Finally I hobbled her front legs and managed to plunge the needle into her neck. I looked away as I pushed in the back of the syringe. Afterwards, I dished out an extra portion of food in compensation for the pain and drama.

Dinner the evening before I left was a greasy affair. Fried egg was scooped out of a pot with a hand that had just been used to wipe a nose and the utensils still had bits of food on them. The next morning I was invited for breakfast in the communal room. Made partly from clay, it had a very low ceiling, a dusty floor and an open fire that served as an oven. It was dark and smoky inside and it took me a while to make out all the faces. Rough, dark, wooden benches stood close to the ground. It was filled with what looked like all their belongings gathered in the one space. Chicken was on the menu so I made my excuses.

"*Solamente pan y agua caliente para mi por favor*" (only bread and hot water for me please).

Next I was offered soup. I was convinced that it came from the chewed chicken bones I spotted in a pot.

"I eat very little breakfast," I lied. Reynalda filled up a plastic container full of chicken and soggy chips.

"You will need something for the road," she smiled.

I could not refuse. I considered it extraordinary that the poor I encountered on my journey were those who gave the most.

Leaving Puesto Grande, we were on our own again. The mountains were quiet and I saw no sign of life. That was until I wanted to stop for a break. My eye caught a man behind the bushes on our left and for some reason he kept up with the pace of the horses. I did not trust him and pretending I did not see him, spurred the horses on to get a safe distance between us. I was in a melancholic mood and Jo occupied my thoughts. How she would have loved to hear my stories from the road. How she would have relished the tales full of drama and adventure. This time last year she was still with us. With a small group of close friends we celebrated my birthday from lunch until midnight. I remembered her sparkling eyes and, as always, she was such good company.

Silent tears dripped on to the saddle.

After three hours on the road my mood lifted. Captivated by the mountains that had turned to red rock, reflecting a luminous rosy glow in the mid-day sun, I began to feel more alive.

The atmosphere in El Puente was jovial. The village with its whitewashed walls and cobbled streets looked fresh and inviting. Everywhere was green and lush and the crops in the fields gave a sense of prosperity to the place. The flowing river reflected the sun like a constant symbol of hope.

A group of men and women sitting in an outside porch, looking comfortable as if they had found their spot for the rest of the day, motioned me over. I was handed a cold drink while my options for accommodation were discussed at a leisurely pace. They suggested that I move towards the heart of the village where the weekly Friday market was in full swing. They indicated that the municipality offices might be a good place to ask.

Initially it seemed that it would not be too difficult to find a spot for the night. But in the end I had to wait for two hours before getting sorted. While a dust storm was brewing I sat outside in the square against a wall, writing my diary. A drunken man came over and I cut him short.

"*Por favor señor,*" I said dismissively.

He got the hint, even in his intoxicated state.

Young boys were standing around and I handed them sweets. Unceremoniously they threw the papers on the ground.

"Hey, hey," I said. "You should keep your town clean. Put it in the bin."

One of the boys obliged but returned rather rapidly, a naughty grin on his face. I was suspicious and got up to investigate. I picked up the handful of plastic wrappers strewn on the ground a few yards away from the bin.

Margarita, an Indian woman with long grey plaits, took me under her wing. Her face was friendly and podgy. She showed me to a field where we collected carrots and carrot leaves. Her apron served as a bag. Later a woman came over to ask if I was travelling *solita*. I confirmed her suspicions and she proceeded to tell me about another couple who also travelled on horseback.

"One of them was murdered," she whispered.

She looked so terrified you would have thought the murderer was standing behind me. I cut her short.

"There are bad people all over the world.... and many good ones too. They were just unlucky."

But as it turned out it was not such a co-incidence that I had to hear that story. Things took a strange twist a few days later.

I joined Margarita for Mass that evening. The other four souls in the church looked lost in the cold, holy building. A statue of Jesus was stretched out solemnly in a glass case. He was covered in a white cloth. The Virgin Mary watched over him. She was surrounded by flowers and fluff that looked like candy floss. She wore a hat and wings and had a banner over her shoulder. She could easily have been mistaken for Miss Teen USA. I refrained from taking bread. I would much rather have had a few sips of wine but the privilege was reserved for the priest.

Margarita and I slept in the same tiny room consisting of two single beds, a small wardrobe and a chest of drawers covered with religious ornaments. I was already in bed when she entered and underneath half-closed eyes, I saw her remove her apron and one sheet of her multi-layered skirt before getting under the covers. I woke a few times during the night to her mumbling. She seemed restless but I could not make out the words.

The following day, Tusa lost himself in an *alfalfa* field. He was not on the leading rope and Mise and I had to cross the same river again to collect him. A family with a pack of donkeys made their way through the water too, watching intently. We went through a village and people peeked from behind their windows. Another woman greeted me happily. I spotted a little girl standing against a mud house. Her ragged-looking clothes were the same colour as the wall from where she was shyly looking at us. I took a picture and passed her a chunk of bread. Going through Las Carreras took a while. Kids followed us and everybody greeted me with questions.

I was not in top form physically. I felt weak and was short of breath. When we stopped for a rest Tusa tried to roll in the dust with the pack still on. I was sitting down and shouted at him.

"Don't even *think* about it."

He awkwardly scrambled to his feet. I unsaddled both horses and they rolled around like two pigs in a mud-bath. They had nothing to eat and picked at plants and whatever was on the ground. After another hour's ride we stopped again. I had cheese with bits of raw garlic to stop my oncoming cold in its tracks. Tusa preferred cow dung.

Villa Abecia appeared like an oasis in a desert. We were greeted with a sign to say we were now 7,575 feet above sea level. We made our way uphill into the village. It was pretty and unusual, set between mountains. We had hardly come to a stop in front of a little shop when a group of children and a man rushed along to look at the horses. I bought a two litre bottle of water and a woman in the shop offered me a chair. The man looked like the 'village idiot' and bombarded me with questions.

"I'm too tired to speak, sir," I said in a weary tone.

He shifted his attention to the horses, handing them bananas and dried beans.

One of the women took me to a house where there were lots of rooms and space in the courtyard for the horses. A bubbly, overweight girl with an alluring smile greeted us. Her painted nails were red and very long. She told me she worked on a project that taught children to become self-sufficient and to utilise the land to its optimum.

The flu-like symptoms had set in and my whole body ached. After unsaddling I crashed out for forty minutes. I would have slept longer had it not been for the orchestra of drums and flutes coming from the school yard next door. Thankfully, a quick rain-shower shut them up. *Ingeniero* Roberto, who also lived on the premises, suggested I go to the hospital for a check-up. I was attended to by two doctors and three students.

When they prescribed medicine, I said, "Maybe I won't need it. Maybe a miracle will happen and I'll be fine in the morning."

They did not understand 'miracle' and I explained in Spanish.

"It's like Jesus in the Bible that turned the water into wine."

They got it after a while and laughed heartily.

I've always preferred to use alternative remedies and purposely walked past the pharmacy without getting the medicines. On the way back we met the Mayor of the town.

"Make sure the horses get maize and *alfalfa*," he ordered Roberto.

He took the prescription from me and smiled with a wink.

"I'll get that for you."

Later I walked with somebody Roberto knew to get *alfalfa* for the horses.

He pointed out to me, "When there's a purple flower it's ready to eat. Before that it's still green and the horses will get colic."

I vowed to remember his advice.

My *alfalfa* helper later brought me a small bottle of *singani* (a 40-proof distilled grape spirit made only in Bolivia). I mixed it with South African Rooibos tea, hot water, lemon and honey. I went outside to use the bathroom and, on return, found I had locked myself out of my room. It poured down and by the time I got through the window I was drenched to the skin.

Despite my assurances to the owner that my horses did not eat flowers we found the following morning that all but a few roses had been savaged by Mise and Tusa. I felt bad. But I felt even worse when I struggled to find breakfast in the village. The first place informed me they served only coffee or tea. The café a few doors down had a sign up to say it was open but there was no-one in sight.

A young girl at another shop said, "Come back in one hour."

I bought two pieces of bread from a kiosk on the street and went back to the first place to ask for coffee.

"*No hay,*" came the answer.

At the market, I had even less luck. The women were so reluctant to serve me that I finally left without getting anything.

I went back to my room and spent the morning cleaning the saddle-blankets, my riding clothes and gloves. I polished the saddle, reins and my boots. The horses' coats got a shining with my machete. A lot of hair came off. I found a man in the village running his own alteration business. He sat behind a sewing machine on the pavement. In a way he was lucky – he had no overheads. He told me to pick up my boots and half-chaps later that afternoon.

Roberto read my palm over lunch.

"You have a good hand," he said, concentrating on the lines. "You're spiritual and money is not that important to you. You won't be rich, but you'll be comfortable."

He pointed at my little finger which apparently is not long enough to ever give me millionaire status. He then focused on my hand for a long time.

"You'll live an extremely long life. You're determined and not afraid of anything." he said.

He showed me how the upper part of my thumb, above the knuckle is very long.

"It means you believe that every problem can be overcome," he concluded.

I nodded my head in agreement. Our food was cold by the time I got my hand back.

Lunch was followed by a nap and, in the late afternoon, a young girl of about sixteen arrived with her boyfriend. She handed me a rose and looked at Tusa.

"Can I have a ride on your horse?" she asked.

She was about to have her first experience on horseback.

"You're a brave girl," I said lifting her up.

I lead her down to the river and Mise joined the outing, overjoyed at the freedom to run where she wanted. You would have sworn she was never allowed out.

I later found a woman prepared to repair my torn tent bag at short notice. She waved me away when I took out my purse.

Instead of breaking up the journey over two days, I decided to do the 46 kilometres to Camargo in one day. It would be a long and tiring day to do such a distance at relatively high altitude. I was in the saddle shortly after 5 a.m. Apart from a few people who were early risers, most of the village were still asleep. We passed a few women, sweeping in front of their houses, their backs in a familiar bend, their faces determined but serene. They looked up and smiled when they heard the hooves.

"*Suerte señorita,*" they said and continued their day's work.

Three hours later, we had our first break on an island in the middle of a shallow river. Just as I got comfortable, I noticed a few men coming in our direction. I turned my back, opened my moneybag and gripped the pistol. I turned around, stood tall and waved with the other hand. They did the same and continued on their way.

I nearly got to use the pistol later that day. As we passed a few houses we were chased by two snarling, vicious-looking dogs. Usually dogs that followed us gave up after a short while, but this time one persevered. He showed his savage teeth, growled like a captured monster and continued to come after us. He bit at the horses' hind legs. I put Tusa into a gallop but the dog was not giving up and grabbed Tusa's long tail in his mouth.

"Kick him Tusa!" I shouted. "Kick him!"

Mise was running alongside us and looked ill-at-ease. I was not so concerned about a nip from a dog but more about the effects that a bite could have. Rabies is a common disease in these Latin American countries. The black dog must have realised he was not winning and at last gave up. He turned around and headed back through the cloud of dust we left behind. He was lucky.

Not long after, we encountered two spaniels sitting quietly next to each other in front of a house. They stared at us with sad eyes.

'They're too scrawny for a chase,' I thought to myself.

A young man peeped from behind the door.

"You should give your animals more food," I said in passing.

His wave, although friendly was more like 'go away, mind your own business.'

Later I picked bougainvilleas from the side of the road and put them in the horses' head-collars. I took a picture with the mountains of Camargo in the distance. It was hot and Tusa especially looked irritable with me trying to doll them up. I laughed out loud. Little did they know that I was simply trying to deal with the monotony of everyday riding and being on my own so much. Anything for a bit of diversion.

A man with his family stopped and asked for my signature. I wrote on a piece of paper in Spanish, '*Marianne, Mise and Tusa are travelling across the Americas. Adios.*'

I was very surprised to see James, the *alfalfa* man from Villa Abecia appear just as we entered the small town of Camargo. He did not explain his presence and I said nothing either. Soon we had an entourage of young boys, some on foot and some on bicycles, who joined us in the search of food for the horses. They indicated they knew where we would find something. But after a long walk all we discovered was a dry river.

"It's *loco*," I said and turned around.

Somebody else suggested we buy food at a house where they knew the people. The man refused to sell. We walked to ADRA, an agricultural corporation on the outskirts of the town. There were offices and a large, fenced-in area with a gate. A man agreed to let the horses stay for the night.

One of the boys offered to take me to yet another house in the search for horse-food. Outside hung a large bell. They rang it a few times. A drunken man with bloodshot eyes came out after a long wait.

"Ask next door," he replied disinterestedly.

The woman was even less friendly.

"We don't have any food," she said.

I was hot and bothered by now and desperate to settle down for the day, desperate to find food for the horses, desperate for us all to rest.

I looked at her and said in Spanish, "Do you know how nice the people have been up to now, throughout my journey?" But here in Camargo I find everybody difficult and slow to help."

I did not give her a chance to respond and shook my head like I was on the verge of exploding.

"*No entiendo, no entiendo,*" I said strongly.

My reaction had the desired effect.

"Come next door," she said.

She indicated to take two arms full of dry hay.

I made the mistake of buying beer for James. I had a suspicion he was already half shot when he greeted me earlier with bleary eyes.

In a small café with plastic flower-patterned sheets on the table, he asked, "Would you like to live in Bolivia?"

"It's a lovely country James," I said impatiently, "but it's not my home."

He started to nag.

"But why won't you live here? Bolivia is the nicest country in the world; it is the most beautiful and it has the best people."

I sighed.

"I'm sure that could be true James but my family and friends don't live here and..."

"Just tell them all to come over," he interrupted.

I looked down my glass of cold beer, racking my brain for inspiration to find a way to get him out of my face. I was not in the mood.

He smiled sheepishly.

"I think I will travel with you to Potosí."

I looked up and shook my head.

"No James, no, you can't," I said emphatically.

I returned his smile.

"I'm travelling alone. *Solita, solita, solita.*"

I did not travel with my saddlebags the day before and by the next morning they still had not arrived as I was promised they would. I spotted a young man standing next to a Land Rover.

"Excuse me," I said. "Are you going in the direction of Villa Abecia by any chance?"

He was Danish but spoke good English.

"No, sorry, I'm not."

When he heard about my travels, he said, "A Polish couple who also went on horseback got into trouble recently not far from here. You should speak to Irene."

Irene, another Dane, had been working in Bolivia for some time promoting and developing sustainable farming among the Indian people. She was tall and friendly and had a no-fuss manner about her. She introduced me to a Bolivian man who was also part of the project. They told me about the attack on the Poles.

"You should get a letter from the authorities," he said. "It should state that you have permission to travel through Bolivia. You also need to get on radio so that people know about you."

I carried my machete with me which was in need of repair. Irene handed me a plastic bag.

"Put it inside," she said with a serious face. "Matters are quite sensitive around here since what happened."

When I went to her office again in the early evening, she told me that Dorota, the Polish girl who was attacked, was actually in town and staying with her.

"She would like to meet you." Irene said.

I went back to my hostel and sat on the porch. I saw a young, slightly built woman walk in my direction.

27. An affectionate young girl in Llacalle, our next stop after Potosí.
28. Reynalda and her daughter waiting for a bus or truck.
29. The horses stealing the show at a soccer match in Lecore in the Bolivian *altiplano*.

30. A chilly, fitful night in my tent in the high mountains.
31. Trying on a traditional dress made by Indian women.

32. Cracked little feet in sandals made from rubber.
33. Tea and crackers in front of my room in Puesto Grande, shortly before my horses ran away.

34. Reynalda's mother in their kitchen, preparing breakfast.
35. The morning after a stay-over in a dentist's room at the Casa de Salud (clinic) in Lahuachaca.

Her skin was pale and when she stood under the glow of the street light I could see scars on her cheek and forehead. We both cried when we said hello. Having been told her story already, my heart went out to this softly spoken girl who had been dealt such a terrible and unexpected blow. Her sadness was still very visible. She spoke quietly and with little confidence.

Dorota who was doing a PhD in Architecture and, her boyfriend who had just finished a PhD in Mathematics, decided to explore the world before work, responsibility and routine became part of their lives. When they got to Bolivia they headed for Tupiza, a town south-west of Tarija. Tupiza is best known as the last resting place of Butch Cassidy and the Sundance Kid.

Here Dorota and her boyfriend bought two horses and continued their adventurous travels through isolated rocky mountains, valleys and forgotten villages. They preferred to sleep in their tent and Dorota told me how they sometimes took turns for night-watch.

"I sat around the fire and I could hear the mountain lions. I was petrified."

However, they preferred to travel this way as they wanted to get away from people and any trappings of luxury.

One morning they descended from the mountains and made their way into a small village. They both walked with the horses. As they entered, they saw a truck with a few men standing next to it. The men were highly intoxicated and without warning, one of them picked up a stone and threw it at the couple.

Dorota told me, "What happened next, was worse than the most horrific nightmare."

Apparently a young boy started to yell from the top of his lungs, "These *gringos* want to steal my organs!"

Before Dorota and her boyfriend could react they had a mob of angry villagers attacking them – men, women and, children. The stoning continued until her boyfriend was half-conscious. They grabbed him. Despite Dorota's desperate pleading they strangled him to death. Dorota was next.

"I am pregnant," she managed to utter in Spanish but said this lie, seemed to make the women even angrier.

They tied her up and beat her relentlessly. What followed was like something out of a horror-movie. The attackers could not decide which method of killing would be best for her.

"She's a witch," one of them screamed. "We have to cut off her head."

They waited for somebody to fetch a machete. Dorota showed me the mark behind her ear.

"When somebody swung to cut me, another woman intervened and pushed the person away. Part of the blade caught me behind the ear."

The crowd was outraged when their method failed. While Dorota lay on the ground, the kids jumped on and kicked the body of her boyfriend a few yards away. Later when Dorota was asked how many had taken part in the attack, she did not hesitate when she gave the number.

"Fifty. I counted the legs while I was on the ground. It was the only way not to go insane."

They tortured Dorota for more than four hours. The crowd wanted a sensationalist killing it seemed and somebody suggested gasoline and fire. They were making their plans for the execution when an ambulance arrived. A doctor from a neighbouring village had been alerted. But his life was not safe either. They accused him of working with the *gringos* and threatened to kill him as well.

"Look in their bags," he told them. "They don't smuggle children's organs. They are simply travellers in your country."

It took him an hour to persuade the crowd to let him take away Dorota and the body of her boyfriend.

Dorota found it difficult to tell me the details and bits and pieces of information came out sporadically. I felt very touched by her story.

'It could easily have been me,' I thought to myself.

She told me seven men were taken into custody after the attack.

"I would really like to travel with you at a later stage when the court case is over," she said.

I told her that it might be possible. I was not sure how I really felt about it but I could not disappoint her at that moment. I knew it was important for her to have something to focus on, something that would allow her to keep believing, hoping and dreaming.

"I am not leaving in the morning," I told her. "I will talk to Vito in Tarija and see if he can get somebody to give your case some urgency."

I tossed and turned that night. My mind zigzagged around as if trapped in a complicated puzzle. Dorota's sad face dominated thoughts of my own journey, the purpose of some experiences in our lives, of life and death.

I spoke to Vito the next day to see if he could help through any of his contacts. He told me he would see what was possible.

Just before I hung up, he said, "Take somebody to travel with you as far as La Paz."

I said I might but I knew it was easier said than done. I sent him an email that evening, outlining Dorota's story again.

Irene offered for Mise and Tusa to stay at her house. Dorota and I collected the horses and rode them bare-back across the river. Dorota looked so happy to be riding again. We struggled to get the horses up the steps and through a little gate. Mise stopped dead in her tracks and I had to lift her feet step by step until she got the idea.

I stayed in Camargo for another four days. I did not have the courage to just leave again after what had happened to Dorota. I also needed time to get my head around the whole safety aspect of my journey. And the more I listened to people the more feelings of fear began to threaten my plans and decisions. Irene's partner was particularly negative. He indicated that his own life was not safe in those parts.

"People are even after *my* blood," he said in his monotone.

Fearing being bored to death I did not urge him to expand. He drew a map and explained to me as you would to a child, all about Dorota's attack and the dangers of travelling in these parts. He was adamant that I arranged transport for myself and the horses to Potosí.

Irene was more balanced in her views and suggested I take somebody along with me. But she was sensible enough to know that this could cause problems.

"You're a leader," she said. "You won't take orders from somebody else and most Bolivian men would expect to be obeyed."

Another Danish man who was involved in community development in Sucre told me about *El Liquichiri* – a name that is given to a stranger who comes into a village and who is believed to bring illness, death and bad fortune.

"If you just arrive in a village and something bad happens to one of its people, they can accuse you of causing it," he told me.

Not everybody was so pessimistic though. A few men I talked to reckoned I would be just fine. They all believed that the attack near Incahuasi was a very rare occurrence and unlikely to happen again.

An email from Dave made up my mind for me;

Hi Mar,

It is now 3.40 in the morning. I just woke up and have been thinking about you a lot since you sent your last email to me. The gravity of that situation has weighed heavy on me and has entered my thinking very much indeed. Turning to my spiritual side I sought signs that you are presently okay and would be safe and in good health. I hoped that this would bridge the unknown, the quandary of not being able to do anything to give you a sense of security. Upon waking up I walked, by chance only, to the balcony and looked up. I saw the plough and the northern star so conspicuously showing off, like glitter make-up in the sky – something I have never seen in the Dublin night sky since moving in here. I was told you are safe and will continue to be. Keep those stars in your gaze.

Ten-year-old Marx was the sweetest little boy who adored Tusa like no other. When I arrived at Irene's house one morning he was there too. The horses were munching contentedly on *alfalfa* he had brought for them. Tusa's mane was carefully groomed and had a fancy plait in it. Marx continued his visits until the morning of my departure. He acted like the man of the day and would not tolerate any kids interfering. Marx was in charge.

Dorota was very withdrawn. Over the previous couple of days I found it harder and harder to be around her. I needed to stay positive but in some way felt guilty about setting off again. Here I was, continuing my journey in a way that caused her so much heartache. I promised to stay in touch and who knows, we might even meet up somewhere along the road.

As we made our way to the hostel Marx kept on getting on and off Tusa. His mother met us at the river.

"I am so worried about Marx," she said good-naturedly. "He talks about horses day and night."

Marx grinned from ear to ear and patted Tusa affectionately.

Crossing the river was not easy; it was full and the water came up to the horses' bellies. The bridle and reins were at the hostel and Marx had no control over Tusa.

"Walk over the bridge Marx and wait for me," I said.

I jumped on Tusa, took him through and handed him to Marx. I walked back across the bridge and mounted Mise. I was hot and sweaty by the time we got to the hostel. My boots were drenched in river water.

The saddle went on Tusa and just as I tightened the girth he turned his head and nipped Marx on the arm. I could not help but laugh when I saw his shocked face. I was sure he took it personally. Tusa was, after all, his favourite. I explained in my best Spanish why horses do that and that it was nothing against him. He looked dubious.

"It's also because he likes you and wants your attention, Marx," I said.

I waved goodbye to the bystanders but especially to Marx. He had his eyes fixed on Tusa. He struggled to compose himself but I saw the tears just before he turned around.

What was most notable about the day's ride from Camargo to Taca Quira was the response of people on the way. It was as if everybody, including myself, made much more of an effort. As if they thought their friendliness would compensate for the attack on the Polish couple. As if they wanted to show they're not all bad people. My waves and smiles were exaggerated too. I wanted them to know I posed no threat and I did not want the people to think that I imagined all Bolivians to be as evil as those in Incahuasi.

We did not linger in any of the numerous ghost villages on the way until we passed a solitary mud house standing just off the road. A couple of kids were playing silently in the dirt. I stopped to give them a chance to look at the horses.

It was a mistake. A man who I assumed was their father walked with a swagger towards me. I only noticed *how* drunk he was when he was already too close. He extended his hand to shake mine. I reciprocated hesitantly. He did not let go and under the guise of wanting to give me a hug, tried to pull me down. My heart missed a beat. I jerked my body to the left and used my foot to push him away. His grip softened for a moment and I seized the chance to make a get-away. He made a clumsy attempt to follow. When we were a safe distance away, I looked back where he still stood in the middle of the road and shouted, *"demasiada cerveza!"* (too much beer).

We left the scene rapidly.

Soon afterwards, the daily monotony resumed. A lopsided pack. The grief. Mise, pissed off, had dashed in the direction of the mountain behind a solitary house. Me, pissed off, chasing her. A drunken occupant of the house following in hot pursuit. He was annoying me with his questions. I had my hand on my pistol ready, just in case he had other ideas.

Will we ever have a plain-sailing day? No hassles, no drama. On the other hand, the daily obstacles were so much part of our routine by now. Maybe I needed something exciting to happen every day. A routine with daily excitement. It was better than a boring one I guess.

Somebody had given me a contact in Taca Quira, too long a name for a place that had only a few houses and no shops. I was grateful to have a bed, even though it had no springs. My feet were elevated at least five inches above my backside and it was like lying in a hammock with my body arched in a 'V'. I had a nap and late afternoon the woman of the house enquired with little enthusiasm if I was hungry. I refrained from reminding her that she insisted on payment for board and lodging on my arrival. I had an early night with only coffee and soup in my stomach.

I found the next day's 45 kilometre ride rather dull. To entertain myself, I made up songs, singing them at full blast. It took my attention away for a while from the monotony of going through the same motions, mile after mile.

The reception in Padcoyo was hostile. An old woman made a 'go away' gesture when I greeted her and a few others. Maybe they thought I was Dorota and they were angry about the men in jail or they just thought I was another crazy *gringa* on a horse. The place was littered with inebriated men. I bought a cold drink and the young girl ignored my *hola*. I greeted her twice.

"Are you sad, is that why you have such a long face?" I could not help but ask.

She managed a smile but remained distant and wary.

At the Flota Express office, I could not find a soul. I knocked next door and asked the young girl if she knew anything about a bag of horse food.

She shook her head.

"The man has gone to San Lucas and won't be back until the morning."

"Does anybody else have a key?" I enquired.

It seemed not but I did not believe her. I looked through the window again and knocked very hard. An old woman appeared from the house where I had knocked first, shuffled over and opened up the door of the office. At first glance there was no sign of the bags. I was ready to kick up a fuss. I continued to search and after some inspection, I stumbled across the treasure in a private back room.

The two hotels in the town looked dodgy.

When I made enquiries about a place to say, a man said, "There is space in our room. You'll be sharing with three other men."

'Fat chance,' I thought.

Somebody directed me to the clinic where after a long wait, a petite woman with a cute little hat appeared. I asked her if I could pitch my tent next to the building.

"You can stay in my house," Mercedes offered. "My husband is away."

I unsaddled the horses and carried the bags to a room that could be locked. I did not notice the low overhanging wall and banged my head against it. I fell back and saw stars for a moment. Mercedes made a concerned noise and rubbed my head. She held me against her chest for a while. The gesture mixed with my tiredness, hit an emotional spot and I put on my sunglasses to hide the tears.

The horses' *corral* was next to the clinic and when I checked on them early evening they were gone... as well as the four donkeys that shared their space. I was frantic and ran to tell Mercedes. I searched the village for the boys who had helped me earlier. I found some of them behind a shop.

"We haven't seen your horses, *señorita*," they answered in a chorus to my question.

But soon they changed their story. They took me uphill.

"This is where we saw them a short while ago," somebody volunteered.

More boys appeared, out of breath.

"We have caught your horses. They wanted to run away."

I did not believe that for one moment. The walls of the *corral* were wide and too high. I had no doubt that the boys had opened the gate. Their scheme was very transparent. Pretend that the horses jumped the wall, hide them for a while, put them in another safe place and charge money to look after them. We settled on twenty bolivianos for the night. After the little ordeal the boys followed me everywhere. They asked me what "*pechos*" were called in English. I shook my head.

"Why are you interested in only that?" I asked. "Why don't you ask me what an arm or a leg is in English?"

They did not even blush. It was breasts that interested them, not other boring body parts that had no fun value.

After two hours on the road to Otavi, I stopped for a black coffee and brown breakfast-roll. I could not get enough of the beauty surrounding us. Even though I was totally alone I felt protected, almost embraced by the mountains as they stood solemn and wise. They exuded calmness and a serenity that could only be acquired with the passage of time. My state of mind in that moment mirrored the peacefulness of the mountains. I was at one with the journey, with all its trials and tribulations. It was part of me and I was part of it.

It was a pleasant day; temperatures were mild. I washed my face, put on some cream and brushed my teeth. At the bottom of a hill I saw the wreck of a burnt-out bus. Motionless, Mise dozed in the warmth of the early morning sun, her eyes shut tight.

The village of Lecore was another food-bag destination and had it not been for the fact that I had to look out for the place, I could easily have gone through it without noticing. The tiny restaurant and the few surrounding houses were empty. There was not a soul in sight. We went downhill and before I spotted anything, Mise's ears stood erect. She also upped her pace. I peered into the distance and could just about make out a bunch of figures on one side of the road. Some stood still, others were moving around. Flags blew in the chilly *altiplano* wind. It turned out to be a soccer match with the whole village in attendance.

The attention shifted fast. One moment people were cheering on their teams, the next everybody came walking towards us. Even a goal by a young boy got completely ignored. A young girl obviously guessed who I was and jumped on her bicycle to collect the bag of food that was waiting at one of the houses. Everybody stared. The children were curious but kept a safe distance from Mise and Tusa.

"Do you like horses?" I asked to nobody in particular.

They all gave a positive nod.

"Not a lot of horses here," I said in a way to keep the conversation going, "more *burros*" (donkeys).

My comment caused the group to erupt into laughter. Maybe I said that *my* horses were donkeys. I'm not sure what they heard.

After Lecore, the landscape changed fast. The mountains were not as close and the trail turned into a dusty, dry, curvy road. Shrubs and thorn bushes were dotted around the place. Apart from the odd bus and truck we rode in solitude. Mise and Tusa had white circles around their eyes. The high altitude was getting to them. From the top of a hill we overlooked another little village.

"This is our next stop," I said to myself.

Two traditionally-dressed women motioned me over. They spoke no Spanish, only *Quechua*, in shrill voices.

A shy young girl said, "There are no places in the village for a horse."

When I asked for water she directed me to a river, a long walk into the distance. Most of it was dry apart from a few tiny patches where women and children washed their clothes. Nobody spoke to me. I asked for permission to let the horses drink some of the soapy water. Tusa went down on his forelegs like a giraffe. He was blind to a spot a few yards to his left where the bank was much lower. I tried to take him there but he stood dead in his tracks like a mule.

The atmosphere in the village was strange and I did not feel safe. Before we left I bought a can of apricots, cold drinks and sweets in the local shop. Two middle-aged drunken men attempted to chat up a group of heavily made up 16-year-old girls. They sat in front of the tuck shop with sparkly bits all over their faces. They were pretty and shy and one hid her head when I came closer.

On the way out of the village a few kids walked in my direction. The older ones were pushing the youngsters in a wheelbarrow. I quickly took out my camera for a snapshot. I looked around to see if any adults were nearby. I had to be careful. Since the Incahuasi attack and the rumours in some Indian communities of foreigners stealing children for their organs, I was cautious about paying too much attention to young kids.

I was happy that we pushed on and it was not too late when we arrived at a village called Otavi. It was tiny and I could not imagine more than sixty people living there. The place and its occupants were friendly and a group of young boys followed my every move. The horses were put in a *corral* with a donkey (which I believe Tusa bullied without respite) for company.

I wrote my diaries at the local diner over a plate of rice, an egg with the white and yellow still running, a tomato, onions and lettuce. Ten pairs of eyes were fixed on me.

'So this is what a monkey in the zoo must feel like,' I thought to myself.

I could not help but smile.

The boys were full of questions. I asked them their names. Next I followed with a lecture about men in Bolivia who drink too much. With sincere little faces they promised not to fall into the same pattern.

"Nunca, señora, nunca."

I wished I could believe them. We soon had more company and the same questions. I turned to those who had been there for a while already.

"You tell the other boys what you know," I said.

It was a great game and they loved to show off their new found knowledge about my travels. I was grateful for the respite.

The accommodation was basic yet sufficient. My room (which the family rented out for the night) had ample space and with two beds I was spoilt for choice. The washing area was downstairs behind three walls and a flimsy curtain. With a primitive hole in the ground for a toilet, at least there was no need to squat behind a wall or a bush like in so many of the places I have passed through in the Bolivian *altiplano*.

A bucket of cold water was the best thing on offer to rinse all the necessary parts and brush my teeth.

On the way to Alkatuyo, 36 kilometres from Otavi, we stopped halfway for a leisurely break. Soon we had a small audience. One little boy climbed up a tree to pick some leaves for the horses. He lost his balance and came plunging down. The others laughed heartily. I joined in when the boy seemed to be fine. I asked one of the older boys to take a picture of me and the horses. He heard a bus approach though, made his excuses and darted off. He stopped briefly for a quick pee. Another boy arrived and took my camera. His adolescent face was fresh and welcoming. He seemed different from all the other Bolivian men. Many of them were unfriendly and showed a reluctance to exchange greetings. They mumbled when you spoke to them and could never look you in the eye.

It was clear to me that, in Bolivia, the women were much stronger. They were the ones that kept the homes and the communities together. They worked and took the responsibility for their families on their shoulders. In every village and town I encountered many boozed-up men hanging around and looking for trouble.

"I went to the woods because I wished to
live deliberately, to front only the essential facts of life, and see
if I could not learn what it had to teach,
and not, when I came to die, discover that I had not lived"
                    — Henry David Thoreau

Belén has to win the prize for the most depressing town in the whole of Latin America. Through a sea of crisp packets, plastic papers and bottles we trotted into the village. The few people I greeted looked back with blank expressionless faces. Everybody seemed down. About what, I never found out.

I expected a food bag for the horses in Belén, and by coincidence the first shop where I enquired had the prized possession, dropped off a few weeks before. Soon a group of about thirty villagers had gathered around.

Some of the women spoke through scarves, covering their mouths.

"Pobrecitas, pobrecitas" (poor little things), they whined.

They did not refer to me but to Mise and Tusa who stood motionless, paying little attention to the crowd of people. One woman suggested I take the horses in a truck to La Paz. I considered it a strange remark coming from a member of a society which could not care less about animals. Everywhere we went I witnessed neglected dogs and an aggressive attitude towards them. They got kicked and beaten regularly and never experienced any affection from their owners. My attempts to rub or pat one on the head usually resulted in the dog cowering away, tail between its legs or growling at me. So, for the women to show concern for Mise and Tusa was rather strange.

'Maybe they see the horses as exotic animals,' I thought to myself.

I sat on Mise for half an hour while everybody stood around, talking, staring, gaping and asking questions. One man picked up Tusa's foot and showed the others his metal shoe. Gasps erupted from the crowd. They had never seen an animal with something nailed to its foot. They looked on in amazement and some hesitantly dared to come forward and touch the shoe. Finally the woman in the shop brought out a chair and told me to get off my horse and sit down. The crowd had no intention of dispersing. Two boys were sent off to enquire about accommodation for us. They came back after forty minutes but reported nothing.

I asked again.

"*Señora*, do you know where in the town my horses can be kept for the night and where there might be a room for me?"

The novelty of our presence had worn off slightly by now and a group of kids were ordered to lead us across the square to a set of buildings. Women sat in the front on the pavement knitting and chatting quietly amongst themselves. It seemed I was having the local 'telephone room' for the night. It was locked though and somebody went in search of the key. The space for the horses was at the back of my room. At first glance I knew it was completely unsuitable. The tiny area was covered in solar panels and wires, a death trap for any moving animal.

I shook my head.

"This is dangerous. My horses can't stay here. Is there somewhere else?"

A young boy offered to go searching. I was surprised to see the state of my accommodation. The room with cement flooring contained a telephone on the wall, a wooden bench and a table.

'Right,' I thought. '*It's going to be an uncomfortable night, no doubt about it.*'

A woman entered and said, "You can leave your bags here but you can't stay in the room yet. It'll be available from 9 p.m. this evening."

I could not believe what I was hearing. I was so looking forward to chilling out and rest, away from the curious stares and endless questions. Nine o'clock was still four hours away. I gave a deep sigh. I had had enough.

I marched to the back, untied the horses and brought them into the square. I had never saddled up so fast. The horses, sensing my distress, stood very still. No one talked to me while I worked away furiously. They kept on gawking and made the odd comment among themselves. I talked to myself out loud, saying what madness is this, it is 5 p.m. and I had nowhere to stay.

"Why did you not tell me two hours ago there is nowhere for us to stay in your town?" I asked the bemused group.

I received only silence for an answer. I shook my head in annoyance, grabbed the 10kg bag of food under one arm and with a *"hasta luego"* I stomped off on foot with the horses.

A group of children followed.

I turned around and shouted, *"hasta nunca!"*(get lost).

A few obliged but the rest ran to the top of a hill to see my dramatic exodus from their town, a lone and furious *gringa* rider, walking downhill into the unknown.

I had no clue where we would put our heads down that night. The idea of pitching a tent in sub-zero temperatures was not appealing. I struggled with the heavy food bag and tripped a couple of times. I eventually looked up, my eyes following the dirt road into unfamiliar territory. I thought I was hallucinating when I spotted another set of houses and cultivated fields in the distance. I was astonished at this unexpected oasis.

We reached the top of the hill and entered a tidy, quiet little village. An Indian girl walked past. She had her hair in a short bob, wore glasses and was dressed in modern clothes. Zenia seemed happy to help. My belongings went to her 'house' – one tiny room that was attached to a classroom. Despite the cement floor and her humble belongings, it was cosy and welcoming. Inside I saw a bed, a table, a small black-and-white television, a battered stereo in the window, a little old two-plate stove in the corner and a chair. A wire stretched across the ceiling. On it hung bits of dried meat looking a bit like a rat.

Together we searched for a *corral* for the horses and found the perfect place. The owner secured the gate properly, placing iron, wood and large stones in front of the flimsy door.

Zenia prepared dinner while I spoke into my dictaphone outside. I lacked the energy to write my diaries. When I walked into the room I noticed a makeshift 'bed' on the floor with two thin sheets and a sleeping bag.

"You'll sleep in my bed," Zenia announced. "I don't want to hear any objections."

I shook my head.

"No, please. I'm just so happy to have a nice home for the night. I'll sleep on the floor. I can't take.... "

"Nonsense," she interrupted with a smile. "It is my privilege to help."

The following morning, I hid ten bolivianos on Zenia's dressing table. I knew she would not take it if I handed it to her. The horses were covered in their own dung and got a rinse-down, despite the chilly air. The kids watched intently while I groomed them. The school bell rang but they were reluctant to leave. One of the teachers urged them on.

"Let them watch, *señora*," I said. "You can see it as part of their day's education."

Zenia strolled over to Mise and Tusa and bid them farewell, formally. It was obvious how fond she had grown of them in such a short space of time.

"I will radio my friends in Kuchu Ingenio," she said. "Dr. Fernando and Sandra will look out for you."

The road was quite flat and straight and we encountered only the odd uphill stretch. The scenery reminded me of the Karoo in South Africa – no colour, shrubs and hardly any trees. The road surface was smooth and apart from one stony stretch, it made for good riding. We had a very brief stop. Just as I had the horses unsaddled I spotted three young men not far away. There was nobody else around and I felt vulnerable. Should they have had any ideas I could not leave quickly with the saddle and bags on the ground. The horses looked confused when saddled up so soon again.

We arrived in Kuchu Ingenio well before lunchtime, a village at 11,745 feet above sea level, only 18 kilometres from Alkatuyo. I found La Posta (the clinic) and Sandra came out to greet me.

"There's a place organised for you at the far end of the village," she said.

A bunch of excited school kids argued over who should lead the horses. Two girls held my hands as we walked the long uphill trek towards the other side of the village. Veronica, a pretty, mature 14-year-old, told me we could stay at her house. It turned out to be the local restaurant and hotel, set high on a hilltop, surrounded by mountains.

"We have a bag of food for the horses," she informed me. "It's been here for more than three weeks."

We walked down a steep slope at the back of the hotel to the bottom of the hill where a narrow stream curved through the trees. On the way down we had to manoeuvre ourselves through broken glass and rubbish strewn everywhere. It looked and smelled like a dump. Pigs and ducks roamed around in search of food. I tied up Tusa next to the water and allowed Mise to explore. I went back to the restaurant and had something to eat. Soon the weather turned cold and rainy. Through the windows was a dark, menacing black sky. I was not happy for the horses to be out unsheltered for the night and asked Veronica and her brother for advice. We brought the horses up to just below the house where Veronica showed me a carved, cement arch, built underneath the road. It was littered with garbage and I insisted we cleaned it out first. They looked at me with surprised expressions.

I made sure we burnt everything in sight.

"Right," I said. "Now I'll take the horses for a walk and hope they do their business. I don't want them to mess up their little space during the night."

They looked at me as if I had gone completely mad but followed nevertheless. Soon we had company. We walked down the quiet, half-dark streets, two horses, a *gringa* and about thirty kids making a lot of noise.

It took some persuasion to get the horses to enter their 'home' for the night. Tusa warily stepped in when he sniffed the chocolate bar swung in front of his nose. Once he was in, Mise followed. It took nearly two dozen wooden planks to block the entrance thoroughly.

Veronica's sister was in Potosí and had the key to my room. By the time she arrived I just wanted to put my head down. While I waited for her to sort out the room her mother came over for a chat.

"There are no houses between Potosí and Oruro," she warned me.

I was not up for that kind of chat and just said, *"Todo estará bien"* (all will be fine).

'Nothing I can do about that now,' I thought to myself. I was hardly going to turn back because accommodation would be scarce.

At last I had the privacy and space I had been craving all evening. I brushed my teeth and crept into the sleeping bag without taking off my clothes. Two blankets weighed down on my weary body.

I was up and had the horses ready to leave by 6:20 a.m. the following morning. I did not feel rested and wished I could have slept more. A window in my room had opened during the night and a steady breeze of cold air on my face kept me half-awake until the alarm on my watch went off.

The trail took us steeply into the mountains from the moment we left Kuchu Ingenio. I remember the scenery as breathtakingly beautiful. The mountains were still partly covered by clouds with the sun shining through behind them with a soft, shimmering intensity. It looked like glittering diamonds strewn recklessly over the hilltops, catching and reflecting the marvellous light. It was spectacular and an image that will stay with me forever. Disappointingly, the battery of my SLR was flat and I had to make do with a black-and-white picture instead.

We were going along nicely on a comfortable road when Tusa decided he had enough and without a sound, turned around. I did what I would usually do and continued with Mise. I was calling Tusa's bluff and was pretty sure he would come back to us very soon. He stood still for a moment, looked back at us and proceeded in the opposite direction. I turned around, frustrated and annoyed.

I yelled at him.

"Dammit Tusa! Potosí is more than 50 kilometres away. Get yourself over here."

As if he understood every word he turned in our direction and walked a few steps towards us. I swung Mise around and kept going.

'I am certainly not going to chase him down a mountain road,' I decided by myself. 'He can come to us.'

It was not long before he had caught up. But his good behaviour did not last for long. We had just passed a stationary truck when he turned around again. I spotted another vehicle in the distance. Somebody got out and chased Tusa back in our direction. He put himself into a gallop and came running towards us, neighing frantically.

Passing through the mountains was just wonderful. In some places men worked on the roads and gave friendly waves. I saw only a few houses. At one the woman rushed her children inside when she saw us coming closer. But she could not contain her curiosity and came out again for a proper look. People were inquisitive and asked the same questions.

"Where do you come from?" "Where are you going?" *"Solita?"*

They all wished us a good trip.

Later, the road split in two. On the left was a wide smooth road and a sign prohibiting vehicles but I took the alternative dirt road.

The variety of the surrounding scenery was mind-boggling. Along the near-desert stretches of the *altiplano* we saw snow on mountaintops overlooking sand dunes, even a delightful trout stream lined with green vegetation at the bottom of a picturesque canyon. I got very excited at our first sighting of *llamas*. They looked at us curiously, twitching their noses nervously. We were obviously a strange sight. They sniffed the air, their funny little faces tilted to one side. It made me laugh.

The road seemed to go on forever, higher and higher. The horses had started to drag their feet. The cold had set in and I stopped to put on a warmer jacket. A man on his bicycle came along and I enquired about the distance. His *"cerquita, cerquita"* turned out to be another three hour ride. I mentally wished for Potosí to appear on the horizon.

I became increasingly conscious of my lack of energy. We were all out of breath. Riding at an altitude of more than 14,000 feet was no joke. I felt weak and nauseous. I had thought that if I ascended slowly at horse-walking pace, I would not be affected by the tremendous heights. But I was not spared. Deep breathing was impossible, my chest simply hurt too much. I felt like suffocating when I walked with the horses so I alternated between walking and riding. The horses obliged even though they were suffering too. I knew that drinking a lot of water could help the initial feeling of altitude sickness and that seemed to work for a while. Until I ran out of water. The cold temperatures as well as the fact that I was engaged in a physical activity added to the sickly feeling.

Numb from exhaustion after nine hours on the road we finally arrived on the outskirts of Potosí, its rooftops shining in the late afternoon sun. I had the name of a farm called Hacienda Cayara and was not impressed when told to go through the city to get there. I had not bargained on that. I attached Tusa's leading rope to the saddle, got off Mise and took on the narrow, curvy road downhill. My patience was wearing thin and I spoke to nobody. I stopped at a little stall erected on a pavement and could not resist a freshly made banana milkshake. A carrot juice was gulped down immediately after it. The women were friendly and did not mind Tusa's attempt to steal their carrots. He got away with a mouthful.

The traffic was heavy and our exodus through the cramped, hectic streets was met with lots of stares and comments. We came to a street through which a railway line ran. Mise stopped dead in her tracks and threw a little tantrum when I urged her to go forward. I got off and detached Tusa. He allowed me to lead him through without blinking. Mise, oblivious to the fact that we were holding up traffic, was still distrustful. She sniffed the ground like a trained police dog and walked to the side to find a 'safe spot' to cross. She stepped on to a metal plate with a bang. People scattered in all directions.

At the bus station I was told my destination was only three kilometres away. I was singing as we continued to go downhill. After another hour on the road, I realised that information was wrong too. Two men stood on the side of the road and received the same question.

They were in agreement.

"Adelante señora, cinco o seis kilómetros mas."

I did not know if I could believe them. Five or six kilometres were achievable but what if they were wrong? I stopped a taxi driver. He scratched his head for a moment.

"Hacienda Cayara is a 30 minute drive from here," he said with confidence.

My heart sank. *'I'll never get there.'*

We went through a security checkpoint. I ignored the policeman trying to make conversation. On the other side we stumbled across a fairly rustic, decent-looking hotel in the village of San Antonio.

When the owner told me it was another four to six kilometres to the Hacienda, I said, "Are you sure? It would make a huge difference on horseback if it's not six but ten kilometres."

Despite threatening clouds and an obvious storm looming I pushed on. We were surrounded by mountains again and it was almost dark now. After quite a while on the road, unsure if I had done the right thing, I stopped another taxi. He was pretty sure it would be about six kilometres to the crossroads and another ten kilometres to the actual farm. Still doubtful I waved down a police car that in turn approached another vehicle to check. The driver confirmed that it was indeed still a long way.

We turned back to the hotel at San Antonio. A strong wind was blowing and the first drops of rain were falling. I had made the right decision. The owner of the four star hotel was extremely amiable and offered the grounds for the horses to roam for the night. It did not bother him that his lawn might be ruined in the morning. For ten dollars (well over my budget), I was shown to a room. It had two mattresses on a cement base, satin pillows and curtains in a sickly green colour. I got under the covers and slept until 8 p.m. I woke when one of the workers knocked on the door, handing me a heater and a plate of food. There was no water in my room and I took a long overdue soak in the sunken tub next door. A cat sat on the bed, watching me through slanted eyes.

Later I lay on my bed, staring at the ceiling. My head felt empty. I had gone beyond exhaustion. I tried to bring up images of the stretch between Camargo and Potosi, six days and more than 200 kilometres of high altitude riding. My mind was a blank. Even while going through the isolated mountains, surrounded by the boundless glory of heights and depths, I did not seem to connect much with myself. I was conscious of the immensity of the beauty and the vastness, but in a way I was also detached from it all. I thought of little else but getting through each day. Does the drowning man look at the beach? Does he think of the feel of the sand, the smell of the sea breeze?

Through parts of my journey it was almost like a child's existence, immersed in a world of new experiences, often without reflection. Survival was the name of the game. Hour to hour, day to day, kilometre after kilometre. Only later would I realise how much I had learned.

A stream of light bursting through a crack in the curtain woke me up well after 7 a.m. I was grateful for the chance to have had a lie-in and felt refreshed. Mise and Tusa were munching happily outside in the green yard. The owner's wife and their four-year-old daughter who told me she loved horses, sat with them. I fed the horses and everybody watched in fascination while they dripped and drooled over each other. I gave the little girl a brush to help me groom them. A puppy was running around chasing his own tail. I patted him and picked him up. The woman looked at me in surprise.

"*Que lindo. Una amiga de los animales*" (How nice, a friend of the animals).

I felt I had achieved Brigitte Bardot status for a moment.

Once the horses were saddled up she suggested I take a short-cut through reception. I laughed.

"I can't do that *señora*, imagine what we would do if one of them lifted a tail!"

We left the hotel with many 'call us if you need help' offers and, after a bit more than an hour's ride, we turned left to follow the sign for Hacienda Cayara. If one of my 'advisors' had been right the previous day, it would still be another 10 kilometres to my destination. We passed the gate of a manufacturing plant and a man called out to us. It was Luis, my one and only contact in Potosí. He indicated that I could unsaddle at his plant where they had space for the horses.

"You don't have to go as far as the *hacienda*," he told me. "Your horses can happily stay here."

Luis was tall and skinny with a thick moustache. Every bit of him was European. He spoke like one and he looked like one. I attributed his pasty coloured skin to his constant smoking. He smiled easily and his eyes were warm. During my stay in Potosí he could not have been more helpful. He was very impressed when he finally understood the magnitude of my journey.

He whistled through his teeth and said, "If I had a hat on, I would have taken it off to you."

He also offered me a room at the plant but I declined.

"I think I need a bit of space from the horses," I said, "and they from me."

I stayed in the city of Potosí for five days. We had gone through a lot the past few weeks and rest was crucial.

Although Potosí is considered a must-see destination when visiting the Bolivian *altiplano*, I refrained from doing any sightseeing. In the small vegetarian cafés I encountered other travellers. They were full of enthusiasm.

"You *have* to go into the mines."

I had no interest. When I asked them why one *has* to go, nobody could produce a compelling reason.

Potosí, which four hundred years ago rivalled London and Paris as one of the richest cities of the world, produced more silver than any other region. Wealth poured into Spanish coffers, which changed the financial balance of power in Europe. Potosí itself was awash with cash and Spanish aristocrats built themselves palaces and dozens of baroque churches. However, the gruelling work of extracting the silver came at a terrible toll of human misery. The work was left to indigenous Andeans, enslaved by the Spanish, who died by the thousand in the bowels of the mountain. Working conditions in the silver mines were so appalling that the Indian and Black miners survived no more than six months.

Today, approximately 18,000 *Quechua* miners still work the mountain in search of traces of silver, tin and zinc. Each morning crowds of weary workers fill the sidewalks waiting for the vans to the mines. In a bizarre daily rhythm these masses are suddenly replaced at noon-time by a flood of schoolchildren wearing bright white smocks, heading home for *siesta*.

For ten dollars curious tourists can have a glimpse of the hardship these miners experience on a daily basis. You can also meet the devil-god El Tío. Respected by Bolivian miners as the guardian of the underground riches, he must be given offerings for the miners' safety.

Tourists are first taken to the market where they have the opportunity to buy presents for the miners, a stick of dynamite, detonator or a string of fuse. Also welcome are cigarettes and Inca Cola drink. And then the essential bag of coca leaves, the only way the miners can cope with the hot, strenuous work in the diminished atmosphere at 14,764 feet. If the tourists choose to crouch uncomfortably, clambering along metre high tunnels, dug at steep angles, they often have to make way for scuttling Indian miners, carrying 20 kg canvas bags of ore back to the haulage level.

I simply had no desire to be a voyeur of such misery.

I also gave a miss to the Casa Real de la Moneda, a large fortress-like building taking up a whole city block. Inside is supposed to be one of South America's finest museums, with the Royal Mint manufacturing silver coins as the main attraction.

For some reason I have never been a fan of museums, with the Louvre in Paris as an exception, so it did not take me long to decide not to go. Still not in 'tourist mood', I felt even less inclined to visit the place when I heard how freezing cold it was inside. The rumour might have been an exaggeration by some brave soul who did the three-hour marathon tour wearing only his shorts, flimsy t-shirt and sandals, but to me it was enough of an excuse. Having had a fair dose of cold and discomfort so far, I was hardly going to look for it. I much preferred hanging out in the numerous cafés around the plaza, studying my maps, writing diaries and watching the world go by.

Despite Potosí being one of the poorest places in South America, the human spirit remained strong as local people are coping with unforgiving economics and the harsh, high altitude environment. In this barren place almost devoid of trees, I saw them walking the narrow streets faces down, persevering against the wind in a city covered with a layer of brown dust. Under the gaze of the mountain these people go about their daily lives, determined to make a life worth living as they have for generations. They take the foreigners visiting in their stride, interactions are distant and respectful but never overly familiar.

A man, sitting in the doorway of his shop, and probably having his bed in the back, allowed me to take a picture of him mending a garment. His manner was regal. He was not hostile but he did not smile. I encountered much of this aloofness, especially through the Bolivian *altiplano*. In the beginning I found it disconcerting but soon understood that it was just their way. They had no malicious intent. I think they just did not want to be bothered. I could accept that. I often felt the same.

On my third day in Potosí Luis drove me out to Hacienda Cayara, an old farm-turned-hotel, now belonging to an uncle of his. This grand estate, founded in 1556 and reputedly the first hacienda in the colony, was typically and necessarily given its location, self-sufficient in almost everything except imported luxury items.

On the way, Luis told me, "The previous estate owners were feudal lords who ruled these vast lands and often big numbers of Indians who were tied to the land as servants."

The place was impressive and the house, a well-preserved example of its type, was furnished with period furniture, paintings and decorations. In one room the ceiling was painted by a previous owner with representations of the four seasons and different continents.

Luis's uncle was a quite a character. He had no bottom teeth and spoke with a lisp, his lower-lip curved upwards to hide his toothless gum. Edgar was an amusing yet dirty old man and grabbed every possible opportunity to talk about sex. He gave me a book he had written. Edgar's portrait, apparently done by some famous artist, decorated the front. His eyes were cast upwards, his expression a naughty grin and circling around his head, in a halo, were six naked angels.

I nearly got robbed that evening in the city. I was having a bite in a somewhat cramped vegetarian café when two men and a woman sat themselves down at my table. In Latin America, it is not unusual for somebody to join you if there are empty seats available. The three kept looking at each other. Next, one of the men touched my arm and dropped money on the ground. I was caught off guard for a fraction of a second but knew straight away what he was up to. He was trying to distract me to give his accomplices a chance to grab my money-belt on the table. I moved away from him and put my arm through the sling of my bag, pretending not to have a care in the world. My heart was beating a bit faster but I managed to nonchalantly point to another table opposite us, which had cleared.

"There you go," I said. "You have a table for yourselves."

They got up and left the restaurant. The diners looked at me with knowing nods. They had seen it numerous times before.

The following day was a Friday and I had the blues. I felt lonely. Everywhere I looked I spotted happy travelling couples reading their guide-books, chatting and laughing, planning the next leg of their travels together. I drowned my sorrows in an ice-cold glass of strawberry milkshake and went back to my hostel.

Although Luis was not travelling with me, he assisted me greatly in preparing for the 500 plus kilometres ahead of us to La Paz. Travelling the distance in a vehicle would take about eleven hours, on horseback about fourteen days.

Together Luis and I planned my route, distances, and where bags of food had to be delivered. The sheepskin on my saddle was falling apart and was handed to a shoemaker for repairs. I bought a bagful of coffee sachets for the road.

In Llacalle, our next stop 30 kilometres from Potosí, a young man called Jesús gave me a hand with the horses. In the early evening we walked around town looking for *chala* (dry maize leaves). But nobody was willing to sell.

"They have to fetch it from far away with their donkeys," Jesús informed me. "They give the *chala* to their cows."

At the local diner a young girl of about twelve hung on to me. Literally. She kept on hugging me and a few times attempted to pick me up, clasping her arms around me from behind. She put her face close to mine and inspected my teeth.

"Are they for real?" she asked.

Her three-year-old sister was teary-eyed and complained about a sore leg. I made her sit on the table and inspected the 'injured limb'.

"I have just the thing for you," I said with a serious face.

She looked on solemnly while I dabbed some Vaseline on. The crying stopped.

"It's much better," she said and hopped away.

The following day after a strenuous climb into the mountains, I saw a couple of houses on both sides of the road and stopped. I used my machete and chopped into the grass shrubs for the horses. A few *corrals* were scattered around and I noticed they had better grass inside. Just as I was about to climb over the stone wall I caught sight of an Indian woman sitting high up on the hill like a Buddha. I thought it wise to ask for permission first. She shook her head – 'no'.

I walked to the other side of the hill in search of some hot water. At first I did not see anybody but could hear a baby's cry. Dogs barked frantically. I walked closer and noticed a woman washing her long black hair over a basin in the doorway. I stood there for 20 minutes before she decided to come out. She took out a breast to feed the dirty crying baby. Over the noise of the dogs' barking I asked her for some hot water so I could have tea.

Her answer was a short *"No hay"*.

Because I did not know how far away Ventilla our next stop was, I started to look out for a place for the night around 4 p.m. There was little activity and hardly anybody around and I felt lucky when I spotted a little settlement consisting of only a few houses not too deep down in a valley. There were *llama corrals* in abundance. An Indian man with a colourful tasselled-hat came out and agreed that the horses could occupy a *corral* for the night. He indicated which one to take. I thanked him but noted that the one he pointed at was high up and not protected from the wind and cold. I hoped I did not appear pushy or ungrateful when I asked if they could be put lower down in the valley. He shook his head.

"Those are for our *llamas* and donkeys."

The weather looked unsettled and just as I started to pitch the tent next to the horses' *corral* a fierce wind began to blow. It was followed by icy cold drops of rain and I struggled to get the tent up on the sloped ground. The saddle and all my belongings went inside, leaving very little space for myself.

I strolled to the houses down below and on the way saw a woman sitting in the doorway weaving. She showed me her work. I loved one particular purple mat and asked her the price.

"It's not for sale," she said. "Too much hard work went into it."

She insisted I buy a blue one for eighty bolivianos but I declined. It was the purple one I wanted.

For some inexplicable reason I felt somewhat uneasy among the people of that specific Indian community. As a result I found myself being excessively sociable and friendly towards everyone. I was on edge and talked too much. I told them how nice all the people in Bolivia had been. I also told a white lie and said that a friend would be joining me in the morning, just in case they had ideas and wanted to dispose of me and keep the horses. I did not know where the sudden paranoia came from. Maybe I was hallucinating because of the altitude. Maybe it was the unsettling thought that nobody I knew had any idea where I was putting my head down that night. Seeing some men walking around with axes did not help to put my mind at ease either.

While I waited for the kettle on the open fire to boil, a woman handed me a traditional dress to try on. I took off my jacket and shivered in the cold evening air. They all laughed. I passed my camera to one of the men for a picture. They refused when I asked to take one of them.

On the way back to my tent, a man asked if I was hungry. I lied and said no. I was queasy about the hygiene and preferred to stick to my crackers and tea despite the fact that since morning I only had a black coffee, a couple of biscuits and a handful of nuts and raisins to eat.

Out of breath, I crawled into my tent just before darkness fell. I squeezed in between all the smelly horse gear. My pistol was ready and extra ammunition at hand. I changed my head-position to the opposite side to what would normally be expected.

'This will fool them,' I thought with satisfaction.

That night was a disaster. For starters I was uncomfortable. I was lying on a slope and kept sliding down. Also, as hard as I tried, I could not get warm. For the duration of the night I was frozen stiff – the thermal sheet inside my sleeping bag designed to give me an extra three degrees Celsius proved to be a farce. The combination of cold and discomfort, fear of an imminent axe attack, a rumbling tummy and the sound of the horses moving around restlessly, blowing through their noses in the biting *altiplano* wind, guaranteed a horrible night. When I did manage to doze off briefly I had bad dreams. I was being attacked and when I shot the man in the head, the bullet bounced back.

I can't really say I officially 'woke up' the following morning. I was unsure if I really slept at all during the night and by six I was up and ready to go. My hands were cold and clumsy as I saddled up the horses. They looked miserable. I fed them a handful of sugar and dished out the rest to one of the children. I received a wide grin when I also handed him a plastic Irish flag.

"I have to go," I informed the villagers. "Please tell my 'friend' I'll see her in the next village."

Once on the road I kept my head down and contact with those we encountered to a minimum. I felt worn out and could only just muster a stiff and formal *"buen dia"*. I encouraged a flagging and hungry Mise and Tusa out loud.

"Only 15 kilometres to do today. There will be a food bag for you at our next stop."

I leaned forward and rested my head on Mise's neck.

"Just hang in there," I whispered, while I wondered whether *I* would have enough strength left to get through the day.

We went round a bend in the mountain and my eye caught sight of a man and woman walking with their three donkeys. We were still a bit far away and I grabbed the chance to take a picture. But the man spotted me.

I passed them and without stopping, said, *"Buenos tardes."*

The man turned towards me and with an unfriendly face demanded money.

"Yo no tengo señor," I said and kept going.

He continued to insist on payment for the picture and walked purposefully towards us. I got slightly worried, especially as Tusa was dragging behind. I did not know what I would do if they grabbed him. I called out to Tusa and kept on shaking my head. The woman shouted something when I put Mise into a trot.

The day continued in more or less the same fashion as the day's ride to Potosí. When, after six hours on the road, there was still no sign of our next destination I realised that I needed to start asking again. But those I encountered on the way did not have a clue how far Cruce Ventilla was. The discrepancies in their answers would have made anyone burst into manic laughter or drive them mad. They varied between 'just another six kilometres' to 'definitely 30 kilometres more' and when I asked another man, "How far *señor*, more or less," he thought about it for a moment and muttered something that sounded like '200 kilometres'.

Those who were incapable of guessing had no qualms about begging. One boy stood on the side of the road and asked for *platita* (a little money) in a whiney tone. I asked him what work he had done for me. Another woman lifted her hat. I initially thought it indicated a sign of respect but soon gathered what she was really after.

I recorded the following on my dictaphone;

It is 1 p.m. I'm in desperate need of food. My hands are shaking and I feel weak. It is cold and looks like it will rain soon. The horses are wrecked and also very hungry. I don't know where Cruce Ventilla is. I spotted lightning in the distance. I am leading Mise who is very tired. We are all tired. I can't sleep here in the open and I can't have another night with nothing to eat. I feel like fainting. We are in the middle of nowhere. There is a man in the front with a donkey but I certainly will not ask him how much further it is.

A short while later, the rain on my face caused a momentary feeling of renewed energy. I contemplated for a moment listening to music on my walkman, something to break the monotony of the long road, but then decided against it. I much preferred riding in silence. It kept things real. I was aware where I was, conscious of my senses, the horses and the surroundings. It was mostly when darkness fell that I sometimes felt the desire to lie back in my tent and lose myself in beautiful melodies. Just me, the night, and the music. Leonard Cohen's melancholic deep voice ironically had a way of lifting me up and giving me hope each and every time I listened to him. Hearing him sing *"Hallelujah"*, a beautiful song of the relationship between humanity and divinity, love and pain, sin and grace, gave me this overwhelming sensation that anything was possible. It is a hauntingly brilliant and moving song. It stirred something inside me like nothing else.

A village appeared on the horizon, well after four in the afternoon. It turned out to be Cruce Ventilla but I was too jaded to care. As we entered, Mise stopped dead in her tracks to allow a sow and her five piglets to cross the road.

I borrowed a wheelbarrow and mixed the horses' food, kept at the police station, into an edible form with water. The station consisted of one room, three desks next to each other and a couple of unmade beds. The horses were led through a narrow alley-way into a small courtyard at the back.

I found a room at the exotic-sounding Copacabana, which turned out to be a filthy excuse for a hotel. The toilets at the back were disgusting. The concrete floors were covered with toilet paper – most of it used. A half-door offered some privacy. Above my head on the one side sat a number of chickens in what looked like their permanent home in the exposed roof. The toilet was the usual squat job and while I was in there a couple of scrawny dogs poked their heads in to investigate. For yet another night, washing myself was out of the question. For somebody used to a shower in the morning and a luxurious bath at night, I was adapting frighteningly quickly to this primitive lifestyle.

After a sickly dinner of greasy soup and a cold egg on the side, I headed for my room. It was small yet almost cosy with a candle burning on an unsteady table made from an old oil tin. A fierce wind blew outside and I felt deliriously happy and contented to be indoors and to have something comfortable to sleep on for the night. An urgent knock on the door got me up. Six little faces tried to say something at the same time.

I was not sure what they wanted and said, "The horses are fine," and closed the door.

The knocking persisted.

'They probably want to have the wheelbarrow back,' I thought.

What did they think? I was going to leave in the morning with a wheelbarrow strapped to one of the horses? I ignored the knocks and was finally left in peace.

Day 131. On the road to Tola Polca, Tusa had yet another episode with a lopsided pack. But this time his reaction was strange and disturbing. He charged past me and Mise and suddenly his legs folded underneath him. He managed to get up and proceeded to kick and snort. I tried my utmost to calm him down but when he eventually stopped, his legs went lame once again. Terrified, I ran over to him and checked for serious injury. I undid the girth and urged him to get up. He was breathing

heavily and shaking. My heart went out to him. We walked slowly uphill to where I planned to stop for a short break. After a few cubes of sugar he seemed to forget his ordeal and nibbled on a few shrubs. I sighed with relief.

We rode through open plains with only *llamas* for company. The tiny village of Tola Polca was situated on a hill. A dirt road divided a small number of tiny mud houses.

A *Quechua* woman managed to utter, *"No hay"* when I enquired about a place to stay.

Further down it took another woman quite some time to decide if she had space for the night. A bunch of kids, mostly girls, had shyly gathered, wearing different variations of traditional hats. A suspicious little face stood out. Her expression was a constant frown and her clothes were ragged – wide, knee-length skirt, a faded purple shawl kept together with a large pin and a dirty woollen cap. Like all the others her feet were cracked, grime-stained and shoeless.

The woman said I could sleep on the floor of her shop. The girls led us to a *corral* at the foot of a small hilltop. They helped remove the stones lying on the ground, inside. We used the same stones to block the entrance.

I pretended to be unable to get out and pleaded in a mock tone, "Help me, help me!"

They doubled up with laughter. When I tried to take a picture, half of them scattered in all directions.

I collected my machete and asked the girls to cut grass for the horses. A short while later they came running over.

"The boys took the machete from us!"

I got it back but the machete turned out to be too blunt and the girls used their hands to pull out the prickly shrubs. A few others pitched in half-heartedly, hoping they too would get paid. I gave a few bolivianos to the three hardest working girls.

I looked up at the sky and saw a powerful dust storm fast approaching. The girls grabbed my hands and ran but it caught up with us before we could make it back to the shop. I could hardly see some of the kids running in front of me. I prayed that the horses would lie down in their *corral*.

A German couple dressed in cycling gear entered the shop. We were going in opposite directions. They had already travelled on their bicycles through Central America down through Ecuador and Peru.

"You can stay with us at the local clinic," they offered.

We chatted over beers and a few cigarettes. Afterwards they helped me carry my belongings to the clinic. Later a Canadian traveller joined us. Rob gave up his job and sold his house to cycle around the world. I laughed when he commented on the confusing O'Brien maps he had used for a while.

"I swear they were made by a pissed Irishman throwing a dice."

The Germans came prepared. They carried a gas stove and water filters with them. They even produced a couple of small containers filled with different spices. I was impressed. We had a meal of scrambled eggs followed by sardines in a tomato sauce with pasta. Coca tea was served for dessert.

It felt strange to spend a night like that with Westerners. Everybody had the same idea about writing a book after their travels – that is about all we had in common. The Canadian cyclist carried a small laptop with him. After dinner as we silently contemplated life, each one occupied with their own thoughts, he put on a song by the group America from the 1970s, *"Horse with no name"*. The raw sounds filled the room and drifted into the cold, dark night.

> On the first part of the journey
> I was looking at all the life
> There were plants and birds and rocks and things
> There was sand and hills and rings
> The first thing I met was a fly with a buzz
> And the sky with no clouds
> The heat was hot and the ground was dry
> But the air was full of sound

Outside, wind, sleet and rain swept through the quiet village. I thought of Mise and Tusa and said a silent prayer for them. I slept in my riding pants and put a pair of comfortable slacks on over them. I also wore two pairs of socks and two long sweatshirts.

The German man kept me awake all night with his loud snoring. He sounded like an injured lion and my sporadic flashes of torch light into his face had no effect.

On the way to Oruro, under a clear blue sky, we went through the villages of Villapujo, Crucero and Pequereque. Small villages letting the seasons pass quietly, only interrupted by the carnivals, Indian markets and the worship of *Pachamama* (Mother Earth). She is the one who, it is believed by the local people, provides maize and the pastures where the *llamas* graze.

It was interesting to see how naturally close to nature the Indian people lived. Conscious of their dependence on the earth, they knew how to respect it instead of violating what was a privilege to share in. The Indian people believe that nature is always interacting with their daily lives. It is never untouched.

Given that I had been so dependent on the earth, the weather and nature, I felt they empathised with me. I guess they also recognised the parallels between their beliefs, the simplicity of how they lived their lives and my chosen way of travelling. They understood my vulnerability, having to rely on the elements, being exposed to what nature threw at me, going through the world in such a primitive way, devoid of luxury and glamour. But many of them also saw me as a poor *gringa* choosing to travel in such a basic way because I could not afford a plane ticket.

Numerous times they would ask, "Why don't you take an aeroplane? You will get to America much quicker that way."

They did not see me as a threat. They did not regard me as a typical tourist, passing through their world, oblivious to their way of life. Some looked at my worn-out attire, torn saddlebags and weathered face with obvious sympathy. In their eyes I had as little or even less than them.

I had a place organised for the horses at the local army base just outside Oruro. I singled out one young man and gave him clear instructions for feeding the horses.

"They need to gain weight," I said. "Please make sure you give them their food twice a day. And don't forget to soak the corn and grains in water overnight."

The outskirts of Oruro were not only filthy, with a river polluted with garbage, but also cluttered with stalls, vendors and trucks. The town was buzzing with the sound of street markets. Everywhere I turned, there was a stall selling fresh fruit, yoghurt, wheat germ and raw egg cocktails, called *multi-vitaminicos*. It was a health paradise. I could not get enough of these nutritious blends and had them for breakfast, lunch and dinner. I dreaded the prospect of poor eating and hunger again.

The next morning I took a minibus to visit the horses. A man got off and the driver turned to me.

"That was the Minister of Mines in Bolivia. I can't understand why he takes this kind of transport for one boliviano when he could easily afford a taxi," he grunted.

He was certainly not impressed at having had a Minister in his vehicle.

I stocked up on a few necessities at the market. I bargained for everything and one woman seemed to enjoy my efforts. She gave me an extra carrot, tomato and banana.

The morning of our departure I was at the stables before 7 a.m. Just as I arrived I noticed my helper pouring water into the *avena* and maize bucket. He did not know that I had seen him. I popped a grain into my mouth.

"Hmm," I said. "They're a bit hard. Surely they were not soaked since last night."

He seemed dumbstruck by my 'expertise'.

It took us three hours to get through the city. I walked with the horses and used vigorous hand-signs to keep the traffic from coming too close. We passed another army base and Mise, recognising the clothes, neighed, expecting to see other horses. Tusa pulled on the leading rope and dragged the saddle back over Mise's hindquarters and down her legs. It happened twice and by the time we were outside the city it felt as if we had already done 30 kilometres.

I wondered how I would manage with Tusa for much longer. He was terribly inconsistent and the pulling-back proved to be a real annoyance. It affected Mise too. She had to work twice as hard, pulling Tusa's weight along. At one stage I detached

Tusa from the leading rope and let him run free. He did not hesitate and turned back to Oruro. Later, I put the saddlebags on Mise but they did not sit well and she seemed uncomfortable. I even contemplated stopping a vehicle and asking for the bags to be dropped off in Caracollo.

45 kilometres of headache and hardship later we finally arrived. I ended up at the local municipality and without a translator had my first interview in Spanish with an amateur television crew. I went to the back of the building while a bunch of kids stared through thick metal bars, thoroughly amused by such unusual visitors. I inspected the horses' feet. Mise's back shoes had a few nails missing causing the shoes to be too loose.

I caught the eye of a girl.

"Can I touch the horses?" she asked.

I let her in and before she knew what had happened she had a hammer in hand. I held Mise's foot while she banged in the nails. We were clumsy and incompetent but pretended to be in control. Suzie was good, willing and not afraid. Sadly I could not say the same about Mise. I tied her to the gate and hobbled her front legs.

But chaos descended in no time at all. Mise, uneasy with the noisy crowd around us and probably terrified of Suzie and I hurting her, moved around nervously. In the process she managed to pull the gate partially off its hinges. Panic erupted everywhere and I feared the whole metal construction was about to crash on top of her. Kids shouted and ran in all directions. I managed to untie Mise before we had a complete disaster. The crowd moved warily closer again, not wanting to miss out on anything. When things were finally under control again I noticed Suzie was still with me. She showed a lot of courage and I praised her in front of everybody.

"Look," I said to our audience. "So many men are standing around but it's a young *girl* that helps me."

After Suzie had nailed in the second shoe she disappeared rather quickly.

It took some time to organise somewhere I could put my head down for the night. I was offered a dusty store-room without a bed near to where the horses would be staying. But really, it was the mouse-droppings that made my mind up to decline. A room in somebody's house above a shop was then suggested. But by the time I was ready to move in I was told it was locked and the key was missing.

My bed for the night turned out to be a thin mattress laid out in an open space under the stairs inside the municipality building. I did not like the fact that I had no security such as a door that I could lock myself. Throughout the night technicians and busy maintenance men walked in and out. I could hear young boys chatting outside. Every now and then they mentioned *"caballo"* and giggled.

I woke up early the following morning bursting to go. Failing to find a public toilet in the building, I went to the back, manoeuvred myself partially underneath a truck and quickly did what I had to do. I collected water from a drum and rinsed my legs and feet.

I was happy to see that the horses had refrained from attacking the apple trees where they were staying. I borrowed a bucket to put the horses' food and water mixture into. Tusa, overly eager to eat, put his foot inside the bucket, cracking the plastic. A man quickly approached.

"I will show you where you can buy a new one," he said, obviously afraid I might do a runner.

I looked behind me when I felt a tug on my shirt. A young boy, not older than seven, explained that I needed to give back the glass bottle in which I had a papaya drink, bought at his mother's shop the night before. I told him to go look under the stairs where I slept.

On the way out of town a woman approached me. I was not in a particularly good mood and did not fancy a chat. She handed me a packet of biscuits and good naturedly wished me a safe journey. I was glad I was not too short with her and thanked her profusely.

On the way to Panduro we encountered numerous groups of school children dressed in pristine red school uniforms. They were not shy and had a thousand questions. In one village, there was a huge sign indicating the distance to La Paz – 200 kilometres.

How far is it to La Paz?" I quizzed the kids.

Their answers varied between eight and two thousand kilometres. Everybody wanted to know the names of the horses.

In another village we walked in the direction of a little shop. A girl spotted us from upstairs, ran down and put a wooden barrier in front of the door. I never found out what exactly made her so afraid.

12 kilometres from Caracollo we stopped at a shallow lake where cows stood knee-deep in the water. I let the horses drink and led them to the edge of an *alfalfa* field. It looked lush and inviting. Just then a man came towards us, his pace fast and determined.

"Your horses can't eat here. I want fifty dollars if they do."

"We'll only be here for five minutes *señor*," I replied calmly. "They won't eat much."

He was not letting it go and walked towards Tusa, waving his arms and saying "shuh shuh".

When he tried to chase Tusa away again, I imitated him and flapped my arms above my head. He briskly stepped back, obviously frightened. Once he had composed himself he moved towards me and waved a threatening finger. He turned on his heels and walked away.

"I know the President of Bolivia," I called after him. "I think I will ring him tonight."

He turned around to look at me, grabbed his crotch and said, "*I* am the President!" and stormed off.

Not wanting to aggravate the Indian man further, I turned around before I burst out laughing. My anger quickly subsided. I giggled about the incident for many more miles and thought of Mark Twain's true words;

Humour is the great thing, the saving thing. The minute it crops up, all our
irritations and resentments slip away and a sunny spirit takes their place.

Not too far from Panduro, I stopped for a tea-break. A man, standing next to a broken-down truck, came over to talk. His timing was wrong. In no mood for chatting, I reluctantly answered his questions, alas not in the conventional way. I pretended to be mute and used a few made-up signs with my hands. It was clear it would be a struggle and soon he said his goodbyes. He gave a sympathetic wave from his truck.

In the small village of Panduro they offered me the use of a schoolroom. Dora, La Profesora, a friendly teacher with an easy manner, provided a big comfortable mattress. She asked the kids if any of them had *cebada* (hay for cattle) at their houses. They all shook their heads until she indicated that I did not expect it for free. On the way to collect the food I asked the children why there was so much paper lying around.

"*Es el campo señora,*" came the answer.

It literally meant 'this is the countryside'. Most of them had probably never been to the city and assumed that in the city you do not litter, whereas in the countryside – who cares?

At the *corral*, I asked who was going to help me. Nobody replied. I commandeered two boys to give me a hand and handed them an armful of *cebada* each. I took some myself.

A girl protested. "It's too much."

"Don't worry," I said. "I'll pay."

They wanted to know how much but were not happy with my answer.

"Our mother would want more."

A girl tried to persuade the boys to take the hay back.

"Look," I said. "You don't understand. My horses are hungry. I know how much the *cebada* is sold for but will give you double that."

Still they were reluctant. The boys did not know what to do so I walked back with only the food I was carrying. The owner of the *cebada* arrived a short while later, angry and demanding a ridiculous amount for the food.

"How much should I give her?" I asked Dora.

The woman was still unhappy and ranted incomprehensibly in *Aymara*. Another teacher put a patronising arm around her.

"Why don't you take the money offered and go back to your home, *señora*?" she tried to soothe.

When she had gone, a teacher shook her head. *"Una mujer muy mala"* (A very bad woman).

Dora invited me to join their basketball training. A male teacher taught the kids and suggested I join them for a game. I lasted less than three minutes.

"It's the high altitude," I explained short of breath.

Dora lived in the school grounds and later showed me her modest living quarters.

"I travel to Oruro every weekend to visit my son who is looked after by my mother," she told me.

I showed her a few TATA articles and she displayed a thorough knowledge about Down's syndrome, mental disability and yoga. A lovely woman, she seemed genuinely happy to know me and delighted that I was staying there.

In the early evening I sat at a school desk in my room preparing a few crackers with sardines, tomato and a bit of cheese. I wrote my diaries by candlelight. Hearing giggles, I looked up and saw a number of noses pressed flat against the window. I gave them a wave to let me have some privacy.

"Ya," they replied and left reluctantly.

My body was stiff and sore and my right arm especially was throbbing. I put a few thoughts on the dictaphone. Even though I carried a phrase book and Spanish CD's with me, I was usually so tired at the end of a day's ride, that I only managed a few minutes before drifting off.

I blew out the candle but the room was still half bright. I lay back on the mattress in the moonlit room, shadows and light making patterns on the white-washed walls.

Dora was one of those rare people in Latin America – someone, who would do something spontaneously without having to be asked. I emerged from my room the following morning and discovered that not only had she given the horses water but she had also gone off in search of more food for them. Just before we left, mothers and teachers came along to get pictures of their children sitting on Mise and Tusa.

After two hours on the road we stopped for breakfast. A little boy walked past and stared openly. I was surprised to see him turn around and walk backwards, too afraid he might miss out on something. Later, the horses had a feast in an *alfalfa* field just off the road. The skies opened and we were pelted by hail stones. The horses were oblivious to this and tucked in. A man and his young son came over and I feared the inevitable. It turned out all he wanted was to shake my hand and satisfy his curiosity about the horses.

Shortly before we entered Lahuachaca the heavens opened again. Mise added her own bit of flair by managing to dump all our belongings on the road after yet another pack that refused to stay on top. I went through the motions as if in a trance. I even managed to smile through the lashings of rain on my face. I was well used to this routine now. I reminded myself that it could have been worse.

Drenched to the skin, we trotted into the chaotic madhouse of the village. It was market day and the hustle and bustle of people, trucks and trolleys left me almost dizzy. Everybody froze in their tracks and stared. Young men whistled and made lewd comments. I tried to ignore them but when two young ones continued to make suggestive noises I finally got the chance to use my well-rehearsed line.

I frowned and said with disapproval, *"Hombres civilizados tienen mas respeto por las mujeres"* (Civilised men have more respect for women).

There was a stunned silence and afraid of a backlash, I stared straight ahead and continued to move through the market, eager to get to the far side. A man standing on the side made a hand-motion to his mouth and pointed to the horses. At first I thought he meant he would like to eat the horses but realised later he probably wondered if I had food for them.

At every village we entered I always attempted to get to the other side of it to look for accommodation. It was a psychological thing for me. It would give me the feeling we were almost 'on the road' for the next day. It also meant that I had gone through the crowds and stares from people the day before and could start the following morning with a clean slate and no agitation or frustration. Well, at least for a while.

In Lahuachaca I first asked at the Casa de Salud (clinic) for a bed. I decided it would make for a welcome change. The German cyclists told me how they always approached hospitals and clinics first when entering a town or village. They claimed never to have been sent away. Travelling with a bike was obviously easier in that sense and asking for accommodation was naturally less of a challenge. I had two equine companions that needed space, food and an area to roll and clean out their bowels, no questions asked.

Great was my delight when offered the dentist's consultation room. Initially I thought I had to sleep in the dentist's chair but then spotted the narrow bed behind a screen. It was perfect. I had privacy and even a basin of my own. The horses, although safe and secure inside the yard, posed a threat to a bed of new plants so I covered each and every one with a plastic bag before heading to the market half a mile away. Dinner was as simple and predictable as ever, sardines and tomatoes on crackers.

On the way to Patacamoya, 29 kilometres from Luhuachaca, we stopped briefly in a village called Sica Sica. A man opened his store-room to give me an armful of *cebada*.

36. Excited school kids walk with Mise and Tusa.
37. A serene man in the doorway of his shop in Potosí, mending a garment.

38. Mise and Tusa enjoying a break in the thin *altiplano* air.
39. A burst of colour at a market in Pisac, Peru.

40. Kids looking to have their picture taken in exchange for cash in Cusco, Peru.
41. Chaco carves Jo's name on a wooden cross.
42. Jo's cross.

43. Tracy and I fishing for piranhas in the Peruvian jungle.
44. Having checked for alligators, getting ready to camp out.

45. My room-mate for the night in her box (the village of Kayo in Beni, Bolivia).
46. Starting early to avoid the worst heat as we go through the tropical parts of Bolivia.

47a. At Espiritu, thinning-out Mise's tail.
47b. Evidence that the mosquitoes were real.
48. A dentist in Australia (Beni) advertises his practice.

49. A handy way of getting the horses across a river.
50. Time to get clean in the dam at Casa Blanca.

51. Kids accompanying me after purchases made at the local (and only) village shop.
52. *Siesta* time when the heat becomes unbearable.

While I had my breakfast – a half ripe avocado, sardines on stale bread and a chocolate – the man puffed on a Marlboro Light I gave him.

He had many curious questions and asked, "Have you been bothered on the road?"

I showed him my machete and joked. "This is predominantly for bad men."

He was very surprised to learn that I had not been 'molested' since I began my journey more than four months earlier.

On the road I encountered two western-looking cyclists. They struggled on their bikes, battling it out against the wind. We did not stop to make conversation. I was secretly delighted to be on horseback and not pedalling a bike. I had been there, done that.

In 1991, I explored Europe on a bicycle, putting about 2,000 kilometres on the clock. Much poorer then than now, I had to knock on doors most nights, asking for a place to put my head down. Sometimes, people allowed me to pitch my tent in their gardens, at other times my blown-up mattress in a garage was the best I was going to get. The mountain passes from Switzerland to Italy were tough and riding for hours into a strong wind nearly broke my spirit, but at least I only had myself to worry about – one agonising body to find a resting place for, one mouth to feed.

This time around I was conscious of the tremendous responsibility of travelling with Mise and Tusa, but still I would not have changed anything. They were the perfect companions. With them I was never alone.

In Patacamoya I headed straight for the local hospital, a large, tidy building with metal barriers in the front, to which I tied the horses. I sat in the waiting room, held the baby of a young woman sitting next to me, watched television and stared into the distance for almost two hours before the hospital manager and his assistant could see me.

One of them asked, *"Solita?"*

Before I could reply the other one used my line and said, *"No, con dos caballos!"*

They both agreed that horses could be much better company than humans. The manager handed me his card.

"Call me if you need help," he said. "My wife is a lawyer."

I laughed and said that if I ever called him, I hoped it would not be to speak to his wife. He organised with the receptionist to take me to her house not far from the hospital. She had space in her backyard (littered with plastic bags and plastic bottles) for the horses and did not mind that Mise and Tusa needed to walk through the house to get there. I was a bit embarrassed the following morning counting nineteen heaps of horse dung decorating the yard but was told it was most welcome.

"We'll use it as compost," the girl said happily.

Día de los Muertos (The Day of the Dead), an ancient, annual Catholic festival held in many Latin American countries, is a celebration of the memory of deceased ancestors. The activities consist mainly of families welcoming the spirits of their dead ones back into their homes and visiting the graves of their close kin. Plans for the festival, celebrated on the 1st and 2nd of November, are made throughout the year, including gathering the goods that will be offered to the dead.

At home members of the family decorate an altar in honour of deceased relatives with *papel picado* (intricate tissue paper cut-outs), candles, flowers, photographs of the departed, candy skulls inscribed with the name of the deceased, and a selection of his or her favourite foods and beverages. The latter often includes bottles of beer or tequila, cups of *atole* (corn gruel) or coffee, and fresh water, as well as platters of rice, beans, chicken or meat in mole sauce, candied pumpkin or sweet potatoes and a special egg-batter bread (*pan de muerto,* or bread of the dead). Interestingly, some people believe the deceased eat the spirit of the food, and even though the offerings of food are consumed after the festivity, they think it lacks nutritional value.

The spirits of the dead are expected to pay a holiday visit home and it is believed they should be provided with adequate sustenance for the journey. Frequently a wash basin and clean hand towel are provided so that visiting souls can freshen up before the feast. The offering may also include a pack of cigarettes for the after-dinner enjoyment of former smokers, or a selection of toys and extra sweets for deceased children.

At the cemetery, family members engage in sprucing up the gravesite, decorating it with large bright flowers (such as marigolds and chrysanthemums), religious amulets and offerings of food, cigarettes and alcoholic beverages. Setting out and enjoying a picnic, and interacting socially with other family and community members who gather there, families remember the departed by telling stories about them.

Simultaneously joyous and sombre, it is a time to welcome the souls of the dead, a celebration, in which the living and the dead are joined if only for a short time. In some ways it is a triumph over death and therefore becomes a celebration of life. Those we love are given back to us if only for a brief time. The souls of children, "*los angelitos*", are believed to return on the 1st of November, with adult spirits on the following day. Because of this warm social environment, the colourful setting and the abundance of food, drink and good company, this commemoration of the dead has pleasant overtones for the observers.

In Camargo I was warned by westerners to be careful on this day. I was told it was a sensitive event and that emotions could run high. My experience however proved the opposite. As I went along towards Calamarca with the horses, we encountered groups of people walking happily on the side of the road, chatting quietly among themselves, carrying arms full of flowers and goods. A few times I got off Mise and led the horses, walking with the locals and answering their questions. Nobody seemed hostile, overly emotional or even sad.

The emphasis was on celebrating and honouring the lives of the deceased rather than fearing evil or malevolent spirits. Not one person seemed bothered to have an outsider even in the form of a *gringa* on a horse in their midst for a short while. This was an important social ritual for them, recognising the cycle of life and death that is human existence.

Having struggled to find decent food for the horses in Patacamya, I was delighted when the next day after about ten kilometres I saw a few patches of *alfalfa* next to the main road. It was not a cultivated field but more like a few seeds that had found their way there and decided to stay put. Neither was it part of a field or in a fenced area. It seemed it belonged to nobody. I had tea while the horses munched happily.

But the peace was not to last for long and soon I saw a man in his early fifties coming over. I knew what was about to follow and when he spoke to me I pretended not only not to understand but also not to be able to speak. The man picked up a piece of rock and aimed at Tusa. Fearing for the safety of my horse, my protective side took over. I knew what I had to do and without saying a word, I pulled the pistol from my money belt. I made a noise to get the man's attention. He looked over his shoulder and his hand froze mid-air when he saw what was in my hand. He dropped the rock and immediately threw his arms up again. I had no intention of shooting but I confess I was pleasantly surprised at the effect the mere presence of the pistol had. The man retreated slowly, his hands still up, his eyes fixed on the gun. He walked in the complete opposite direction of the fields he was minding. Only then and from a distance did he request permission to return to his field. I gave him a nod but kept the pistol aimed.

When we left half an hour later I saw him in the distance and gave a warning finger. My hands were still trembling. I had stood my ground but I wished I could have done it in another way. I did not like the fact that I felt it necessary to pull a gun on somebody. I hoped I did not act too hastily. Also, thinking of the startled Indian man I felt sorry for him and regretted very much my actions. Surely I could have just walked away. All I had proved was that I was willing to retaliate in a similar negative and combative manner. For quite some time after the encounter I wished I was not carrying such a dangerous weapon. The responsibility of having something that could cause devastating consequences weighed heavily on my shoulders. Yet, I felt safer for knowing it was near.

By the time we had reached Calamarca, the last town before La Paz, Mise's left back-shoe was split in half. Large numbers of trucks and buses roared past and it was clear we were coming closer to a city. The sheepskin I was sitting on was falling apart and the wooden bar on the front of my saddle had nearly cracked in two. It was also that time of the month and after forty days of hunger, cold and high mountains, I felt thoroughly frazzled and shaky.

A friendly bearded young man stopped his pickup truck. It turned out Gonzalo knew my contacts in Tucumán. He looked at Mise's shoe.

"You can't continue to ride her like that," he advised.

I asked him if he knew a farrier in town.

He laughed.

"In Calamarca? No way. I suggest you organise a truck from here. It would be reckless to enter La Paz with two horses."

I nevertheless continued on foot in the direction of San Antonio. I was bursting for a pee and hid in a ditch off the road. On my return I discovered Mise had just soaked my money belt which lay on the ground, in her urine. A storm was brewing and I knew the writing was on the wall. Gonzalo looked me up again.

"I can't find a truck for you," he said. "Leave the horses at one of these houses, take the bus to La Paz and organise transport from there."

It was excellent advice.

The man sitting next to me on the bus tried to make conversation but I answered his questions with a *"no entiendo"* most of the time. I needed to be quiet and wanted to use the short journey to La Paz to think, plan and reflect. Later I offered him a biscuit. He took the whole packet (they were my favourite) but neglected to give it back. I said nothing. At one stage he asked if I wanted to buy *"leche de vaca"* (milk from the cow). I declined.

The bus had no designated stops and picked and dropped off people when and where they requested even if it meant stopping three times in twenty yards. We went through the poor city of El Alto with its half a million inhabitants.

Gonzalo had warned me earlier that day.

"You don't want to travel through El Alto on your own. It's a dangerous place."

It was a disorganised sight with hundreds of pedestrians, cars and buses careering precariously through the noisy streets. People ran and dodged cars, hooters echoed non-stop. In the midst of the tumult, vendors were trying to sell food on the streets.

And then suddenly from an altitude of 13,287 feet the world opened up and the city of La Paz appeared in a canyon, looking like a large fish-bowl. It sprawled untidily all over the valley below the plateau with thousands of houses lining its walls. To me it looked like the perfect setting for a futuristic film. I almost expected a character out of *Star Wars* with its combination of science fiction, mythology and romance, to appear from one of the canyons, leaping from one roof to the other, to suddenly disappear out of sight into a large cloud. Snow-capped Illimani, Bolivia's second highest mountain hovered mysteriously on the distant skyline.

Still dressed in my riding gear I headed for a phone box to let my contacts know I had arrived. First I tried Chacho who was a good friend of Carmen in Tarija. During our brief encounter there he had offered a place to stay once I arrived in La Paz. Stupidly I had not made contact with him since Tarija and found he was not at home when I rang.

Fernando who had arranged accommodation for the horses was out of town. Maria the cousin of Ciro and Vito sounded preoccupied and did not invite me over and Peter from the Irish Consulate was apologetic and suggested I booked into a hotel.

After my unsuccessful attempts to find a helpful friend in a big strange city I took a cab to the three dollars a night Alojamiento Universal, a place geared to backpackers with whom I had no desire to mingle. At that moment my world did not cross over to theirs. I felt strange and deflated. I had been fantasising about this moment for many weeks. I had visions of arriving in La Paz having conquered the infamous Bolivian *altiplano*, excited and on a high.

But here I was alone with nobody to pat me on the back to say, "Well done, you did great."

The tiny room closed in on me and I headed out in search of a cinema to occupy my thoughts. By accident I walked into a porno film and left swiftly. I went to an internet café and among the thirty messages was one from Fernando telling me to contact a friend called Louis to make arrangements for the horses. The city was alive but I felt very much alone and close to tears. I could not wait to get here and now all I felt was desolation and emptiness.

It took a cup of milk to push me over the edge. The woman in the shop was unfriendly and tried to overcharge me and on my way back to the hostel the tears started to flow. There was nothing I could do to stop it and I bawled all the way until I was in the confines of my room. Once on the bed I really let it rip. I cried for Mise and Tusa and what they had to go through, I cried for the silent demands of the *altiplano*, the struggles and the tribulations. I cried for the magical beauty of what I saw, the poverty of its people, the scrawny, sorrowful dogs. I cried for me and for everybody in this world that felt lonely and sad.

I cried for ten minutes. I wiped away my tears and looked into the cracked mirror.

"You have so much to be grateful for. Stop whingeing," I said to myself.

I tucked into muesli I bought from a Hare Krishna café in Oruro and listened to Prince's "*Condition of the heart*" on my walkman.

The Club Hipico Los Sargentos in the suburb of Obrajes in La Paz was located in an impressive setting. They had space for sixty horses and there were three large riding rings. The jumping arena was spectacular, nestled at the foot of cliffs, streaked white and yellow, with views over the city. The exclusive club also had a shooting range (where I tried out my pistol for the first time), tennis courts, an indoor pool, fitness centre, a bar and a restaurant.

Los Sargentos was also going to be home to Mise and Tusa for a number of weeks. When I initially spotted the fancy jumping horses I worried what impression my horses would make.

'Mise and Tusa will look like mules against these fancy ones,' I thought to myself.

Louis, the friend of Fernando, was a member of the club and turned out to be as friendly as his voice. I was introduced to another Louis, the club manager, of jovial disposition and wearing a wide-brimmed hat.

"What can I do for you?" he asked in perfect English with a smile.

My requirements were simple, a place for the horses where they would be well fed and looked after until my papers were in order and we were ready to tackle Peru. Both men showed genuine support in every possible way. The horses were collected the following day.

Fernando and I had lunch later that week in a Basque restaurant. He looked like an Arabian Knight with his tanned, friendly face, black hair and manners to match.

"You have to excuse my trendy handbag," I joked, pointing to my green saddlebags.

He laughed.

"I wanted to meet you, not the fashion queen of La Paz."

Over chilled white wine and a tasty meal we shared a relaxing time talking about everything. Fernando listened attentively to all my stories. A few weeks later, just before I left La Paz, we met up again for a quick coffee and cake rendezvous and great was my surprise when he handed me a hundred dollar note.

"This is to make sure you eat properly at least for some part of the way," he said as he stretched his hand across the table.

My protests fell on deaf ears. He was not going to take no for an answer. His face gave away the pleasure he felt at being of assistance.

It took three days before I managed to get hold of Chacho who was visiting another part of Bolivia. He urged me to get out of the hostel and head straight for his apartment. On the way I had my shoes cleaned on the street by what looked like members of a cult. The young men had their faces covered with balaclavas and wore baseball caps.

Chacho, an elegant 62-year-old man with grey hair combed back, sometimes gathered in a little pony tail, loved wearing hats and designed his own clothes. He had tremendous zest, his attitude to life truly admirable and inspiring.

Chacho González Roda left his parents' house at the age of twenty-two, not even taking his clothing with him. "It was a matter of 'we or she'," was how he described his parents' response when he started a passionate romance with a divorced woman. They spent seven years together and she is also the mother of his first son. Four subsequent marriages gave him two sons and two daughters.

"I have excellent relations with my ex-wives and a deep and warm bond with my children," he told me.

His CV reads like something out of a Bond film. He had lived in more than half a dozen countries, working as an industrial and systems engineer, film maker, director of the information department in the biggest mining corporation in Peru, journalist and editor of four different magazines over a thirty-year span, economist specialising in international relations, secretary for economic integration in the Bolivian Government, chief of projects in the Latin American economic system and international consultant in local productive development. During his vibrant career he worked for the United Nations Development Programme, UN Industrial Development Organisation, the International Labour Organisation and others.

Politically he belonged to the seventies generation. He was a leftist who dreamed that changing social conditions was possible with the will and the sacrifice of the people.

He was also the political secretary to President Siles who had re-opened the democratic process in Bolivia and Chacho acted as his representative in-hiding inside the country during the dictatorship. Twenty years of 'democracy' in his country made him abandon politics because he believed that what they had was a corrupt government, based on money oriented electoral processes.

Chacho had turned his life-long passion for food into his final (although I do not believe it for one minute) career move, that of running his own restaurant near the city of Santa Cruz in Bolivia.

At Los Sargentos I also met a few very chic, pretty girls. One of them commented how small my horses were.

"They seem suitable for children," she said with a wry smile.

The girls were all my age, married to rich husbands. They were pleasant in a glamorous way but I found it hard to connect with any of them. Their mornings consisted of turning up at the club immaculately made-up, dressed in designer clothes and fired up to do a few jumps with their horses. The highlight seemed to be feeding their equine pets a few carrots. I never saw any of them pick up the foot of a horse or brush it down. Maybe their horses were seen as just another fashion accessory.

Gabriel, the vet, was a great help during my stay and whatever the horses needed he was happy to oblige with. He floated their teeth using a metal file to smooth out the rough pointed parts, administered anti-parasite paste for worms, gave the necessary injections and assisted in organising any official veterinary papers required to cross the next border.

At the clubhouse, the supervisor, a small compact little man with no English, offered me free massages. They were good and every time I left, my face, hair and upper body were covered in honey. I made use of his generous offer regularly until his hands started to wander too much.

I relished the food eaten at Chacho's apartment. Breakfasts were made by his house-help and were simply delicious – *chirimoya* fruit shakes, hot rolls and aromatic freshly brewed coffee. For a number of nights Chacho cooked and the combination of spices and flavours he used were out of this world. He had a natural flair for food and a passion to match. We liked red wine in equal measure and it was not long before I fell ill. I committed the two sins of living at high altitudes – I ate spicy food in abundance and had *vino tinto* as if it was about to be taken off the market.

Not only did I have an upset tummy, a few sores formed in the corner of my mouth as well. I was pretty sure it was also an accumulation of the rough living through the *altiplano,* stressful situations, the extreme climates and my unwholesome diet over many weeks.

While I rested and meditated on our next stretch, I had a visit from Tracy, a friend and patron in Ireland. She arrived with twice the weight of her own luggage allowance, carrying a backpack full of surprises and goodies for me from friends in Ireland. I picked her up at the airport and she appeared out of breath.

"I think I suffer from asthma," she said with a serious look on her face.

I laughed. "No, you don't, it's the high altitude. Nothing that a cup of coca tea won't sort out."

Tracy and I decided to spend a few days exploring Peru. It was terrific to have a girlfriend with whom I could giggle and be silly with. As we set off from La Paz, we saw Lake Titicaca through the small plane window. The highest navigable lake in the world, its vivid blue waters shimmered under the blistering sun. They say this is where the Incan Empire originated.

"We must go there another time," Tracy said as she squeezed my hand. I could only nod while trying to fight off the nausea.

I was never a good flyer. The slightest turbulence would set me off, sometimes even causing me to hyperventilate. I was grateful when we finally set down without having thrown up, but probably not as much as Tracy, who could not find a sick bag for me.

For numerous reasons, but mostly because we did not feel like competing with scores of backpackers destroying the magical atmosphere, we decided *not* to visit Machu Pichu the ancient Inca fortress city in the Andes northwest of Cuzco. Instead we visited the Peruvian jungle and had a great time – on the cheap. Tracy fancied the luxurious Sandoval Lake Lodge but I insisted we take the shoe-string option, ignoring the guest tarantulas, no running water, an outside toilet and the same menu every day. I caught my first piranha and the following day we were brave enough to jump into the waters where these carnivorous creatures swim.

Tracy left too soon and once I was on my own again my focus turned to what lay ahead. I headed for the Peruvian Consulate but the Vice Consul seemed more interested in playing solitaire on his computer than helping me. Judging by his weak handshake, I had no great hopes of assistance from him. He indicated that I might have to leave my horses for fifteen days at Desagaudero, the border point between Bolivia and Peru. I asked him if there were facilities for horses and somewhere I could stay. His answer was negative.

That evening I told Chacho about the situation.

"I can't leave my horses for two weeks at a border in the middle of nowhere," I said. "It could be a disaster."

He agreed and we looked at his wall-to-wall South American map hanging in the hallway.

"Maybe you should enter Peru on the right side of Lake Titicaca. There is no immigration point there," he suggested.

"Well, I don't have any problems with that," I said. "But what if I'm halfway through the country and get stopped by police with no entry stamp on my passport and no official papers admitting the horses into the country? They could deport me or even take the horses from me."

He agreed that it might be too risky an option.

"I am not happy with you riding through the Peruvian Andes, girl alone," Chacho said. "It's just too dangerous, especially after the guerrilla war."

Over the previous decades, Peru had fought a bloody and brutal war against the Shining Path guerrilla terrorists, with 30,000 Peruvians killed by one side or the other. The goal of the Shining Path was to defeat the existing government and replace it with a totalitarian socialist utopia. In their quest they had no hesitation about slaughtering peasants who got in the way.

According to Chacho's explanation, the Fujimori government proved to be as vicious as the Shining Path and the military and the police continued to be responsible for murders, arbitrary detentions, torture, rapes and disappearances. Violence against women and children were continuing problems.

Chacho's face lit up. "Why don't you travel to Chile and take a boat from there to Central America?"

I sighed. "That means going south again, through the *altiplano*."

"True," Chacho agreed. "That and about 90 kilometres of desert before you will reach Arica. No, there has to be another option."

He rubbed his face vigorously. "I've got the solution! Why did we not think of this before? You must travel through Beni, the northern part of Bolivia that runs parallel with Peru and then cross into Brazil, straight up through Venezuela. As easy as that."

"That's funny," I said. "I'm reading a John Grisham book that takes place in the Brazilian Amazon. The place sounds intriguing."

"You'll love it," he said enthusiastically. "I worked in both countries. The people are amazing."

Chacho suggested I go to the respective Consulates in the morning and check the requirements for entering their countries with two horses in tow.

I lay in bed that night with many troublesome thoughts spinning through my head.

'How would I know which route was the best to take? Which country to go through? Which ones to avoid? How would I know which paths were safe to travel?'

But I knew I could not let thoughts of the unknown, the obstacles and the trials which followed me like a ghost on my journey turn into fear. To me fear was a paralysing emotion that took up too much packing space. There were no straight answers for what was on my troubled mind but I had to keep the faith that things would continue to work out as they should.

A week before I left La Paz a man approached me on a busy street.

"Careful!" he said.

There was urgency in his voice. I did not know what he wanted but before I could reply he took my arm and pointed to a man looking at us from a distance.

"He has a knife and is planning to steal from you. Quick! Follow me."

My first reaction was to be suspicious of my 'rescuer' but I followed him nevertheless to an office building where he claimed he worked. Once inside, he made me look over my shoulder. My back was covered with sticky *dulce de leche,* a well-known ploy with the aim to distract. I felt a bit shaken. This was the third time somebody had attempted to rob me in La Paz. A few days earlier a man tried to open the zip on my small backpack and shortly after I was spat on – a trick like the *dulce de leche* to catch the victim unawares and rob them off their goods.

I was much more alert when I walked uphill where I found shops, booths and street vendors, offering a staggering array of goods. I soon forgot the near-robbery and immersed myself in the wonderful woven goods of alpaca and *llama* wool, musical instruments, antiques, foodstuffs and hardware. What I found most fascinating were all the items a well-equipped *brujo* (witch doctor) might need, including herbs, potions and most intriguingly, dried *llama* foetuses.

Towards the end of November I began to feel more confident about my trip and proposed route and for the first time since arriving in La Paz I felt ready to go again. On the last Saturday of the month I visited the horses and spent more time with them than usual. I groomed them thoroughly and trimmed their fringes and manes. After the few weeks break I was worried I might be uneasy with them. Surprisingly it was not the case and I felt strong and in control. Edwin, the stable-boy, would not take the money I offered in exchange for his help.

"God will protect you on your way," he said with conviction. "Do you have a gun? Just in case God was not looking and you needed help."

He was full of suggestions.

"You should take a dog as well. He can guard you when you sleep alone in your tent in the middle of nowhere."

I told him I had thought about the idea at one stage but was not sure if I would be up for the added responsibility. Two horses were enough of a handful.

Mise and Tusa also got new shoes. They would not stand still for the farrier though and needed to be tranquilised. I only realised later during my trip that it had less to do with their character and more to do with their lack of trust in the farrier.

Things were looking good for travelling through Brazil and Venezuela. It took me ten days to get all the official documentation sorted. We had a visit from Chacho's doctor friend who advised me to buy Vitamin B injections, apparently an excellent guard against mosquitoes. The three of us shared three glasses of red wine with a fast waltz, called "*Palabras para Julia*" playing in the background. The words, '*You never say on the road you can't no more, there are others waiting for you,*' were most appropriate.

Three days before my departure, Chacho's right-hand man took me for my compulsory yellow fever injection, a prerequisite for entering Brazil. I am not keen on injections and looked away as the needle pierced my skin.

I was warned by those in the know *not* to attempt the Cumbre Pass with the horses, a notorious road that drops 9,850 feet from La Paz to Coroico in Yungas. The road is known to be the most fatal in the world and the number of casualties per kilometre higher than anywhere else. With blind corners every hundred metres, landslides, rock falls and no barriers, it is easy to imagine that any slight lapse in concentration, for rider or driver, could result in a freefall catastrophe. At some points the road is only ten feet wide. Crosses, shrines and rock memorials dot the road as you descend, each telling a tragic story. I was told that drivers sprinkle their trucks with alcohol for good luck before setting off downhill.

The night before our departure by truck from La Paz, Chacho and I shared a last farewell glass of *vino tinto* while he concentrated on carving Jo's name on a piece of wood he nailed into the shape of a cross.

The following day, not far from the start to the Cumbre Pass, I spotted an open space on the side of the road, a deep valley, covered in heavy mist spread out below. I indicated for the driver to stop. It turned out to be a spot where people brought offerings to the mountains in thanks for protection. An emotional moment for me and already having cried twice that morning when asked about the cross, I slowly walked to the edge, not wanting to forget the moment. Jo's face was very clear and vivid in my mind. It was as if she was there. I could feel her presence and although sad, a sudden peace swept over me. It was as if she was consoling me, urging me not to worry, to go on, and to continue to live life. I inhaled the heavy misty air, a weight falling off my shoulders. I could almost hear her whisper. *'Go on. Everything is going to be okay.'*

I erected Jo's cross at the edge of the mountain, a few stones helped to keep it upright. I lit a piece of incense and said a prayer to a wonderful woman, mother and friend. Her spirit will live forever.

Even though the drive down the Cumbre was spectacular, I cannot say that I enjoyed it. Even from the safety of a truck cabin the experience was nerve-racking. The horses stood steady in the back, secretly pleased I am sure for not having to walk that dangerous road. At a snail's pace we crossed the high Andean passes before descending through cloud-forest, under waterfalls on to steamy Amazonian jungle.

"If you think you're too small to make an impact, go to bed with a mosquito"
— Anita Roddick

The heat was oppressive when we arrived in San Borga. A cute little boy jumped on the step on the side of the driver's door and chatted enthusiastically while the truck kept moving, sharing all the gossip of people that had come through. All this was said with an earnest face, punctuated by many laughs. Winking, he agreed to having his photograph taken.

While we waited in the scorching heat for Romeiro Ferreira, the manager of Espiritu farm, four people on a motorbike whizzed past. I had to do a double-take when I saw a woman sitting at the back, breastfeeding.

At Romeiro's house his family could not have been friendlier. They were laid-back and relaxed and had an attitude about them that you only get from people that live in hot, tropical areas. Their reluctance to move in a hurry was understandable; it was simply too damn hot to exert any unnecessary energy. They gave me my own room with netting instead of glass covering the window-area. A cold shower only helped momentarily and soon the sweat was dripping from my face again. One of the girls took me around town on their family motorbike in search of a long-sleeved cotton shirt I could use while riding. Everybody was out on their bikes and I struggled to discern any clear road rules.

Back at the house I administered my first Vitamin B injection in the upper right leg. In a perverse kind of way I was looking forward to doing it – the thought made me feel quite adventurous, like a real explorer. But the reality was in harsh contrast to my temporary Indiana Jones-like excitement. It burnt like hell and the novelty of sticking a needle into my own flesh lost its daredevil appeal rather quickly.

Romeiro asked two *gauchos* who did a regular cattle-run between San Borga and Espiritu to accompany me through off-the-beaten-track roads and farms, 120 kilometres of swamps, grasslands and tropical forest. Our first day's ride started on a leisurely note. I noticed that the women stayed very much in the background and the wife of the owner of the farm where we were getting ready acted mainly as nurturer. She brought us all cold drinks, said nothing and stood by for re-fills.

I received silent respect from all the horsemen standing around when single-handedly I saddled up the horses, connecting the ropes on the saddle bags very fast and without hesitation, and tying up everything smoothly and accurately.

'If only you could see me now, Zavaletta.'

My two companions admired my saddle and equipment – I glanced at their basic, poor-looking gear and felt a bit embarrassed. Edgar was a healthy-looking young man with very white teeth. He rode a mule. It had long ears that flapped in all directions like a windmill as we walked. It looked comical but I tried not to laugh in front of him or his owner. Ernesto, a man in his fifties with a pleasant demeanour, rode an ordinary grey horse. Initially we all talked a bit and I answered their questions but soon we fell silent. Mise and Tusa struggled to keep up with the pace and every now and then I had to put them into a trot. I got the impression that the two men were not overly keen on my horses.

Edgar did notice my relationship with them though and said, "I can see your horses are obedient and listen when you say no."

They thought it very strange that I talked to Mise and Tusa while I thought it quite peculiar that the mule and horse they rode did not even have names.

The landscape was flat, the wide dirt road smooth with not many curves and no surprises. The trees on both sides were short making it possible to see very far. A couple of times large numbers of Brahman cattle appeared from the opposite direction, kicking up dust and driven on by men on horses. Other than that the road was quiet.

My guides had their routine set out and after a few hours on the road we stopped for lunch. Edgar took out his hammock and attached it to two trees. He must have read my mind and offered that I lie in it. At 4 p.m. we stopped at another farm. A woman brought out a tray with three glasses of water, no questions asked.

Once on the trail again we got caught by a sudden rainstorm that lasted no more than twenty minutes. While still on their respective animals, Edgar and Ernesto huddled closely under a torn plastic poncho. Just before I was completely soaked I managed to get my rain poncho on. By 6 p.m. I was really tired. So too was Mise. Tusa was not on the leading rope and I could hear him stumble a few times at the back. We rode for more than an hour in the dark through long plantations of palm trees forming a roof over our heads. I could hardly see the two men riding in front displaying a jovial camaraderie with much shared laughter. I trusted Mise to keep us on the trail.

The woman on the farm where we eventually came to a halt for the night knew Edgar and Ernesto. We were greeted with a soft handshake and four kids hiding behind her, big-eyed. We were offered a strange tasting sweet drink with unidentifiable bits in it. A weak paraffin lamp provided the only source of light and it was difficult to make out any of the faces. I felt wrecked and my body ached. I could barely manage a conversation and instead sat back and listened. Later I pitched my tent with the kids holding the lantern. The woman was preparing food outside and strange smelling odours drifted in our direction. I struggled to work up an appetite despite the sizzling sounds of hot oils splashing in the large black pan. I was barely able to force down the greasy egg and chips.

"Why don't you eat meat?" Edgar asked.

I mumbled something and he did not pursue the matter.

"I feel the distance tomorrow to Espiritu is too much for one day's ride," I said.

They tried to convince me that it was not that far and Ernesto laughed when I said *"en serio"* (in all seriousness).

Four hungry dogs stared longingly, saliva dripping from their mouths, while Ernesto sucked the last bits of juice from his chicken bone. I soon excused myself and went behind a building to brush my teeth and have a pee in pitch darkness. Nobody could tell me where was most appropriate to go. I could not find a soft, grassy spot and ended up with urine splashed all over my leg. Just as I put the toilet paper in the V of the tree, I sensed movement and heard a growl from nearby. I did not linger to investigate and made a beeline for my tent. I removed my pants and top once I had turned off the torch. The tent was flimsy and I did not fancy being seen in only my underwear. It was still hot and I kept the cover in front of the netting of the tent open. I used my flip-flop to squash an orange cockroach settling in for the night right above my head.

The two men had put their mosquito net make-shift homes behind me. They seemed to have no qualms about sleeping on the cement ground. My situation was not much better but I was grateful for at least a thin yoga mat and sleeping bag underneath me.

We were up at 5 a.m. the following morning. Little did I know that the stretch between that farm and Espiritu would end up being the longest day's ride of my entire journey. Had I known that we would reach our destination seventeen hours after we had saddled up that morning, I would have said it was utter madness and something I had no intention of undertaking.

We were still off the beaten track and travelled through water, long grass and muddy terrain. Mise and Tusa sloshed through the swampy areas, their metal shoes making it difficult to move easily. The mule and grey horse were not shod and seemed to struggle much less. We stopped a few hours later at a big pond and the horses stood knee-deep in the water. It took a few 'mud bombs' to get them moving again. Tusa tried to escape and a chase resulted in me tripping over and falling into a mud bath. I looked and felt a real mess.

When we had yet another stop, late afternoon at Hacienda Tucumán, I became increasingly agitated.

"Do we have much further to go?" I asked wearily.

My guides looked at each other. "About 15 kilometres more," said Ernesto.

I was not sure if I was up to another two hour's ride but I was also keen to get there. "Right," I said after some thought. *"Vamos."*

But they were not ready yet. We sat in a dusty room with the sun throwing soft long shadows through the horizontal slats framing the windows. Only after they had three slow helpings of a salty bleak-looking chicken dish did we get going again.

We were hardly on the road for five minutes when I discovered Tusa had gone in the opposite direction. I put Mise into a gallop and went after him. The pack had gone loose and he had simply turned around to get my attention. There were puddles of water everywhere and while I secured the pack, mosquitoes attacked me and the horses with equal vigour.

As we rode through muddy grasslands, Brahmans grazing in the distance, I looked up at the sky, a spectacular cocktail of pinks and blues hung over the enormous open spaces for as far as the eye could see. I felt overwhelmed by emotion at such a beautiful sight and fought back the tears. In that moment my desire was simple. All I wanted was an understanding companion on my side, one with whom I could share these places, the highs and the lows, the victories and the frustrations. I had always been adamant that I wanted to travel alone but at that moment, I wished so much for a trusted friend with whom I could be happy and sad.

I composed myself before Edgar and Ernesto could notice they were riding with a cry baby. A cool breeze swept over my face as I rocked back and forth to Mise's comforting rhythm.

Darkness was beginning to fall. We kept up a steady pace, passing through palm trees curved in arches over the dirt road, birds' chatter echoing from the green forest. It made for eerie yet strangely fascinating riding. Once outside the density of the forest, the trail was lit up by the moon, sometimes partially obscured by rain clouds.

By 9:30 p.m. my whole body ached and the pain, especially in my knees, was excruciating. There was still no sight of Espiritu. I took my feet out of the stirrups and let them dangle by the sides but this caused friction on my thighs as they rubbed against the saddle. It was a matter of deciding between the lesser of two aches. At 10 p.m. both Mise and I went into auto-mode. In the distance to the front I could just about make out Tusa behind the men and their horses. Everything was happening in slow-motion and I had stopped caring if and when we would ever arrive. It was nearly 11 p.m. when I spotted an aeroplane in a field. I sat up straight on Mise. This must be it. I envisioned pure luxury at the farm – a hot shower and a comfortable bed...

We were met by an Indian man called Victor, standing motionless in the dark. He said very little and only motioned us over to where Mise and Tusa could be unsaddled. I said a quick thank you and goodbye to Edgar and Ernesto who disappeared quickly into the night.

I was taken into a small house and while I wondered where my bedroom would be, the lady of the house proceeded to move the dining table away to make space for my bed. I was crestfallen. An ancient-looking mattress was brought out. I sighed but Victor's wife appeared unfazed by my irritation. There was no shower and I rinsed myself down using buckets of water out in the open in the back.

After I had thoroughly sprayed the outside of my mattress to keep away spiders and other creepy crawlies, I crashed out. I was sure that most likely it was flea-infested but sleep beckoned before I could fret any more.

It was probably most appropriate that Monday, the 16th of December turned out to be a respite for us. In South Africa my home country, it is a public holiday called the Day of Reconciliation, the hope being for understanding and harmony between different racial groups at the end of Apartheid. Ironically the day was previously called Dingane's Day, referring to the Battle of Blood River when 470 Boers took on 10,000 Zulus and came out on top.

But for me, six months after I had commenced my expedition, no battle or politics entered my mind on this day. For me it was just another timely opportunity to rest and chill out.

Victor gave me a lift on his *moto* (motorbike) to the room where I would be staying the following night and then dropped me off at the house of one of the workers where I was going to have breakfast. I was struck by the tidiness of the small settlement. Caribbean music with that typical laid-back beat was playing quietly and chickens scratched in the early morning sun. His daughter, a girl of about nine, set the table. Like all kids who grow up having to work and take responsibility from an early age she had an appealing mature attitude and friendly manner. A hammock in the middle of the room swung gently back and forth. Inside a tiny baby was sleeping peacefully. I could see the mother in the kitchen through netting where you expected there would be walls. She had the help of a few other women preparing breakfast. They were not invited into the dining area and made no attempt at contact although that did not stop them from listening attentively to the conversation which revolved mostly around questions and answers about my journey.

The following day I was accompanied by yet another guide to lead the way to Santa Rosa, 65 kilometres away.

At one farm where we stopped for breakfast one of the girls asked, "Would you swap Mise for one of our horses? She is beautiful."

"Never," I replied.

She wanted to know if I would stay for the night.

I gave her a hug. "No, sorry, next time."

"*Cuando?*" she asked.

My guide left to check out the river-route which could make the day's ride about

15 kilometres shorter. He came back a short while later.

"I think it'll be difficult, but it depends on you."

The girls at the house, keen for some action, saddled up their own horses, grabbed a gun, their hats and a plastic container and left with us. Three dogs ran alongside barking excitedly. At the river, my guide scooped the water out of a canoe, took off his shoes and put on short pants. I proceeded to take off my boots as well.

"No, no, you go in the canoe," he ordered.

I felt a bit disappointed, the idea of going through the water bareback on the horses had the potential for a thrill. I had nothing to complain about though. The close brush with a yellow cobra a short time later while going through a narrow trail of grasslands gave me enough of an adrenalin rush. I did not notice this lethal poisonous snake until he was nearly on top of us, swishing past aggressively right in front of Tusa's feet. Thankfully he wanted to put as much distance between us as we did, and disappeared quietly into the greenery.

In another town the old man of the house where I was staying gave me the rundown on all the dangers I could expect en-route through tropical Beni. He mentioned tigers, long distances and no houses or people around. He fell asleep in his chair shortly after, content that he had done his duty by warning me.

Riding through Bolivia was done mostly in solitude. It gave ample time for thinking, recounting memories and reminiscing, especially about my days as a young girl.

According to my mom I was a go-getter and self reliant from an early age. In fact, she claimed I was doing my own thing even before I could walk properly. She used to tell people with pride how I bathed and dressed myself at the age of two. It is funny how the memories I have of myself as an eight, nine or ten-year old were different. Even though I had an independent streak, I would have described myself as shy and cautious, self-conscious in front of people and easily embarrassed when too much attention was paid to me. It was a nightmare to have people over for dinner. I was fine if I could listen, join in the laughter or kick my youngest brother under the table. Just do not ask me a question. I was known for biting glasses to pieces if I found all eyes on me waiting for a response to something that somebody had asked.

Our farm in South Africa was 35 kilometres away from the local school and the everyday commuting wore me out. So, at the vulnerable age of six, my parents made the heart-wrenching decision to send us to boarding school. When my mom realised I was serious about my journey on horseback, she mentioned those years.

"I always knew it would stand you in good stead. You learned to fight your own battles and be strong."

It did make me strong but they were tough times too. For both of us. One time I had the blues by mid-week. I could not bear the thought of two more lonely nights without my mother. So I pretended to be ill. I wailed for hours, until the matron finally called my mom who stood at my bedside an hour later. I had my bag already packed. I was ready to go home. But mom knew that would have been a mistake, so after a while she kissed me and reluctantly left. It felt as if my heart had been ripped out. I followed her down the long cold corridor, shouting and crying. She upped her pace and closed the double glass doors behind her, before rushing off to her car. I banged on the glass and called out for her. She did not look back.

Years later we talked about it.

"I so badly wanted to turn around and give you one more hug," she said, obviously sad at the memory, "but I could not. I could not allow you to see the tears on my face."

I was nine and still at boarding school when homesickness 'forced' me into yet another stunt. Pretending to have a serious stomach ache, a doctor was soon called out. An uncomfortable internal examination followed. Next I found myself tucked into a hospital bed, conscious of nothing else but the disinfectant smells and heavily starched linen scratching my skin. My mom and dad were there with the 'devastating' news.

"They are going to remove your appendix. The doctor says it is serious. He is treating it as an emergency."

There was nothing wrong and I do not know how I managed to keep a straight face. The operation duly went ahead. I got a week off school and even though the pain was severe when I laughed or coughed, it was worth it. I was home.

As I swayed back and forth to Tusa's lazy walk, deep in thought, I realised that maybe all those experiences did serve me well. It must have toughened me up somehow, enough anyway to have braved these unknown roads with gusto, although inexperienced and unsure. If only mom could see her little 'glass-eater' girl now.

Everyday when we rested, I had a constant battle with ants. They seemed to congregate exactly where I planned to plonk myself down for a while. The big ones bit unbelievably hard and the little ones seemed to infiltrate every pore of my body, just because they could. Usually for the duration of the rest I would lash out at them with the crop, squashing them as they crawled frantically around my yoga mat.

For most of the journey through Beni the roads were deserted. At times I had the pure luxury of opening up my shirt soaked in perspiration, to let in a cool breeze. I would sit there on my mat, saddlebags behind my back, watching the horses, sometimes playing my Irish tin whistle. Mise had no appreciation for my musical abilities and usually walked away after the first few notes.

The day I lost my tent, probably my most valued and critical possession at that stage, is one I remember clearly. It was strapped on Mise and when I looked back again it was gone. There were no cars on the road and when a bus appeared I knew the driver would have seen the tent on the way and probably picked it up. I tried to flag him down but was left with a cloud of dust in my face. His refusal to stop confirmed my suspicions. Still, I did not want to take any chances so I tied Tusa under a tree and started backtracking. After four kilometres I knew the tent was gone.

The tent was my comfort blanket. I knew that if we were in the middle of nowhere, at least I would have something over my head for the night. My knees ached and I felt miserable. I blamed everyone. Nobody had showed me how to tie up the pack properly, the shape of the tent had not been practical and Tusa was giving me grief, trotting like a crab, making it impossible for me to have Mise (acting as packhorse for the day) on the leading rope where I could keep an eye on her.

Ultimately I had to admit that it was my fault alone.

When we arrived back to where Tusa was tied up, I discovered that three pigs had ransacked my saddlebags and finished off all my biscuits and bread rolls. They trampled the bags, smearing them with their filthy trotters and rotten smells.

Three days before Christmas, I left the horses behind and took a truck to Riberalta, the last major town before the Brazilian border.

I knew I could not continue through Beni without a tent. The truck was full of Brahman cows and four little piglets. I sat in the front with Angel the driver and Karan – a woman who suffered from a bad case of verbal diarrhoea and who just could not keep quiet for a minute. She invited me to stay at her house in Riberalta.

"*No cobro*" (I don't charge), she said.

I would have preferred arranging my own accommodation for more privacy but could not find a way to decline the offer. I knew the move would also help me save money, especially as I had to buy another tent.

The cows were restless in the back and I cringed every time the boys used a stick to get the weaker ones to stand up, poking their backs without mercy. The poor piglets got trampled on and every now and then loud squealing erupted when yet another one got squashed under a cow's foot.

I frantically planned my route as we drove along (the distance calculator in the truck was broken), trying to calculate distances and work out where I would sleep and find food. Checking the availability of water along the way was important too. The road was quiet and isolated. The few settlements I spotted were poor and very basic.

Karan had a lot of questions which Angel answered as if he were the newly appointed Manager of the TATA Challenge.

He was quite impressed by my trip and pointed out to Karan, "Other people might have come through here on their bicycles from the United States but this girl is travelling alone. *Solita.*"

I blushed when he looked at me with admiration.

"*Que valiente*" (what bravery), he said, shaking his head.

Riberalta was not what I imagined as I had expected a more developed, bigger town. First we unloaded the cattle that were heading for the slaughter house. I could not help making a comment about my dislike for these places. Young boys were standing around aimlessly. They were throwing fire-crackers in the street, enticing dogs to investigate, just to have them explode in their faces. Roars of laughter followed. The boys looked over at the truck and I shook my head furiously in disapproval.

Karan's place, which she shared with her sister, mother, 84-year-old father and many other young children and teenagers, was an interesting, dilapidated mad-house. An open area between a number of rooms and the main house served as a washing place for the women who came in to scrub clothes and bed linen. On the other side, not far from the door of my room, was an area where animals were slaughtered. For the duration of my stay there was the constant smell of dead meat and blood hanging in the air. I was amazed at all the kids running around, clothes strewn everywhere and TV's blaring. Lights did not work, the mosquito netting in my room was torn and toilets did not flush. Chickens had the run of the place and one speckled hen in particular loved the warmth of my saddlebags. The soundtrack to the chaos was provided by the Christmas tree, which repeated "*Jingle Bells*" over and over again. A rainstorm not only brought more mosquitoes but completely drenched my bed. I had never seen a house with so many leaks.

But I was grateful for Karan's generous offer and not having to worry about finding a place to stay.

Christmas came and went.

On the 26th of December I received an email from Dave;

Hi Mar,

I'd say you had a different Christmas day and will have a different new year, which I have to say is quite a nice thing to do. You know what to expect here at all times, so newness is a great adventure. I wish you every safety and happiness for the New Year. I know it will bring each side of that equilibrium of adventure, the bad inherent in the good parts and vice versa. See it, live it, hear it, touch it, smell it and above all live it as a whole. In that way we can keep all facets of it in perspective.

I'll stay in touch while you stay safe.

In the town of Riberalta young people hung around the square Plaza. Almost everybody between the ages of fifteen and twenty-five had a moped and early evening the place was busy with youngsters going round and round, flirting, chatting and arranging dates for the disco later. The girls pulled out all the stops, wearing short mini skirts, flashing smooth brown skin and skimpy, sexy underwear. They were all obviously extremely conscious of their bodies and how they looked. Here women had only two shapes, they were either skinny and trim or, for those who seemed to have given up on the notion of true love, obese.

While in Riberalta, I made up boxed parcels each containing canned peaches, a bottle of water, crackers and tomatoes. For a treat, I put a pineapple into some. These boxes were dropped off in different locations as I made my way back again, two days after Christmas to where the horses were waiting, 400 kilometres away. I would ask the truck driver to stop in a village, jump off and ask the unsuspecting villagers to mind the parcel for me.

"I'll be here in about one week with my horses," I would say enthusiastically.

In one spot there was only a deserted house next to a tiny chapel and not a soul in sight. Somebody told me the place was called Hacienda Buena Hora, meaning 'farm of good hour'. While the truck-driver waited, the back filled with passengers, I went into a dusty room that was open and left my parcel under a mattress. I calculated I would be there in about four days.

Back at Casa Blanca (where I had left the horses behind), after an eight hour journey in the truck, I put on my bathing suit and joined a local woman scrubbing clothes on a long wooden plank in a large dam. With the horses grazing happily a few yards away, I gave my clothes, trainers, the horse-blankets and girths, a thorough wash. I hung everything on the wire fencing just as the sun was setting.

Afterwards, I took the saddle and reins outside and started polishing the leather. A teenager, about seventeen, came over to have a look and soon there were about eight of his friends standing around. One read the message on my sheepskin from José the *gaucho* in Tucumán and raised his eyebrows in a mock gesture. He brought out his colourful silver, leather-thong reins.

"Would you like to swap?" he asked.

I said thanks very much but his was too heavy for the horses for everyday riding.

I heard them later discussing the journey and telling those who did not know the details, bits about my travels. Had you not known any better you would have sworn they had taken every step with us.

I struggled to eat dinner that evening after I had witnessed a piglet being dragged from the truck, his fore-legs and snout rubbing on the gravel. He hardly made a noise and it seemed had already accepted his fate. A while later my soup contained no meat even though I had no doubt that the flavour was pork.

A scary-looking flying cockroach was twitching nervously on the ceiling in my room just as I was about to settle into my sleeping bag. I attacked him with my crop but it took about six hits and a number of bangs from a shampoo bottle before he stopped kicking.

I fell asleep quickly but the night was not a peaceful one (maybe the bloody death of the cockroach brought me bad karma). I woke up only after a couple of hours sleep to men chatting loudly outside and the radio on full blast. One man was continuously spitting deeply from the back of his throat. I finally got up when I could not stand it any more. My pleas to the group to be a bit quieter fell on deaf ears. Why would they care that I had to face the heat the following day and do about 40 kilometres on horseback?

When I finally dragged myself from my bed at 5 a.m. the majority of them were still downing beers outside.

Even after five days rest Tusa was dragging his feet. I did not urge him on too much. I could understand his lack of energy. It was early morning and I struggled to stay awake myself. The fierce heat forced us to keep the pace slow. A warm wind was blowing as we passed grasslands with pools of water almost every hundred yards. We stopped for an early breakfast when we reached the fifth one.

I spotted a large log a few yards away from the water and considered it ideal on which to prepare my rolls and tea. I let go of the reins to allow the horses drink. I strolled over to the log and nearly collapsed. It had moved! My jaw dropped when a large alligator, his sunbathing interrupted, edged his heavy body into the muddy pond. There was no splash, just a few ripples on the surface of the water indicated his departure. I stood frozen and then looked over at the horses, slurping water blissfully.

"Mise, Tusa! Get away from there!"

I managed to half roar, half whisper. I rushed over and was horrified when I saw Tusa, walking deeper into the water.

"No Tusa, no!"

I was frantic but too afraid to go after him, not knowing where the alligator was heading. I grabbed Mise and prayed that Tusa would follow when he saw us heading towards the road. He looked at us and neighed. I walked backwards and kept on calling his name.

"Come on Tusa, come on!"

I let out a sigh of relief when he finally turned around and came running towards us.

After we had passed a number of ponds with numerous alligators spread out along the banks (nobody had warned us of their existence in these parts), I finally let Tusa run free again. But it turned out to be a mistake. I knew he was lingering behind, nibbling on grass every now and then but when I looked again he was going in the opposite direction. I chased after him but he went into a gallop, literally running away from us as if it was a game.

When I finally caught up with him (he came to a stop to eat some more), I was not in a good mood.

"What the hell are you thinking?" I shouted.

He looked at me sheepishly as I got off Mise. I walked over to him, took the rope on his halter in my hand and out of frustration, gave him a rap on the hindquarters with the crop. It was a stupid thing to do. Without warning, he broke free and charged away from us into a large open space next to the road. To my horror, Mise followed. I ran after them, past alligator infested ponds and through long grass.

The surface of the ground was very uneven, lumps of dried clay that looked like miniature mountains made progress difficult. The plus side was that the horses struggled too. They did not look back once while I continued to plead and shout. I tried to catch them by going in a loop but Tusa broke into a trot every time I came too close. The gods were looking down on us when Mise's foot got tangled in the reins and she was forced to stop. Tusa, realising that Mise was not running with him anymore came to a halt a bit further on. With Mise in tow we walked slowly in his direction until I could get hold of him. With the sun burning down and sweat streaming down my back we stumbled back to the main road.

I had a fair idea that the stretch between Puerto Therezal and Hacienda Buena Hora (where I had left my box of food under the mattress) was going to be a long one. So when my alarm went off at 5 a.m. I was up in a flash. On the other side of the bridge curious bystanders wanted to inspect the horses' shoes.

"Your horses are in good condition," they commented.

I smiled proudly. "Yes, I do not like to see any animal that is too thin."

I could not let the opportunity pass and added that neither could I stand people who treat their animals badly.

I gave this lecture regularly, hoping that my words would inspire others to take better care of their own animals and pets. Just the night before, I had seen a girl hitting a cat when it came closer for a rub. The animals here acted strangely when you wanted to touch them, most cowered away, expecting to be struck by an angry hand or kicking foot.

Outside town I noticed a dead horse in a field, his legs in the air, tummy blown up. It was a sad and disturbing sight. I hoped Mise, who always seem to be affected when we stumbled across a dead or distressed animal, had not seen it.

When we took a break three hours later, two *gauchos* came along. We shook hands. They did not ask the usual 'what are you doing here, where do you come from' questions, which made a refreshing change. Their horses wore elaborate reins. Heavy leather tassels and silver bits decorated their foreheads and the sides of their faces.

"Don't the horses find those reins uncomfortable?" I asked.

"No *señora*, they love it," the man answered in all seriousness.

In the late afternoon, I saw a few men on the side of the road. I asked them the distance to Hacienda Buena Hora.

"Are you going to stay there tonight?" one of them asked.

"No, of course not," I lied. "I'm pushing on past that to spend the night at a house where people live."

"Sure," they said. "You'll find something, probably two hours from Buena Hora."

I did not want those men knowing where I was putting my head down that night. Too many people already knew, a thought I did not find comforting. The whole area was particularly isolated and should I have received unexpected visitors with bad intentions, a cry for help would have had no effect at all.

Jaded and hungry, I could not wait to put my feet up, watch the sun go down and tuck into the box of food waiting for me. After 60 kilometres on the road my back was in agony.

When I finally led the horses through the small front gate at Hacienda Buena Hora, a door creaked open up with an eerie sound, then slammed closed with the wind. The three of us jumped. I took out my pistol and entered the room where I had left the food. A lizard on the wall watched me intently with beady eyes. The silence was heavy and disconcerting. Afraid to breathe I slowly walked to the back room and lifted up the filthy mattress. The box was gone.

A wave of disappointment swept over me. I did not know if I should cry or shout. I ended up doing neither. I was deflated, numb and exhausted and could not quite believe that somebody would maliciously have taken my food. I knew that it had to be somebody that was on the truck the day we drove back from Riberalta.

I strolled to a pond a few hundred yards down the main road. I stripped down and with a bar of soap in hand ventured into the muddy water. I kept a watchful eye on the road in case any vehicles approached. There was neither sight nor sound of anyone around. Once dry I let off three shots into the air. Not only did I want to make sure my gun was still in working order, I also wanted to scare away anybody harbouring ideas to rob me. The loud bangs helped ease the anger and frustration I still felt about the stolen food.

Shortly before darkness a young man on his motorbike stopped to chat for a while. I hinted about my lack of food. Although he lived nearby on a farm he made no suggestions for assistance. He did however show me a well near the side of the house, indicating that the water from the muddy pond, despite my purifying tablets, would not be suitable to drink. Before I settled down for the night, I administered an injection to keep the mosquitoes away. I also hoped the sardines and raw garlic I consumed in large quantities in Puerto Therezal would help.

I spent the night in my tent in a restless state, alert and conscious of every sound.

Australia, a tranquil village, little thatched houses on both sides of the road, open porches and hammocks and a river down a slope, was 'home' for two days over the New Year. Cows, horses, dogs and chickens walked around freely. I was offered a room with crumbling mud walls, a dirt floor, a large hole where the window was supposed to be and a mosquito net with numerous gaps, hanging over the bed.

I asked the lady of the *pensión* if I could have something to eat.

"I'll pay *señora* and please if possible, no meat. Anything else is fine."

She mumbled something and returned a short while later. I stared at the tray, consisting only of a few slices of white bread and a mug of black tea. I could feel my strength waning, not having eaten since the morning before.

"Do you think I might have something more?" I begged.

She grunted and appeared after a long wait with rice, tomato and a fried egg on a plate.

The woman had two young boys who scrutinised me with great curiosity. They asked me to translate Spanish words into English but their understanding of even the most basic words was poor. The younger of the two sat next to me, slurping and chewing loudly with exaggerated movements of his mouth. I made my excuses and had a shower outside, standing in a basin under a hose pipe. My hair got its first wash in twelve days.

I woke the next morning with four girls staring through the hole in the wall, not uttering a word.

"What do you want?" I said rather grumpily.

Their eyes searched my room with belongings scattered all over. They had misunderstood my question and were actually looking for something they might like to have. I laughed and shook my head.

I bought eggs and sardines in the one and only local shop. Well, the word 'shop' might be an exaggeration, it was more like a dark, stuffy room with a narrow counter and crooked shelves behind, stocked with a few basic necessities. I answered the woman's question as to where I was staying.

"Aah, down at the Hotel," she said with a knowing nod.

Later, as I was sitting on my bed reading, a sharp desperate noise from an animal outside caught my attention. What I saw made me feel sick. A young boy was swinging a terrified chicken by its legs, round and round. Next he would aim it at his brother, standing about ten yards away, attempting to hit him by throwing the helpless creature in his direction. I was fuming. I ran towards him and grabbed his arm.

"It's very bad what you're doing!," I shouted.

He looked at me wide-eyed, slightly shocked but embarrassed as well. Nobody had ever told him off for doing *that*. I grabbed the injured chicken and stormed off. It seemed unable to walk and I put it down on a spot of grass, away from the thoroughfare. It sat there motionless for the next two days. I brought over crackers and water. I had a strong urge to use my machete and relieve it of its misery but feared the reaction from the owners.

Looking back, I doubt if I would have had the guts to decapitate the chicken. I remember as a young girl I once stepped on to a baby chick by accident. It lay there half-paralysed, making awful noises. I was mortified to see it in that condition but had to ask somebody else to kill it. I walked away with my fingers in my ears.

I know two girls from Portugal who believe it is crucial to put on a pair of brand new knickers on New Years Eve. Apparently, it means a good start to the year. I did not have that luxury but at least made sure to put on a fresh pair for the evening after I had washed myself in the river below.

Despite the man of the house tucking into a plate of hot food, nothing was offered for dinner and I had to be content with my last can of peaches and some olives. I asked the woman if I could have hot water for tea. By her expression I might as well have asked if I could borrow her husband for the night. Her movements and body language exuded laziness. When she did not waddle around the house, she rocked back and forth in a hammock. It took too much effort to use one of her legs to get the hammock moving again, a large stick served that purpose.

A New Year's service was in full swing and the sounds of the evangelical hymns drifted through the quiet air. I blew out my candle long before midnight.

On the way the following day, I saw a sign that read 'Restaurant 24 hour Service'. I tied the horses to an old wagon and proceeded to ask for bread. I was told there was none.

Frustrated and hungry I said, "But it says restaurant on the outside."

They shrugged their shoulders and without saying another word, I proceeded to unsaddle the horses. I made myself comfortable against the wheel of the wagon, preparing tomato on crackers and coffee with lukewarm water. A short while later, a girl with a friendly manner came over and shook my hand. She had two small kids hanging on to her hands. The little boy had a cute smile and was talkative.

"Why do you sit on the ground and eat?" he enquired. "Can I have some of your chocolate biscuits?"

His mother gave him a look that kept him quiet but only for a short while. She asked if I fancied sitting inside.

"No thanks," I replied, "It's nice to sit out in the breeze."

The girl left only to appear with a plate full of plantain, rice, sausage and something that looked like spare-ribs. I felt overwhelmed at such a hospitable gesture. Even more surprising was when a boy of about fifteen came over to give the horses water. I loved their initiative, something you would seldom find in the *altiplano* where you had to ask for everything.

From Sheraton onwards the scenery became much more tropical with palm trees and a chorus of chirping green parrots everywhere. The trail was narrow and the dense trees nearby threw long shadows over the red dirt road. We stopped at a place called Comunidad Delmira where I wanted to buy bread. I got the usual *"no hay"* and even though I was greeted with handshakes, I sensed their suspicion.

'Thank God, I don't have to overnight here,' I thought to myself.

They asked no questions and I left rapidly.

After eight hours on the road we arrived at our next port of call. A girl not older than ten, with an endearing smile, opened a gate made from heavy wooden planks so I could enter their property. They called the place America, a tiny one-room house sitting on about two acres with an open porch and outside cooking area.

"Los Mesposa is still far away," she said with sparkling eyes, not hiding her excitement at my arrival. "You should stay with us tonight."

Her father told me to get comfortable in one of the hammocks and proceeded to unsaddle the horses. There were a lot of animals around, three dogs, chickens, ducks, two piglets and even a baby ostrich. I pitched my tent just before the rain started and relished a tasty lunch of crisp fried plantain, salty porridge and rice. Clearly the animals were all hungry and scrambled as if in a race for survival when I chucked the ostrich a few grains of my left-over rice.

I washed my grubby shirt in a half tractor tyre that served as a basin. When I indicated I would like a picture of the family, they all went inside for a change of clothes. A chicken, still alive but not moving, was lying on a bench made from rock. I could not imagine what had been done to get it into such a state. I handed the girl a few newspaper articles about my travels. She blushed.

"I can't read."

She took them from me nevertheless and studied the pictures intently.

The man and his wife had a relaxed attitude with their kids and I observed no shouting or screaming. The children were very obedient and sweet in manner. When the little boy spilled his cup of tea, nobody made a fuss. The mother quietly changed his trousers and handed him another cup. He suffered from a runny tummy and I was glad to have had something in my first-aid kit to help.

Dinner was fried sweet porridge and I kept a bit for breakfast. Suzie, the young girl noticed and handed me some of hers. I gave her a hug.

"I'll remember you on the road tomorrow."

Her big smile said it all.

The shower area was behind torn maize bags, hooked on to wire. Suzie brought me water in a container. It took some effort to wash all the important parts without being seen. I ignored the rooster right above my head, nestled in a tree, getting comfortable for a night's snooze.

In my tent, I listened to a song from Dido, "*Here with me*". For some unexplained reason, a wave of sadness swept over me.

'*Nobody knows where I am tonight,*' I thought to myself.

I missed everything that was dear and familiar to me. Music was an emotive tool. It made me think of times and places. I did not need it now. I turned off my walkman and listened to the sounds of the night. The sun will shine again tomorrow.

It was still dark when I got up. My watch read 4:30 a.m. I tip-toed around the house, trying my best not to wake the family, each of whom was sleeping outside in a hammock with a large mosquito net over it. But they soon rose from their slumbers and without my asking, the man collected the horses. It was a tremendous luxury and what a difference to start the day like that, not feeling hot and bothered before I even got on a horse. They commented on how expertly I got the pack together and tied-up. I laughed.

"After six months, I *should* know."

I received no 'good luck' goodbyes or words of encouragement when we trotted away. But it did not matter. They were simple people whose world revolved around the battle for survival. But they had helped me.

A strong wind was blowing and it got warmer with each passing mile. A woman, selling *chicha* (a maize drink with sugar) appeared like a godsend on the side of the road. I bought three cups and enough to fill up my thermos. It felt good to hand her twice the asking price. She was very sweet and quite inquisitive about my travels.

"God will look after you," she said, handing me a drink on the house.

Her kids did not utter a word.

Having noticed the horses' unenthusiastic trots, I stopped for an early lunch. The first spot was not great with long grass, where, maybe, snakes were lurking. We got to a dried up, semi-muddy pond where I pitched my tent. There was no shade and soon it was like a sauna inside. I picked up the dome tent and moved it to where the horses were partially shaded under trees. When I got into the tent I discovered an army of angry red ants ready to attack. I squashed them until there were none and turned my attention to the horses moving around restlessly. The horse-flies were a real nuisance and for every two I killed four more started to feast on their blood. Realising we would not manage to nap or rest I saddled up again. The clouds had gathered and I was hoping for rain to cool us down.

The reception we received in Kayo could best be described as lukewarm if not unenthusiastic. When I dropped off the box of food a week ago, I do not think anybody really took me seriously or thought they would see me again. Also for them, a visitor with two horses was maybe after all not such a thrilling event. I had to remind myself that I actually preferred people not fussing too much. Maybe I was getting too accustomed to big welcomes.

After a while a wooden bench was brought out for me to sit on and when I asked where I could pitch my tent, Walter, who seemed to be the one calling the shots in the village, ordered one of the girls. "Get a room ready."

My room turned out to be a sort of 'shed' with no solid walls. Around the double bed were wooden poles stuck together with large gaps in-between. It was not difficult to notice the dirt, or the chicken in a box at the foot of the bed. The mattress, covered in a pink synthetic throw, was in a permanent elevated state, rendering the use of pillows unnecessary but also indicating I would be sleeping practically upright.

"We can pitch my tent for some of the kids to sleep in," I offered, thinking that somebody might be minus a bed that night.

On request, a girl brought out the box of food they had minded for the past week. I sat on my bed and opened the carton. I reached inside and felt something strange. I jerked my hand back, slowly peered inside and saw three cockroaches scurrying away. I jumped up, horrified they might get underneath my clothes. I was shocked to see that the packet of crackers, tomato and pineapple had been destroyed. I felt sick with disappointment.

When a market-truck selling food from one of the bigger neighbouring towns stopped in the village later I was first in the queue.

"Where can I put my food where there are no cockroaches?" I asked Walter's wife.

She led me to another house where there was a refrigerator.

'How wonderful,' I thought. 'No creepy insects would get near my food and it'll stay cold as well.'

My elation was short-lived when she opened the door of the fridge. The dirt and smell hit me in the face and at least twenty cockroaches were crawling around. When the woman saw my face, she suggested putting it into the freezer box. It was no better.

"The fridge is not even turned on," I observed.

"We have no electricity," she replied dryly.

I put the cheese and veggies into a plastic container and then into my saddlebags, which I hung on a pole in my room.

It was getting dark and I prepared myself for the night. Worryingly my torch seemed to have little battery power left. I blew out the candles and lay down on my bed. The hen, tied up in the box had quietened down. I must have dozed off for about an hour when I was woken by a sensation of something crawling on me. I shook my arm vigorously and reached for the torch. It only gave off a dim light but enough to see the two cockroaches staring me in the eye, an arms-length away.

'Dammit. Bloody hell!' I shivered. There was no way I could sleep in that room. My torch had ceased to work completely and with a candle, the hot wax dripping over my hand, I made my way outside.

When I reached my pitched tent I said out loud and as sweetly as possible, "Hello. I have a question. Can we please swap? I can't sleep in the room with all the cockroaches."

There was only silence. I repeated my question and a woman, dressed in her underwear, reluctantly peered through the netting. It seemed I had disturbed a moment of passion.

"Ask somebody to put up a mosquito net for you," she suggested.

I was not convinced.

"I don't think that would work *señora*. They come from underneath the mattress."

But she had no intention of leaving the cosy confines of my tent and I had no choice but to go back to my room. I heard her mumble *gringa* and *loca* a few times followed by chuckles from the amorous couple.

The following morning, for reasons unknown to me, I was not called to the breakfast table. Feeling a bit sorry for myself, I headed to where Mise and Tusa were grazing, for a bit of consolation. Fighting back the tears I talked to myself. *'Pull yourself together. You're part of a unique and interesting journey and these upsets are part of the package. Deal with it and get on with it.'*

I felt better and approached Walter a while later.

"Can I please eat as well? Don't worry, I'll pay. But please, I have to eat!"

A plate of food arrived shortly after with a spoon which looked as if it was licked clean. Half of the rice went to the hungry dog at my feet.

I had a world map with me and asked the kids, ranging between eight and twelve to indicate where on the map they lived, where South America was and if they could locate the USA. They did not have a clue. I was not sure if they even attended school and guessed that whenever they were taught something, it was mostly cooking skills and tree-chopping techniques. They had no curiosity and none of them asked me any questions.

One of the women sat nearby eating a piece of fruit, her lips extended to the front, exposing pink gums and half of her teeth missing. She was a dirty mess with food and snot all over her shirt which was a tattered garment she also used to blow her nose. Earlier I had to look away when she and another woman inspected each other's armpits like two monkeys.

The young girls of about eight and nine had many responsibilities. They minded their younger siblings, carrying them on their hips or backs all day and even cooked for them. A girl of about four, her hair tangled and dirty, had taken to me and nestled against my leg while I wrote my diaries. She had a doll with blue hair, attached to her breast.

"Look *señora*," she said in a husky voice. "I'm feeding my baby."

I touched her cheek. It saddened me to think that in eight or nine years she would most likely nurse a real baby of her own.

I calculated three more long days of riding, covering another 160 kilometres before we would reach Riberalta. Little did I know how tough those three days would turn out to be.

On the first day we were surrounded by a swarm of bees during a stop. I spotted a few buzzing around and within minutes there were about thirty circling me and the horses. I was forced to put on my 'mosquito hat' with netting covering my face and neck, and gloves, before I started waving a towel vigorously in the air to get them to disperse. They kept on coming back and I lit a cigarette, circling the smoke round and round in the air. I must have looked quite comical having every part of me covered, flapping my arms and dancing like a tribeswoman around a fire. We were fortunate not to get stung but in my hurry to leave I left behind a couple of things I had hung on a tree to dry. Tusa and I backtracked the half hour ride, hot and bothered.

I missed the entrance to Villa Lourdes, a place I had intended to spend the night. Some people said nobody actually lived there. My only option now was to look for a place where I could pitch my tent. Spotting four men on the side of the road all dressed in white and sporting shotguns messed up my plans. I passed them with a quick and formal *"buenos tardes"*. There was nobody else around and I could not take the chance of having them witness me pitching a tent, or worse having them come over. They could have been decent folk but I just could not risk it. It was a tricky situation. I was on my own, nightfall was looming and I had nowhere to stay.

I made the decision to continue into the night until I found somewhere that looked safer, even if it meant going through the night and leading the horses until daylight broke.

53. Frank (left) and Brian carrying bags of saw-dust for bedding on the boat for the horses.
54. In my tent on the boat that would take us from Porto Velho to Manaus (Brazil).

55. Antonio, the captain's assistant on the boat, doing a shuffle while I play the Irish tin whistle.
56. A duck on the boat awaiting his fate.

57. The best shower is a bucket of water from the river.
58. Mise and Tusa's home on the barge for five days.

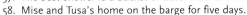

59. Street artists in Manaus.
60. Remembering Tusa.

Before we were completely swallowed by the arms of darkness, I stopped to have some left-over potato I had put in a plastic container the night before. It was now mashed.

Two trucks passed but nobody stopped to enquire if I was okay. I know a girl with two horses was a very unusual sight in these parts and I found it strange that all we received were quick glances and no further curiosity. When we got going again Mise displayed a burst of renewed energy, trotting beautifully at a perfect pace.

"You're a queen Mise!" I sang into the quiet air.

But she could not sustain the pace for long.

While still on Mise I took a picture of a magnificent deep blue sky and smiled to myself. I was quietly amused that given the circumstances, I was still in touch with my surroundings, experiencing feelings of happiness and contentment. Taking into account my fear of the dark as a small child, I was surprised that I was neither afraid nor overly bothered that soon it would be pitch dark and we would still be on the road.

But the good feelings only lasted until I could not see my hand in front of my eyes anymore. The only sounds were the rhythmic clip-clop of the hooves on the dirt road and the occasional blow through their noses. I turned my head to the right and imagined somebody in the long grass with a light, keeping up with us. My heart missed a beat. I talked to the horses in a put-on deep voice, wanting to give the impression that I was a man. I continued my baritone monologue until I realised the sporadic flashes of light were innocent fireflies, getting busy for the night.

Plants, trees and logs became strange, weird creatures in the shadows of the night. A bus rumbled past, hooting and throwing light on the dark gloomy road for a few seconds, only to leave even deeper darkness and a cloud of dust in our faces.

And then, all of a sudden there was light, a friendly smiling half-moon, shining with brilliance and throwing long shadows through the jungle on my left. I felt much less alone.

It was past 9 p.m. when I spotted a steady but subdued shine in the distance. My suspicion that people had to be close by was confirmed when I saw two kids on the side of the road holding kerosene-lit lamps, their faces full of suspicion.

Their mother had no problem that I pitched my tent outside their humble shack and the girls held the lanterns while I got busy. I changed clothes inside the tent and the girls left only after I had said *"gracias"* three times. The mother made a fire outside and they all sat quietly around the warmth, waiting for the man of the house to return. Late into the night I felt comforted by their quiet murmurs

I must have drifted off because I was woken by one of the girls.

"Your horse is running away," she announced in almost a whisper.

I could hear Mise's hooves on the dirt road. Tusa, who was tied up, called out for her. I quickly got dressed, ran to the road and shouted her name. On hearing my voice she stopped, turned around, and came galloping towards us, neighing as if we had not seen each other in years. I scratched her ears in a comforting gesture and returned to my tent when she seemed calmer.

I was up before daybreak and far from being rested, made my way over to where my horses were dozing together. I tied up Mise and let Tusa roam, hoping he would get enough grass on the side of the road to sustain him for a while.

During my journey, if the horses were not put in a stable or a *corral* for the night, they had to take turns at being tied up. They had grown very close to each other and I knew one would not leave or go too far away without the other. More often, however, I allowed Mise to be free at night purely because she pulled her weight much more during the day.

A pathetic-looking dog with a tiny body and no tail lay in the ashes of the fire from the night before. His eyes were devoid of hope and it looked like he had given up on life. Bones protruded through his tight skin when he suddenly lifted his head and threw up.

"Is he sick?" I asked the woman.

She said yes. I shook my head. How could he not be ill if he most likely had not eaten for God knows how many days? He was clearly not a priority, this was a large family and nine mouths had to be fed first.

Later, a few men turned up claiming to want to see the woman's husband who had still not returned. I was bombarded with the usual questions and got the impression their early-morning visit had more to do with their curiosity about the visiting *gringa* and her horses than anything else.

Another man arrived full of arrogance and macho bravado. He winked at me all the time and kept on shouting 'hey!' to get my attention. He was also drunk and a bit aggressive.

"Would your mare go with my stallion?" he asked in a slurring voice, making a thrust-action with his hips.

I gave him an abrupt 'no' and tried to ignore him but when he asked me for the third time I gave him my line about civilised men. It kept him and the others quiet. Not having much else to talk about the men soon left. Only a couple said goodbye.

After I had shared my hot chocolate with the kids, I put one of the boys on Tusa and with him clinging on, walked down the road with some of the others following. It turned out the water-well where we were heading belonged to some of the men who had visited us earlier. Thankfully they were still in too much of an intoxicated state to remember the icy atmosphere of earlier. I made a mental note to try to bite my tongue the next time somebody annoyed me. I depended too much on the goodwill of people and burning bridges was not going to serve me well.

By lunchtime I had arrived at Triangulo, a non-descript place consisting of a petrol station and a *pensión* (boarding house). Lunch consisted of salty scrambled egg, rice, plantain and a carbonated raspberry drink. The heat was fierce outside. The horses nibbled on grass in an area that was also used as a rubbish-dump.

I sat at one of the tables in the *pensión*, put my rolled up tent under my head and tried to catch a snooze. Sweat was dripping from my face and rolling down my back and red ants were crawling over some of the sticky, spilled raspberry drink.

I was in relatively good shape when we left just after 4 p.m. But my patience wore thin when suddenly a swarm of horseflies descended on us, attacking the horses' heads, their ears and anywhere they imagined they would have easy access to blood. I stopped and sprayed both horses with insect repellent but it only worked for a short while. The flies stuck with us and while we kept going I lashed out at those I could reach. Mise did not flinch when the crop or my hand suddenly struck down on some part of her body. It was as if she knew I was doing it in her own interest. I had to stop again to rinse the blood from my hand.

Later I took a picture of a rainbow as we went downhill. The sky was dark in the distance but despite my silent pleas for rain, it remained hot and dry.

Invariably a journey offers a chance to learn and grow. Mine was an opportunity to reach out for my dreams, to go beyond the surface and search for a deeper meaning, maybe to find a better understanding of others, but maybe ultimately a better acceptance and tolerance in myself. With all the ups and downs that realising my dream entailed, it never ceased to amaze me how things eventually turned out fine.

It could be because I have this strong belief that when things are bad, they have to get better. It could be the fact that I was simply willing to give it a go, grasping opportunities when they arose and trying to make the best of whatever came my way. I believe that inevitably, resilience and determination are rewarded, sometimes in less obvious ways, an unexpected smile from a stranger, a rainbow after the storm, an offering of food when hunger is overtaking the body and mind, a friendly nudge from a horse, soft rain on my face when the heat became unbearable.

Almost seven months gone and every day there was something new to be discovered, something waiting to surprise. I remember the planning stages, scheming and trying to imagine scenarios, possible experiences and obstacles on the way. It was just one big unknown out there and my imagination was filling in the blanks. Little did I know how rich a journey was in front of me. Little did I know how extending my boundaries by living to the limit of my abilities would make me stronger and better, broadening my views and understanding of the world and its people.

Day 205. When I saw the sign for Villa Luz we turned left on to a narrow path running through thick forest. Having seen the turn-off only briefly on the way back from Riberalta in the truck, I had no idea what to expect and continued hesitatingly down the winding road. It was quiet apart from the echo of hooves on dirt road. The trees overlapped above our heads, making the trail dark and eerie. The horses seemed ill-at-ease too and Tusa, rolling his eyes nervously, kept on pushing close against us. After one kilometre and still no sign of a house or life I quickly turned around. We could not get back to the main road fast enough.

It was getting late now and the sun had gone down. I dreaded the thought of having to go through the same difficulties and hardships as the night before. The sky was less friendly and there were only a few stars, struggling to lighten up the dark patches above us. The moon was hiding its face and the surface of the road was rough. My back was aching.

We were riding in complete darkness for at least two hours when suddenly Mise stumbled and tripped over, falling to her knees. Without hesitation she quickly got herself up and continued at a fast trot. Although I managed not to fall off, I got an awful fright but more than anything else felt terribly sorry for her. My dearest Mise, always the brave fighter, giving all she had. I talked out loud into the quiet night and apologised to my horses for having brought them out there. I asked for their forgiveness for the days that they were hungry and tired and I asked for their understanding. I promised them days and days of spoiling and tender loving care once we got through that demanding stretch.

The lights that came from the odd passing vehicle highlighted the rows and rows of trees on the side of a long, never-ending, isolated road.

My prayers were answered when after another half hour of riding I heard a dog bark. A man followed by his family came out of their small house to greet us. His wife was dressed in only a skirt and white lacy brassiere. I received a sweaty bosomy embrace and assurances that it would be no problem for me to stay the night.

While I pitched my tent the man held a small drum, smoke pouring from it, close to the entrance in an attempt to keep the mosquitoes away.

I was brought to a well and had no choice but to strip down and wash under the watchful eyes of the half-naked woman and her two children who soon got rid of their clothes too. Mosquitoes landed on the wet parts of my body and one of the kids waved a towel to keep them at bay.

Despite the smoking drum the mosquitoes still managed to settle in my tent and once the light was gone they commenced their attack. Throughout the night they kept on biting, even through my clothes and the thermo-liner that was wrapped around me. They were vicious and relentless and I hardly slept a wink.

Throughout the frustrating night I could hear the man's guttural snoring drifting through the open hole in the wall of the two-roomed house next to my tent.

I could not have slept more than two hours and somehow managed to drag myself out of the mosquito-infested tent just after 5 a.m. It did not help that my 'monthly visitor' had decided to arrive prematurely. I had to ask the man very nicely, almost pleading, to collect the horses while I packed and folded my tent. My one and only long-sleeved top was filthy and I threw a T-shirt over my head, lashing sun block on the exposed areas. When I tied up my last few belongings, I noticed that my rain poncho was missing. I cursed myself. It must have slipped away from underneath the saddlebag the night before.

The dusty deep-red road to Riberalta was wide and full of long, rolling hills. For most of the way the vegetation was dense and thick on both sides.

When we got to a river a group of men pulled up in their 4 x 4.

"I know Europe well," said the driver after we had exchanged a few words.

I contemplated for a moment sending my bags with them to Riberalta but fear of them getting lost made me change my mind.

The bank down to the river was too steep and I continued uphill where we stopped at a small house to ask for water. It was a welcome surprise when the man produced one of my food boxes. I did not recognise the place and had completely forgotten that I had dropped one off there as well. The woman gave the horses corn on the cob which they devoured eagerly and I shared my tin of sardines, can of apricots and biscuits with everybody, including a tame baby parrot. After an hour's rest I thought I was ready to tackle the road again.

Neither of the horses shared my feigned enthusiasm to continue in the oppressive heat. After another few hours ride and about 15 kilometres from Riberalta I took a small dirt road that led to a farm to ask for water again. Mise and Tusa rushed to the patches of green grass scattered around the house as if they had not eaten in days. The man offered me a chair. He joined me in the shade and we sat in comfortable silence.

When we got going again with me leading Mise, Tusa was in an even less co-operative mood than usual and kept on pulling back. We were going very slowly. The sun was burning relentlessly, even the shadows offered no respite. A man in a *camioneta* (pickup truck) stopped to chat.

"Do you have something cold for me to drink?" I asked in a desperate voice, my dry tongue sticking to the roof of my mouth.

The man suggested a place, two kilometres off the main road.

"There is a lake and a resort," he informed me nonchalantly.

I thought I was hallucinating when I heard his words.

'The idiot. He obviously had no idea what that meant on horseback in fierce heat. A four kilometre round trip could break us. He must be insane.'

I did not share my thoughts with him but said a silent prayer that he would be my oasis in the desert and offer to get me something. But this hope faded rapidly when he switched on the engine of his pickup and accelerated towards Riberalta without as much as a backward glance. Dejected I sat down on the dusty ground. I cursed myself for not having handed the man money and asking him to buy me a cold drink. He was not a mind reader. He did not know that I had already done 40 kilometres that day, thirty-seven the previous day, forty-five the day before that. I should have just told him. Surely then he would have had more sympathy? Did pride stop me asking or was I afraid of rejection? Maybe I was the crazy one.

I discovered I could get Tusa to walk alongside Mise (and not pull back) if I walked in front holding something edible just out of reach, at arms-length. Every now and then I would allow Tusa to take a bite but it only worked until he got fed up with the tasteless crackers that were on offer. I was drained by having to drag them along and at one stage got behind the horses and urged them on, swinging my crop in the air. We managed to cover not more than thirty yards when Tusa pushed Mise into the long grass on the roadside where they came to an annoying stand-still. Walking behind them I also discovered that Tusa's back shoe was about to fall off and Mise was limping.

I had never experienced such devastating numbness in my legs and back. Even stretching did not improve things much. I had absolutely no energy left and the cruel red-hot dirt road continued into the distance with no sign of civilisation. I was as dirty as a pig, sweating profusely, sunburnt and completely worn out from pulling the horses, the heat, and lack of food and sleep. I was also desperate for water.

I had no control over my emotions when I suddenly broke into a flood of tears, chanting, "I can't go on anymore, I can't go on anymore," over and over again.

I cried my heart out until I had no more tears. I reached into my saddlebag for a cloth to wipe my face when my hand touched a water bottle. After a couple of sips of warm water, I threw the last few drops over the horses' faces to cool them down. What followed was the most hilarious face that Tusa pulled, curling up his lips and exposing his huge teeth in an open grin. I looked at his funny face and laughed out loud through the tears.

In the late afternoon, just when I thought I could not do another fifty yards, a farm appeared as if from nowhere. I was met by one of the workers and she led me to where her boss was supervising the slaughter of cows. I approached reluctantly, dismayed at the sight of cut-off legs, strewn around and a freshly killed cow on the ground. What disturbed me most was to see half a dozen cows, standing a short distance away, watching the brutality with obvious fear in their eyes. I swallowed my disgust and trying not to look at the slaughtered cow, asked the owner for shelter for the horses.

The trip on the back of a motorbike taxi into town was exhilarating and I could not get enough of the wind rushing through my hair. The young boy drove like a lunatic and wore a baseball cap which had *'No Fear'* written on the front. He eyed every pretty girl we passed and oblivious to the traffic would then stare into the side-mirror until they were out of sight. But I did not care. I felt deliriously happy to have arrived, closed my eyes and enjoyed the ride.

After a thorough scrub-down, I walked to the nearest café and devoured a plate of fish fillets, chips and salad. My first decent meal in twelve days.

During my stay in Riberalta I met a kind woman my age, bubbly and talkative, called Patricia. She was keen to learn English and sat in her shop everyday, studying books. One day she took me for a spin around the square on her moped where we joined about fifty other bikers.

"I would like to get a bigger bike," she roared to the back. "They're expensive but it's possible to get a stolen one from Brazil."

She returned a smile to a dashing young boy who overtook us.

"Did you see him look at me?" she asked excitedly.

I was bemused by this speedy and unusual form of flirtation and courting between members of the opposite sex.

Patricia also mentioned the macho society and how there was a lot of domestic violence.

"All the men here have affairs," she said in a matter-of-fact manner. "This is completely unacceptable to women but there's nothing we can do about it."

She told me how she was the local 'psychotherapist' in town with endless numbers of women coming to talk to her.

"Most women want to tell me about their husbands' infidelities. I love to be able to help and advise them."

She showed me her books on metaphysics and one about unfaithful men.

"This is where I get all my information to help people," she said seriously. "I use the books and my own experience. My husband is unfaithful too and likes women too much."

She looked wistfully into the distance.

"I'm a romantic and I believe in love but I want to learn to work the internet and find myself a boyfriend."

She looked at my surprised face and laughed. "Don't worry, I told my husband about my plan!"

Laughter and humour were what kept me going a lot of the time. My journey provided many comic moments. I also tried to see the funny side of any situation I found myself in. Sometimes the laughter came during the event, many times afterwards. Some emails I received also had the chuckle factor. I received few jokes though. In hindsight I wish I had encouraged friends to send me more. The one below had me in stitches;

The old cowboy came riding into town on a hot, dry, dusty day. The local sheriff watched from his chair in front of the saloon as he wearily dismounted and tied his horse to the rail.

"Howdy, stranger..."

"Howdy, Sheriff..."

The cowboy then moved slowly to the back of his horse, lifted its tail, and placed a big kiss were the sun don't shine. He dropped the horse's tail, stepped up on the walk, and headed towards the saloon.

"Hold on, Mister..."

"Sheriff?"

"Did I just see what I think I just saw?"

"Reckon you did, Sheriff... I got me some powerful chapped lips..."

"And that cures them?"

"Nope, but it keeps me from lickin' em.

Guayaramirim, a small border town on the edge of the Mamoré River, never slept. It is a busy place with ample accommodation, a few internet cafés and a large market where you can just about buy anything. It is also the place where 7-minute boat trips are taken across the river to and from its modest and sleepy little Brazilian neighbour town, confusingly called Guajará- Mirim.

Crossing the Mamoré River a few times, it did not take long to organise my entry into our next country. I stayed a while longer though, not wanting to break my promise to the horses to give them a good break. Frankly, we all needed it badly.

The whole process of getting my horses legalised was thankfully much easier than I had anticipated and I fell in love with the Brazilian people there and then. Everybody from the official vet to those at the Agricultural and Customs offices went out of their way to accommodate me, making jokes and offering strong espressos. Solutions were sought and nothing was a problem. I spoke Spanish, they all conversed in Portuguese and I got my business done smoothly. There were long queues at the local bank where I tried to withdraw Brazilian real, the local currency.

During the two hour wait I could not help but notice the patient demeanour of the Brazilians, chatting and waiting good-humouredly until they could be served.

At the pier, waiting for the next speed-boat to cross the river back to the Bolivian side, I used the restrooms and was astonished by the cleanliness. It was better than a lot of toilets in private homes not to speak about the public ones in South America. There was not a trace of dirt or a whiff of urine. I complimented the girl standing outside the door hoping she understood.

Before I officially crossed over to Brazil with the horses I spent time at the local market on the Bolivian side to stock up on a few necessities. I asked the boy from whom I had bought a Gillette razor why they were so expensive.

"They are expensive *señora* because they are original and one razor will last you five months," he replied in earnest.

I could not help a giggle.

"Yeah sure, that's if I put it in the bathroom cabinet and use it twice over the next twenty weeks."

His cheeky smile secured the sale. The thought of having smooth legs and hairless armpits after roughing if for many weeks filled me with joy.

I also found the ideal hat without searching too much. The style was not too cowboy and certainly not Mary Poppins.

Arriving back at the Eco Lodge where I was staying, I was gutted to discover my walkman, a present from a friend, had been taken from my room. I found the door I had locked that morning, ajar, and knew the cleaning girl was the culprit. I approached the proprietor who first responded with a "We've never had a theft here," before committing herself to handling the matter internally.

"We don't want the police here," she said with a distressed expression. "We take full responsibility for your loss."

Sadly her tune changed when she realised how expensive the walkman was. She even felt brave enough to inform me that the cleaners claimed that they had never even seen it in my room. The woman went back on her word to reimburse me and I made the decision not to pay for my accommodation. I calculated that I still lost out and felt even more disappointed by having something personal stolen after so many months on the road.

But this experience did not change my perceptions of a country that stood out in my mind more than any other. There was so much that enchanted me in this sparse, silent place. Bolivia is one of those countries like certain people that will stay with me forever. They say beauty is in the eye of the beholder but it is impossible not to appreciate the impact that Bolivia has. It is a country that warmed my spirit. It brought out a zeal for life and living in its most basic form. It is a place to discover. It is a place where culture, geography and a rich history blend themselves into an elaborate tapestry of colour, smells and real adventure. To me, Bolivia is one of the most all-embracing South American countries with a variety of awesome landscapes, peopled by communities whose lifestyle has changed little since the time of the Spanish conquest.

To try to put words to my experiences, the highs and the lows, could never really do justice to the uniqueness of this place. I probably went through the most physical hardship in this magical country, shedding more tears than anywhere else. But I also had the most exquisite moments of beauty, tranquillity and peace. Bolivia's enormous vastness and the faces of its innocent people – these are the memories etched in my mind eternally.

11. FORTY DAYS AND FORTY NIGHTS

"When experience is viewed in a certain way, it presents nothing but doorways into the domain of the soul"
— *John Kabat-Zim*

The morning of my departure it did not just rain, it poured. A knock on my door brought the news that the boat was leaving in forty minutes. On the way, I hailed a taxi, asking the driver to go to the port and tell them not to leave without me.

When we arrived, drenched to the skin, they had already started to load the trucks. Tusa was frightened to go on board as I pulled him from the front. A man stood behind him, my crop in his hand. This did not impress Tusa and without warning he gave a vicious kick, crushing the man's knuckles leaving them bloody and raw. I apologised profusely and the man, in some shock, left to get himself a stiff drink and have his injury attended to.

I mounted Tusa to attempt riding him on to the barge but he pranced around the place, retreating and then rearing up on his hind legs. I got off and handed another man the leading rope. Standing behind Tusa, I urged him on but he stood dead in his tracks. Feeling safe in the knowledge that my horses had never kicked me, I lifted my crop to give him a light rap on the bum. Just as my arm was in mid-air, I felt a blow to my left elbow and it took me a moment to realise that Tusa had just kicked me hard. Stunned and clutching the injured limb, I tried to pretend it was not serious.

I asked a curious bystander to lead Mise on to the barge and everybody stared as she walked on as if a well-rehearsed queen of the catwalk. Tusa co-operated fully after that and I could not believe my stupidity not to have thought about taking Mise on first. An official came over to check my papers in the pouring rain but the men running the boat gave him a hard time, leaving him only a couple of minutes to scan through my documentation.

By the time I got on the barge where the horses were standing, my arm had turned purple and green. It was painful and I bit on my lip while a kind man rubbed ointment on to the multi-coloured bruise. He also brought along a cloth to wipe the mud from my poncho.

Arriving on the Brazilian side, people could not have been more helpful. Luis the vet, a charming man with friendly eyes, a warm demeanour and a big tummy, was concerned when I could not shake his hand.

"We need to get you to a hospital," he said after inspecting the arm.

The public hospital did not have an x-ray facility and things at the private one were not much better. After a long wait with my arm throbbing, the doctor finally put a thin bandage around the injury. He then tied the bandage like a sling behind my neck. It cut into my skin and actually caused more discomfort. We were told to wait for x-rays.

Luis and I waited patiently but he looked relieved when after more than an hour I suggested we leave.

"I don't think my arm is broken," I said. "I'm pretty sure it will heal itself with time."

On the way to the pharmacy to buy a proper sling, he said, "The best hospital in Guajará-Mirim is an aeroplane out of the place."

We both laughed at the madness of it all.

Second in length only to Africa's Nile, the Amazon River carries the greatest volume of water of any river in the world. It flows eastward about 6,275 kilometres through South America from its source in the Andes to its mouth at the Atlantic Ocean. Navigable for almost its entire length, it provides an important commercial route through the continent.

The Trans Amazon Highway is impassable for much of the year and the rivers are the only practical means of communication and transport. I found myself making arrangements to get myself and the horses on a five-day boat trip, exploring the waterways of the Rio Madeira, the Amazon's longest tributary, linking the city of Porto Velho with Manaus, 901 kilometres on.

While in Porto Velho, I was fortunate to meet Frank, a Dutchman, and his North American colleague, Brian, both of whom worked on contract for a US telecommunications company. Frank and I got on very well and it helped that they both spoke Portuguese and so could assist with some of my preparations.

It was also Frank who told me it would be impossible to go on horseback from Manaus to Venezuela as one had to pass through a private Indian Reserve.

"Although you're allowed to enter the Reserve, it's prohibited to stop in that area and with you travelling on a horse, it'll take more than three days to cross," he informed me.

He also told me how the Indians living there are still used to their old ways and I shivered when he mentioned cannibalism.

From what I gathered, the Manaus Boa Vista Highway, called the br-174, has a violent history. Its 125 kilometre stretch of road cuts across the 25,000 square kilometres Reserve called the Terra Indigena Waimiri Atroaris.

The Waimiri-Atroari Indians live deep in the Amazon Rainforest in this part of Northern Brazil. Their territory is one of the most feared and impenetrable in the Amazon. Having been in constant open warfare for over 300 years, the Waimiri fiercely defended their land against the construction of the road, combating the forces of the Brazilian army. The retaliations against the Indians were always disproportionate. They were unequal battles, first in terms of weapons – one side using firearms, the other, bows and arrows. Furthermore, 300 Brazilians were arrayed against a much smaller number of Indians according to the reports of casualties on both sides. These were unjust wars in which one side attacked while the other defended their territory, their honour and their communities.

With right on their side they fought to reoccupy their traditional territories, part of which was occupied by a large mining company. In 1968 a Catholic priest and seven nuns were found dead in Waimiri territory and more than 200 soldiers were killed by poison arrows during the confrontation. The number of Waimiri killed in retaliation was never released. The Waimiri-Atroari were simply reacting against repeated acts of plundering and violence against them. Since the sixties and seventies, when the BR-174 highway was built, they have been dominated and subjugated by the Army. In this process, 2000 Indians disappeared and their lands were reduced by four-fifths. A hydroelectric power plant, which led to severe flooding within the Waimiri territory, also caused irreversible damage to the Indians' habitat.

But the Waimiri Atroari faced up to these challenges and negotiated with Brazilian officialdom so that today they enjoy secure reservation boundaries, cultural vigour and population growth.

A local man called Geraldo worked as an agent for the ferries in Porto Velho. For two days we rushed through the city on his powerful bike, visiting different boat companies. Despite the fact that I love motorbikes, I was in a state every time I sat behind him, clinging to his midriff with all my might as he sped through the busy streets, far too fast. More frightening was the fact that I was never given a crash helmet to wear.

"You're doing a hundred, Geraldo!" I shouted one morning as we zigzagged around. "This is madness, we're going to crash."

He turned his head side-ways and grinned. "Relax. I know what I'm doing."

It turned out he did not.

Two days before my departure, I could not get hold of him on his phone. I knew he had had a late night (I was invited to the party but declined) and left a message for him to ring me on Frank's phone. When he finally returned my call I did not recognise his voice.

"I cannot speak," he mumbled in a croaky murmur.

I had to pass the phone to Frank who shook his head for the duration of the conversation, making a lot of sympathetic noises.

It turned out that Geraldo had been involved in a very serious accident on his motorbike when on the way back from the party. He had fractured his skull and broken numerous bones including ribs.

Before the accident Gerald had made arrangements with a cargo boat to transport me and the horses up the Amazon after it became clear that the passenger ferries would not accommodate us. They were not keen on having animals on board and mentioned potential difficulties with health and safety. I cannot say I was overly disappointed, especially after I had been on one of those ferries. Hammocks were lined up like sardines in a tin and I was told theft could be a problem.

A day before our departure, Frank and Brian helped me to cart bags of sawdust to the port. These would go on the surface of the barge area where a section was cordoned off for the horses.

The barge was about 20 x 6 metres and also carried four cars and hordes of bags of spaghetti and beans. I pitched my tent between the bags of food and the cars. The small boat pushing the barge was managed by a laid-back and very friendly crew, the captain, his assistant, a mechanic and his wife who did the cooking. Accompanying us would be a missionary and his son, from Brazil, and later, a duck.

On the day I was told we would be leaving I rode the horses to the harbour wearing only knee-length shorts, a sleeveless top and trainers. The neighbourhoods we passed through had a distinct market atmosphere about them, with music stores blaring out their sounds, traders shouting out their wares and stallholders chattering on about their predominantly cheap plastic goods. Every other lamppost seemed to have had a loudspeaker attached to it. We received a lot of friendly stares, thumbs up and waves as we headed down towards the port. My spirits were high and I did not even get annoyed at some men making flirtatious gestures. I even gave a group of jubilant kids a spin on Tusa.

Not too far from the port a car stopped. I barely recognised Geraldo in the passenger seat. He looked terrible. His eyes were bloodshot and swollen and the area around them was badly bruised. He still had dried blood on his face, ears and neck.

"You should have stayed in hospital," I scolded him.

He shook his head, "No, now I work for you."

The port area was bustling when we arrived around 6 p.m. A man suggested the horses jump from one barge to the other but I insisted on finding two wooden planks so they could cross safely. Mise strolled on as if she did that kind of thing just about every day and true to his nature, Tusa boarded more warily, his legs trembling slightly.

I loved the atmosphere on the boat and had a real feeling of excitement, knowing that the journey up the river was going to be a memorable and unusual one.

Before the sun went down, I fed the horses a cocktail of wheat and proteins in their brand new powder-blue buckets. While the crew was still getting everything loaded, I crawled into my tent, fatigued yet pleased and gratified. I was asleep when we eventually got moving.

I awoke the following morning to a beautiful sunrise and the sound of water splashing against the barge. I peeked through my tent and felt on top of the world when I realised that we were actually cruising up the Amazon. Completely relaxed and in great form I made my way over to the little kitchen, checking on the horses first. They were standing around calmly waiting for their buckets to be filled with more food. I attached a rope to a bucket and scooped water from the river.

Sipping coffee and tucking into crackers, I sat in my chair (purchased especially for the boat trip) on the tiny deck, watching the world go by, contemplating life. I had absolutely nothing to do and nowhere to go. Dense, lush vegetation and towering trees lined the river and the odd, small settlement nestled in the forest or on the shores. For the sake of the horses I was happy it was an overcast day.

That evening I sat in the opening of the kitchen, my feet dangling over the side of the boat, eating spaghetti. Life was good. I had a beer and asked Valcilene the cook if she would like one too. She declined politely.

"I suffer from depression and shouldn't drink or smoke."

I found her openness very interesting although it was not the first time in Brazil that somebody, without shame or embarrassment, had admitted to being depressed. They stated their condition simply as a fact of life.

These were tranquil, easygoing days. Occasionally pink-grey river dolphins surfaced, a sight which never ceased to amaze and excite me. I wished that the days would pass by even more slowly. One day though was particularly hot. I asked the men what we could do for protection for the horses. They brought out large plastic sheets to tie over the area where the horses were standing. However, the horses were disturbed by the noisy, flapping sounds of the sheets in the wind and I feared they might jump overboard. Noticing that Tusa was sweating profusely they cut open the sides to allow for more air to blow through.

Mise was in heat again and bullied Tusa, giving him playful bites which hurt I was sure. She also intimidated him when they were eating, moving over to his bowl, pushing his head away. They had a container each but somehow Mise must have thought that Tusa's food was better.

A number of people living on the edges of the river made their living from providing food and provisions to the passing boats. They arrived in a type of motorised canoe and attached this to the moving boat, using a rope. The inside of their canoes were filled not only with a number of family members but also with everything ranging from fruits to fish or a slaughtered animal. This is how we acquired the duck but in this case he was still alive. He was tied up in different places on the boat and I made sure he had food and water. On one occasion the crew even chucked him into the river for a brief spell to cool down. I dreaded the moment of his slaughter and had an urge to throw him overboard, pretending he had escaped.

For lunch one day Valcilene prepared fish we got the day before. I took pictures from the top deck as she cut them open expertly, tossing their bloody insides into the river. Later, I noticed the heads and dismembered parts floating in a pot. I could not stomach the white, uninviting pieces of fish, their eyes still intact, and made my excuses not to join in the meal.

The horses' diet worried me. So when one day we passed close to the banks of the river, I ran to the side of the barge, went down on my knees and started to pull reeds sticking out of the water. Soon, I was joined by some of the crew who helped to gather a good quota for the horses. They loved the bit of greenery and afterwards their systems appeared much more regular.

A full bladder at night turned out to be the biggest hassle on board. First of all I had to get out of my tent in the dark and make my way over to the toilet, stepping carefully on the narrow side of the barge past metal obstacles and bags of dried food. A wrong step to the left would have seen me plunging into the perilous waters of the great river.

The toilet, next to the noisy engine, was the smallest I had ever encountered, much smaller than those on planes. Not only was it a struggle to get my pants up and down, but to actually sit on the toilet was an achievement in itself with my knees almost pressed to my ears. When I stood up, my head knocked against the ceiling. A kind of squatting position was mercifully possible due to a strip of wood attached to the wall on the front left on which I could distribute my weight. The tiny room was newly renovated and the combined smells of fresh paint, lavatory and engine, made for a nauseating experience.

I woke up one morning around 3 a.m. bursting to go. Once I had reached the toilet I discovered the door was locked. I had to make a decision fast and walked to the back of the boat and dropped my pants. I grabbed on to a metal hook that was fixed to the deck and literally hanging over the edge of the boat with my bottom hovering over the mighty Amazon, I managed to find relief. The flow seemed to last forever and I could feel my arms and legs tiring from the strain of holding my own weight.

Later, back in the tent I could not help smiling to myself at the thought of what a sight that must have been.

Antonio, the Captain's assistant, had been seeking my company since our departure from Manaus. He came over almost every time as I sat on my chair writing my diaries. He would touch my knee a number of times in a sweet manner indicating his eagerness to chat. But I had difficulty understanding him so usually we would have a three-minute conversation, discussing the different currencies in each country. One day he brought out a book to show me all his notes.

"I studied mathematics," he said while proudly showing me the figures on the pages.

One evening as the sun was setting he came out to the deck just as I had started to play a few tunes on my tin whistle. He pretended to do a slow shuffle with himself, his eyes closed as he moved around. He looked thoroughly happy and content with his life, enjoying the moment and not thinking about tomorrow. I could share in that feeling. The time I spent on the boat was probably the only time during my travels that I did not worry about the future and what obstacles we still might have to face. Being surrounded by water and the hypnotising easy rhythm of the boat brought with it a serenity that must have rubbed off in some way. I actually forgot that there was another world out there.

There were no washing facilities on the boat and most of the time I would rinse myself, clothed in a t-shirt and mini-skirt, with a bucket of water scooped from the river. Twice during the journey, the boat came to a halt when we reached clear waters, noticeably different from the murky waters for most of the way. Stopping in such waters meant a thorough body wash and clothes were rinsed clean. I was watchful in the water however, especially after I had witnessed the biggest fresh water fish I had ever seen. I was told they did not bite but those assurances did not really put my mind at ease and I made sure not to linger unnecessarily.

The second last night was rather an uncomfortable one. I was in bed well before 8 p.m. and at midnight woke up, bursting to go. It was another 'over the side job' and when I finally got back to my tent, I had so much horse and journey stuff on my mind that I could not go back to sleep again. Then at 2 a.m. it started to rain really hard, a downpour that went on for two solid hours. There was nothing I could do as I saw the inside of my tent becoming progressively wetter. I had hardly slept a wink and was delighted when the day broke just after 5 a.m. so I could get up. The sleepless night was my own fault though, as the captain had offered me his bunk bed, given that he had planned to continue his watch through the night.

So when Antonio offered me his bed on the Saturday, our last night, I took up the offer without hesitation.

"I'll sleep in the hammock downstairs in the kitchen," he said, delighted to be of assistance.

I was aware of the spiders and cockroaches roaming in the cabin but also liked the idea of sleeping with the crew. The thought made me feel as I was almost one of them and not another strange *gringa* travelling through their country. During the night, I could swear I felt something crawling on me and when I began to itch, I got up. Standing outside around midnight, I stripped and shook out my clothes and sleeping bag.

I slept peacefully after that.

We arrived in Manaus to an industrous port on the 3rd of February 2003, six days after having left Porto Velho. Looking in my diary I also realised that we had now been almost six months 'on the road'. It was with a mixture of pride and disbelief when I reflected on what Mise, Tusa and I had gone through since Argentina, more than 4,000 kilometres away.

Our travels had presented their fair share of challenges but also moments of exquisite reward and insight. I was regularly racked by self-doubt and problems but there were so many joyful moments too. In a way, I believe that the combination of my experiences, good and bad, prepared me mentally for what was in front of us. We had been through some rough times but looking back, I would still rank the days I spent in Manaus as the most difficult and challenging of the entire journey. Certainly on a psychological and emotional level, I was tested to the limits.

A ramp was put down for the horses and they were required to step from the barge on to a higher platform.

"The planks are too shaky," I told the men standing around but they insisted they were fine.

Surprisingly, Tusa did okay but Mise stepped on to the wood cautiously, panicked when it started to wobble and attempted to jump the last bit. As she connected with the platform of the other barge, she began to slip, falling backwards towards the river. I was in the front, holding the leading rope and it took all my strength and another man's help to pull her away from the water. She kept on sliding on the slippery surface and ended up falling down over a kind of solid piece of metal. I was mortified. She tried to stand up a few more times but to no avail. I knelt down and rubbed her face.

"Don't get up Mise, please don't get up," I pleaded with her.

I rushed back to the boat and grabbed some of the empty food bags. I tied these around her feet and shoes to give her better 'footing' and I felt utter relief when she awkwardly managed to get up without sliding again. I was dismayed to see a number of open gashes on her legs and inner thighs. One week of solitude and no drama and now this. She seemed to be okay and I made a mental note to get her antibiotic cream as soon as possible.

I had to leave the horses at the port and after I had secured a helper who would look after them, I took a bus into the city. I did not know a soul and had only a name and number of someone given to me by a man in an equestrian shop in Porto Velho.

Manaus, capital of the Amazonas state, is where the two great rivers, Solimoes and Negro merge to form the Amazon. It is the chief port and a hub for the region's extensive river system. Interestingly, after meeting, the black waters of the Negro and the muddy brown of the Solimoes do not mix and the two rivers run side by side for a considerable distance with a defined colour contrast, a phenomenon known as the 'meeting of the waters'.

Because of its location in the middle of the Amazon Rainforest, Manaus attracts a substantial number of Brazilian and foreign tourists who usually spend not more than a couple of days in the city, while planning boat excursions and overland trips into the surrounding jungle. My experience in this city turned out to be quite different.

Tammy, the contact given to me, turned out to be the perfect person to know in Manaus. Not only could she make a living out of talking, she was also full of energy and enthusiasm, wanting to do as much as she could for us while we were in her city. Within minutes of our meeting she made a phone call to the army base to arrange for my horses to be picked up and brought to her place. She also negotiated a fee with her farrier to look after the horses' feet.

Brazil, I found, had a totally different feel from the other Latin American countries we travelled through. The people seemed to be so easygoing and full of joy. 'Flexibility' could be their middle name. True to Chacho's words, life in Brazil positively vibrated. Incredibly dynamic, it was impossible not to be impressed by the unique energy.

On my second day in Manaus, I received an email from the Irish Ambassador in Mexico, who also has responsibility for Venezuela. It read as follows;

Your email to Peter Macaulay, Honorary Consul in Venezuela, about your intention of riding through Venezuela has been passed to me. I suggest, in the strongest possible terms, that you should not attempt to proceed with your journey by way of Venezuela at the present time. I do not know what Consular Information Sheet you are referring to, where you read that the greatest turmoil is in the cities. Our consular advice now is that no-one should travel to Venezuela unless they have pressing reasons to do so. 'Pressing reasons' would not include the kind of project you have set yourself.

At the present time you should not cross into Venezuela with or without your horses. Most consular services are giving similar advice. It would be very unwise of you to think that it is alright to go through Venezuela provided you avoid the cities. Indeed, if you told me you were taking a flight home, transiting through Caracas airport, I would take a much more relaxed view than I do of your intention to cross Venezuela by land. Please understand that I am giving you very serious consular advice. If you decide to press ahead in spite of what we are telling you, you must accept the risks yourself. There would be little we could do, as a consular service, to extricate you from any situation in which you might find yourself.

I had no doubt that I had to trust my instincts in this matter. Consular advice about perceived dangers was often exaggerated and often the situation was not nearly as bad as it was made out to be. During my stay in Manaus I spoke to a number of people, one of them living in Caracas, the capital of Venezuela. He told me to avoid protests and demonstrations due to their potentially violent nature but that otherwise I would be fine.

"Travelling through my country is like anywhere else," he said. "You have to be careful where you go in some cities."

He told me to keep my eyes open and be sensible.

"I live there and I would advise you to continue your journey," he said. "Look me up when you reach Caracas."

A friend in Ireland contacted the Venezuelan embassy in London to get their opinion and initially the woman appeared shocked when she learned of my plans to ride through Venezuela on horseback. However, she changed her view when told where I had been riding from.

"Parts of Bolivia are much more dangerous than Venezuela," she said.

Realistically I had no other choice but to continue northwards. Retracing our steps to Bolivia was not an option. Heading west towards drug and crime ridden Peru and Columbia would have been silly. Lastly, but most importantly, I had no intention of aborting my journey at that point.

After my third day in Manaus I moved to a cheaper hotel. Even though it was in a less safe area, the rooms at least did not smell of mould. They also had a fridge, double bed, balcony and they served better breakfasts. It was a good move especially as I ended up spending many more days in that city than originally planned.

Tammy's place was well out of town. It took a rambling forty-five minute ride on a bus and another fifteen minute walk to get there. I went almost every day to check on the horses.

After a week in Manaus I visited the Ministério da Agricultura where Guillermo, the vet, told me they were still waiting for the Venezuelan consulate to inform them of the requirements to enter their country with two horses.

"I suggest in the meantime you sort out the horses' anaemia tests," Guillermo said. "It can take a while as the blood has to be sent to Sao Paulo in the Southeast of Brazil.

I was told that the horses would also be tested for *mormo*, a highly contagious disease that was prevalent throughout the Amazon area three months prior to my arrival. From what I heard, large numbers of cattle and horses had to be put down as a result.

A woman vet from the Ministério came out to take blood from the horses. Both Tammy and I considered the 120 dollar bill excessive. Tusa had developed a fungus on his neck, stomach and hindquarters, but the vet seemed unconcerned when I pointed it out. The following day, Tammy mixed a strong solution in a container and sprayed Tusa all over. Afterwards, I put on a special fungus cream, using a toothbrush to get it thoroughly underneath the hair. In the absence of a professional, the Web can be a great tool.

Mise's wounds on her legs, although superficial, also received daily attention. One morning, Tammy's partner helped me with the horses but Mise would not stand still when he tried to put cream on her inner thigh. Without meaning any harm she gave light side-kicks in his direction. They were more warning 'mind you' kicks than anything else. In retaliation Johnny lifted his foot and kicked Mise hard on her belly. I was so shocked it felt like it was me who had received a blow to the gut.

"Don't *ever* kick my horse again," I said with angry emotion.

He looked only slightly embarrassed. "Sometimes that's the only language some of them understand."

I shook my head and walked away.

Tammy and I both differed with Johnny on how he treated horses. He mocked her regularly for trying to understand the 'psyche' of the horse. He thought she treated them unnecessarily softly. I could see how their different ways of thinking was a cause of tension in the relationship.

One evening after dinner at an Italian restaurant where they served wine tasting like vinegar in a coffee cup, I ended up in the local plaza with a bunch of people from literally all over the world. They were all recounting their experiences of travelling on a ferry down the Amazon. Never having been a 'group person', and after so long travelling on my own with just Mise and Tusa for company, I felt out of place. I ended up talking mostly to an interesting, down-to-earth girl from Buenos Aires, who worked in the USA with refugees. My attention was caught by a local boy, no older than eight, trying to sell peanuts and tiny eggs.

"*Não obrigada,*" I said and continued my conversation.

I was aware of him again when I felt an arm around my neck and before I knew what had happened, he had planted a kiss on my cheek. I laughed.

"Go away," I said. "I don't want to buy anything,"

But he stood his ground, standing there with velvety skin, dark brown eyes and an irresistible smile. He moved over again and pinched my cheek, wiped away the hair from my forehead and rubbed his nose against mine. I could feel myself blush as everybody looked on. I had not met an adult man in all my life that had been as charming and seductive as that little boy.

I bought all his eggs and the last few packets of peanuts in his basket.

Men and women in Brazil make a real effort when it comes to their appearance and it isn't strange for men to have their nails manicured, all buffed and shiny. I was tickled by how forward women were but when I was told there were seven girls for every man, it made more sense to me. Tammy also told me about the five second rule of flirting.

"If it lasted that long, it means serious interest," she said, "and holding hands almost for sure means you'll end up sleeping together."

She laughed when I told her about men making comments on the street, whispering in passing, "Feeling hot, beebee?"

When I asked her why people took their pet birds, stuck in cages, for walks, she said earnestly, "It makes them sing better."

The Jesus signs and messages about the Messiah arriving soon were everywhere and hard to miss. People were obviously committed to their faith and I noticed some bringing bibles into their place of work, others carried them around on their person.

I will not easily forget the morning of the 20th of February. It started like any other day since I arrived in Manaus. A breakfast of fruit on the balcony outside the dining room of the hotel, a few hours on the internet, but instead of visiting the horses that day, I took the bus to the Cavalaria, the equestrian section of the Army. I was told they had a therapeutic riding program. I had an interesting conversation with the therapist and great was my delight when I saw they used a Criollo horse as part of their programme.

When I got back to my hotel there was a message waiting from Tammy to ring her urgently.

"Tusa has tested positive for equine infectious anaemia and inconclusive for *mormo*," were her first words on hearing my voice.

I struggled to give a proper response. The news had taken me by surprise but I had not realised the full significance until I went to an internet café to gather more information about something I really knew nothing about. Having travelled from Argentina, it was standard procedure to have the horses submitted to these tests for equine infectious anaemia (EIA), also called Coggins tests, but I could never have guessed the impact of a positive diagnosis. This is what I learned about the disease from a variety of sources on the Web;

> Equine infectious anaemia (EIA) is a blood-borne disease transmitted mainly through the natural feeding of large biting insects, principally horseflies and deerflies. It is also known as Swamp Fever, an infectious disease of horses, donkeys and mules caused by a virus. Horses infected with the EIA virus carry it for life. Most infected horses show no symptoms but they remain infectious, endangering the health of other horses. EIA is a viral disease that affects the horse's immune system. The virus reproduces in the horse's blood cells and circulates throughout the body. The horse's immune system produces antibodies which attack and destroy its own blood cell components. The result is anaemia and organ-damaging inflammation. The clinical symptoms of EIA are variable and include fever, anorexia, depression, swelling of the underside of the belly and legs, muscle weakness and wasting, jaundice of mucous membranes and infertility. EIA can leave a horse vulnerable to other potentially fatal diseases. At this time, there is no treatment or cure for a horse that has contracted EIA. There is also no vaccine available to protect a horse from the EIA virus.

Thoroughly upset I read the information over and over again. Later the letters became blurred and nothing made sense. I sat with my head in my hands, not sure what to think or what to do. Obviously testing positive for carrying the virus was much more serious than what I ever thought. I could not believe that Tusa had to be so unlucky. He did not deserve it. I hoped and prayed he had not suffered too much discomfort during the previous few months. Maybe his habit of pulling on the leading rope and seeming less than eager to trot alongside Mise at times had a good explanation.

Tusa was ill. He did not feel well. A wave of guilt swept over me. Why hadn't I paid closer attention? I thought he was lazy and stubborn. I was wrong.

Poor, poor Tusa.

Disastrous news arrived that evening. In Brazil, by law any horse testing positive for EIA must be destroyed. Tusa had to be put down. My heart felt like breaking and I could not get my head around the devastating thought of losing him forever. Teary and emotional I rang a few close friends in Ireland that evening. They all shared in my pain and tried to console me as much as possible. Deidre broke down when we had to say goodbye.

The following day in a coffee shop, a couple from Guyana who sat next to me, made small talk. I told them about Tusa. As they left, the man turned to me.

"I wish for a miracle for Tusa," he said with sincerity.

I could only nod.

Later I met up with Tammy and Johnny. He expressed his concerns that their horses might become infected but Tammy shut him up.

"I think you should get two new horses. Mise might show to have EIA at a later stage," he said. "She and Tusa did after all share the same bit."

I was gobsmacked by his comment and had to refrain from giving him a sarcastic answer.

"I won't leave Mise behind just because she *might* be infected. She tested negative and that is all that matters."

I also added that EIA is mainly transmitted by blood and even though the horses shared the same bit, the chances were very slim for the disease to be transmitted that way. I was in a flood of tears when the conversation turned to how Tusa would be put down. I longed for some empathy and understanding for what I was going through. All I really needed was a hug from somebody who cared, a hug that said it was going to be alright.

I received an outpouring of sympathy when I broke the news to family and friends about Tusa carrying the EIA virus. The care and support from everyone carried me through those difficult days. I knew I was not alone. An email from Tom Phelan (a friend of a friend) in Ireland said it all;

Marianne, I never met you and those two magic horses, but in some kind of odd way, I know you well. The three of you. Tonight is the end of a sunny Spring Saturday in Dublin, the kind of day you'd almost have to invent bad news, and yet uninvited in it comes. Tonight Marianne, I'm sad too. All I can say for now to Mise and Marianne is, 'Ride on, see ya, I could never go with you, no matter how I wanted to'. You must both now redouble your intent and *Allez au bout*. Even at journey's end, you will always be the trio that started out. Tusa will remain a special pal. He was a founder member of the boy band.

Two days after I had received the sad news, I managed to face Tusa for the first time. He was standing alone in his *corral* and walked up to me when I climbed through the fence. I burst into tears. He stood very still while I brushed him down. Still sobbing, I kept on talking to him. I thanked him for his wonderful spirit and the hard work he had done for me. I also apologised again for the times I might have pushed him too hard or scolded him. He kept on nudging me softly with his nose and turned his head in my direction while I spoke. A young boy who had been cleaning out the stables had seen my distress, came over and asked my name. He stood a polite distance away and somehow his mere presence brought me comfort. Later his young friend came over too.

"Do you need anything?" he asked sweetly.

Later I checked on Mise who could not understand being separated from Tusa. Her eyes looked sad and confused. Tammy said they called out for each other all the time.

Sunday was market day and I forced myself to go, hoping that it would be a distraction from my sadness. But even the lively drone of people selling colourful handcrafts could not lift my morbid mood. I walked around aimlessly, hardly aware of my surroundings.

Tammy was reluctant to use a vet in Manaus to put Tusa down.

"Johnny and I are concerned that the rumour will spread about an infected horse on our premises," she said. "We fear that might result in our premises being put under quarantine and we won't be able to hold our rodeo shows."

I could understand their concern but I was not going to have somebody without experience put Tusa down. I had indicated a number of times that I wanted Tusa to die by lethal injection. Shooting him was not an option.

"I want him to go peacefully," I reiterated numerous times.

Earlier I had read something about the humane destruction of a horse. Even though it was written with sensitivity, it read like an execution job and I could not control the chills running down my spine. It also brought the question of what would be done with Tusa's body. Bury it or burn it? I had heard of people selling the meat of a horse that had to be put down but I was adamant that that would not be Tusa's fate. My sentiment is that horse flesh should not be eaten, ever. They were far too noble and regal to end up as food.

At the Ministério de Agricultura, Guillermo and Gilbert gave me contradictory advice about what needed to be done with Tusa, with regulations in general, and border crossings. Guillermo informed me that Tusa needed to be tested again for *mormo*.

"He can't be put down, just yet," he said.

He explained that if the second test came back positive, then Mise would have to be tested again. The whole procedure could take another month. I felt helpless and upset. Gilbert acted the 'good cop', telling his colleague that he could not understand the rules himself.

"It just doesn't make sense," he said as he moved his chair over to where I was sitting.

He put his hand on my knee.

"I can understand that you are feeling very lonely in a strange country where you think nobody cares," he said in calm, counsellor's voice. "But I think God has a plan for you."

Dr. Vera who took the blood from my horses denied that she had ever told Tammy and Johnny that Tusa could be put down by us and not the Ministério.

"We cannot give you a health certificate for Mise before the second *mormo* test for Tusa is back and you could face prosecution if you destroy Tusa before we know the results," Guillermo said.

I was becoming increasingly frustrated at the discrepancies and contradictions.

Johnny visited the Ministério later as well and showed his annoyance that Tusa could not be put down as soon as possible. Guillermo suggested that Johnny 'sprayed and prayed' referring to the horses that Johnny was afraid might become infected with Tusa still around. When ten days later, we still had not received the results of the second *mormo* test, Johnny and I agreed to have Tusa put down, with or without official permission.

"I'll tell them Tusa was bitten by a snake," suggested Johnny.

Emotionally, I felt drained and just wanted to get it over and done with. A vet was found who would do the job by lethal injection for sixty dollars. We agreed to meet on the 6th of March at 4 p.m.

I spoke very seriously to Pedro the vet, telling him that I did not want Tusa to suffer in any way.

"I want you to use a very strong anaesthetic and once he's asleep, you can inject whatever is needed to make his heart stop. I don't want him to have any anxiety or fear," I said, looking him straight in the eye.

He spoke perfect English and nodded that he understood.

It felt like a bad dream as we walked towards where Tusa was standing in solitude between the shrubs. I shivered when I saw the hole – apparently it took three days to dig it to that depth. I led Tusa gently towards the open grave. I stood very close to him, hoping and praying that my presence would give him some comfort.

His head started to hang after the first injection and not long after the second one, his knees buckled and he went down on his side, making deep sighing noises.

"Why are his eyes still open?" I asked the vet.

He said it was normal for an animal under anaesthetic.

Johnny took a picture of Tusa lying on the ground for the purposes of the Ministério. *'How horrible,'* I thought.

He even suggested we took off Tusa's shoes, which were still brand new. I shook my head.

"No way. He'll die with dignity. I want his shoes kept on."

I was amazed at his suggestion.

'How could one think about money at a time like that?'

I moved away when the vet approached to inject the chemicals. We waited but nothing happened. He gave Tusa a second shot and then to my horror, Tusa tried to get up. He managed to rest on his bent front legs, his head up in the air.

Anxiously I asked Pedro what was happening.

"I think he needs more anaesthetic," I said before he could reply.

I could not believe my ears when he said he did not have any more.

"Then go back to the shop and get some," I said impatiently, my voice trembling.

"The shop would be closed now," he replied nonchalantly.

He mumbled something to Johnny about fetching a gun. I was mortified and could not believe their attitude, both he and Johnny standing around clumsily and no-one seemed to care. My worst nightmare was coming true. Tusa was going to be destroyed in a way that I was fighting against from the very beginning. I knew we had to act fast. I could not stand the idea of Tusa being in distress and already he appeared disorientated and very uncomfortable.

By the time Johnny finally left to find somebody that possessed a gun, Tusa was standing on wobbly legs, quite close to the open hole. He seemed disturbed and although still partially sedated, made long neighing sounds. I had to restrain him when he attempted to move around. I spoke to him softly, hoping he would calm down.

The heavens opened up and within minutes Tusa, the vet and I were soaking wet. I became increasingly agitated at seeing Tusa like that and turned to the vet.

"The way you've dealt with my horse today is shocking. I asked you more than once to bring enough sedative but you were more concerned about profit than Tusa's welfare. My horse is suffering and it's your fault."

He gave me a challenging look. "No, he's not."

"Well, did you ask him?" I replied. "You'd have to be stupid not to recognise that he was suffering."

He responded in a sarcastic manner. "Why don't you go and ask him."

I felt like murdering him. He continued to say how he felt under pressure to do the job but I cut him short in a fury.

"Listen, no one has put a gun to your head, forcing you to do this," I shouted. "Tusa is not a pet hamster and if you felt you did not have the experience to do this, you should have fucking well said so before."

I was shaking with anger and my heart was ripped to pieces for Tusa's agony. I held his head close to my chest while the rain poured down. The vet and I did not speak another word.

When Johnny and his friend arrived, I kissed Tusa on the side of his face and walked away. I put my hands over my ears and chanted the same line over and over again.

"It will be over soon. It will be over soon."

Unfortunately I could still hear the single muffled shot.

I walked into Mise's stable, put my arms around her and cried sad tears, I had no more.

"It's all over now Mise, it's all over."

I did not pay the vet. He knew what was good for him and did not pursue the matter.

The following morning, I went over to where Tusa was buried. I put a wooden cross bearing his name on his grave and decorated it with pretty wild flowers.

It was time to move on.

For a while after Tusa's passing, Mise's eyes were still sad. But she always appeared calm in my presence, no tricks or anything. I sensed a special bond between us, as if she knew we only had each other now. I loved her so much.

I found a replacement horse without too much difficulty. It was not a Criollo, they were few and far between, but I liked the look of our new companion who I called Tu Fein. It means 'yourself' in Irish.

I decided to buy him despite the fact that he was highly-strung. He had enough of a troubled look on his face to bring out the protective instinct in me. It was as if his eyes pleaded with me to take him. I had a suspicion he was mistreated before. It took weeks before he would trust me enough to take food from my hand. It was a good feeling to see our relationship progressing, Tu Fein getting more used to me with each passing day. It was not long before he stopped rolling his eyes nervously when I approached.

At the Venezuelan Consulate they were friendly and helpful but there was confusion as to what I needed in the way of papers for the horses. I gathered that they had never had a request like that and did not know what to say to somebody requesting permission to ride across the Brazilian border into their country.

Five days after Tusa was put down I was still waiting for the results of his second *mormo* test. They did not know at the Ministério that Tusa was not with us any longer and I simply kept quiet.

I was over the moon when a couple of days later I got formal clearance. The test came back negative and Mise did not need to be tested again. But things were not that straightforward. Guillermo had not yet received the formal veterinary particulars from the Venezuelan consulate, so he could not provide me with an International Heath Certificate.

I was exasperated.

"You have to look *outside* the framework of what your handbook tells you Guillermo," I said. "This is an unusual situation. The Venezuelans cannot give you the information because they don't know themselves what is needed."

I convinced him that the Venezualan Consul General was happy for me to proceed with the horses and had assured me that I would have no problems at the border.

"Just give me the GIA (a certificate that allows you to travel from one state to another in Brazil) please," I asked Guillermo, "and I will negotiate with Venezuela onwards."

After numerous phone-calls to the chief, Dr. Neuza, he finally agreed.

"And that's why I have to go back, to so many places in the future,
there to find myself and constantly examine myself with no witness
but the moon and then whistle with joy, ambling over rocks and clods of earth,
with no task but to live, with no family but the road"
— *Pablo Neruda*

Entry into Venezuela was not as smooth as I had hoped. Officials on the Brazilian side demanded export papers for the horses. After a frustrating half hour explaining and much exaggerated sighing, they finally let me exit Brazil with the papers I had.

On the Venezuelan side everything was scrutinised and it seemed only a small number of people could give permission for us to pass through. If one of those people was on an extended lunch break or was not going to return until the next day, that was it, you had to wait.

I got part of my official documentation for the horses seen to by a co-operative woman vet but had to hang around for hours before another official could give me the final stamp to enter Venezuela.

I also had my first experience with bribery after some papers 'disappeared' only to be 'found' again. The man who approached me with my documents had a suspicious look about him. He had difficulty maintaining eye contact for longer than three seconds and I just knew he was a thief. I had noticed him earlier hanging around idly, bearing the demeanour of somebody that had all day to contemplate his next move. With shoulders slumped, he stood casually against a wall. The only movement came from his jaws as he slowly and deliberately chewed on a piece of gum.

Even though I knew that bribery was part of the culture in some South and Central American countries, I had made a vow to myself never to succumb to these crooked ways. Unfortunately I had no choice this time. I was very vocal about the corruption and made sure everybody around knew what I thought of the man, but nobody seemed to care about having a criminal in their midst.

In Santa Elena, an American man staying at the same hostel as me made an interesting comment about Venezuelans.

"I find them very distrustful," was how he put it. "They are not keen to find solutions and everything is a huge mountain. Basically they are very negative people."

His viewpoint surprised me and I hoped he was just biased.

"Well, we'll have to wait and see," I said optimistically. "Every person's experience is different."

As Mise, Tu Fein and I trotted out of town we were joined by a friendly-faced dog that appeared out of nowhere. He paid no attention to my finger waving and commanding voice, urging him to go back. He stayed with us until we had reached the outskirts and reluctantly turned around. For a moment I fantasised about having a dog travelling with us but thoughts of the added responsibility put a damper on my dreams. Tu Fein's trot was smooth and easy and he almost needed no spurring on. He gave me an offended look once when my crop accidentally tapped his backside. There were very few cars on the road and I enjoyed the feeling of space and the wide sweeps of open savannah. The immense blue skies gave the feeling of being on the roof of the world.

My rather basic map did not indicate the tiny settlements on the way and by four o'clock I started to look out for anywhere secluded to overnight. A couple of houses were dotted on a hilltop but apart from barking dogs there was no-one around. I pitched my tent very close to the main road in a deserted bungalow with walls three quarters high. It had no door but at least I was partially protected and obscured from general view. A bridge about one hundred yards on was evidence of water and the sight of a lush-looking patch of green grass on the bank persuaded me to tie up the horses there. I changed into my bathing suit and had a wash in the stream. Afterwards I wrote my diaries until darkness fell and climbed into my tent. I had the pistol loaded but was not overly wary about being alone. It was only when I woke up to men's voices in the early morning hours that my heart started racing. They did not spot the tent and I relaxed when their footsteps faded away.

The following morning a movement caught my eye as I was saddling up the horses. I looked up and saw a man on the hilltop in front of his house, standing motionless, watching us. I waved twice but received no response.

The officials at a police point on the way to San Francisco de Yuruani were not the friendliest. Maybe they were bored.

Without looking at me, one asked his colleague, "Why would somebody want to travel on a horse?"

He pulled an ugly face as if he was thoroughly confused.

His friend replied mockingly, "Oh, they go on bicycles, horses, just about everything."

I ignored their sarcastic comments and waited patiently to get my papers back.

I took a break further on when I spotted a sparkling river on the side of the road, curving invitingly between rocks and trees. Just as I had unsaddled, a car with a group of boys stopped to chat. I answered the usual questions and when they heard where I had ridden from, their eyes widened.

"Felicidades!" (congratulations) they said with broad grins, some shaking their heads in disbelief.

While the horses splashed about in the shallow water, I sat on a rock, sipping a hydrating drink from my water bottle and munching on a handful of pumpkin seeds. I inspected my heels where blisters were forming from the friction of my boots. I walked a lot and the socks I was wearing were not thick enough.

In San Francisco de Yuruani, a tidy Indian village with a school and a small number of simple houses, many of them with thatched roofs and pink bougainvilleas abundant, I left the horses in the care of a young boy eager to earn a bit of pocket money, and took a minibus back to the border town of Santa Elena, about 70 kilometres away. My pack had become too heavy so I decided to go to a courier company to have my trainers and other excess baggage sent on to Caracas.

While having a sandwich and tea in a small café, I watched CNN news in Spanish on the television mounted on the wall. The war in Iraq seemed imminent and I wondered what dreadful consequences that would have, not only for its many innocent citizens but also for the world at large.

World events and affairs of the day have always interested me. During my journey I missed not knowing what was going on in the world. Sometimes it added to that sense of isolation I felt. Most important news would be passed on through friends and family via emails, even though it sometimes meant receiving the information well after the event.

What bothered me was being completely out of touch with the day to day happenings. In a weird way I worried that if I 'forgot' the world, then the world would forget me. What I was busy with was so far removed from reality and I wondered if my cocoon existence would be to my detriment later. Would I still have the curiosity in me? Would I still want to know? Would I still care? Or would I find out that not-knowing is actually better. It is simpler. There is less to worry about, less to keep you awake at night.

Later I bumped into Eva Hernandez, the vet who helped me with my papers at the border. Her husband was with her and we discussed my route.

"Don't stay over at Las Claritas or San Isidro," he advised. "It's too dangerous and you'll be shot for your money."

I nodded my head showing that I understood the warning. He continued.

"Even as a Venezuelan man, I wouldn't go there."

He suggested I stay with the military police and get them to look out for me. I promised to avoid staying in that area and would push on beyond it.

That evening, the village of San Francisco de Yuruani appeared very dark with only the odd candle burning on a few open porches, creating a special ambience. People sat peacefully in front of their houses.

61. Waterfall in Kama Meru, Venezuela.
62. A typical vista of the Gran Sabana shared with Mise and Tu Fein.

63. Writing diaries under the remaining light of the day.
64. A long road stretches ahead as we go through the Gran Sabana.

65. Idonia and her mother doll-me-up.
66. Smiles from a hospitable family, one stop before Ciudad Bolivar.

67. Resting weary bones.
68. On a Jet-plane (courtesy of DHL) from Caracas to Costa Rica.

It was so quiet I felt like I should whisper. Every now and then somebody would say something. Sometimes nothing was said. The smell of food drifting through the evening air led me to the house of a woman cooking out in the open in front of her house. She was willing to prepare something for me. An hour later I picked up the bread, chicken and rice; my lunchbox for the following day.

There was no water coming from the shower in my room and I rinsed myself in a bucket of water. The mosquito net fitted awkwardly over the bed and I ended up sleeping with my head at the foot of the bed.

The Gran Sabana, a rolling grassy highland in Venezuela's far south-eastern corner, is one of the most celebrated landscapes of the country. It encompasses Canaima National Park, Angels Falls and a wealth of cultural and biological diversity. In this almost alien landscape, the dramatic views of the scattered flat-topped mountains, called *tepuis,* adds to a sensation of great distance and enormity. It had a lasting impression on me. Riding in such unique surroundings somehow made me feel separate from the ordinary realities of life.

I was struck by the number of waterfalls on the way. The one in Kama Meru, although small, had a large flat rock that extended out from the base of the waterfall. It was incredibly smooth and sported an unusual red colour.

It was in Kama Meru, a popular stop-over not only because of the waterfall but also its old-fashioned thatched bungalows, that I met a woman called Blanca. She was holidaying with her family in the south of her country during the Easter period. Meeting her was just another of those encounters in life, and specifically on this journey, which seemed destined to happen. As it turned out, she played a crucial part in my journey. Her nieces urged me to make contact with them when I reached Puerto Ordaz and Blanca gave me an open invitation to her house once I arrived in Caracas.

When I told her that the horses were my main concern on this trip, she shook her head.

"You are very important too," she said, her tone warm but serious. "In fact, I think you are the most important."

I tried to explain how *I* decided to make this journey. It was not only my responsibility but also my duty to ensure that first and foremost the horses, who had no say in the matter, were happy and well looked after.

Blanca and her family were worried about how I would manage to travel on from Cuidad Bolivar. It was not the first time somebody had expressed concern about that.

"What will you do when you have to cross Puente Angostura?" was the repeated question. (Puente Angostura, outside Ciudad Bolivar, is a suspension bridge built in 1967, with a main span of 712 metres across the Orinoco River).

I shook my head. "I don't know, probably like I would cross any other bridge."

They shook their heads. "You can't. It's illegal for anybody to walk across."

I did not know what to say.

"Well, I'll have to cross that bridge when I come to it."

Only those with good English understood the irony of my remark.

Tu Fein never seemed comfortable with being tied to a long leading rope and kept getting tangled up. The friction from the rope cut into the sensitive, lower side of his back feet, called the pastern, a part that extends from the fetlock to the top of the hoof. It was a bloody mess and I wondered if he would behave while I tried to clean it. I was surprised at how he stood perfectly still while I rinsed the wound with a salt solution, using a cloth to wipe away the blood. He did not mind my fingers touching the sores when I put on antibiotic cream and it was Mise who gave a jump when I sprayed repellent to keep the insects away.

I was extremely pleased with the positive changes in Tu Fein's behaviour. He had also stopped being paranoid whenever I handed out a carrot or something sweet to nibble on. In the beginning he would regard me warily, head turned side-ways, whites of his eyes showing. He would bring his head closer very slowly and when within reach, would grab the food like a hungry dog. With time I sensed that he trusted me more and more. To me this proved once again that all animals have the potential to be well behaved and a pleasure to have around if handled with tender care and patience. I do believe that pets are reflections of their owners and how we treat them.

Blanca and her family left the day after we met but I decided to hang around for another day. In the early evening I walked over to the little restaurant but found the door locked. I walked to the house of one of the workers and asked the women where I would find food.

"The man of the kitchen won't be back today and I can't do anything, I'm alone with my child," she said.

I told her I was really hungry and that I did not have a morsel of food left with me. After some nagging she agreed to have chicken, rice and salad ready at 8 p.m.

Not much later there was a knock on my door. A young girl with a sheepish expression informed me that only rice would be served.

"The woman who said she would make the food has problems with her husband. She cannot make you anything else," she said.

Not happy with the news, I searched my bags for something to nibble on. I found a tiny piece of stale sweet bread which I ate slowly, savouring every bite. I was tempted not to answer another knock on my door but got up when the banging persisted. I eagerly took the plate my neighbour handed me, consisting of a slice of thin pork, cheese, six chips and a tiny portion of rice.

Maybe there was a God after all.

The road through the Gran Sabana was not the best for riding. The sides, although open spaces of savannah, were uneven and in many parts had large stones scattered around. We had to go on the tarmac too often and I knew that before long, the horses would need new shoes. That was not my only concern. The hard surface was also tiring for the horses and with the heat they displayed less and less energy.

Kamoirán was probably my most pleasant stay in the Gran Sabana. With only a gas station, grocery store, a restaurant and rooms for accommodation, it was basic but ideal. The people were friendly and open but did not intrude. They were curious though to know the names of the horses. My tummy full after a tasty pasta dish served with fresh bread, I led Mise and Tu Fein to a cascade behind the complex and had a beer, my feet dangling in the cool water. Feeling happy and content, I spontaneously burst into singing *"What a wonderful world"* at the top of my voice.

The following day I came back down to earth when I had to secure the pack on Tu Fein four times over a short stretch. I could not figure what I was doing wrong and felt frustrated by our lack of progress. While I was adjusting the pack a minibus approached and from a distance I could see people's heads sticking out of windows, cameras flashing. They were French tourists, curious and excited to have stumbled across a female rider and her two horses.

"Give us your address in Ireland and we'll send you some of the pictures," they kindly offered.

The same day I also met another interesting French traveller. Just as we reached the top of a hill, I spotted a cyclist. I was sure he was foreign but refreshingly he was not parading in the usual flashy gear. Matthieu was wearing ordinary very dirty shoes, equally dishevelled trousers and an Arran sweater (Irish traditional knitwear) that looked as if he slept in it. Over his panniers were a number of towels, spread out to dry. He was cycling through Latin America and planned to tackle Asia next.

"The children from ten schools in France are following the journey," he told me. "I send them regular updates about the countries I go through, my experiences and also typical recipes."

We had a pleasant chat and then headed off in opposite directions, tracing each other's footsteps through foreign lands.

Arriving at Luepa, a military base, late one afternoon, I made the mistake of entering the grounds instead of presenting myself at the Control Point further down the road. I was met by urgent whistling, stern faces and guns pointing in our direction.

"You are in a prohibited area," said one stern face. "You should immediately go back towards the main road and make your way over to the Control Point."

Still sitting on Mise, I looked to my left and said, "Surely I could just cut across this field. It'll be much shorter than having to go back to the road."

He shook his head adamantly. "No, you can't,"

I could never come to grips with that kind of inflexibility.

"It just doesn't make sense," I said. "I'm in the restricted area already so it'll be just the same if I cut across the field."

I was amused by their stiff-necked attitude.

"Why do you all look so serious?" I asked lightly. "Have you received bad news?"

A number of them could not help but smile back.

"That's better," I said as I turned and steered Mise and Tu Fein across the field towards the Control Point.

The horses were tied up and one of the men took me to a high ranking official.

"Commandant, excuse me, hmm, eh, um, this girl from Argentina..."

The formality of his tone and him shifting timidly from one foot to the other nearly had me in a fit of giggles. With a smile on my face I cut in and introduced myself to the good humoured Commandant who led me next door to meet the Major. I told him that my horses needed new shoes and I planned to travel to the nearest town that evening.

"Your horses can stay," he said.

But it turned out to be a huge dilemma when I mentioned that my bags would have to be left behind as well. Finally he agreed.

"Fine, but only for one day."

I did not know the size of the horses' feet in Venezuelan terms and had to think quickly how to measure them. The horses were standing in front of the office door at the Control Point under a canopy, protected from a light drizzle. I asked for sheets of paper and put these under the horses' hooves and with a pen, I traced the shape. Next thing, both horses lifted their tails and did their business right on the spot. The man managing the office looked thoroughly displeased, throwing his hands up in the air, ranting. I tried to soothe his fury.

"It's only horse manure and the world hasn't stopped. I'll clean it up in a minute."

There was only one woman in the battalion. Her name was Ana and she was also the major's wife. A real character, she was delighted when she realised we would be able to converse in English. She took me under her wing immediately.

Her yes was a long 'yeeeeesh' as she sang it loudly from a low C to the top. I was invited for dinner in the communal dining area and after that everybody retreated to the 'casino', a leisure room with couches, two pool tables, a television and a bar.

Cruz, a young man of about twenty-two, was told to stay at my side at all times and to make sure I did not feel left out. Patriotic songs about Venezuela were belted out and after numerous rums and cokes they began to dedicate every song *"para Marianne"*. I had never witnessed so much testosterone and macho bravado in one room as the men jumped around, roared, bumped chests and gave high fives.

I was relieved when at 11 p.m. a soldier alerted us to the arrival of a bus. It was like something out of a secret military operation as Cruz and his assistant escorted me to the waiting bus. Cruz got in, had a word with the driver and led me to my seat. The bus was packed with sleeping passengers. My seat turned out to be wet from a leaking air conditioner above but despite that and the large, snoring woman next to me, I fell asleep straight away.

We reached Upata just after five the following morning.

After going round the town for two hours in a taxi, I finally found a farrier who was willing to travel to Luepa. He wanted one hundred dollars, everything included. I shook my head.

"I might be a *gringa* but I don't have much money."

He laughed and we settled on half of that.

After an extensive search, we found the right size shoes. Well almost right. The horses were a five and all that were available were fours and sixes. I settled on the latter, knowing it would be easier to make a metal shoe smaller than having to stretch it.

I nibbled on a toasted sandwich while we waited for the bus. Two men sitting next to my table asked if I needed a taxi. I declined.

"So, how are you travelling through Venezuela then?" they asked curiously.

When I said by horse they burst out laughing.

The ride in the bus was bumpy and uncomfortable. The driver drove like a madman. A strange-looking fellow sat next to me. He stared at me a few times and without uttering a word, handed me his golden ring. I shook my head that I was not interested in taking it. He continued to sit in stony silence and when he was getting off, he shook my hand formally and departed, again in silence.

It was past 6 p.m. when we arrived at our last stop, 56 kilometres from Luepa. The farrier and I were the last ones to get out. When he went to the back of the bus to retrieve his bag of tools and the horse shoes, it was gone. He and the driver jumped back in the bus and rushed in the direction of the second last stop. They arrived back quite soon, the farrier displaying a satisfied grin. They had caught the thief just as he was going through the bag on the side of the road.

A man gave us a lift in his 4 x 4 and we arrived at Luepa just as dusk was falling. A group including Ana gathered to watch the farrier at work. She turned to the man.

"I hope you're doing a good job because she still has to go to New York."

The farrier smiled wryly.

"You are asking a lot from a simple pair of horse shoes *señora*."

Day 285. Ana gave me a long hug the following morning, obviously sad to see her only female companion going.

I looked back to wave and she shouted, "Remember your best friend is God and Venezuela is the best country in the world!"

We were warmly received at Cierra de Lema, another Military Control Point, 22 kilometres on. They suggested I keep the horses inside the fenced area for the night.

"There are tigers around," one of the men said.

I shivered. In a way, I would have preferred not to know. Although my bed was comfortable and I knew the horses were safe, I did not sleep well and was up well before 5 a.m.

The road twisted downhill from Cierra de Lema, tropical forest and dense vegetation on both sides. Initially I did not hear any birds but later the forest came alive, sounding like an orchestra fine tuning their instruments before the start of an opera. I walked with the horses and stopped regularly to allow them to munch on luscious palms on the side. I took the bit out of Tu Fein's mouth so he could eat more comfortably.

There were green tapestries of fern everywhere looking like soft, inviting beds. I could hear water but not see it. A short distance on I spotted a small waterfall, water tumbling over rocks through the greenery.

'This is something a motorist will never see,' I thought to myself.

Often when we travel in conventional ways, the focus is on the big picture stuff, the sunset, a mountain in the distance, a flowing river. Because the pace is sometimes fast and often confined inside a vehicle, we do not see the magical little things on the way. Slowing down and noticing the tiny insects, the browns, greens and yellows of the leaves, the sound of a sparkling stream over rocks and stones, catching the expression on a cute little animal in the bushes – each and everything adding and enriching our experiences and perceptions of the beauty of the world around us.

A twig fell from a tree and a monkey's face appeared from among the branches. He was curious and came quite close. When we moved on he gave an exaggerated leap to another tree, making both horses jump. A number of large, oversized trucks came crawling past, grinding their gears. The horses did not flinch.

Further down the road it was Mise that first spotted movement between the dense bushes and sure enough, twenty yards on we encountered two young men, squatting on their haunches, almost hidden from sight in the undergrowth, doing nothing. One of them asked if we came from Santa Elena. "Yes," I said formally and continued without speaking another word. I did not like their presence and once we were out of sight, I put the pistol in my moneybag as a precaution.

Tu Fein, a perturbed look on his face, did not know what to make of all the curious bystanders when we reached the town of San Isidro, often simply called 'KM88'. Earlier some over-excited kids came to see the horses and one ignorant boy hit Tu Fein on the mouth. I did not blame my horse for being wary when yet more people approached. Not wanting to leave the horses alone, I handed a petrol attendant money.

"Could you please buy me a fruit juice?" I asked.

A dodgy-looking character hiding behind dark glasses strolled over to talk. Once I had my juice I made a quick exit despite 'come on, come here' sounds, whistling and continuous remarks from more questionable-looking men sitting idly in front of shops, cafés and houses. Some of them sported large guns.

We crossed a small bridge. Women and children were in the water, washing clothes in yellow and turquoise buckets. People drifted from their houses when they heard the clip-clop of hooves on the road. Children incessantly shouted, *"Caballos, caballos!"*

Only three kilometres on we entered the dirty ramshackle town of Las Claritas. Music was blaring from every eating place. A few men shouted, "Looking good beebee," when we passed. I lowered my hat and looked straight ahead.

On the outskirts of town a car pulled up next to us. A German guy sat in the passenger seat. He enquired about my travels in Spanish.

"So, what are *you* doing here?" I asked.

"I'm walking through Latin America," he said proudly. "It took me fifteen months to get from Mexico to KM88."

"Well done!" I said.

We exchanged a few more pleasantries before I continued on.

But we did not go much further. The sight of a few wooden houses in an open area surrounded by green grass and water just off the main road, made me stop. A shy woman indicated I could pitch my tent. Once the horses were settled I washed my face and shirt then brushed my teeth in a shallow stream. Nobody bothered me. Before I crawled into my tent I saw a car coming down the road. It stopped, lingered and then turned around. I slept lightly that night.

The following morning as I saddled up I was watched intently by a man standing by the roadside. He was still there when we left and he tried to shake my hand in the

African friendship way. You shake and with both parties still holding hands, you hinge your wrists, let the thumbs interlock and shake again.

I did not like his over-familiar manner.

"Can I have a ride on your horse?" he asked.

I said no as I continued to walk on.

"Sorry, my horses only like women."

He offered to walk with me. It was just after 6 a.m. and the road was isolated. Because we were going downhill I knew I would not be able to get away from the man fast enough. Trotting was out of the question. He carried a small backpack on his chest, clutching it as if he was holding something rather valuable. His body language made me uneasy.

I stopped.

"Oh gosh, I forgot something," I lied and quickly turned around.

I returned to where I had stayed the night before. Members of the family were standing by the roadside, waiting for a lift into town. I asked a young man if he would walk me downhill. He made an excuse.

"My leg hurts," he said lamely and suggested I asked his elderly father.

The man obliged.

When we got to the bottom of the hill, the other man was still there, waiting for me. I handed my 'bodyguard' a few notes and trotted away. We were getting ahead but the man's pace was fast as well and I never made the gap between us wide enough so I could relax completely.

I was relieved when a few kilometres on, I saw movement and people around. I stopped. It was another small Indian community called Araime Comunidad, the place where I had intended to stay the previous night. I was told that the people there were open and trustworthy. Without hesitation they came closer when they saw me getting off Mise. We were warmly welcomed and as they were from British Guyana, they all spoke perfect English. It made for a welcome change. To be able to communicate without searching for the most appropriate words in Spanish and to express myself properly was wonderful.

"I fear somebody might be following me," I said to the chief.

He invited me to sit down. "Stay here for a while. We'll look after you."

Within minutes I was handed a freshly toasted cheese sandwich and cold, milky tea. To a very hungry woman it tasted like a gourmet meal.

"Everyday we get bread freshly delivered from a man on his motorbike," somebody said.

I had no food with me for the day's ride and asked them to tell the baker to stop if he spotted me on the road later. Out of the corner of my eye I saw the suspicious-looking man of earlier take a side-road. I sighed with relief.

A group of about ten kids from the Araime community ran alongside Mise and Tu Fein as I set off again. The boys showed off, pushed out their chests and strutted like peacocks. One of them lost both his shoes in the process. They were good humoured and in great spirits. When some of the children turned around, two young girls appeared and started to run with us. One of them with long, shiny black hair had a mature, gracious attitude. In a well-mannered way she asked for the horses' names and mine and where we were heading. We met her grandmother and sister coming from the opposite direction carrying containers filled with food and water.

Soon I was on my own again. Dry leaves covered the ground and I saw lizards and a few small snakes trying to blend in with the shades of nature. When we got too close they scurried away, obviously more afraid of us than we were of them.

Often I had to place my trust in complete strangers. I was always aware however that the people I encountered, those strangers, needed to trust me as well. In some ways I could understand if they were more guarded than the other way around. I was definitely a more unusual sight, a tall girl, sporting a large machete, travelling alone with two horses in Latin America. A bizarre scene, no matter how much I 'normalised' it in my own head. When I asked for help, those I sought assistance from had to grapple with their own worries and fears. They had to be comfortable with opening their doors and lives to a complete stranger. In a short space of time they had to decide if they could trust a person and a situation more alien than probably anything else they knew.

I stopped for a rest around midday when I saw an open sided thatched roof building on the side of the road. The shade was welcome and I unsaddled the horses. A man came along, his manner friendly. It was dry and there was nothing for the horses to eat.

"Why don't you bring them to the back of the house where there are reeds," he suggested.

His house was a five minute walk away. I had to make a quick decision. If he had bad intentions it would not have been a good idea to go out of sight with a man I did not know. But something about him told me it was okay.

Later, I sat out in the front writing my diaries at a table he had brought out for me. Standing behind me, he smoked a cigarette in silence. We did not feel the need to converse. There was a comfortable stillness in the air. I wondered for a moment what he was thinking. He was not asking any questions. He understood. He did not need to be curious. He already knew the answers.

Not far from there I encountered more excited children. They came over when I smiled at them. An older girl wore an oversized army shirt and her little brother had underpants on and one sock. Another girl of about five was dressed only in frilly knickers and carried a toy gun. I told them to come closer and touch Mise.

They warily reached out for her nose.

"It is so soft," one girl said and giggled shyly.

I asked for water when we entered a village. An elderly woman, walking slowly as if she suffered badly from arthritis, came over to chat. She liked Mise in particular and patted her neck. I mentioned that she was female and had more energy than Tu Fein most of the days.

"Yes," the woman said with a naughty toothless grin, "men are always tired, aren't they?"

The last seven kilometres to our next destination was difficult. Mise could not sustain a trot longer than a couple of minutes and Tu Fein continuously pulled on the leading rope. I had a sore back and my legs ached all over. As we entered the km 33 mark I spotted a pretty, heavily pregnant mare at the side of the road. She neighed and came running towards us. Mise greeted her in an impersonal manner and Tu Fein tried to make her acquaintance. The neigh he gave sounded hilarious. It was croaky and had you not known he was a horse you could have sworn he was on thirty cigarettes a day. It appeared as if he was embarrassed by the sound himself and did not attempt another one.

A Coca-Cola sign in the distance grabbed my attention. It turned out to be the place I had intended to stay at that evening. The vet's husband in Santa Elena had indicated that it might be a suitable place to overnight. My tent was pitched in a barren room next to a loud generator. The horses escaped during the night after somebody had left the gate ajar. I was woken with the news by a young boy who shook the tent with vigour until I got up. He went back to bed while I chased after Mise and Tu Fein. The night was short and not very restful.

A young woman was having breakfast as I entered the room to say goodbye the following morning. She offered me coffee with strange bits floating on top. I emptied the cup behind a corner. She and her husband were watching early morning television and hardly looked my way when I thanked them for my stay.

I was looking forward to El Dorado, our next destination. Matthieu, the cyclist, had told me about a cosy campsite on the edge of the River Cuyuni. I planned to stay there a couple of days. After 12 kilometres we had our first stop on the far side of a village. There was a small single-roomed house and enough grass for the horses to graze on for a while. The occupants of the house were absent and just as I opened up my saddlebag to get something to eat, a cute, very skinny puppy appeared. He seemed afraid at first but came closer eventually when he saw the *catalinas* (dark, sweet bread) on offer. He gobbled up the first one and when he had enough, used his paws and nose to bury the other piece among loose pebbles. I shared the last drop of my water with him.

He was so clever and cute I had a strong urge to take him with me. Unfortunately, the neighbours could not contain their curiosity and before long a crowd gathered. It messed up my plans so I wrote the owners a little note which I stuck between the door and wall;

Hola, I am a *gringa*, travelling with two horses. Your dog is hungry and thirsty and very thin. Please give him food and water. *Gracias. Con Dios.*

I was walking downhill with the horses when I saw an animal in the distance moving at a snail's pace very close to the ground across the tarmac. At first I thought it was an injured monkey but on closer inspection I recognised it as a sloth.

I have always been fascinated by sloths, so when I spotted this one I had to stop. He had that eternal, good-natured smile on his face and did not make any of the usual hissing sounds when I approached. With a childlike excitement I softly stroked his fur. I really like the sloth. He is calm, quiet and has a face that looks a thousand years old. This one was small and had a burn wound on his back. The local people burn the forests at that time of the year to get the tortoises to come out of their holes. They are caught and killed for Easter. The burning sadly destroys not only the forests but also the wildlife.

The sloth kept on moving painstakingly towards the edge of the road. On the ground it is capable of crawling 250 metres in an hour but when moving along the bough of a tree in its characteristic upside-down position it can cover roughly 400 metres.

Just as the sloth moved into the long grass an Indian man and his son approached. They tried to make conversation but I pretended not to understand, hoping they would leave before they could see the sloth. But the grass was dry and when the sloth continued to move, they heard the sounds and came closer to investigate. I did not leave before they did and I said a silent prayer that they would not go back and capture this magnificent animal.

I was in no mood to take out my papers when we passed a police control point so instead I peppered them with questions and simply trotted past.

Travelling in solitude and having no real opportunity for conversation meant one had a lot of time to think. On the way to El Dorado two days before the 1st of April I decided to send an April fool's joke to family and friends. I sent it from an email address I had created specifically for the outrageous, made-up story below;

A big hello to all my family and friends,

This message is typed and sent by somebody else and my hope is that it'll reach you safe and sound, especially due to its important content. In a nutshell...

Two days into the Gran Sabana in Venezuela, I went off the beaten track and stumbled across a remote Indian village, the tribe which is called Pémon. I did not know I was in a prohibited area until I felt and saw a small arrow sticking from my thigh. I was lucky it had nothing poisonous on the tip. I was stunned when I spotted at least fifty strange-looking creatures, emerging from the long grass. I was captured unceremoniously. I was told after a 12-hour meeting between the most senior Indian men in the village that they were very suspicious about my presence and also that they considered a girl, travelling alone with two horses, the most curious thing they had witnessed since the big birds with deafening sounds that regularly flew over their heads. I was told I would be staying with them indefinitely until they were clear about my intentions. I was informed that I will act as seventh wife to the chief of the community. He is about 91 years of age and goes by the name of Uguani, meaning 'the most virile' in Pémon language. Due to his mature age and unstable heart, I am pardoned to be a wife in the true sense of the word. I am reminded though by his six other wives, whose ages ranged between 55 and 89, with 48 kids between them that I will need to execute a number of duties on a regular basis. The most important of these is to be able to distinguish between edible and poisonous berries which I collect around 5 a.m. every morning. These I have to squash into a pulp and spoon-feed to my husband who has no teeth left.

I was taken shooting a few days ago and by some miracle managed to kill three rabbits using only two arrows. As a result I was relieved of my nightly duty to rub palm tree oil into Ugauni's blistered toes and have become the first woman in the community to lead the hunting team every morning... after I have collected the berries of course. The wives have decided that as a *gringa*, I will not take the surname of the chief. It was whispered in my ear that this decision had more to do with their concern of me inheriting some of Uguani's extensive and elaborate macaw feather head designs he has assembled over the years. The only times I seem to have the wives' goodwill is when I take pictures of them and it sometimes takes hours for them to get ready for these photo sessions. I have long run out of film and by the time they find out I hope to be in another place.

I have very few fears and anxieties here and the best part is never to have to worry about what to wear. I was given three leather thongs by the women in the village as a wedding present and the novelty of white, exposed breasts has worn off for most of the villagers by now. The horses are fine. They have food and water and it was decided that they will not be slaughtered for the Pémon Todos Santos religious festival in three weeks time after all. I urge you not to be worried about me. I don't feel that the situation is life-threatening as long as I play my cards right. I do miss stimulating conversation though but have to be content with a parrot which belonged to a previous captive who died of dysentery not too long ago and who's only line is 'we have to get out of here alive.'

Love Mariuyani (my new adopted Indian name)

As luck would have it, only my mom and dad believed the message and without hesitation somebody in Ireland was phoned to see what could be done to secure my 'release'. I felt really bad for the upset my email had caused them, never having thought for a moment that it would be taken seriously.

Friends replied in different ways but the theme was generally the same, "Get off the coca leaves."

The entrance to the River Cuyuni campsite was covered with numerous international flags, welcoming the visitor to a rustic experience of tranquility, sun and no-frills excursions. These included a miner-guide taking people on day trips to show them the process from extraction of ore-bearing materials to amalgamating it. They even let you pan for gold.

The Swiss owner Bruno, entertained guests playing his authentic Alpenhorn (a curved wooden horn, sometimes as long as 6 meters, used by herders in the Alps to call cows to pasture), while his Venezuelan wife, Vanessa, a former actress, added a different dimension playing the guitar and singing.

"We don't have our rooms ready yet," said Bruno when I entered the premises, "but you're more than welcome to pitch your tent, overlooking the river."

He also had no problem with my horses roaming on his property.

Before sunset I had a refreshing wash in the river and also led the horses into the water. Mise panicked initially but soon got to love the feeling of weightlessness as she went round and round, making little snorting noises.

Cesar, the helper at the site and miner-guide, accompanied me into town the following morning.

"The women here are very good at panning for gold," he told me on the way. "They're much better than the men as they don't spend all their profits, which could be up to 130 dollars a day, on drink. The men go into town after a day's work and start boozing. They buy drinks for everybody in the bar and leave at the end of the night with nothing. Tomorrow they repeat the whole process," he said, shaking his head.

He also told me how the women in that Indian community do all the hard work.

"Men only hunt and they wouldn't even think of washing their own plates," he said. "Then there are the 7th Day Adventists," he laughed. "All they do every weekend is lie around all day. You might think there is nobody in a village until you spot all the swinging hammocks."

Cesar certainly did not fall into the lazy category. He was smart and willing and when the horses went off one day for a little exploring of their own he had no hesitation in spending hours helping me to find them. Another time he rescued me when I was overcharged almost five times the normal price by a taxi driver in town.

"That man is an ass, a big ass," he said numerous times, pushing his bike alongside me as we walked the four miles back to the camp in darkness.

In Venezuela a lot of people keep exotic animals or birds and these seemed to have a much better life than the common domestic animals. At the campsite, a cat meowed constantly for food but the colourful pet parrot got fed three times a day. I also heard about Bruno's pet tiger which was shot by a Columbian poacher.

"I spread the word that I would cut the man's throat if I caught him," said a still angry Bruno.

I shook my head in sympathy, directed more at the animal than its owner.

I felt like saying, "But what was a tiger doing on a chain in the first place?" but held my tongue.

Leaving El Dorado I had at least the name of a *finca* (farm) to look out for on our way. Just before I reached the farm of Antonio Gometz at around 5 p.m., a boy came out of his house to greet the travelling trio. He had a severe haircut, trimmed far too short, his scalp visible. By his crooked smile and first few rambling words, I gathered he had some kind of mental health problem. He was very sweet and hungrily wolfed down the *catalinas* I passed him. Kindly he offered Mise a couple as well. Not long after, his father joined us.

"Do you have some cigarettes," he asked upfront. I handed him three.

I smoked much less these days and sometimes weeks would pass without me lighting up. I simply did not need them any more. In stressful situations, instead of smoking, I now used deep breathing as a relaxation technique. However, I always carried cigarettes with me on my journey. They came in handy and were always useful in showing goodwill. Even those who did not smoke would accept the offer. Some of them would light up just for the hell of it and I had to keep a straight face amidst all the coughing and spluttering

I spent a relaxing evening at Antonio's farm. He did not live there but I was warmly welcomed by a worker, his wife and their seven-year-old daughter. I pitched my tent while the horses nibbled on mangos that were strewn on the ground. Later they were fed *alomiento*, a type of horse food that looked like rabbit pellets, in a tractor tube. The dogs growled and tried to nick some but Mise took no nonsense, scaring them away with a kick and an exaggerated head-butt.

The little girl helped to put my belongings in my tent. She copied my body language and folded her arms in exactly the way I did. When I sighed or laughed, she did the same. The picture I gave her of me and the horses immediately took the place of another one she had on the mirror in their small house.

A few men arrived later and some stared open mouthed when they were told about my journey. Newspaper articles were scrutinised under candle light. They discussed distances and could not hide their admiration when I corrected their guesses of how far the towns are spread out from Santa Elena northwards.

"Calculating distances is an important part of what I need to do everyday," I said with a smile.

I was invited to join in a game of dominoes but only found out after the third game that we were actually playing in teams. There was a good atmosphere around the place. Those who did not play games sat around chatting quietly, among them an ancient-looking couple who listened attentively and gave only the odd gummy smile.

I went to bed without dinner. I had only a poloni sandwich that morning, a packet of crisps, a handful of nuts and one sachet of my *maximuscle* protein drink. I needed more than that.

Puerto Ordaz stands out as a bit of an anomaly in Venezuela. Founded in the 1960s compared to its neighbouring towns such as San Felix which were founded centuries ago, the city has a very modern feel. During my time there, I missed that air of history that permeates the atmosphere of most towns. The people of Puerto Ordaz have taken good care though to preserve and savour the natural beauty around them and the parks around the city showcase the area's flora and fauna.

The concrete jungle of this city became my home while I stayed in an apartment with a family that rented out one of their rooms. The horses were kept in a large parking area not far from there. Fearing they would escape when cars came and went, the owner insisted that both horses were tied up at all times. This arrangement turned out to have disastrous consequences.

On the evening that I arrived, I received a phone-call from a neighbour in the apartment block.

"Your horse is tangled up in a rope," she said with urgency in her voice.

I sped down to where they were kept and got a mighty shock when I saw the state that Mise was in. A lot of people were standing around.

Apparently, a group of young boys walked past and saw Mise on the ground struggling with a rope around her neck. It seemed that by some accident it got caught in her shoe, tripped her up and had somehow wound itself around her neck in the process.

"We struggled for an hour to free her but she was kicking so frantically we could not do anything," they said.

My heart was breaking. Mise's right eye was swollen and bruised and around the other eye it was raw with most of the skin rubbed off by the kicking.

"A man came along and managed to cut the rope," one of them said.

I was shocked and felt so bad for her. In trying to be nice and to give her a bit of roaming space, I had left the rope too long. I could never have envisaged an accident like that would happen.

I led Mise away from the group. She looked shaken and in a fragile condition, standing motionless, her head hanging. I borrowed a t-shirt from one of the boys and wiped away most of the mud on her face and body. I stayed with her until I felt confident that she would pull through.

Wearily I crept into my bed at 3 a.m.

'What a night. What a lesson learned.'

It was meant to be that Mise did not die that night. If she had, I do not know if I would have been able to continue.

The following morning a vet with a happy face and pleasant demeanour came out to look at Mise. He was very taken by my journey.

"And here I am," he said, "married to a Venezuelan wife who can't even go out on to the patio by herself."

He did not want to discuss fees and with a wave of his hand dismissed my insistence on paying.

"We'll talk about that later."

He prescribed eye drops and an antibiotic injection and promised to come out again.

"Your horse will be much better soon," he said

I did not leave for another three days. Michael, the ten-year-old boy of the family where I stayed, loved to help me with the horses. He also started to call Mise, 'Mishie' and did whatever I asked of him. He seemed to like the responsibility of holding the horses while they got their vitamin injections. I was taken by his sweet manner.

During my last dinner with the family, his sister said, "Give it to her now Michael."

He was the colour of beetroot but finally pulled a small brown bag from his pocket. He handed it to me.

"This is for you," he said, casting his eyes away.

Inside was a pretty silver bracelet. He looked even more embarrassed when I planted a big thank you kiss on his cheek.

People were making worried noises about the three-day stretch to Cuidad Boliviar.

"There is nowhere to stay on the way," was the general concern.

I could not quite believe that.

"Well, there has to be something, somewhere," I said.

The apprehensive look on their faces did not go away.

I was dismayed at the amount of broken glass and whole beer bottles strewn along the side of the road. As a result, we were forced to go on the tarmac for most of the way. Mise's eye was still swollen and she seemed to have lost much of her energy. I put some of this down to the hot and stuffy climate. Tu Fein stumbled a few times and I wondered whether his shoes were a proper fit or if he was just worn-out. I suspected it was a combination of both.

Soon I ran out of water but a small road leading to what looked like a farm yard was a godsend. Three men were standing around collecting water in big containers that were then loaded on to their pickups. The water was ice cold and I filled all my bottles. I must have drunk about two litres there and then.

"There is really nothing ahead," an older man commented.

One of them mentioned a small community not too far off the main road about 15 kilometres from there.

Not much further on I saw a sign that said 'breakfast', then a sign for 'lunch and breakfast'. Another hundred yards on was a sign for 'juices' and then one for *chicha*. The last sign read *"hay sopa"*, literally meaning 'there is soup'.

I was nearly salivating by now and quite conscious of my empty stomach. I stopped when I saw a man sitting under a thatched roof. He greeted me with a *"hola cariño"* (hello honey).

I returned his greeting.

"Hola señor. I'm starving, what do you have on your menu?"

"I have nothing to sell you," he said with a pained expression on his face.

He continued to tell me about the problems with the government and petrol shortages in Venezuela.

"That's why I have nothing," he concluded.

"That's fine. I understand," I said in a disappointed voice.

He asked if I had cigarettes and I handed him two. He waved me off with a big smile.

On the way there was a great deal of religious graffiti painted on rocks. Some said 'Christ is coming soon,' others read 'Christ has arrived'. I wished they could make up their minds.

Later in the afternoon I turned off the main road when I saw a sign for Santa Fe close to where I was told there was a small community. A dirt road brought me to a communications tower and a house surrounded by a high fence.

We nearly got savaged by the pack of barking dogs that a man with a big belly had difficulty controlling. With him were another man and a boy of about fourteen. It took the big bellied man a while to agree to my request to stay.

"There is no woman here," he said cautiously.

"That's no problem, the police told me that this is a safe place to stay," I lied.

Later when I wrote my diaries at an outside table the man brought me a plate of rice, eggs, thin yucca and dry bread. I was even fortunate enough to have a mattress on a floor in my own room. The bathroom with cement flooring was rather dirty and covered in religious pictures. Their obvious fanaticism with religion actually made me feel safe, I could not imagine being harmed in any way.

By 7 a.m. the next morning the sun was already out, burning mercilessly. We made numerous stops on the way, always searching for shade and water. After one stop I took the reins off Tu Fein and rode him with only a halter on and without a bit. I was surprised how easy it was to control him by just using a rope attached to the halter. The sensitivity on his nose and neck forced him to obey my commands.

In the late afternoon I noticed a settlement just off the main road and without me having to steer, Tu Fein led the way to it. Two boys explained a short cut to a nearby village. Next, a woman, looking more African than Indian, came out of the house. She handed me ice cold water and then a sweet espresso in a small plastic cup.

"Why don't you stay here tonight?" she asked in a friendly voice.

Before I could even answer, a chair was brought out and I was told to sit down. Her two sons spontaneously took the horses from me, unsaddled them and gave each one a thorough wash. I felt like I had just won the jackpot.

Their 16-year-old sister with mature breasts and a pretty face, called Idonia, asked me later if I wanted my hair done in plaits like hers. I said yes and soon she and her mom got busy on my head. Her young brother held the pot of gel as they applied their expertise, lashing on handfuls of the sticky stuff.

Early in the evening I handed the father of the family money to buy food and drink for all of us. He did not need a second invitation and sprinted on his bicycle to the nearest village. I declined the change when he returned.

"Why did you not want your money back?" Idonia asked me later.

I was not sure how to respond. They were proud people and she showed me her possessions – a hairdryer, a small black and white television and a camera. There were three rooms in the house, two had a number of hammocks hanging from the ceiling and one a double-bed. Given my lack of experience in sleeping in a hammock, it was decided that I would share the bed with Idonia. She asked if I wanted a window open. When I said yes, she removed a piece of wood from the wall, exposing a hole with no glass in front. I wondered about the mosquitoes but was glad for the cool breeze. I fell asleep while she was reading out loud a letter she had just written to me. During the night I was aware of her snuggling up and making sounds like a small puppy, her arms around me.

The day's ride to Cuidad Bolivar was a scorcher. Nowhere could I find a shaded place to stop for a break. There was burnt grass everywhere and not a tree in sight. When we finally found something half suitable I noticed Mise's breathing. It was very fast – 124 breaths per minute compared to Tu Fein's fifty. After the rest, Mise's had gone down to eighty-eight and I felt it was safe to proceed. She just was not cut out for such extreme heat.

In Cuidad Bolivar, heading to the house of people who had invited us, we were peppered with mangoes by a group of school children. At first I was annoyed but later had to laugh. I probably deserved it and it was my own fault for ignoring their shouts and attempts to get a response or at least a wave.

I had difficulty finding the home of my contacts.

When I stopped to ask people they said, "It's very far, about three kilometres from here."

I nodded and said nothing. Explaining that I had done more 'three kilometres' in the past ten months than I would care to remember, would most likely have invited more questions and strange looks. Keeping Mise in a slow walk and savouring the last few kilometres of peace and silence, my thoughts drifted back to Argentina...

Unsure and green I had set off from San Diego almost one year ago. With saddlebags full of hope and stars in my eyes I had steadily kept my gaze on the road. I was adamant that the glass had to be kept half-full. That had not changed. The optimism was still there, the inquisitiveness for what might lie around the next corner had not disappeared. I was hoping that after all those months I could now add more wisdom to my repertoire with maybe a pinch of increased patience on top. On the practical front I was so much better with the horses, so much more confident and in control. I was nearly the boss now.

Ciudad Bolivar has the feel of a small town despite its 100,000 inhabitants. Pink, yellow, green and blue paint decorate the fronts of little houses in the historical centre, close to a statue of Simon Bolivar – the South American revolutionary leader who was credited with leading the fight for independence in what are now the countries of Venezuela, Columbia, Ecuador, Peru, Panama and Bolivia.

With the relentless heat, I soon found out that siestas were a necessity and gladly followed suit during the few days I spent there. Afternoons were enjoyed socialising in the shade and strolling along the promenade along the Orinoco. The family I stayed with in Cuidad Bolivar was extremely hospitable. They had only one concern. My well-being. As long as they thought I was happy there, enjoying the food and having the time of my life, they were satisfied. Life was really good some days.

On my second day, a journalist arrived and had one beer after another. He was a terrible listener and I had to tell him to be quiet when he interrupted me for the umpteenth time. He asked no relevant questions and did not have any batteries for his tape recorder.

"You don't have to pay for this interview," he slurred after we had nothing more to say to each other.

It was difficult to refrain from laughing out loud.

Alberto, a jovial character and man of the house, arrived with friends of theirs just as we had finished. The men were pretty jolly too and I could smell the alcohol from a distance.

"This girl has travelled from Patagonia with her horses and is going to Australia," Alberto announced proudly as he opened yet another can of beer.

I knew they were far gone when he later compared me to Simon Bolivar.

"You are our modern day Liberator," Alberto announced for the whole neighbourhood to hear.

I shook my head. It was obvious the beer was now talking.

"I don't think so," I laughed, pretending to be pleased with their flattery. "Bolivar was a hero in these countries and his perseverance in the face of overwhelming odds made him a role model to many," I said, showing off what little knowledge I had of Venezuelan history.

"Exactly!" roared Alberto's friend. "You are our hero."

I stayed another two days at Alberto's house. They were easy-going and kind and his sister living next door could not do enough for me. She considered her eldest son a perfect match for me.

They were easy to amuse and chuckled when I said, "If I don't leave soon I'll be here for *navidad* (Christmas)."

Crossing the Puente Angostura (looking quite like the Golden Gate bridge in San Francisco), which I had been warned about so much, turned out to be much less of a nightmare than everybody had imagined. I nonchalantly pulled up with the horses, ignored the officials at the tollgate, waved to another man and even took a picture before we crossed. The metal surface with gaps in-between, presenting a view of the river waters forty-five metres below, was not the best for horses. They sniffed the ground cautiously and proceeded slowly. I had my left arm extended to keep cars a safe distance away. Most of them obliged.

We were about three quarters of the way through when a policeman pulled up.

"What you're doing is illegal. Did you not know you're not allowed to walk across this bridge?" he asked through his car window, not overly anxious.

I pulled Tu Fein in for a moment.

"What was I supposed to do? Swim across the river? We're on our way to New York, *señor!*"

The policeman scratched his head.

"Well, I guess you are almost on the other side," he said after a while. "I'll pretend I never saw you."

In Venezuela, I had the privilege of spending some time with Yurubi, the most interesting woman I had ever met, not only on this journey, but probably in my entire life. She was related to Blanca, the woman I met in Kama Meru in the Gran Sabana. I stayed with Yurubi and her Texan husband Jimmy for more than a week.

The horses were in need of rest and recuperation after days of relentless heat, the dry climate and lack of food, especially since the Gran Sabana. Mise had started to pull back a lot when on the leading rope, something she never did before. I imagined her legs were hurting from going on the tarmac so much. We had little choice. When it looked as if it was suitable to ride on the side of the road we encountered not only stubby burnt grass making the surface uneven, but bottles, cans and rubbish everywhere. It was terribly frustrating and I could not take the risk of the horses injuring themselves.

While I stayed at Yurubi's a number of interviews took place. With every one I made sure to mention the terrible litter and dirt I encountered on the way. To our surprise that part was edited out of every single interview.

During my time in Venezuela it was clear that this was a divided society. It was as if people had lost their own identity. They were known less by their names than whether they were *chavistas* (supporters of Hugo Chavez, the President) or anti-*chavistas*. Some families were polarised to the degree that they had stopped communicating altogether.

Yurubi was not a *chavista*. But she was politically very active, consistent with the dominant Venezuelan culture since the beginning of their democracy in 1958. However, the political debate had not always been so tense. So involved was Yurubi with the troubles of her country that for safety's sake one of her sons was sent to the United States to finish his schooling.

One day she took me to the house of a woman whose sister she believed could help with the painful tendons I had been suffering from for weeks. The conversation turned political and I watched wide-eyed as Yurubi got more and more agitated.

After ten minutes in the house she jumped up and said to me, "Come on, let's go and find a real doctor."

I smiled uneasily at the stunned women as we left in a hurry.

"It is impossible to talk to those *chavistas*," Yurubi said once we were in her pickup, still visibly upset by the exchange of words. "They all have tunnel vision and along with Chavez are destroying our country."

She told me how thousands of people had lost their jobs as a result of the strike that started in December 2002.

"The middle class is disappearing," she said. "Chavez is a manipulator who has thrown his lot in with the masses of the poor and downtrodden. Our country is a mess."

That was of course only one side of the coin. Those supporting Chavez would say that his radical policy of attempting to share the wealth generated from the export of his country's vast oil revenue with the majority peasant population, had to be acknowledged. That, as well as his attempts at creating a health care system accessible to all. The supporters felt that his policies, a radical change from the previous governments, had upset the apple cart, causing various degrees of disgruntlement among the more affluent members of society.

It seems that Chavez is trying to replace the North American cultural influence by national and holistic values. He wants to see more participative democracy, the growth of the country's population and increased rural development. He prefers national production over imports and wants to replace lack of self-esteem by belief in the empowerment of the people. Instead of singing the praises of other countries, he wants Venezuelans to have faith in their own.

The 'anti-*chavistas*' describe themselves as the 'democrats'. They describe the President as a 'communist' and a 'dictator' and his supporters as 'hooligans', 'delinquents' and 'killers'. But realities are more complex.

In April 2002, Chávez survived a coup by dissident generals, backed by opposition media tycoons and many in Venezuela's upper class. US officials knew of the plot in advance and Washington welcomed his arrest and apparent overthrow. But the mutiny collapsed two days later when hundreds of thousands streamed out of the poor areas of Caracas, calling for his release in a huge display of 'people power'.

In fact, in a country that was still a dictatorship 45 years ago, democracy is not yet a cultural conviction, particularly among the economic elite. That might be the reason why they have also overestimated their capacity to mobilise an electorate that has serious doubts about their democratic vision.

The *chavistas* see themselves as the 'people', the vast majority of the Venezuelan population, in contrast with the 'very few' from the opposition. They even call themselves the 'anti-few', meaning that they define themselves in a clear opposition to the rest of the society. They describe their opponents as a corrupt oligarchy and middle class that have robbed the oil revenues from 'the people' for their own particular benefits. Consequently, 'the people' have to take the power and fight against them if social justice is to be achieved.

It often crossed my mind that both sides might actually be closer to each other than they imagine, because they belong to the same culture. It was interesting to see how the Venezuelan flag was used by both sides as a demonstration of their patriotism.

In Ciudad Bolivar I was presented with a t-shirt bearing the colours of the Venezuelan flag.

"Make sure you wear this all the time," my hosts, who were anti-*chavistas,* said.

I am sure, had I stayed with the 'other side', they would have had exactly the same sentiments. Not long after, I had my picture taken with a girl, dressed from head to toe in the colours of the flag.

"Chavez our President is the best," she said to no-one in particular while we 'cheesed' for the camera.

Yurubi was a strong woman with definite views but what I remember most about her was how easily she laughed. And I could not remember when I had laughed as much as the time I spent with her. She and Jimmy had a comfortable, fun relationship. She was her own person and he accepted her unconditionally.

"I've told Jimmy I would like to be with another man just once," she said tongue in cheek. "He knows it's not because I don't fancy him anymore but I am curious what it would be like to be with somebody else."

She told me how she reckoned she knew Jimmy better than he knew her.

"He bought me a ring for Valentine's Day and I hate jewellery," she said. "I told him I did not want it especially when he told me the girls in the office suggested it would be a nice gesture."

She shook her head, obviously mystified.

"Why did he not buy me a hosepipe or something for the dogs instead?"

While Yurubi smoked like a chimney and drank one coffee after another (she claimed there were more benefits than vices from her habits) she told me about their honeymoon.

"We went to the States as Jimmy wanted to visit all his family, most of whom are very old. So we ended up having our romantic dinners in numerous nursing homes across the country."

She was fascinated by my journey and indicated she would have loved to join me on horseback.

"But really I am too lazy," she admitted. "I would have to sit down every hour or so and would need a break every two days."

On my second day with her, I was tucking into a plate of food she had prepared.

"You'd better eat all you can now," she said with a serious face.

"I know," I said after a mouthful, "I don't know what is ahead once I leave your house."

She chuckled.

"No, you misunderstand. I mean you might not get another proper meal while you are here!"

I nearly choked with laughter.

My tendons continued to give me trouble and Yurubi took me to a paediatrician, the only doctor she knew well enough to see me at such short notice. There was a couple with their tiny baby in the waiting room sitting quietly opposite us. Soon Yurubi was chatting to the woman who suffered from post-natal depression. It was not long before she and her husband were in stitches from Yurubi's anecdotes and funny remarks. If I remember rightly, she also recommended sex as great therapy for any kind of mental or physical condition.

Once in the paediatrician's room she said, "There is no charge for this lady."

The kind doctor had no choice but to obey. He prescribed a long list of antibiotics, none of which I bought. Instead, that evening I put hot and cold compresses on the inflamed parts. There was some relief but it took weeks before I managed to walk with ease again.

Yurubi also introduced me to friends at her 'club', a tiny corner shop in the village. A few of the regular customers were there, all of them characters. One woman did embroidery and needlework in exchange for beer. They listened attentively to Yurubi's tales about my journey, making tut-tut and aah noises in all the right places.

Gajao, her helper on the farm, was mad about horses.

"He is very poor," Yurubi said, "but he always makes sure that his horses have something to eat."

Gajao looked after Mise and Tu Fein and also administered an injection to make up for any vitamin deficiencies. It worked a treat especially for Tu Fein. I took him out the next day and made the mistake of riding him with only the halter on. I realised I had no control once I turned his nose back towards the house. The vitamin injection must have given him a burst of renewed energy because he sprinted off like a horse possessed. I thought an accident was imminent and could only cling on for dear life. He came to a halt when a fence forced him to stop. Yurubi thought she might be able to handle him but suffered the same fate. Ditto for Gajao. We stood there with white faces and trembling legs, cursing ourselves for our bravado in thinking we could have ridden him without a proper bit.

It looked like our travel plans were going to be slightly adjusted when more and more people indicated that I would probably find it easier to locate a boat that went from Puerto La Cruz in Northern Venezuela, close to the Caribbean, to Central America than from Caracas. I was still adamant that it was not worth the risk of travelling through Colombia.

Leaving the horses behind, I made my way to the port city of Puerto La Cruz, the major gateway to Isla de Margarita, Venezuela's number-one mass tourist beach.

Yurubi and I were put in touch with Olga, a professional dancer, who with her toy-boy boyfriend really wanted to help. Giving up their time, they kindly spent half a day with me at the port in an attempt to secure transport. When we did not get far she told Yurubi to ring a General whom she believed could pull a few strings with the boats.

"I'm in Margarita," he said over the phone.

This turned out to be a fib when another contact confirmed to Yurubi that the General was indeed in Puerto La Cruz that week.

Yurubi spoke to Olga again.

"There is a boat in Caracas," Olga said, "and it will take her and her horses *anywhere* in Central America."

It sounded too good to be true.

We were then put in touch with another woman, who together with her husband, we were told, not only had lots of money but good contacts too.

Just after we had greeted one another, she announced, "I believe in God and of course the Virgin too."

Yurubi and I looked at each other but I quickly cast my eyes away. We were both on the verge of cracking up at the tone of the heavily made-up pretentious woman serving us rum and coke in her fancy kitchen.

"My husband is a witch and can arrange anything," she said full of melodrama.

We left their house somewhat suspicious and as it turned out, their promises never materialised and we never heard from them again.

Back at Olga's house there was suddenly no boat anymore.

"You have to pursue all the contacts," she said as we were getting back into the car.

As we pulled away Yurubi, Jimmy and I could not help but chuckle among ourselves at her innocence.

After more enquiries and contact with Blanca, a friend of Yurubi's whom I had met when travelling through the Gran Sabana, I decided that after all Caracas would be the place from which to organise our entry into Central America.

I sent an email to a German couple who were travelling on horseback as well, asking them for advice about routes through Costa Rica, a country they had gone through already. I was not sure whether it would be better to go along the Pacific, the Caribbean side or through the middle of the country. I was keen to find a route where we would not have to go on tarmac so much.

Their response went along these lines;

We only ride with topographical maps which in our view are the basics for such a trip. We write down every day which places we pass through, but I think it makes no sense to give you the names of the (mostly) little villages when you don't have the appropriate maps. It is not a secret where we travelled through, but I just think it will not help you so much if I write down all the detailed names. Some trails were shown to us only by people we met, and they had to open some gates for us or lead us along. But you will never meet the same people by chance or travel the same trails we took. I think everybody will find their own way anyway.

Their reply was rather curious. I asked for very little but you could have sworn we were in competition. I thought that we might have been kindred spirits, the same kind of people understanding the joys and magic of travelling in the way we had chosen. I thought they would embrace the opportunity to share and assist. I could not understand their cagey attitude. Numerous people wrote to me during my journey, asking for help and advice about long distance horse riding. I spent hours replying to them, sharing my experiences, where to go and what to avoid. To me that was what it was about, trying to help the next person to have an even smoother experience with less hassle for both rider and horse.

Blanca met us at the Cabaleriza, the stables she had organised for the horses in Caracas, with an enthusiastic 'you crazy girl' and a warm hug.

The horses were led down steep steps to open individual paddocks, where they would reside until we were ready for Central America. There were flies everywhere and I handed one of the helpers repellent to spray on the horses. I was promised the horses would receive special care. Experience had taught me to be dubious about such a promise but I could do nothing but hope and believe.

At Blanca's house I was warmly received by her sister and nieces. Her mother, who suffered from Alzheimer disease, also lived there and was looked after by two Indian women. Blanca's sister suffered a terrible ordeal just a year earlier when her husband was shot dead at point blank range, in the city.

"He tried to help two girls who were robbed," Blanca told me, "and then *he* lost his life."

Her sister kept up a brave face but it was not hard to detect the sadness behind her smile. It was not only his death she had to come to terms with but also the loss of her job as a judge, due to the political situation in Venezuela.

The day after I arrived, Blanca made one phone call after another to see if we could find a boat that would take me and the horses to Central America. We shifted our focus once somebody indicated that it would be almost impossible. Instead they suggested we contact one of the international courier companies. DHL Ireland was one of my major sponsors but not even in my wildest dreams did I think that they would actually transport horses by air. It turned out that not only could they, but more importantly, they actually would. I was ecstatic and Blanca and I danced around the computer when we received the green light.

The city of Caracas has grown into the political, economic and cultural capital of Venezuela, despite being torn by earthquakes, burned, and plundered by English pirates from the time it was founded in 1567. In started off as a small settlement, separated from the coastline by 7,800 ft, a colonial city nestled in a long, green valley surrounded by lush forested mountains. This city has grown enormously and now stretches the length of the valley, up the hillsides and into intersection canyons.

It is a large, noisy city with nearly 3.3 million inhabitants. Like any other metropolis there are dangerous areas to avoid, traffic jams and slums called *barrios*. The latter are assembled in a patch-work fashion from pieces of plywood, corrugated metal, sheets of plastic, and any other material that will provide cover. It was not difficult, driving past these shanty towns dotted like ants on a heap and every square inch occupied, to notice the distinct contrast between the levels of society. It truly brought back the reality of the poverty and the struggle that is now almost an accepted part of Venezuelan life. I found a sign outside a small supermarket in one of the more middle-class neighbourhoods quite amusing. It said that it was prohibited to enter if your shirt was hanging out of your pants. I guess that was one way of combating the ever increasing theft in this increasingly poor city.

Blanca told me about the devastating floods and mudslides of 1999 which destroyed masses of houses and buildings, leaving between 30,000 and 50,000 people dead and about 150,000 homeless. According to the Red Cross it was Latin America's worst natural disaster of the century.

Blanca took me to an area that was worst hit, La Guaira outside Caracas. It was never properly re-built despite all the foreign aid, and, four years on it was still possible to see the impact of that terrible disaster. I saw buildings that looked as if a bomb had hit them and houses standing askew, almost pulled from their foundations.

"Chavez did not serve the people well during that time," Blanca said bitterly.

She told me how he had sent back a boat full of military troops that arrived in Venezuela to assist, with a 'thanks but no thanks' attitude.

Before my journey commenced I was warned that I would have a fifteen percent chance of getting the horses from Mexico across the border into the United States due to a widespread tick-borne disease throughout Central America, called piroplasmosis. I also understood that the lush and steamy jungles of Panama were a breeding ground for this virus, and having already lost one horse to a tropical disease, I came to the conclusion that it would be best to avoid Panama altogether. I could not contemplate losing another horse and was not willing to take any unnecessary chances.

In the Hippódromo at one of the bigger and better veterinary shops in Caracas, I met Carlos the vet. He spoke good English but I found him rather odd and wondered why he appeared to have a chip on his shoulder. He indicated that he would shoe my horses for free if I purchased the seventy dollar plastic shoes from his shop.

The next thing, he said, "Altogether it would be one hundred dollars."

I looked at him in surprise.

"I thought you said the shoeing was for free?"

"Don't you want to pay then?" he asked with a strange look on his face.

He continued to tell me how lucky I was for all the free advice I was getting from him.

"Giving should come from the heart," I said, forcing a smile.

In a patronising tone he replied, "Your smile is enough for me."

I bought weight-gain supplements for Mise and Tu Fein and left before a row could start. On the way out, a girl working in the shop handed me rosary beads. I was not sure if they were meant to protect me from Carlos or from evil on my journey.

Just as well I kept my cool with him. As luck would have it, he was the only vet in Caracas who had the different injections the horses needed to enter Costa Rica.

On another visit he showed me an article about himself in an equestrian magazine. He pointed to his picture and said with exaggerated self-pride.

"This is Carlos! I'm on the wall of fame in Texas."

Blanca treated me to a badly needed haircut and afterwards we visited the equestrian part of the mini zoo where they had riding facilities for people with special needs. The riding was done in complete silence and I found it far too serious. It was sad to see a woman who used to be a competent rider being led around on her horse.

"The muscles in my upper legs are almost non-existent now," she said with a bitter-sweet smile on her face.

Heading back to Blanca's house I noticed a number of Venezuelan flags hanging at half-mast.

"Somebody important must have died," I said.

She nodded. "Yes, our country. We are all very sad people now."

Blanca spent all her time trying to assist me in every way and I could not have asked for a kinder friend and ally. We still had so much to organise and with a 'let's get on with it' attitude, she put all her energies into what I needed done.

On Mothers' Day I met Carlos at the stables to give the horses the necessary jabs.

He appeared highly-strung and gave Blanca a sarcastic answer when she apologised for being a few minutes late.

When he and I walked down to Mise and Tu Fein he asked, "Why are the horses in such a dump?"

I did not get the chance to reply. He seemed distracted and tried to climb over the rails into the paddocks until I showed him the small metal door. The head collars were not there and I suggested I would walk up and get them.

"We don't have time," he answered impatiently, "anyway, that would not make me a gentleman if you have to go up and collect them."

Strangely he did not make an attempt to get them himself. Instead, he walked aggressively towards Tu Fein and without even holding him, jabbed the needle into his chest as if he was stabbing him. I could not believe my eyes. Tu Fein went berserk. Carlos grabbed a thin piece of string that was lying on the ground and put it around Tu Fein's neck. But Tu Fein would not stand still and the thin nylon cut into Carlos's hand, making him even more agitated.

I whistled to keep Tu Fein calm but Carlos turned to me and said, "Don't make that noise, you're scaring him."

I exhaled hard with relief when we were finally done.

He gave me a lift home and the conversation turned to politics. His father was president of PDV, the largest oil company in Venezuela and was without doubt well-connected with Chavez.

"The changes that are now taking place in Venezuela are great and I have a very good life," Carlos said with satisfaction.

When I tried to picture the other side of the coin he told me I was getting too excited.

"Let's meet up for coffee and continue the discussion," he said when the time came for me to get out.

I gave him a half-hearted answer but did not commit myself.

The day before my departure from Caracas, Blanca and I headed into the city to get the international health certificates for the horses officially signed. I remember the traffic being wild and fast and I closed my window when I saw the dark cloud of pollution hanging over the city.

"The roads are very busy because people working for the Metro (subway) are on strike," Blanca told me.

At the entrance to the building we were told that they did not work that day. Nevertheless, we took the lift to the offices and were met by a lot of people sitting on chairs, blocking the entrance. The walls were decorated with banners complaining of not receiving any salaries from the government for three months.

Blanca made a passionate plea to a woman called Margarita who was part of management and who had helped us on a previous occasion.

"It is imperative we have the papers signed by the director today," Blanca said in a desperate voice. "Her plane is leaving tomorrow!"

Margarita indicated in a whisper that she would talk to her supervisor. Under no circumstances could she be seen to work while a strike was on. She informed us every twenty minutes or so that things were starting to happen.

Then after a two hour wait she appeared and said, "I'm not sure if the director can sign the papers after all."

Blanca and I stared at each other in disbelief.

At 1 p.m. she beckoned us over and in a hushed, secretive tone said, "Take the fire staircase and go down to the floor below. Wait there for me."

We discreetly did just that and stood in darkness, awaiting the next instruction. A door opened and my heart missed a beat. But it was only Margarita, looking flushed.

"Quick quick, go up again, the leader of the strike-syndicate is coming up."

Blanca and I rushed upstairs and after a while were called down for a second time. Margarita told Blanca to follow her and turned to me.

"I'm sorry but you have to stay here."

I did not care. All I wanted was that crucial piece of signed paper. I sat on the cold steps and waited. A door opened again. It was Blanca with an exuberant look on her face.

"We have it!" she said breathlessly.

Margarita was waiting on the fire escape, another floor down with an envelope in her hand. She gave me a quick kiss on the cheek.

"*Suerte,*" she said softly and disappeared through a door.

Blanca and I scurried down twenty flights of stairs and out of the building into bright, welcoming sunlight.

Roll on Costa Rica.

The fate of my pistol was another matter I had to consider. Given that I had not declared it going through borders since Bolivia meant that I had it illegally. Blanca's niece suggested taking it apart and hiding the different components in the saddlebags. But that was too risky an option. I would have been in serious trouble not only with the officials but also with DHL if such a weapon were found hidden among my belongings. Blanca detested guns in any shape or form and could hardly look at it.

"Just put it in the bag," she said and turned her head away. "I'll keep it for you until we meet again."

It was just as well. Security was tight and twice my bags were thoroughly searched.

Although I was at the airport at 10 a.m. it was not until 1 a.m. the next morning that the horses were loaded on to the plane. The men had difficulty getting the horses into their narrow boxes and I was secretly pleased when I was called to assist. Tu Fein did a lot of eye-rolling but Mise showed no emotion once they were lifted into the air and deposited into the belly of the aeroplane. It was as if she saw it as just another opportunity to gain air miles. I was terribly excited at the notion of flying with my two horses to another country. To me it was almost as great an adventure as any other part of our travels.

I sat with the three pilots and peppered them with questions. Once we had taken off I went to the back to check on my two faithful companions, tucked in-between boxes and parcels. It was stuffy and warm. I noticed Mise was perspiring but otherwise they seemed to be doing fine.

"Far better it is to dare mighty things, to win glorious triumphs even though chequered by failure, than to rank with those poor spirits who neither enjoy nor suffer much because they live in the grey twilight that knows neither victory nor defeat"
— *Theodore Roosevelt*

We had a pit-stop in Panama at 2 a.m. and I got to take a nap in one of the blacked-out staff rooms at the airport. Back in the cockpit, the pilots explained everything to me before take-off.

"There seems to be a problem with the third engine," one informed me as he went through an instruction manual on his lap. I managed a worried smile. I would have preferred not to know. We got moving but had to turn back when the ventilation lights ceased to work.

"The manual says 'continue with normal procedure'," one of the pilots announced.

I closed my eyes and forced myself not to be concerned. I would have much preferred to be in the back with a gin and tonic in hand, hearing the dulcet tones of the captain explaining that there was only a slight delay and soon we would be in the air.

A dog had to sniff my bags when we got off the plane in Costa Rica. I walked over to my pallet of belongings and found the bag of hay I brought over for the horses. An official rushed to my side.

"You're not allowed to take out the food," he said. "It was not on the list of items."

I was met by Arturo, a former vet. He was a contact of the director of *Chanelle,* my veterinary sponsors in Ireland. I only learned later exactly how much Arturo had to organise to get clearance on the Costa Rican side for my horses to enter. He was meticulous in his approach and went to so much trouble to make sure everything would fall into place. I felt very much indebted to him for all he did for me. We were in touch since my arrival in Caracas and a week or so before the flight I received this email from him;

1. I can have a truck at the airport. Need date and flight or hour to coordinate.
2. I've talked with a vet (I'm more of a desk vet now) and she will gladly check your horses.
3. We have a lot of offers of places to stay for your horses but for health reasons I believe that a secluded place, with no horses or few, is better for Mise and Tu Fein. I have a place like that, 7 – 8 miles out of San José.

69. Arturo and Melania in Costa Rica.
70. Talking about my travels to a group of school children in San José.
71. Maria Del Rosario and Iris doing a traditional dance in their house in Bajo Rodriquez.

72. Alternative work for a pretty white horse.
73. Walking the girls to school.
74. Marco (2nd left), Allan (4th left) and Lalá (middle bottom).

75. Lalá and I watch on as Allan is shoeing Mise with great expertise.
76. Mise hot and sweaty after crossing the bridge in the background.
77. Cooling down time.
78. Marco and I.

79. A perfect spot on the side of the road in Nicaragua for refreshments.
80. Bright happy smiles despite having to do the dishes.
81. An Official checks my passport at the border.

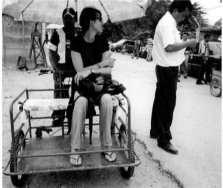

4.   You are most welcome in my house. My family looks forward to receiving you.

5.   I have a 'horse man' working with us as sales representative. He can help with routes and other data. In any case, we have clients and friends along all the roads in Costa Rica and we can help you feel comfortable along your route, if you wish.

Arturo, along with a couple who were both vets, was waiting at the airport for us to arrive since 3 a.m. A driver was there as well, yawning as he leaned against his truck. We arrived at the farm of the amiable Juan Rafael in time for an early breakfast. His helpers, Guido and Pedro, were courteous and obliging and had already prepared the large cosy stables.

Arturo's wife, Melania, received me warmly in their tastefully decorated home. With its colourful off-beat paintings, use of wood everywhere, ample light and even a tree growing in the middle of the living room, every corner and every space spoke of an individual, personal touch.

Melania understood when I made my excuses just after we greeted. I had a shower and went straight to bed. I woke a few hours later to find her in the kitchen, putting the finishing touches to a mouthwatering spread – a variety of cheeses and cold meats, olives and French bread in abundance. Soon two horsemen both known to Arturo, came around to talk about my route through Costa Rica. Solid characters with quite shy demeanours, I liked them immediately. Arturo told me later they were so thrilled to have been asked to be there, sharing their expertise.

I had two 'firsts' during my stay with the Iglesiases. We visited the Poás Volcanoes and I could not help being fascinated by this active crater. Like an overlarge boiling kettle, steam was rising from the bowl, creating strong sulphur-like smells in the air. We also travelled down south towards Panama for a few days. I was as excited as a child when I got the opportunity to wet my toes in the Pacific Ocean for the first time.

Melania lent me some clothes when we went to their daughters' school to attend a music evening.

"You can borrow anything you like from me," Melania said with a wink, "but not my husband."

She was an interesting, intuitive woman with a lot of soul and wisdom. Her job was decorating houses, but in her case, it was decorating with a twist. She would initially visit the family to get a feeling for the energy of the place. Many times, she would first suggest change within the dynamics of the family before she commenced her work on the house.

One evening, Melania tried hypnosis on me.

"You are not necessarily brave," she said, "but you simply don't have any 'stops' in your head. In your mind, everything is possible."

I did not ask if that was a good or a bad thing. She told me she was happy knowing me, sharing my energy. I felt pleased by her flattering words.

Arturo walked with a limp and needed a cane to get around. But it was not always like that. Arturo was a keen hang glider and during the Holy Week of 1988 he organised the annual Central American Hang Gliding Championship – the first time it was held in Costa Rica. Despite his better judgement and knowing that his focus was not only on flying, Arturo could not resist competing as well. He was third up and after a kilometre in the air the wind began to gain speed and strength – apparently racing up to sixty knots. His flight was interrupted when a nightmare began to unfold. He was losing control. Despite fighting with all his might to regain his position, he was thrown from 2,500 feet above ground to the lee side of a mountain, crashing into a coffee plantation minutes later. He was found unconscious in the bushes, bones protruding from his legs and feet.

With an ironic smile as he was telling the story, Arturo said, "I had organised for the Red Cross to be there. How could I ever have guessed that I'd be the beneficiary?"

According to Arturo, the next thing he remembered was waking up in intensive care a month later. At that point he had already had four operations. Bone and muscle were replaced by metal bars and screws in his legs, hips and vertebrae. Somebody took the time to count his eighty-four fractures which included some broken ribs. His legs were twisted in different directions.

But the day Arturo was diagnosed as a paraplegic, he gave back his wheelchair. What followed was nothing short of sheer courage, determination and a will of steel. He promised himself he would walk again. After being bed-ridden for ten months, the long and painful road of recovery began. After seven years of therapy he was able to more or less lead a normal life.

"I limp a lot and I fall once in a while," Arturo admitted, "but I can walk with a cane and even manage a few dance steps with Melania."

Arturo insisted that his accident gave him more than what it took away.

"It made me a stronger and better person," he said with moist eyes. "It showed my capabilities and the strength we carry inside ourselves."

Hearing his story gave me a lot of strength and encouragement to continue my journey despite the hardships. I decided that if he could overcome what he did, then I could see through what I had started.

Marco was another fascinating character I met while in San José. He was a large, jovial man with an open manner and a hint of innocence in his demeanour. He was a successful businessman but also a horse fanatic who called himself 'a helluva rider'.

He was smitten by my journey and invited himself to join me.

"It's a pity though," he said. "I have to go to Brazil for a few weeks and you'll be gone by then. Otherwise I could have travelled with you to New York."

I silently sighed with relief. I was not too sorry. It was nothing personal but I still felt comfortable with my choice of travelling solo. It just worked much better for me that way. However, as it turned out, my encounters with different people through Costa Rica threw a spanner in the works for a while.

The farrier, originally from the USA, who looked after the horses' feet during our stay in San José, was built like a giant. He was in his early fifties but looked younger. He wore cut off t-shirts, purposely showing his massive sun-tanned biceps and strong physique. He was good at what he did. He was also a dreamer. In his car on the way to the stables he shared his 'life-story' with me. Less than twenty minutes later I knew he had fought in the Vietnam War, was chief of police at some stage in his life, a pilot, a captain of a ship, a falconer and rode Harley-Davidsons. I 'oohed' and 'aahed' in all the right places when he told me about what was clearly a fantasy story about his involvement with a secret plot which involved salvaging 150,000 dollars out of Botswana.

"But it all went wrong," he said. "We found out that another group was planning exactly the same stunt."

He got a bit rough with Mise when she would not stand still and I had to hold my tongue.

"The previous shoeing you had done was not a good job," he said. "They did not trim the hooves and the nails drew blood."

He also indicated that the shoes were too small and did not give enough protection. That probably explained part of the horses' reluctance to go on the hard tarmac as we travelled through Venezuela.

The veterinary couple came over too and both horses got their teeth floated. Tu Fein had two sharp teeth near the front of his mouth which were filed flat. We put him back in his stable afterwards for the tranquiliser to wear off.

Both horses were so much happier when they were outside. I cannot understand it when people keep their horses cooped up in stables for days on end. It is torture for an animal that is first and foremost a free creature. Being in a stable is a lot like jail for a horse. You can see it in their eyes. They get frustrated and angry at the lack of stimulation and exercise, and then people wonder why their horses go crazy when allowed outside only occasionally. It does not matter how much they have been domesticated, their spirit is wild and they are at their best when allowed to roam, roll and explore. Marco told me how a horse can cover 24 kilometres a day by just grazing and walking around a field. He shared my sentiments about horses needing to be outside most of the time.

I also met a likeable girl who ran an equestrian shop and did endurance riding. She was anorexic thin.

"They have to put extra weight on my horse when I enter a competition," she said. She felt she wanted to give up the endurance riding.

"I don't care what anybody says but it is just too cruel and tough on the horses." She gave me a rain poncho as well as a saddle blanket she made herself.

I felt happy every time I headed back to Arturo and Melania's house after a long day out. The good vibes were tangible and I enjoyed the interesting conversations around the table in the kitchen. Their two delightful girls were great fun too and both spoke perfect English. Arturo was a mine of information and remembered statistics, names of places and figures, like most people would recall what they had had for breakfast that morning.

"I don't read," Melania said. "It's not necessary because Arturo can tell me everything!"

They teased me about my appetite and with reason. I ate like a horse during my stay with them. It became a joke as we travelled through Costa Rica. Arturo 'warned' most of my hosts in advance about my ferocious appetite and most days I found myself presented with enough food to feed a small army.

Marco decided that he and a couple of good friends would accompany me for a few days riding in the north of Costa Rica. He was so excited about the idea that I could not refuse. He vowed to organise everything and promised me the time of my life, all expenses paid.

Over a Mexican meal he gave me advice.

"You have tits," he said. "I think you should wear something for back support when you ride."

I tried not to laugh at his choice of words. The manager, whom Marco informed about my travels, asked if I would allow a picture to be taken with him. For some reason I went red. Marco noticed and grinned.

"You are blushing. I like that!"

Back at his house he presented me with a large machete and showed me his vast horse tack.

"See which bits you might like for your horses," he offered good-humouredly.

The evening before I left San José I shared a bottle of red wine with Arturo. I was out of practice and I could feel the alcohol going straight to my head. Arturo took a phone-call from Manuel, one of the men who had offered to accompany me to my next stop. Afterwards he told me how the men were so excited at the prospect of riding with me.

"Manuel asked me if it was okay if he bought you a Coca-Cola on the way," Arturo laughed. "I said to Manuel: of course you can. She is human!"

Weeks later I found the note below from Arturo and his family, written in a book they gave me as a momento;

> It has been very special to share these days with you. Not every day a girl comes riding along the Americas, giving the opportunity to become part of a dream for a precious time. I hope that you will remember your time in Costa Rica and with my family with a smile (that place where everybody was waiting for a chance to ride along). I'm sure that when we meet again, we will both be riding our dreams with your strength and joy. We wish you to complete your voyage safely and fulfilling all you want.

Costa Rica is a country that has never had a war and does not have an army. Its democratic government voted for its removal in 1948. Monies used to support the army were saved and put back into the community to further the development of Costa Rica's growth, culture and conservation. The country is, and has historically been, a sea of tranquillity in a region that has been troubled by turmoil for centuries.

Its reputation was justified – I felt safer in Costa Rica than any other country we had travelled through. The relaxed attitudes of the friendly locals appealed to me. The place was also pristine. If I think about a colour for Costa Rica, it would be green. It reminded me of a poem by Jeremy Schmidt I once read;

> All around me, shrubs and ferns pressed tight. Vines spiralled upward into the tops of huge trees draped with hanging plants. Filtered through all that vegetation, even the light was green.

Manuel and Louis waited for me at Marco's farm and had their horses already tacked up. Tu Fein bucked when I mounted him, made a high pitched noise and jumped towards Mise. She was in heat again and Tu Fein felt insecure with the other two geldings around. I looked at my horses and felt tremendous pride at how well they looked. They both seemed happy and displayed an abundance of energy. I decided to carry only the small saddlebags for the stretch to Tilirán where the plan was to meet up with Marco and the others. It was a great respite for whichever horse was not ridden on any particular day.

Before we reached Antenas, our next stop (whose claim to fame is having the best climate in the world – never hot, nor cold with constant mild temperatures all year round), Manuel handed me his card with a note saying I could contact him for anything I needed.

"I am your friend now," he said with emotion.

Breakfast the following morning was not the promised fried rice and beans.

"What did you eat at Arturo's?" my hosts asked.

Within minutes I had cereal and scrambled eggs in front of me.

At the edge of the town I was met by a man I had never seen before, sitting confidently on his white Peruvian horse. He handed me a hat that said 'Costa Rica' and looked pleased when I put it on my head immediately. Further down the road we were joined by another eight riders, ranging in age from six to eighty. I did not ask any questions and demurely followed the group as we went up a steep, rocky road into the mountains. The man on his Peruvian horse was the only one who followed my example when I got off and led the horses downhill. After half an hour of tough riding, white foam seeped from the sides of their horses' mouths.

I cannot say that I found my first ride with a group of people especially rewarding. I was so used to being on my own that all of a sudden I found it strange to have so many people for company. It was frustrating that I could not stop where I wanted to or just sit quietly for a while when I felt like it. But I did not show any irritability. Everybody was genuinely excited to share in our journey. I knew it would only be a few hours until it would be me, the horses and beautiful silence again.

Mist billowed across the mountain and it was difficult to see more than a few yards ahead. We continued uphill over rough stones and muddy ground. At one point the leader took a wrong side-road and we had to turn around. When we got to the top of the mountain the riders announced they were heading back to Antenas. I thought they were joking. But they were not and soon I was left on my own. I continued to navigate my way carefully through the thick fog until we stumbled across a main road two hours later.

As on so many other occasions while riding through Costa Rica, I got caught in a rain storm and was soaked to the skin. It helped a great deal that I had proper accommodation every night and the opportunity to have a warm shower and dry my clothes.

Three *gauchos* met us on the outskirts of San Ramon on their Peruvian horses – the air was electric with the high stepping gait peculiar to this breed of horse. There was an abundance of energy, testosterone, bright rain ponchos and warm handshakes. Small bottles of whiskey were dished out and I eagerly accepted one, hoping it would warm my chilly bones. We trotted together into town, creating a bit of a commotion with our arrival that coincided with the 5 o'clock traffic.

The following day on our way to Bajo Rodriquez, the rain started well before noon. We were drenched within minutes. Even the inside of my shoes did not escape. Two hours later I took a turn-off onto a small road when I saw a sign for a hotel. I envisaged a cup of tea or hot chocolate, but one kilometre down the road and still no sign of civilisation, I stopped at a little open construction. I gathered it was once some place of worship when I spotted the cross outside and an even bigger one inside. I pulled the horses underneath the roof. Mise lifted her tail when nature called and I could not stop her in time. I put on a dry shirt. I noticed a man walking past. He carried a machete and looked back twice. I kept a vigilant eye but was not afraid.

Reaching Bajo Rodriquez, it was still pouring down. But it did not deter my hosts who were waiting with excited faces for my arrival outside the basic little café they ran. Maria Del Rosario, their eight-year-old daughter, blew me a kiss full of warmth and charm when I said hello from Mise's back. Her 'adoptive' sister, Iris, a pretty girl from Nicaragua who had been living with the family for three years was as sweet and had endless questions. Shivering from the wet and cold I gratefully accepted a bowl of vegetable soup followed by the hot chocolate I've been craving all day. I had to patiently sit in my wet clothes for another hour while every customer that came in was told the whole story and shown an article that appeared in one of the Costa Rican papers a couple of days earlier. Margarita, mother of Maria Del Rosario, snapped one picture after another.

Despite the rain, the girls were adamant that they wanted to walk into town with me and the horses. Iris walked behind with Tu Fein, chatting incessantly to him as if he understood every word.

Margaret had commandeered half the population, sheltering from the rain under umbrellas when we entered the town.

"Nobody would believe me when I told them you were coming to stay with us," she said, beaming.

At the house it was a collective effort to get us sorted. The horses were led to a grassy hill behind the house and Margarita rinsed, spun and then hung my clothes behind the refrigerator to dry. The family, although not well off, was tremendously rich in spirit. On my bed I found a small toothbrush, toothpaste, a packet of instant soup and thoughtfully, a sanitary towel. Everybody, including the man of the house and his young son who were both very quiet, were reluctant to leave my room. It took a while before I had a bit of privacy. Soon afterwards there was another knock on the door. Margarita handed me hot water in a kettle, enough to fill a plastic tub in which I had a leisurely rinse. I had company again the moment I stepped from the bathroom. A malt drink and crackers were served on my bed for dinner while I tried to write my diaries.

For the rest of the evening I only had to sit back and enjoy being entertained by the girls who showed me every picture they possessed and wrote heart-warming little notes to remind me of my stay with them. Later I was called to the kitchen and dressed in yellow, blue, red and green shiny skirts and pretty embroidered white tops, they did a traditional dance round and round to music coming from a small radio.

They got on to Mise and Tu Fein the following morning and I led them to their school nearby.

"Te quiero" (I love you), they whispered in my ear when we parted with tight hugs. I knew I would never forget their sweet, innocent faces.

Umberto, who was Marco's friend and my next contact, met me halfway to La Fortuna on his mule. As an introductory gift, he handed me a *fusta* (crop).

"It's made from the penis of a bull," he said grinning.

He told me he knew a short cut and led us to a wide river.

"You need to check the depth first," I suggested.

He entered with his mule and halfway through, they suddenly began to sink deeper and deeper into the water. At one stage it looked as if the poor mule was going to go under. Umberto slid off his back and swam and I held my breath as the mule struggled to the bank. When he reached solid ground he charged in my direction and before I could react, he had gone past me, straight down the road without looking back once. Umberto grabbed Mise and without a saddle or reins, chased the mule. It took us forty minutes to get back to the main road again.

Just before La Fortuna the heavens opened up. Umberto reckoned my poncho was too thin and not suitable for heavy rains. He surprised me with a brand new light-green one including a purpose-made piece of canvas that fitted over my hat, causing the rainwater to drip off instead of soaking my head.

Later that evening after dinner at his parents' house, he took me in his pickup to look at my route for the following day.

"Bring your bathing suit along," he shouted before we headed out.

Umberto turned off the engine of his vehicle when we got to a small dirt road.

"Wait a while and then look to your left," he said mysteriously.

I did not hear anything until a burst of colour caught my eye. The active Arenal Volcano was grumbling quietly. It was a memorable sight – red hot lava pouring down the slopes into the balmy evening air.

On the way back to the house he stopped next to dense, tropical trees and bushes.

"Can you see a narrow trail going down?" he asked.

We got out and made our way on foot through the thick trees to a natural hot spring. It was dark but for the light of the moon. The sensation of the warm bubbling water was magical and I was enchanted by the atmosphere, the absence of artificial light and the sweet smell in the air. Umberto looked at me, his toes sticking out of the water.

"You shouldn't trust all horsemen helping you the way you trust me," he said in a serious tone. "Not all of them are decent."

My route the following day took me alongside the shimmering blue Lake Arenal, an artificial expanse of water as far as the eye could see. Passing the Arenal Volcano again it rumbled like thunder, seemingly getting ready for yet another impressive outburst that evening. The thick, green forest was alive with sounds. Hummingbirds and woodpeckers provided a harmonious choir as we went on little pathways that curved left and right. There was nobody around and a few times the strange sounds from the forest made me jump. We encountered a group of wild horses with long manes and attitudes that said, 'We're free'. Under the disguise of being curious one approached Tu Fein, who was bareback and unattached, and unceremoniously gave him a nasty bite.

In the late afternoon, I was met on the road by my next hosts, and after the man had secured a place for the horses to stay, I went with them to spend the night at their house. The following day I still had eight hours riding to do before we arrived in Tilirán. It was a long and tiring day but the spectacular views more than made up for it. It was a painter's dream with steep inclines, twisting roads lined with small farms and green rolling hills. Cows lazily grazing, hardly looked up as we passed. The few shallow rivers and streams we crossed were cool and welcoming and the horses, courageous as ever, strolled with poise and confidence over an unstable-looking wooden bridge.

Accompanying us for the five-day expedition with Marco was Lalá, a 50-year-old rich divorcee with a terrific personality, Allan, a cool laid-back guy who was also the farrier, and Eduardo, my host in Tilirán. Marco's driver was also there and his job was to travel with the group, carrying belongings and stopping when refreshments were needed. I wondered how I would cope with such decadent luxury. Along the way, our group expanded for periods as more people joined the adventure.

The wet conditions left the frog (V-shaped area on the underside of the horse's hoof) on Tu Fein's feet soggy and almost unrecognisable. Allan showed me how a piece of cotton wool, soaked in iodine and inserted daily into the gap on the foot would help the condition. He was worth his salt and after a few days the bacteria had dried and the frog had developed more shape to it.

Whichever horse had the privilege of running free and without a pack, had a ball, and Tu Fein especially, was like a child in a sweet shop. He rolled in the grass whenever he wished and even had a quick wash in a stream that we crossed. Once, he became overly involved with a couple of horses across a fence and it took Allan a while to get him back. He recounted later how he had used my high pitched call that he had observed the day before – much to the amusement of a couple of men who were working on the telephone lines.

I was disappointed to observe that neither Marco nor Eduardo, who were heavy men, ever made an attempt to get off their horses when we went downhill over rocks and uneven terrain. During our stops I was the only one who unsaddled my horses. The others could not be bothered to even loosen the girths. I did not want any bad feelings so I kept my mouth shut.

Alcohol was high on the agenda for some of the men and on the first day of our ride, vast amounts of whiskey were consumed. I was riding out in front on my own when I heard a horse galloping up behind me at a fast pace. Marco, carrying a water bottle filled with liquor was as drunk as a lord. When we went through a river he steered his horse in the opposite direction. At one point he pulled up next to me and tried to touch my breast. I said nothing and moved away. I noticed that he hung to the left side of his horse, sitting completely unbalanced.

"You are going to injure your horse if you continue to ride like that Marco," I lectured him.

He struggled to string a sentence together and I was not surprised when he tumbled down to the ground after his horse gave a little jump when crossing a patch of water. Arriving at Hacienda Tenario, Allan pinched the skin on Marco's horse.

"He's very dehydrated," he commented.

The horse had also developed a saddle sore.

I noticed that a bottle of liquor was still being passed around.

A band consisting of five musicians playing a large wooden marimba was organised specially for us and Lalá whispered in my ear.

"You are the guest of honour."

She also kindly thanked everybody for their hospitality and received loud applause from all the farm workers who observed the festivity with curiosity and amused expressions.

As I was getting my bags ready the following morning, Marco came into my room and made himself comfortable in my sleeping bag. He was in a chatty mood. I laughed it off when he hinted I should cuddle up with him.

He chuckled and said, "I decided not to bring five pairs of riding trousers as originally planned for this trip when I heard you've been using only one pair of jodhpurs since your journey started a year ago."

The rocks we had to climb on the way to Hacienda Rejoya were of concern to me. I held my breath as Mise and Tu Fein scrambled awkwardly over difficult terrain. I feared a broken leg or serious injury. It made for exciting riding but it was no fun if you needed your horses badly and still had a long and arduous road ahead.

At nightfall we rode through a field covered in fireflies. The surreal, mystical atmosphere in the air was spectacular. Eduardo rode in front and shouted out warnings about low hanging tree branches so we could duck in time. I could only make out his white shirt and the backside of Lalá's horse.

The farm of Hacienda Rejoya was bustling with activity when we arrived. Don Alex, the owner, a small gentle man, had the reputation of being a master of horses.

"He can ride three at one time," I was told.

Don Alex's philosophy was that you did not need to mistreat a horse to teach it.

The local men observed my every move and a few came over to ask questions. There was a lot of activity in the big barn and I noticed Mise standing on her own untied and looking a bit lost. On seeing her, a wave of emotion swept over me. I called out her name and she turned and came over, much to the delight of the spectators, surprised at our close bond.

Mise and Tu Fein were the only horses important enough to sleep inside the barn, protected from the rain. I was grateful for the kind treatment we received everywhere.

It was a pleasant surprise to find that our hotel had thermal baths, just what was needed for aching bones and sore muscles. Lalá gave me a Watsu massage holding me lightly in her arms as I floated weightless on the water, the tension and stiffness in my body melting away.

We had such a slow start the following day that when we had not left by 11 a.m., I suggested we stay another day. The loud cheers indicated overall agreement. Lalá pulled me aside at one point.

"Have you talked to Marco about his drinking?" she asked.

I indicated that we did have a chat about health and his diabetes. She smiled.

"He has definitely eased off with the alcohol."

We were both pleased.

I woke early the following morning to the thundering voices of Marco and Eduardo. My head was throbbing and it felt as if a cold was coming on. I sniffed a handful of lukewarm saltwater in an attempt to clear my blocked nose.

The foreman on the farm, a friendly sincere man, seemed impressed with my journey.

"I hope God gives you strength to finish these travels so that you can be united with your family again," he said warmly.

Marco sent his driver to the nearest town to get me an extra blanket to put under the saddle. He was concerned that the front part of the frame was pushing into Mise's withers. Later, he mentioned how the lads at Don Alex's farm were in awe of my trip.

"They say they have noticed you never complain," he said.

Once everybody was saddled up, our guide, jovial and full of jokes, mounted his donkey and within minutes we were climbing again.

Around the middle of the day, Marco and I were riding together as the others trotted on, way ahead in the front. We got to a river and a precarious-looking wooden bridge. Without investigating Marco urged his horse to cross. After two steps, the wood cracked and gave in underneath them – both fell down but fortunately not into the river. Marco's horse managed to get up, retreated and dragged Marco, whose foot was stuck in the stirrup, along. I got an awful fright but managed to catch the horse. Fearing that Marco might have hurt himself I urged him to lie still. But he got up after a few moments, unfazed. Apart from a few gashes on the animal, both rider and horse seemed okay.

Arriving at Buenos Aires de Upala, a romantic setting with rustic cabins and lapas, we headed out early evening to yet another natural hot spring. The water was soothing and warm. Unfortunately a colony of mosquitoes had their sights set on me and unable to stand them ambushing my face and ears, I retreated to the safety of the pickup cabin.

The following day, the owner of Buenos Aires de Upala joined us for a day's ride.

"My son kept the hair that came from the brush that you groom your horses with," he said. "We are all very happy to share in your adventure."

Another man, accompanying us for the day, considered it necessary to completely exhaust his horse before we had even started. He attempted to show off the speed of the horse and how abruptly he could make him stop. The silly man was far too big for the animal and when he hit him for the third time, I coughed loudly. He looked at me and could see by my expression that I was not impressed.

It struck me as interesting that the only horses in the group that were called by their names by the others, were Mise and Tu Fein. Not once during the five days did I hear anybody referring to or calling their horses by a name.

40 kilometres on was Los Inocentes, a spacious wooden lodge, geared towards tourists with its cool rooms and large porches, overlooking enormous gardens and a volcano. It was also our last stop before I was on my own again.

Allan expertly shoed both my horses while we looked on. He was without a doubt the best farrier I encountered throughout my journey. He was fast, knowledgeable and thorough but more importantly, he genuinely loved horses. The way the horses responded to him while he lifted up feet and banged in nails was a clear indication of that. He liked Mise a lot and thought she was a very good horse. He told me that her two white rear socks, the stripe on her back and the black points on the tip of her ears, were all an indication of that.

Another man chopped into the horses' thick tails.

"They will be much more comfortable with lighter tails in this hot and wet climate," he suggested.

Physically I was not in top form. My body, especially my shoulders was stiff and sore and I could feel a cold developing in my chest. I also had an uncomfortable rash on the inside of my legs, a combination of saddle friction and the wet conditions almost every day. I showed it to Lalá who asked if I minded she called Allan for a second opinion. I did not. I so badly wanted it better. Later he handed me a tube of cortisone cream to ease the discomfort.

After dinner, Lalá helped to sort out my pack. She gave me a light thermal riding top, underwear, a torch, water bottle, sewing kit, metal clip and a body support. As if that was not enough, she also treated me to a deep neck massage. I slept like a baby afterwards.

I was sad when I said goodbye to my friends the following morning. I started bawling when Lalá hugged me warmly. She had become a best friend and soul mate in a short time. I still wanted her near. It was too soon to part. But Nicaragua was waiting and I needed to keep my eyes on the horizon.

Despite my initial reluctance to ride with others, I found the time spent from Tilirán to Los Inocentes a real treat and a wonderful memory from my journey. What a terrific luxury not to have had to worry about food, accommodation, the horses' feet, safety or anything else for five glorious days. It was going to take a while to get used to my own company again.

"Sometimes you don't achieve your goal but the intention means everything"
— *Ingrid Betancourt*

Day 373. At the Nicaraguan border, a vet on the Costa Rican side had to inspect the horses and prepare the documentation so we could go through. Four hours later I was on the other side. An official wanted to check my bags.

"No time," I mumbled and continued.

The women standing around were friendly and smiling but I found a lot of the men quite sleazy and I was unimpressed by their innuendos.

All of a sudden Tu Fein developed a fear of the black and white painted stripes on the walls of the bridges we had to cross. He reacted every time by jumping nervously as we approached, breaking the leading rope a few times.

Our first day in a new country did not start well when the farm that Marco had told me about did not appear, four kilometres after the border. While I looked out for the place, I witnessed the most spectacular sunset ever, with extraordinary colours in gold, yellow, orange, blue and pink. A volcano on the right hand side was covered in pastel-coloured fluffy clouds.

Four drunken men came out of a house while I roared for somebody to assist me, standing at the locked gate of a farm. They told me I could stay with them but I politely declined. It was dark by now and not even the moon felt like showing its friendly face. I realised I might have to continue to the next town, 25 kilometres on. A number of cars passed. I hoped that somebody might see my distress or even wonder what I was doing in the darkness of night on the side of the road with two horses, and stop. But nobody did.

I was overjoyed when a few hours later, I saw a light flickering in the distance. I stood at the gate and called out to the occupants of the house. After a while a man appeared, studied the arriving trio for a moment, then slowly opened the rickety gate. While the family watched soaps on television, unperturbed by the unexpected stranger in their midst, I quickly got ready for bed. I had not eaten since that morning but hunger was the last thing on my mind. I let the sounds of the television lull me to sleep. I was grateful to be safe.

The following day when we were on the road again a noise caught my attention and looking back, I saw a young boy pedalling like mad on his bicycle, holding a small bag in his hand. I blushed when he passed me the knickers I had accidentally left behind.

Some days I had very little to eat travelling through Nicaragua and once I went for nearly two days without food. I remembered arriving at a house and shaking so much from hunger that the people considered calling a doctor. I indicated that I only needed something to eat, a pineapple, anything. They obliged and with my blood-sugar level back to normal I could function again.

I enjoyed the spirit of the people along the way. A woman approached as we went through a small town.

"I've just heard you on the radio. One of your horses died," she said.

She ordered me to wait until she could serve me a tiny espresso. She apologised for the small amount of sugar but when I mentioned that I liked it exactly like that, she was pleased.

We were met by a lot of friendly banter on the way and comments from young men, trying to show off their English with 'oh my God', 'goodbye goodbye' and 'yes yes yes' remarks. One passed on his motorbike and in the process of taking off his helmet to shout *"buena suerte"*, he nearly rode into a tree.

I noticed a man on the other side of the road with a foal pulling a cart stacked high with grass.

"Your horse is too young to carry that load," I commented in passing.

"Then give me one of yours!" he shouted back.

I continued my crusade against animal abuse and while on the way to Nandaime I spotted three horrendously scrawny-looking horses tied up on the side of the road. They had severe-looking saddle sores, in fact the worst I had seen so far. I took pictures and headed for a house nearby. The occupants claimed the horses did not belong to them and neither did they know where the owner was. I asked them to pass on a serious message to the man.

"Treat your horses right or I'll come and get them."

I noticed for the first time blood-sucking ticks on the horses. Whenever we took a break I inspected their ears and lifted their tails, looking for those red, detestable creatures. I pulled them off, wrapped their wriggling bodies in tissue paper and with satisfaction set them alight.

The long, hot 47 kilometre day's ride to Nandaime did not improve. We got there just before darkness fell, but the guard at Arrosera, a rice processing and packing plant, where it has been arranged for the horses to stay, did not want to let me in. He did not believe me when I told him the owner had given permission for us to stay there. An argument followed and I left in tears of frustration.

A good Samaritan at a petrol station took me under his wing. Edgar directed me to stables just outside the town and took me to one of his farms where he had a room available next to where his workers lived. He put the fan on full speed in my room to keep the mosquitoes away. He left to go to another farm where he shared a house with his mother, and, whistling happily that things had turned out so well, I prepared myself for a good night's sleep.

I went to the outside tap to wash my hands and next thing I heard the door behind me close. I was locked out. I woke one of the workers and the woman told me she had no key and neither did she have credit on her phone to ring Edgar. She brought out a tiny camping bed and put it in a large, barren, dilapidated room next to hers. I had only a sheet over me and the moment I put my head down the mosquitoes attacked. After half an hour of vicious biting, I could not stand it anymore and called the woman.

"Do you have some repellent please?" I asked in a desperate voice.

She did not, but brought out a bulky container with wood burning inside and put it next to me. But the mosquitoes still would not give up. I held the sheet over the billowing smoke then put my hands and feet, even my face over the drum – but to no avail. I tossed and turned and miraculously managed to fall asleep hours later, still conscious of the little devils gnawing at me. Having to wake up to the deafening sounds of a radio, voices and the clatter of pots and pans, all before 5 a.m., put me in a foul mood.

Thanks to my encounter with kids on the way that day and many other days that we passed through Nicaragua, I continued my travels in high spirits. They had no hesitation in making contact, had quick smiles, easy responses to my questions and always gave enthusiastic, cheerful waves.

We went through the tiny village of Cuatro Esquinas, meaning four corners, and I indicated for an ice cream man on his bicycle on the opposite side of the road to stop. A few kids were standing outside their modest dwelling and I called them over.

"Ice cream for everybody!" I yelled.

Within minutes I was buying for thirteen excited little faces. It felt great seeing them getting so much enjoyment from something so simple.

Further down the road, as I was still licking my chocolate lolly, a pickup truck passed and stopped in front of us. A woman in her fifties got out and as she walked towards me said, "One year is a long time to go on horseback."

Joan was a missionary, originally from New York, who had been living in Nicaragua for fifteen years. She had a soft manner and after our encounter I suddenly realised how much I missed my mother. Joan sent me an email a few days later;

> I forgot to tell you... Nicaraguan men are passionate, warm, convincing and gross
> *mujeriegos* (womanisers). Please be careful.

In another email she invited me to her home, suggesting I rest there with the horses for a few weeks. She was sincerely caring but the road kept on calling and I did not take her up on the offer. We met up again a week later when she interviewed me. Afterwards she presented me with a bible and forty dollars. I knew she needed that money herself and I was surprised at such a thoughtful gesture. When I objected she said the Lord told her to give it to me. I could hardly argue with that. She urged me in a later email to keep on reading the Bible and to ask the Lord to help me understand it. For the purposes of the article she hoped to write, she sent me at least twenty additional questions ranging from my height, how many siblings I had, if I wore make-up, to queries about my adventures.

One question in particular had me in stitches. It said, "Your breasts are large, did you have them enhanced?"

I answered 'no', not knowing whether she was joking or not.

One of the magical things about my journey was not knowing what was around the next corner. Had I known what awaited me, I most likely would have turned around and ran, very fast and as far away as I could. By not knowing what would come my way, I was content in the belief that I would cope with whatever was thrown at me. If my path was clear and there was no mystery to it, why would I have wanted to explore that road? Why would I have wanted to continue had I known the daily grind, the blood, sweat and the tears? It was the not-knowing, blended in a mixture rich with curiosity that urged me on.

Having had positive experiences for most of the way through Nicaragua, I never imagined that not only would a stop in Tres Cruces, meaning 'three crosses', bring a lot of agony and stress but that I would have difficult times in a number of other places, right up to the border with El Salvador.

Waking early on the morning of the 28th June in the house of Juan Carlos in Tres Cruces, I had a strange feeling. So anxious was I that I did not even get dressed before I went out to check on my horses. I walked around the house and looked for them but to my horror, they were gone. The yard was fenced in, apart from a tiny gap between shrubs, and had a gate at the front which was closed. I could not believe the horses would first of all have noticed the opening, and secondly gone off, despite the abundance of grass and water available. A woman worker whose room was next to the house indicated she heard a commotion during the night. But it was her husband I was keen to speak to.

Manuel blinked at a hundred miles an hour, claiming that he had an infection in his eyes.

"I heard the horses going past my room," he said, struggling to look at me. "They escaped around midnight and I saw them running down the street and I... "

"You saw them running away and you did not call me?" I said incredulously.

"I thought they would come back," he answered uncomfortably.

I was panicking now.

"Come with me Manuel," I ordered. "We must find them immediately."

Our first stop was the local police station, a one room operation, consisting of only a typewriter on a bare table. The place was deserted but eventually a man in a vest appeared. Our call was far too early for his liking and he was reluctant to help. He finished mopping the floor first before he came over to speak to us. His colleague came out later half dressed and proceeded to zip up his trousers and put on his shirt and cap in front of us. At his own leisurely pace he sat down, took out a pen and paper and painstakingly began to write down the details. I counted to ten. Patience was a necessary virtue here.

Afterwards Juan Carlos and I drove around town, showing people a picture of the horses and asking if they had seen anything strange. Things were not looking good.

I spoke to Roberto Rappaccioli, a friend of Juan Carlos. He indicated that Danilo his brother knew the area, the police and the people, and would be able to help. By now I was so upset I could not even continue the conversation with him.

Lalá, my friend in Costa Rica, gave me the details of a good friend of hers, called Enrique Zamorra. He was from a well-known, affluent and influential family in Nicaragua. They owned banks and hotels and everybody knew them. I spoke to Enrique and within thirty minutes he was in Tres Cruces with his driver.

"I suggest we find ten horse riders and pay them to go and search," he said in a helpful manner.

It was not a bad idea but easier said than done. Enrique rang a local radio station and within minutes they made an announcement about the missing horses. We listened to it in his car and I could not help but smile wryly at the special sound effects, complete with horse-hooves and neighing. It was not long before a journalist from the La Prensa newspaper arrived for an interview. I broke down when she asked me what I would do if I could not find the horses.

"I would rather not think about that now," I said tearfully.

I felt numb and for a moment got a glimpse of what people might go through when a loved-one goes missing. It was a feeling of utter helplessness. I got very emotional when somebody suggested we go to the nearest abattoir. I forced myself not to think about the implication of Mise and Tu Fein being sold for their meat. Enrique reckoned we consider that possibility after we had tried all other avenues.

I got a lift to Managua the capital, and was dropped off at a Xerox office. I made a number of 'lost' posters with enlarged pictures of my missing horses.

Feeling drained and distressed, I spoke to a special friend in Ireland.

"I will come over if you need me," he soothed. "No matter what happens, you will finish your journey."

I needed his strength and encouragement so much.

Not long after our phone call late that afternoon, Juan Carlos stopped outside the house.

"Your horses have been found in a field 40 kilometres from here by Danilo and his workers," he smiled broadly.

The relief on his face was visible. I could not believe my ears. I danced and jumped, laughed and cried with joy. Juan Carlos opened a bottle of red wine and despite not having had anything to eat since that morning, I gulped it down. I was delirious.

"How do you think it could have happened?" somebody asked.

I shook my head. I did not care whether my horses had been stolen or had run away. All that mattered was that they were safe. We could go on. It was not over yet.

Riding one of Danilo's stallions I participated in a horse parade through the town of Rivas the following day with Danilo and many other riders. My horse was a handful and tried to mount every mare within range. I scolded a boy riding in front of me who, without any reason, hit his horse continuously. I saw more brutality later. The culprit answered with a 'We do what we want in Nicaragua', when I pointed out the raw, bloody sore on his horse's nose on top of which a heavy mental band rested. I was exasperated. The bloody cruelty everywhere was wearing me down. What would I see next? A goat hanging by its tail? It was a heart-warming moment when another man stepped forward and put a handkerchief under the offending piece of metal.

The parade was followed by a presentation, drinks and dancing. I was called out to the front and handed a trophy for being the most *simpatica* (friendly) towards horses. I was so pleased.

I got a lift back to Tres Cruces with Francisco, a pleasant man who used to be Ambassador for Nicaragua in Washington. His bodyguard and driver sat quietly in the front, pretending not to hear our conversation.

"I will be President in 2006," Francisco said with confidence. "I will buy you a first class ticket for the inauguration, no matter where you are."

Weeks later and now in another country, I spotted the favourite Guatemalan Presidential candidate, Oscar Berger, having lunch with family and friends a table away from me. When they got up to leave, I boldly approached the group and asked Mr Berger if he would pose for a picture with me. He happily obliged. He was sworn in as President a couple of months later in January 2004.

Funnily enough, not long after, I received a short note from F.W. De Klerk, the last State President of Apartheid South Africa, who served from 1989 to 1994. In the hand-scribbled note, he said he had heard about my journey and lifted his hat in admiration.

In Nicaragua, the differences in responses from people on the side of the road as I passed with the horses, were always interesting. In some places people knew about us having heard something on the radio or having noticed a newspaper article. Many times as we passed I would hear somebody telling tales of my travels to the others, as if I was not even there. Sometimes people returned my greetings, other times they looked as if I was a witch approaching.

At another place where I stopped one day, the owner of a little shop appeared displeased when I gave what he considered to be too much attention to a two-year-old boy playing outside. On the other hand, two men spontaneously approached the horses in good humour and adjusted the loose pack on Tu Fein. You could sense by their manner that they were not threatened by me. On another occasion, a woman running a little café on the side of the road took me by complete surprise when she would not take money for the *tortilla* and coffee I had. She refused point blank and I was amazed by her generosity.

Just as I was about to cross a bridge one day, two young men sitting in the long grass motioned me over.

"I don't understand," I pretended in Spanish and continued.

A little further down the road I saw a herd of goats tied to ropes. The ropes were tangled up and too short and the goats could not reach the grass. I looked back and saw the men still sitting there and although not feeling a hundred percent comfortable, I jumped off my horse and began to untangle the ropes. The goats bleated gratefully. I had two more to do when my eye caught one of the men walking towards me. I swallowed hard and could feel the butterflies in my stomach. Call it intuition or paranoia but I did not trust him at all. He waved his hand and indicated I should wait but I made sure I mounted Mise at the speed of lightning. I urged her on and looked over my shoulder.

"You should check on your goats more regularly," I shouted and put Mise into a trot.

There were no villages on the way to León and in the late afternoon we came to a halt in front of a locked gate. Behind it in the distance I could see a small house. The woman reluctantly came down to talk to me but would not let me in.

"You have to ask my husband, he has the key," she said.

I sat on a stone and waited. When the man arrived I was subjected to a lengthy interrogation and finally invited in. They were poor and as I pitched my tent I wondered if I would get something to eat. As dusk fell I sat myself down on a chair, watching the kids swinging silently in a hammock on the porch. A few words were exchanged and after that the only sounds in the quiet evening air were that of the dog's rumbling tummy. No food was forthcoming so I dug into my saddlebags and shared my last packet of biscuits with the family and their dog. My own hunger did not bother me too much. I would be in León the following evening, staying at a comfortable hotel I had been invited to, where there was sure to be an abundance of food available. My hosts that night though were not so fortunate; for them the daily struggle for survival would continue.

In most parts of Latin America, the people have to think of every possibility to earn money. One particularly interesting enterprise was run by kids who waited on the side of the road, shovels in hand. They were not begging but in fact provided a valuable service. They scooped up loose earth and filled in the numerous potholes that pitted the road. Motorists, trucks and bus drivers would pass, handing the youngsters money in exchange for their help. It was a win-win exchange.

My stay at Los Balcones, courtesy of Carlos the owner, was a real treat and happened at the time when I needed some creature comforts and a diet other than *tortillas* and beans. The horses were cared for on Carlos' farm a few miles out of town.

On my second day I took a bus, first to Chinadega 42 kilometres on, and from there to Potosí, a small port town on the Golf of Fonseca, not too far from El Salvador. The bus was a hive of activity with children loudly advertising their wares, ranging from fried chicken to chewing gum, to water. The driver stopped whenever somebody wanted to get on or off and what should have been a one hour journey, took almost three and a half hours. I arrived in Potosí (not to be mistaken for Potosí in the Bolivian *altiplano*) covered in dust and feathers from the live chickens that were on board.

I made the decision to organise transport across the Golf of Fonseca to El Salvador for three reasons:

1. Tschiffely went that way in 1925.
2. We could skip Honduras – one set of veterinary documents less to organise.
3. It was shorter and had the potential to be a different kind of adventure.

An adventure it sure turned out to be but in a different way to what I had imagined. I was introduced to a man who owned a *lancha*. It was a kind of canoe, only bigger and deeper, and ran on an engine. He agreed to take me and the horses from Potosí to La Union in El Salvador, a forty-five minute journey on a good day. I asked him if he had a hoisting system in place.

"No problem," he said. "We transport cows all the time."

I told him the horses were still in León and that it would take a few days' riding to get them there.

"See you in about four to five days," I said as we shook hands.

Back in León, I organised a farrier to shoe both horses. Once the first shoe on Tu Fein was taken off, the man surprisingly did not cut or trim the hoof. Instead, he proceeded straight away to nail on the first new shoe. I stood in front of Tu Fein who was quiet, his head resting in a submissive manner against my chest.

As the man was hammering the nails in, I noticed he did not finish them off properly, leaving the long pointy bits exposed. This was dangerous, not only for him, but for my horse too and for anybody standing around. I thought he held Tu Fein's foot awkwardly when he banged in the last nail. He used too much force and before anybody knew what had happened, Tu Fein jumped forward and kicked strongly to the rear, catching me sharply on the hip. The pain was ferocious and became more and more acute with each passing second. I felt like collapsing. I could not stand on my right leg and the farrier carried me to where our taxi driver was waiting. He made an effort to drive very slowly towards Leon, yet I still felt every bump on the road.

At the hospital, I had an embarrassing moment. When a doctor asked me to take off my trousers, I called over a concerned Carlos and whispered in his ear.

"I need to talk to you first."

With a red face I explained that I was not wearing any underwear. He looked amused.

"Don't laugh," I said. "This is serious. I have only one pair of flesh coloured knickers I can wear under these thin trousers. This morning when I got dressed, I discovered the pair I had rinsed out last night was still not dry. I don't have another pair of trousers and was forced to wear this one, minus the underwear."

He kept on looking at me with a playful grin on his face. I knew he would get great mileage out of that story.

Thankfully the x-rays showed no broken bones but I was warned that it would take a while for the torn ligaments and bruising to heal. I was given a pair of crutches and spent another week in León, receiving physiotherapy every morning.

Another farrier was organised and once I had gained a bit more mobility I proceeded to plan our departure from León. Mounting a horse was painful, trotting even more so and I continued to have trouble with the hip for quite some time after that.

It was always pleasant to find somebody selling food or drink on the side of the road when it was least expected. At one such place on the way to Potosí, a woman prepared a milk and corn concoction which is drunk from a plastic bag with a straw.

Her mouth literally fell open when I answered her question as to where I had ridden from. Her two daughters were standing a respectable distance away, conscious that their mother would not want them to interfere in the conversation.

"How sensible of you not to have too many children," I said. "This way you will be able to give them more opportunities and a better education."

She laughed.

"I have two daughters and ten sons. I kept on trying until I got my girls."

Further down that same road I caught up with an elderly man on his horse. We chatted as the horses moved forward and I noticed he had hardly anything under the saddle for protection for his horse. I noticed the horse was limping and asked the man if he knew why that was.

"Yes, his leg is sore," he replied.

I told him that I reckoned the horse's back was sore and that was why he was in pain. I stopped, took the saddle bags off Tu Fein and gave him a blanket I did not really need. He thanked me profusely, put it *on* the saddle underneath his own backside and proceeded happily on.

Mise's shoe had come loose and my attempt to hammer in a few nails failed. They kept bending so I gave up after a while. I walked the last 20 kilometres on foot.

In Potosí I went straight to the pier. The *lancha* was there, already waiting in the water. I could not see any hoisting facility. I asked the owner about it and he mumbled something I did not understand. It was clear that the horses would have to board by other means.

The next two hours turned out to be an outrageous farce as more and more people joined the spectacle, making the craziest suggestions, thinking *their* idea was going to be 'the one'.

Omar, the owner, believed we only needed to take off the engine, pull the horses and make them step up over the back and down into the deep interior of the boat. I dismissed his idea straight away.

"Let's take them to a lower pier on the far side, pull the boat alongside and then push the horses into the *lancha*," somebody else suggested.

I looked at the thirty-strong crowd, all eyes on me, waiting for my answer. The suggestion was ridiculous and I said so. We moved to the other side and the boat was brought out of the water, on to the sand.

"We tilt the boat, the horses will step in, we tilt it back and off you go," said one.

"Do you really imagine a horse would walk on to a tilted boat?" I said.

I showed! them what I meant and they shook their heads in agreement when both Mise and Tu Fein stuck their heels in the sand, refusing to move another inch towards the boat. Another suggestion was to tie a rope around the horses' feet and necks and using the 'surprise element', tip them over.

"And then what?" I asked, not taking the idea seriously at all, but more curious about what might follow.

"Then ten of us lift up the horse and put it in the boat."

I put my head in my hands. We were not going to go through the Gulf of Fonseca after all. The owner of the lancha became grumpy when I told him we were going back to Chinadega and from there on to the border with Honduras.

"I want money for my time," he sulked.

I shook my head.

"And what about *my* time?" I replied.

I left the horses behind in Chinadega while I took a minibus to the border. I showed the equine veterinary papers I had to an official. They seemed to be in order.

"Just come straight to this office when you arrive with your horses," the friendly man said. "There should not be any problems getting you through."

Tent living was never comfortable and it took a while to get used to constantly having aches and pains after a night's sleep. I did not have a blow-up mattress and the smelly saddle blankets proved to have only limited use as far as comfort was concerned. The worst night in my tent must have been the second last stop before we reached the border with Honduras. The saddle blankets were too sweaty and I rolled out my yoga mat. Two sheepskins on top of the saddle served as a pillow. I was woken during the night by growling and barking. When I peeked out I noticed I was surrounded by a pack of dogs. The presence of the tent had attracted their attention and they would not leave. I roared at the security guard but he failed to control them.

"Shut up!" I shouted to the dogs from inside the tent and after a while a worker living next door appeared.

She chased the dogs away but they were soon back again. I called for her a second time.

"I need to move my tent *señora*," I said.

It was 1 a.m. when she patiently helped carry the dome tent to another outbuilding. The room was dirty, full of chicken manure and the woman first had to remove a hen and a rooster. There was a disgruntled pig outside the door, unimpressed to have his sleep interrupted. An hour later the rooster started to crow and soon he was joined by a meowing cat. The cement surface underneath me was unforgiving and I was relieved when music from a radio began to blare well before sunrise and I had to get up. I could not have had more than an hour's sleep.

The road surface to Somotilla was rough and through the shimmering haze I spotted a tiny eating place on the side. The man helped me with the horses and gave me free water in small bags. He turned to his young daughters, both of them with a baby on the hip.

"See what a girl can do?" he said to them.

They were a courteous family and did not intrude with questions. Once I finished my meal he helped to saddle up the horses. He put Tu Fein's leading rope around Mise's tail. I gently showed him where it was supposed to go. He nodded warmly with a toothless grin.

The twenty dollars they asked for a room at a small motel in Somotilla was far too much for what was on offer but I was too drained to bargain or look for something else. A woman insisted I paid upfront. There was no space for the horses and I arranged for a young boy to look after them in a field next door, keeping guard throughout the night.

Without dinner, I showered and wrote my diary in my room. All I could think of was sleep. I went outside and asked for hot water.

"You must have a lot of dollars to be able to travel like this all the time," the woman said curiously.

"I don't," I said. "I can travel like this because I get a lot of help."

When she brought my water she lingered and tried to peek into the room to see what belongings I had. Her manner was strange and I did not trust her. Something was brewing.

It was before midnight when I was woken by loud thumping music outside. I looked from inside my door and saw groups of people sitting around drinking beer and watching a large flower display on a truck that was lit up by candles. When the music had not stopped two hours later, I got up and approached an elderly lady, and asked her to turn the music down a bit.

"Please *señora*," I said. "I have to get up very early. It's impossible to sleep."

She was drunk and aggressive, waved her hands in my face and said, "*se va, va, va*," meaning, 'go, go, go'.

I was not prepared to have a confrontation at that hour of the night and went back to bed. Fireworks followed, my bed shaking with every bang. A brass band picked up where the fireworks left off and continued belting out their tunes until 5 a.m. Feeling like a zombie I dragged myself out of bed when my alarm beeped shortly after. Little did I know what was to follow.

Outside a woman approached while I tied a few things to my saddle. I ignored her, went inside my room and shut the door. There was a knock. Another woman filled the door frame. Her bloodshot eyes and the strong smell of alcohol left me in no doubt about her condition. She rubbed her fingers together.

"Dollar," was all she said.

"You must be joking," I replied.

I pointed to another woman standing outside.

"I paid her last night when I arrived."

I told her to leave me in peace.

The old witch from the previous night came over, stood at the door, also drunk and demanded more money. I was getting fed up.

"Listen," I said. "I am not paying forty dollars for this dump of a room. You got your money and I'm going now."

With that I pushed her out and shut the door. The old one went ballistic, picked up my machete outside and began to bang on my door, shouting and roaring. I opened the door and she kept on swinging the machete, inches away from my face. She ran to her room and I followed, asking her for my machete back. She reached for something on her bed. I was staring into a revolver, pointed directly at me. My stomach turned. The woman was off her head and I knew it was madness to try and talk to her. I stepped back.

"I'm going to the police to file a charge against you," I said in my best Spanish.

Shaking, I turned around and heard a clatter behind me. I looked back, picked up the machete she had thrown after me, grabbed my saddle and bags and left rapidly.

My first instinct was to go to the police but I had doubts too. They would be taking statements from a group of drunken people and I would have to explain the whole situation in a language I still struggled with. It was my word against theirs and I could not be bothered with more complications, and precious time was being wasted. I was five kilometres away from the border and just wanted to get the hell out of there.

At the border my passport was stamped, papers inspected, and with a lighter heart I made my way to the bridge to cross into Honduras. I was stopped by a Nicaraguan policeman.

"The chief wants to talk to you," he said.

I was annoyed at the delay. "They've checked my papers," I said. "Everything is fine." But he insisted I followed him.

The sullen-faced policeman kept it short.

"You have to go back to Somotilla because the police there want to talk to you."

"What for?" I asked.

"A woman in a hotel has pressed charges against you for damaging a room," he said.

I looked at him, shocked.

"That is such nonsense. They are after money."

I tried to explain to him what had happened but he insisted I go back to Somotilla.

"I can't," I said. "That woman is drunk and crazy. She has a gun and she might actually shoot me the next time."

I told him I was more than happy to speak to the police but they needed to come to the border. He insisted that I go back.

My mind was racing.

"I need to make a phone-call," I said.

He reluctantly agreed.

Enrique Zamorra, the man who helped me when the horses disappeared in Tres Cruces, mercifully answered the phone and I explained my dilemma.

"I will ring you back in fifteen minutes," he said. "If I don't get through, ring me."

The policeman was unhappy about developments and that his authority might be overruled.

"Enrique Zamorra is nothing," he said. "I will only listen if the President of Nicaragua tells me that I should let you go. If Enrique does not ring back in fifteen minutes I am taking you to Somotilla."

My heart was beating faster.

"Why are you so hostile and unhelpful?" I asked.

He replied by accusing me of being aggressive.

"No, I'm not," I said. "I'm tired, frustrated and shaken."

The phone rang and I jumped up, expecting Enrique to be on the other side. It was not. The policeman spoke to a colleague in Somotilla.

When he ended the call he looked at me unhappily and said, "The charges are dropped, you can go now."

I felt such relief. I had another quick word with Enrique and thanked him for his help and understanding. I hope I managed to convey my deep gratitude.

Despite the bad experience just before the border, I will always have fond memories of Nicaragua, a country that satisfied all the senses with its beauty and charm. What happened in Somotilla was an isolated incident and the behaviour of those people was certainly not indicative of Nicaraguans in general. The warmth of the people was tangible everywhere, most of them truly wanted to help. However, I will remember the children most when thinking of this country. You could not ignore them. They were everywhere and their easy smiles were hard to miss. Their genuine infectious laughter, friendly waves and jubilant jumping up and down wherever we went made me feel very special. I sensed their optimism despite their circumstances. Most of them were desperately poor and I wondered how bright their futures would shine, what opportunities would come their way. Still they lived their daily lives with joy and grace. The spark in their eyes said it all; they were just so happy to be alive.

"And when you have reached the mountain top, then you should begin to climb"
— *Kahlil Gibran*

The friendliness with which I was received on the Honduran side eased the earlier bad feelings. Even though I had to wait for hours before official permission was given from Choluteca for the horses to enter, I did not mind. I was simply too wrecked to care. The office was air conditioned and the officials had no problem with my presence while bureaucracy took its course. A girl working in the office kindly invited me to stay at her house that night, 14 kilometres from the border.

"We have no electricity," Wilma apologised.

"That is no problem at all," I said, meaning every word.

She could not have known how much that invitation meant to me.

Later that day her father, a man in his sixties with a respectful demeanour and a firm handshake, waited on the main road for me to arrive. Wilma was there too and together we walked with the horses on a dirt road full of stones to their humble yet immaculately clean house a few kilometres away. One or two people we encountered on the way tried to make conversation but Wilma's dad maintained a fast pace and did not engage. Later he explained his hurry to get home.

"For your safety I do not want to give the people here too much detail about you," he said. "The less they know the better. A *gringa* to them spells dollars."

Not having slept for more than a few hours the past two days I would not have exchanged my bed that night for anything in this world. I was not sure what to make of a large wooden coffin standing in the corner of my room but said nothing. Later Wilma told me it was for the grandmother who was still alive but near the end.

"It was very expensive but we had to buy it when we had the money," she explained.

The family was friendly and dignified, giving me space but still showing interest in my journey. They understood however, when after dinner, I made my excuses. The television was turned down and voices lowered. The following morning I was told that the man of the house had stayed up with my horses all night.

"We've had our donkeys stolen," he said. "I did not want to take a chance with your horses."

Those were the moments of my journey that I would never forget. The unselfish assistance I received countless times, the generosity from the poorest, the hands extended in true friendship. I believe we have so much to learn from people like that, who may have little material wealth, but give of themselves wholeheartedly and with no strings attached.

I declined an invitation to a communal bath and Wilma's mum walked a shortcut with me through fields and across tiny streams until we reached the main road an hour later.

Throughout the day, I saw groups of boys standing on the side of the road, trying to sell live armadillos, iguanas and even a porcupine. The trembling body of the armadillo, held upside down by his tail, greatly upset me. I felt guilty for quite some time afterwards for not having bought him. At least I could have released him back into the wild, giving him a second chance to live.

The people on the way through Honduras continued to be kind and helpful. However, the suffocating heat stood out most from our three days of travels. The sun beat down relentlessly every day. I had a constant headache and often felt dizzy. Mise struggled much more than Tu Fein. She had no energy and dragged her feet all the time.

The road in and out of Choluteca was well maintained and the tarmac looked new. We did not stay in any of the bigger towns but instead sought routes off the main roads where I asked for assistance from people living in small settlements in the countryside. I received many positive responses and as I found in Nicaragua, the kids were inquisitive, smiley and open. Near the village of Agua Fria, my eye caught two young children, oblivious to the world, singing and whistling while washing colourful dishes outside their little house. Shyly they agreed to have their photograph taken.

This most southern part of Honduras was the least typical face of a country considered very much a hidden gem in the middle of Central America. I was told about lush rainforests in the north-eastern parts, untouched cloud forests (which can rise up to nearly three thousand metres above sea level), savannas and mountain ranges laden with pine and oak trees. Honduras also harbours a priceless ecosystem, the largest coral reef in the western hemisphere. In the Bay Islands it is not unusual to swim with bottlenose dolphins, parrot fish, schools of blue tang and even the colossal whale shark.

While we fought the merciless heat, I could only daydream about the white sands, tall coconut palms and the relaxed Caribbean atmosphere that this beautiful part of the world is best known for. The rest of the country still remains on my list of 'must-see' places to visit one day.

The border with El Salvador was all hustle and bustle. There were enough eager helpers at hand to look after the horses while I sorted the veterinary papers. The atmosphere was friendly and relaxed. I had everything organised in less than half an hour. I had a feeling they knew we were coming.

Going through Santa Rosa I heard a noise behind us and Mise charged forward. I looked back and saw we were being chased by a wild-looking man with a mop of hair which was sprouting in every direction. He was swinging a plastic bottle and shouting at us. When close enough he threw the bottle, hitting Mise on the leg. I decided to ignore him but when he did it a second time I swung the horses around and chased him. He ran away but was soon back. I followed him into a petrol station but he hid behind a petrol attendant when I lifted my crop to give him a rap. I pointed to my machete.

"Next time I will use this," I said, trying not to laugh when he pulled a comical face.

He made one last attempt to throw something at the horses and then gave up.

We passed a *gaucho* on the way and I greeted him with a friendly *"hola"* and a smile. He responded with one of the dirtiest looks I had ever encountered – possibly disgusted to see I was a woman travelling on horseback.

I entered a small farm settlement for a break later that morning. There was only one man there. His face was half paralysed and he had no teeth. I unsaddled the horses and they eagerly began munching on the grass. I sat on the ground and wrote my diary. The man sat on steps and watched me. We did not speak. I was sleepy and leaned back against the saddle-bags, my face covered with a hat. When we got going again, I silently lifted my hand in a 'thank you' gesture. He did the same.

Back on the road large trucks whooshed past us for most of the way. They were going too fast and came very near, keeping me constantly on edge. One wrong turn or lapse in concentration from one of the truck drivers and we would have been mince meat. It made for dangerous riding.

We arrived in a village at 3 p.m. but I was unsuccessful with our first attempts to secure accommodation for myself and the horses. I thought I had found a perfect spot when I saw a neat house and garden with a large field next to it. The woman refused, claiming that the horses would damage her trees. At another place I was told that the man of the house was not there to give me permission. We finally got sorted out on a farm outside the village. The owner agreed that I could pitch my tent and indicated he had ample space for the horses. He was full of questions and advice and he wore me out.

"You won't be able to enter New York with your horses," he said with a know-all tone.

"Anything is possible," I said. "I'll find a way."

He asked to look at my US maps.

"I'm in El Salvador now *señor*," I said impatiently. "I'll get maps for the States when I get there."

His house was in another town and he invited me to stay there. I declined.

"I can't keep my eyes open," I said. "I'll be fast asleep in my tent by 7 p.m."

He looked disappointed but I did not care. He had not mentioned a wife and I had no intention of spending a night alone with him in his house.

I am not sure how long I had been in dreamland but through a sleepy daze I was conscious of somebody standing at the front of my tent. Through the netting I could make out a large figure. My heart missed a beat when I saw a man peeping inside, fumbling with the zip of the tent.

"What do you want?" I managed to blurt out.

"Would you like some company?" the stranger replied.

I jumped up and with shaking hands tried to open the flap to get out. I ordered him to stand back so that I could talk to him. My fear disappeared once I could look the intoxicated man straight in the eye. A few yards on his left stood the guard, torch in hand. He had obviously escorted the man to my tent. I was now furious.

"What the hell are you thinking?" I roared at the drunken man. "I've only had good experiences on my travels and here in El Salvador you try to come into my tent and scare me."

He did not know what to say.

"I want peace, now leave me alone," I ordered.

He tried to say something but I cut him short.

"What's your name?" I asked, not expecting an answer.

"Orlando *señorita*," he replied sheepishly.

He mumbled an apology, walked away and got into his 4 x 4 at the gate.

The guard also got an earful once I had composed myself. The following morning the owner appeared as I was getting ready to leave.

"I think a friend of yours paid me a visit last night," I chanced. "He was lucky I did not have the machete in my tent."

The man appeared surprised and pretended not to know anything.

Marco, (who, with his friends, travelled with me in Costa Rica for a few days), put me in touch with the people from DIANA, a multinational company that he worked for. He was a friend of Hugo the owner, and urged me to get in touch with him once we reached the capital.

"Hugo would have been president of El Salvador if he had not come from a middle class family," Marco told me.

In San Miguel, those at the DIANA offices were expecting us and during my one-night stay in his town, I was treated extremely well by Mario, the supervisor.

He not only generously organised my accommodation but also paid for the horses' food and stabling.

The next day as we left the busy town of San Miguel the traffic was already thick and heavy by 7 a.m. Fumes, dirt and rough tarmac made the exodus even more unpleasant. Two hours later Mise was dragging her feet and I got off to give her a Vitamin B injection. A man stopped in his pickup and invited me to his house up the road.

"There's lots of grass for the horses," he said.

I trusted him and followed him uphill. He gave me an apple and hot water to mix with my instant sachet of cappuccino. While the horses grazed happily, we swung in hammocks and chatted. It turned out he had worked in the US for twenty years as a landscape gardener and made good money.

"I still have an apartment and a car there," he told me.

He asked if I sometimes got fed up with my journey. I laughed and said I came to the conclusion that being fed up was not necessarily a bad thing. It was a state I had to be in to change those little things that were not bad enough to make me properly angry but had the cumulative effect of robbing me of my sense of humour. If I got fed up with Tusa pulling on the leading rope, I put the saddle on him. If I got fed up with the mosquitoes feasting on my arms, I put on a long sleeved shirt. If I got fed up with the heat, I stopped and hoped for a breeze. If I got fed up with stares, I kept my head down.

"Funnily enough," I said while chewing on my apple, "I also discovered that the best way to get rid of being fed up was getting fed."

He looked amused but then his face turned serious.

"I think you should stop now. You have done more than enough."

I smiled silently and thought to myself, *'There is so much unknown yet to be known. I could never stop now.'*

Later, we crossed a bridge over the River Lempa on the way to San Nicholas. When Tschiffely was there in 1925 things were more basic and he had to take a boat across. We stopped on the side of the road where a woman and daughter were selling shrimps. There was a gate behind them leading to a corn field. I asked the woman to open it for me. She obliged but appeared shocked when the horses began to nibble on the corn.

"The boss will be angry if he sees you," she said worriedly.

To keep her happy I tied up the horses and with my machete, cut a bundle of corn for them to eat. Later as we were going past construction workers and large machinery, a man approaching from the opposite side stopped abruptly and jumped out of his vehicle. He wanted to know if he could do an interview for a local paper. I agreed, glad of the opportunity to rest.

82. At the border between Nicaragua and Honduras.
83. Rested after a night at Wilma's family's house.

84. Graffiti in El Salvador.
85. At the border between Honduras and El Salvador.
86. A tomato entreprise at the side of the road.

87. A little Indian girl who stole my heart.
88. A picture that appeared in an El Salvadorian newspaper.
89. Two policemen who were my escorts on a road in Guatemala, notorious for assaults.

90. A guide taking us through mountains despite his intoxicted state.
91. Leaving Guatemala via lush mountains.
92. Entering Mexico in not exactly the usual way.

After two refusals late that afternoon I met Christa, a kind woman who invited me to stay at her house. While I swung in the hammock in the sparsely furnished communal room she prepared something to eat. Christa told me how she had worked at a petrol station in Boston for two years to enable her to buy things for the children.

"Things like a television and a stereo," she said.

Her children had to stay with her mother. Her husband was still working in the US and Christa admitted she fretted about him dating other woman.

"There is no gain in you thinking like that all the time," I said. "You have no control over the situation. You must just believe that he will stay true to you."

Christa was one of twelve children.

"When the war broke out I was ten years old. I had to work in the fields and look after my siblings," she said really not looking for sympathy. "Thank God we are moving forward now," she said as she handed me a large plate of food.

She made up a mattress for me to sleep on in the room she shared with her three children.

"I'm so happy you are here," she said warmly while I slid under the sheet, yawning. "I recently had a dream that somebody that speaks English would come to my house."

During the night a storm broke out and I had to move the mattress when I was woken by water dripping on me.

I handed Christa a ten dollar note the following day. She indignantly refused to take it.

"You must keep your money to buy food. You are too thin," she said in a motherly tone.

A police car stopped next to us after we had gone not more than a few hundred yards. They had a copy of a newspaper article about my travels that appeared that morning. They passed it on to me.

"You can have it," they offered kindly.

Not long after, Mario, a man in his early thirties came along on his motorbike.

"I saw the article this morning," he said. "I was looking out for you."

He offered me a place for the horses further on in San Rafael.

"I'll come out later and check your progress," he said.

It was not a pleasant day's ride. I had a sore stomach, diarrhoea and felt nauseous. It was hot and I was hungry, dirty and sweaty. I could not wait to get to San Salvador for a decent rest.

At the the Palomos house, my hosts in San Salvador, I beamed when I saw the satin sheets on my bed. *'This is rather dangerous,'* I thought. *'I might never leave.'* There was a basket-full of gels, shampoos and divine smelling cosmetics in the bathroom.

"Tell me if you need anything else," Leah, the tall blonde American wife of Eduardo, said.

I was put in touch with Eduardo and Leah through Arturo in Costa Rica. I knew that I also had an invitation to stay with Hugo Barrera, Marco's friend, but unable to divide myself in two, I had to make a decision. I chose the Palomos mainly because of their fluent English.

I had not eaten in almost two days and declined a full meal, fearing it would give me an upset stomach. I had wine, olives and yoghurt and after a good night's sleep, felt like I could face the world again.

Leah noticed that I arrived with a limp and I relayed the story of the kick I got on my hip. She suggested I joined her for a water aerobics class. I threw my whole heart into it, kicking so vigorously under water that even the instructor noticed my commitment. Clearly it worked – after two sessions the pain and discomfort had disappeared completely. I was over the moon.

Hugo, the owner of DIANA, invited me to his house for dinner. A security guard with a mean-looking gun opened the large metal gate that led to an expansive mansion. The house-keeper was friendly and courteous and had the comfortable air of somebody who was with the family for years.

The following day Hugo took me to his factory for a look around. "Ninety-seven percent of managers in my company are women," he said.

I was given a tour and unlimited tastes of all the variety of sweets, different flavoured popcorns and snacks. I felt sick afterwards but said nothing.

El Salvador is a country that has had more than its fair share of disasters and turmoil. There was the bloody twelve-year civil war that killed 70,000 people, hurricane Mitch in 1998 and then early 2001, two earthquakes struck the country within a month, killing about a thousand people and leaving many homeless. When I travelled through this hospitable country, little did I know that seventeen months later, another earthquake would kill nearly 700 people or that an increase in gang-related violence would lead to army patrols on the streets.

During my stay in El Salvador I was presented with a certificate from an endurance riding group in recognition of my journey. Some of the group accompanied me on their horses out of El Salvador ten days later. I remember Carlos in particular. He was easy to talk to, a good listener and gave intelligent responses. Felipe, his friend, surprised me when during the day's ride he got off his horse and walked. Carlos did the same later and I noticed how gently he treated his horse, patting his neck affectionately.

Mise stole the show with her obedience, easy manner and big eyes but poor Tu Fein received no compliments. I made sure to give him extra attention.

Dr. Reina, my host in Santa Ana, was a medical doctor but they were not well off. I received excellent hospitality though and he even gave up his bed so I could be more comfortable.

Instead of going through the usual border crossing into our next country, I went through a farm which had half of its land in El Salvador and the other half in Guatemala. A guide escorted me from the farm on his mule to the first small town on the Guatemalan side. Almost every woman I greeted responded with a *"que te vaya bien"* (may it go well for you). At the local bank I changed dollars into quetzales, paid my guide and set off on my own. We had another 24 kilometres to Jutiapa.

The tarmac road led us straight into the mountains. A man on a bicycle passed and then stopped in front, pretending to be busy with his bike. I greeted him but when we reached a curve in the road I got off Mise, not only to take a picture but also to check out the man whom I did not trust completely. He whizzed past again and said *"nos vemos"*, meaning literally 'we'll see each other'. I took my machete out and kept it in my hand as I walked with the horses for a while.

A short distance on, the police arrived.

"This is a dangerous road," one of them said.

I was surprised.

"I haven't seen much traffic so far," I replied.

He shook his head.

"We're not talking about trucks and cars," he said. "This road is notorious for assaults."

They could not believe I had not been warned about it. They offered to escort me. I thanked them and continued.

For the next 10 kilometres or so they lingered behind us and then passed. A few kilometres on they would be waiting. I would overtake them and wave. Soon afterwards they would pass again and wait further on. This was the pattern as we continued to go along the winding roads. I imagine they did it for diversion. Because I was going so slowly it would have been utter boredom if they were to drive behind me. There was a fair bit of downhill so I got off and walked with the horses. The bushes were dense to my left and right.

Mise jumped when a man appeared like a ghost from the mountain on to the road. I greeted him. The road had a 180 degree curve in the front and exactly where the bend was, I saw another two men, handkerchiefs over their mouths. In my innocence I thought they were working on the roads... until I saw one produce a machete, the other a silver revolver. I froze and turned to the man who had just stepped from the bushes.

"Please sir, I need help," I whispered.

But he had no intention of coming to my assistance. He turned on his heels and disappeared into the greenery again. I felt the blood drain from my face.

I looked at the thieves in front of me pointing their weapons at us. They moved around tensely. There was still about fifteen yards between us, which gave me the opportunity to think of a plan. My police escort was oblivious to what was unfolding as they were sitting in their vehicle further up the road waiting for me to come past.

The thieves were coming closer and I shouted, "The police are both behind and in front of me!"

My words stopped them in their tracks. One tried to get back into the bushes but his braver friend motioned him over.

"*Venga, venga,*" (come here, come here) he said.

I kept on walking backwards slowly, still talking to them. They did not know if they could believe me when I said the police would be there any minute. I was praying for a car to appear. After what felt like an eternity I heard the roar of an engine and a pickup truck came round the corner behind me. The thieves disappeared into the bushes. I ran to the middle of the road and the pickup stopped. I was shaking and burst into tears when the driver put his hand on mine to comfort me. I pointed to where the thieves had been a second before.

"Please don't leave me here alone," I begged.

The man said he did not have a gun and I offered him my machete.

"I have one," he said. "Just stay on this side and we'll shield you."

We went quickly round the bend and once we were on a bit of a straight, still on foot, I started to run with the horses. The police appeared shocked when I told them what had just happened and made a beeline for the scene of the crime. But the thieves had long gone.

It was already dark when we arrived in Jutiapa. The policemen took statements from me and I handed them some quetzales, thanking them for their assistance.

"We are happy for the money," one of them said, "but our job is to protect you."

In Campero I was invited by my hosts to attend a wedding with them. Not in the mood for a late night I declined.

"I have nothing to wear."

It was the truth but it did not deter them. Soon I was handed a pair of masculine-looking jeans with narrow legs and a high waist belonging to one of the boys. The sister lent me a top that had even fewer feminine qualities. My boots were in bad shape and I finished off the attire with a pair of flip flops. I think I received more attention than the bride. Every single woman was dressed to the nines in elaborate evening dresses and sparkling accessories. People could not help but stare at my outfit.

Nobody really paid attention to what was happening at the top table and there was constant chatter among the guests. The groom's mother even took two calls on her mobile phone while the bride's father was making his speech. I was introduced to the Mayor of the town but he was incapable of stringing two sentences together. I did not know whether he was just stupid or already drunk. Macho-looking men wearing golden chains and guns attached to their belts walked around, beer bottles glued to their lips. Crackers were set off with a bang, and when the couple had their first kiss it was accompanied by loud cheers. The two of them sipped sparkling wine from crystal glasses while the guests downed theirs from plastic cups.

Day 421. The hold-up on the way to Jutiapa put me in a different frame of mind. All of a sudden I was much more aware of danger and possible assaults. Many people warned me that the places I had chosen to travel in Guatemala were really dangerous and they warned me to be careful.

In Pueblo Nuevo, the Mayor of the town arranged for a guide to show me a short-cut through the mountains. A group gathered while I was getting the horses ready. It was Sunday morning and most of the men were still recovering from a boozy night out. They stood around half sloshed and had red, bleary eyes. A strong smell of alcohol filled the air.

Everybody had an idea as to how I should tie the pack up. I explained to them the reasons for the system I had been using for many months, but they kept on interfering.

"It just seems that some men can't accept it when a woman might be right," I said with a wink.

The one and only sober man in the group nodded and said to the others, "She has experience and we should leave her to do it the way she's used to."

My guide, a man of about sixty, was also in an intoxicated state, but at least he did not fall over himself. He took Mise from me and after a photo was taken, we set off. I bought a two litre coke, crisps and juice on the outskirts of the village. A man on his stallion joined us for a short while but once the trail became narrow and steep he turned around. The guide and I walked behind Mise and Tu Fein, spurring them on. We crossed several little streams and slow-flowing rivers. Between the mountains we passed fields where a family worked on the land in silence. I turned back and gave the kids handfuls of sweets from my saddlebags.

The roads uphill were tough but going down over big stones and rocks was not much better. I slipped a few times. Tu Fein spotted a trail that branched to the right and mischievously took it. Mise followed. We chased them but they kept going. I managed to grab Mise's tail and she literally dragged me along as if I was water skiing. I slipped and stumbled but finally managed to get alongside her and grab the rope. Once Tu Fein realised he was running alone he stopped and turned back towards us.

The thick vegetation opened up later and around midday we began to pass through small settlements. We had a rest at a house where my guide knew the owners. The face of Florencia, a little girl of about three, lit up when she saw us approach. Her eyes were exquisite deep brown pools and she had the cutest smile.

She stared at my half chaps and laughed.

"I love them *señora*," she said sweetly.

Her mother asked how much I would charge to take a picture of her little girl. I was surprised by the question. I was told that it was not wise to attempt to take pictures of children in Guatemala due to rumours about abductions and organ theft by foreigners.

The woman changed the girl into a pretty dress and I put her on a wall for the picture. The woman even suggested that she took one of me holding her daughter. I was smitten by the little girl and gave her a picture of myself and the horses, as well as my tin whistle.

Despite their obvious poverty the woman handed me a plate of beans and *tortilla* and a glass of water with lemon and sugar.

My guide was not happy with my suggestion that we push on to Guanagazapa.

"It's another five to seven hours to get there," he said miserably.

I insisted that I wanted to continue and started to saddle up. Without uttering a word my guide got up, walked to the road in front of the house and jumped on a bus that had stopped briefly. Disbelief gave way to feelings of momentary anxiety but truth be told, I was not too bothered.

'The coward,' I thought, 'and he still had two packets of my crisps.'

Failing to find anybody else willing to accompany us and without knowing the way through the mountains, I proceeded with the horses alone. I was vigilant travelling off the beaten track but it was a case of hoping for the best. Just before I took a turn that led into the mountains, two men came from the opposite direction on their horses.

"You can't go to Guanagazapa on horseback from here," they said. "There is a bridge you won't be able to cross. It will be better if you take a truck and go the longer route."

I thanked them for their advice and continued.

I did not see another soul for at least two hours. Two boys were walking on the narrow road.

"Is this the way to Guanagazapa?" I asked.

They nodded. Late afternoon I saw a house just off the trail, the garden neat and clean, surrounded by fencing. The girl who answered my call indicated that she could not allow me to stay there.

"My father isn't here," she said.

An hour later I still had not reached the bridge I knew we had to cross. There was a little house nestled in between the mountains, and a little boy who heard my shouts from the gate called his mother. It took her a long time to agree for me to stay.

"I am alone," she said. "My husband is not here."

I told her that I was a woman alone too.

I pitched my tent while the kids watched shyly from a distance. I gave them sweets and struggled to open my tin of tuna with the machete. I shared my Rooibos tea with the quiet woman. Later, I sat on a tree stump and wrote my diary in the remaining light of the day. I was woken during the night by a bright light shining into the tent. But there was nothing to fear. It was only the glow from a full moon.

I found a tick on my thigh the following morning. Noticing that it had done a good job of sucking into my flesh already, I made sure I removed it properly, head and all. It was important that nothing was left behind. I was careless another time when bitten in Costa Rica. Part of the tick's body did not come out, and months later the spot would itch and flare up regularly.

I left just after sunrise on an empty stomach. We made our way up a narrow, rocky trail, bordered by lush greenery.

We crossed a river and I noticed an Indian woman sweeping in front of her house between the trees. The road split in two and I asked the way to Guanagazapa. She indicated to the left and we went uphill along a very narrow, stony trail. When we got to the top I was surprised to see a man, machete in hand, waiting for me like an angel in the night.

"You just asked my wife for directions," he said. "Follow me. I will be your guide."

I obliged with a grateful look on my face. His unexpected presence turned out to be crucial. Soon the trail got even rockier with deep inclines like miniature gorges. The two of us and the horses slid and stumbled and I feared they might get a shoe stuck between the rocks.

We finally reached the 'swinging bridge' I had been warned about. It was not as bad as I expected but it certainly was not solid. Mise stopped dead in her tracks when I urged her on. My guide took Tu Fein who cautiously obliged. The wooden bridge swayed as they stepped on it. Mise and I followed slowly. She was clearly afraid and at one point when the bridge became too unstable, I thought she might attempt to turn around. I soothed her speaking softly. With baited breath we all made it to the other side.

My guide's help was invaluable. I would not have known which way to turn at the numerous forks in the mountain trails. He received a generous tip once we reached another community. He was extremely appreciative.

"Call me when you're back this way again," he said before we parted.

I continued to be on guard every day as we travelled through Guatemala. We encountered a number of shifty-looking men not making eye contact but instead focussing on the money belt on my hip. In most places the people received us warmly although I sensed they were cautious about opening their doors to a stranger.

Before the town of Esquintla, an Indian woman and her husband, who were the care-takers of a spacious property behind high walls, agreed that I could stay a couple of days. Great was my delight when Esperanza pointed to the sparkling pool outside, right in front of the room they had offered. I spent a lot of time in the water to stretch my sore muscles. I did not know if I would have such luxury on my journey again.

Later she made excuses for their humble house. She told me she could not have children and instead had a lot of animals. They loved the Rooibos tea I offered after dinner. They talked non-stop about assaults in Guatemala, obviously afraid of being attacked themselves.

"You should continue your journey by car or in an aeroplane," her husband suggested.

Esperanza shook her head. With exaggerated hand movements and emotive facial expressions, she loudly explained to her husband exactly why I was travelling that way. She was a real character and laughed easily.

"What will you do next?" she said with mischief in her eyes, "travel on a giraffe or a buffalo!"

But there was melancholy behind her bubbly demeanour and she shared her stories with me. The fact that she could not have children saddened her a great deal.

"My husband made another woman pregnant," she said with tears in her eyes. "The baby was born a week ago."

She offered to give me a massage and I noticed the purple and blue marks on her arms. I was in no doubt as to what had caused them.

"He cannot hit you." I said.

She told me she had nowhere to go and that he spent all their money on prostitutes and alcohol. Instead of giving her money for my stay I went into town and bought her bags of groceries. At least that way he could not squander the money and she could eat.

The sun continued to beat down most days and usually the three of us were drenched in perspiration. Sometimes space on the side of the road was almost non-existent and I felt uncomfortable with the large number of buses and trucks that brushed past us, literally an arms-length away. We survived but I feared it might have been just a matter of time. The margin for error was very small and at some point I thought our luck would run out and we would be in an accident.

Our fate was taken out of our hands when Mise had one of her shoes torn off – how, I do not know. A farrier showed me why he could not nail on another shoe.

"The hoof is damaged," he said, "and there is no space to put in a nail. If I try, it will go through the sensitive part and she could go lame."

He told me it would be a few weeks before she could be shod again. I could not ride Mise on the tarmac without shoes and was advised to organise transport to our next destination an hour away. One glance at the terribly narrow road to Retaluleu, full of traffic and with no space on the side of the road confirmed that it was the right decision.

Annie and Tirso, a young couple with a charming boy of five, were waiting for me in Reu. I could not have asked for better hosts. They were relaxed and easy-going and I thoroughly enjoyed my stay with them. Their vet friend suggested my horses rested for at least fifteen days.

"They need to recuperate, get fatter and Mise's hoof has to heal," he said.

I listened to his expert advice and used the time to organise our entry into Mexico.

I was fortunate that while I prepared for Mexico, I had a bit of time on my hands to explore other regions of Guatemala, each part clearly contributing to the beauty and diversity of a spectacular country rich in culture and history. Most notably is the legacy of the Mayans, the western hemisphere's greatest ancient civilization, long revered for its sophistication and hieroglyphics, which show evidence of dentistry and brain surgery from 800 BC to 800 AD. Their influence is still evident today among the life and traditions of the Guatemalan people. The only difference is that now it is witnessed in a modern and picturesque setting.

A good example was the town of colonial Antiqua, the oldest and to me, one of the most beautiful in Central America. Strolling along cobbled streets, I marvelled at all the well-preserved baroque buildings, wooden and brass-studded doors and a church painted vibrantly in bright yellow. I found the town a true expression of colour and life. I spent hours sitting in the square plaza, people-watching and thinking — where I was, what I had gone through, and what might lie ahead.

A day-out to the town of Chichicastenango (also called Santo Tomás) in the heart of the Guatemalan highlands was an unforgettable experience. With a maze of winding streets surrounding the main plaza, this charming little town also has one of the most colourful native markets in Central America. An intoxicating combination of colour, dialects, costumes, smoke and smells, the place was packed with vendors, street musicians and tourists. I found the 400-year-old church of Santo Tomás, which is situated next to the market, fascinating. The stairs leading to a temple remains venerated, each of the eighteen steps representing one month of the Mayan calander. While I sat outside on the steps, engaging with delightful kids trying to sell their wares, a procession was taking place up the stairs. Men dressed in colourful orange and pink attire were waving small containers through the air, releasing a sweet-smelling smoke that slowly drifted through the crowds.

Lake Atitlan was another highlight for me and it is impossible to disagree with author Aldous Huxley who once described it as 'the most beautiful lake in the world'. Lying snugly in the midst of three volcanoes and various Indian villages, the place had a magical, tranquil effect. I am not so sure though that I continued to have some of that quietness and peace within me, when soon after, I found myself confronted by more obstacles than I would have wished for.

I received no response from the Mexican authorities after I had sent an explanatory letter about my travels, including every health certificate that I possessed for the horses. I knew it was possible to enter but for some unexplained reason they did not want to know about me. This left me frustrated. I had a nagging feeling that my request was going to be one of those cases which would get lost in a black hole of red tape and bureaucracy. I had to start thinking of Plan B, when after a month, I was still trying to get information from them. All I wanted to know was what other conditions I needed to comply with to gain entry to Mexico.

After days of deliberations with friends in Reu the decision was made that I would take the horses in via the mountains. With the help of Riki, a brother-in-law of Tirso, we planned my route and he organised a place for me and the horses to stay every night for the four day ride up to a border farm. A guide would bring me from there on an 'alternative' route into the country.

The turn-off to the farm where we were expected was about four kilometres from the border. I left the horses at a small roadside café and got a lift in a taxi. My next move was paramount. I needed to get a stamp on my passport to show I had left Guatemala and then another stamp for entering Mexico. Once I had that, I needed to go back into Guatemala without being noticed. That was risky. If my passport was checked in Guatemala, I would have been illegal. This meant serious trouble not only for me personally but also for the future of my journey. After calculating the risk, I had no other option but to proceed with my plan. I tried the legal way, wanting to do everything according to the book, but the doors were closed.

The official on the Mexican side asked how long I was going to stay, "thirty, sixty or ninety days?" he asked.

"Ninety days," I said.

Feeling jittery, I made small talk and told him I was a photographer and that I thought Mexico was beautiful. He complimented me on my good Spanish. I thanked him profusely, nauseated by my exaggerated friendliness.

I tried to stroll back to the Guatemalan side as unobtrusively as possible, conscious that a tall white girl dressed in horse gear was not an everyday sight. Two policemen stood at the barrier. I took the assertive approach, walked up to them, holding a Guatemalan phone-card in my hand.

"Where is the nearest phone box?" I asked.

One indicated towards Mexico, the other in the opposite direction and with a definite "*gracias*" I walked into Guatemala again. My heart was thumping and I forced myself not to look back. I was waiting for an official voice to call me back. Once I was out of sight, I jumped into a taxi and headed back to where Mise and Tu Fein were waiting. The plan was working. So far.

An hour later we reached the farm high up in the mountains in pouring rain. The whole area was spacious and fenced in, and a cobblestone path led to the houses of workers, dotted around the place. Once I was helped through security I was taken to a room consisting of only a bed and a thin springy mattress. Outside, two macaws in a cage were causing a racket. I had to ask for a sheet and later for food. The latter was brought to me in a plastic bag, still warm *tortillas* wrapped in a leaf. Delicious *frijole* (black beans) and scrambled eggs completed the tasty menu.

A frog crept underneath the door and sat quietly in the corner of the room. I caught him in a T-shirt and put him outside before I took a cold shower. Not long after I turned out the light. I had been warned that the following day would be a long and difficult one.

The horses were grazing all over the place and the next morning I was surprised to see them on my doorstep. I do not know how they knew where I was. I had small round chocolates that looked like miniature soccer balls wrapped up in paper in my pocket. Tu Fein heard the crackling of paper and came to investigate. The chocolate rolled on my hand as I extended my arm towards him and I bent my fingers upwards to prevent it falling down. Just then Tu Fein bit and my little finger ended up between his teeth. I rapidly pulled my hand back but the damage was done. He had bitten through to the bone and within minutes I could not bend the throbbing finger. I was in agony and one of the workers gave me a painkiller. My guide arrived and I asked him to help me saddle up, pointing to my injury. He fumbled awkwardly with the pack while I struggled on with only one 'working' hand.

On leaving the farm we were straight into mountainous terrain. The surroundings were dense, leafy and like jungle. The air was moist and dew sparkled on shrubs and trees in the crisp morning light.

Some rocky surfaces were slippery and slimy and I fell a few times. The horses were not completely sure-footed themselves. We passed a few locals on the way. They looked on curiously but neither my guide nor I paid them much attention. We entered a village and the guide commandeered two men he knew to accompany us. The surface of the trail was uneven, rough and muddy as well as extremely narrow in parts. The footing was treacherous and the horses struggled and tripped occasionally. We all found the going hard.

A group of men approached from the front.

"Where are you going?" they asked.

My guide pointed in the direction of Mexico. The men looked surprised and one said we would not be able to cross the river.

"The current is too strong," he said.

We did not pay attention to the comment. Mise walked in front and stopped and waited when Tu Fein and the rest of us fell too far behind. We were still quite high up but I could hear the sound of the river far below.

'Maybe the men were right,' I thought somewhat concerned.

We descended slowly through mud and over rocks and stones.

Five hours after leaving the farm we reached the river.

"Which one of you will test the strength of the water?" I asked the guide and his friends.

The blank stares from the three men spurred me into action. I ripped off my shoes, grabbed a long rope and tied it around my waist. I handed one end to them.

"Hold on tight," I said as I made my way backwards into the river.

The stones hurt my bare feet. Halfway through there was a sudden powerful surge of water and I felt as if I was about to lose my balance. I shouted at my guides to tighten the rope. They did not hear me over the rush of water and instead gave more slack. With that I lost my footing and was swept downstream. Two of them jumped in the water and pulled vigorously on the rope until I managed to find solid ground underneath me again. With worried expressions they pulled together until I was back on the bank.

After a moment to catch my breath, I took Mise in with me, slowly braving the waters again. She did very well, staying at my side until we were through. I left her on the far side and went back for Tu Fein but he was too eager and, not wanting to be away from Mise, jumped into the water, heading straight in the direction of a strong rapid. I roared at him and panicking, he returned to the bank. I took him across as well and waited for the men on the other side. My guide, standing only in his underpants, was tiny and had to hold on to his taller friend, who holding a long stick, led him through the water. The water came up right to my guide's chin. I was continuing with only the original guide and after handing the two men some money, they turned back again, clearly pleased that their job was done. My guide put on fresh clothes and slapped me good-naturedly on the back.

"Welcome to Mexico," he said with a grin.

We were in Mexico! I was legal, having the necessary stamps on my passport but the horses were in a less secure position. We reached the village of Santa Domingo three hours later. My guide indicated my route from there and quickly turned back towards Guatemala. The injured finger throbbed like hell and every inch of my body ached. I knew I would soon be purple and blue from all the knocks I got going through that challenging mountain trail. But I decided it was worth it. Nothing would stop us now – or so I thought.

Heading for Tapachula I had two encounters with local men that could easily have turned into something nasty. A man on the isolated road engaged me in conversation. He was eyeing my sunglasses and saddlebags. I did not want him to think I was travelling alone and told him I was waiting for my 'boyfriend'.

"He wouldn't be happy to see you talking to me," I said.

He sprinted away on his bicycle but I saw him further down the road again, picking oranges from a tree.

"Do you want some?" he asked.

I did not speak to him but just shook my head. He had a menacing look and I took out my machete. As I walked past him, I lifted the collar of my shirt and 'spoke' into my shoulder, pretending to be in contact with the local police. My suspect heard as I gave a thorough description of what he wore and looked like.

"The police know about you," I said, feeling a bit more empowered by the charade I was putting on.

He did not bother me again.

Further down the road a pickup passed with three men inside. They stopped.

"We're not thieves," they announced in advance having probably noticed the suspicious look on my face. "We just want to know if you would sell your horses."

I did not make it to Tapachula that day and had to overnight in a village where I was offered a couch in a house to sleep on. The horses were tied up on the other side of the road in an open area with ample grass around. During the course of the evening a man approached me.

"Your horses are not safe there. There is a man in the village who is a thief and will probably try to take them."

We moved them to another spot. Another man offered to be my guide the next day, claiming he knew a shorter route to Tapachula. We agreed to meet at 6 a.m.

I had only a black coffee for dinner and had to ask for a blanket. I was woken at midnight, feeling a hand on my shoulder. It was the man of the house.

"What are your horses' names?" he asked.

I was wide awake. He told me he was going to check up on them. Rather suspicious I told him I would go with him. Both horses seemed fine. The man and I walked back to the house. He turned to me.

"Does everybody in your country have sex with everybody like here?" he asked.

I looked at him as if he had gone mad.

"No," I replied. "In my country, it does not work like that!"

I said goodnight abruptly and headed straight for the couch. I changed the position of my head to make sure I was aware of anybody approaching me during what remained of the night.

There was no sign of my guide twenty minutes after our arranged time and I left while it was still dark outside. Two men on bicycles passed, one stopped and looked back. There was not enough light to make out his face. My heart was beating faster but I simply continued. So did they.

The day was breaking slowly and the light was inviting and soft. It was a wondrous feeling to be on horseback while the world was beginning to wake up. There was a cacophony of moos, crows and barks, almost in harmony with the clip-clop of my horses' hooves on the tarmac.

Three kilometres into the day's ride I heard the dreaded sound and checked Tu Fein's feet. A shoe had come loose. I approached a man standing in front of his house. He ordered his son to get tools from their shed. His wife brought out coffee later, which Tu Fein unfortunately pushed over when he put his nose too close to sniff what was in the cup. I could have strangled him.

Neither the man nor I had the proper tools and it took him an hour to get the shoe off. He did not complain and seemed pleased to help. I took out my camera to take a picture of him standing next to the horses but when I pressed the shutter, I realised I had run out of film. He looked so happy to pose and I did not have the heart to tell him so I just pretended that it was done.

In Cacayutan, the town was getting ready for Independence Day celebrations. I had not eaten for some twenty-four hours. A sandwich and coffee hit the spot. I complimented the man on the cleanliness and tidiness of his shop. He beamed and standing behind the counter, began to vigorously rub the already immaculately clean glass top.

The police let me through barriers on the road that was closed to traffic.

The horses were going to stay at Lienzo Charro, the cattle association located on the outskirts of Tapachula. They had a number of horses stabled there. I discovered a large number of ticks in the horses' ears which they must have picked up as we were going through the lush mountainous areas. Elias, one of the helpers at the stables offered to give them a proper spray the following morning.

A few days later I took a plane to Mexico City to arrange a face to face meeting with the officials so that we could proceed through their country. I had little luck as the responsibility for making a decision was passed from one person to the other. I was kept at arms length with promises that *"mañana, mañana"* things would be sorted.

"We'll call you within a week with an answer," they promised.

Back in Tapachula I was told the president of the Lienzo Charro wanted to see me urgently. Having found out about the horses' illegal status, he was distressed about the effect it might have on his organisation.

"Our members are worried," he said "They think you smuggled the horses through because they carry disease. They fear that these stables might need to be quarantined because of that."

I explained that I had anaemia tests done in Reu and that both horses had all the vaccinations they needed. I also mentioned that the place where they stayed in Guatemala was immaculate. I told him my position, why I had entered Mexico the way I did and that I was waiting for the authorities to grant me permission to continue my travels.

What dismayed me more was not whether the horses were legal but the condition I found them in on my return from Mexico City. They neighed when they saw me. I was disgusted to see them standing miserably in a dirty *corral* with the cement floor covered in manure and no protection from the sun. There was not even a bucket of water to be seen. Mise had a few bald patches on her back and Tu Fein seemed to have some skin condition as well. They obviously had been exposed to the elements and were in much worse shape than the previous week.

"They have been there since you left for Mexico," Elias said. "We did not have room for them in a stable."

I was distraught and cursed out loud. I had no doubt that they needed to be moved somewhere else.

Within half a day, and with the help of contacts, another place was found outside the town. Dressed in a denim mini skirt, flip flops and an umbrella to protect me from the sun, I led the horses on foot to their new accommodation. It was a struggle in the heat and they were in no mood to cooperate. I arrived drenched in perspiration, two hours later. The dirt of the yard bothered me and the sight of a half-dead calf on the ground made me question my decision to bring the horses there. All I could hope was that the stay would be brief.

The call from the authorities never came. I contacted them repeatedly and was told to wait. And wait I did – for more than four weeks. Friends tried to figure out why the authorities would not tell me one way or another. Riki had an explanation.

"They don't want to say yes to you, fearing you might get into trouble on the road and that it would be bad for tourism in Mexico if there was publicity. And they can't say no because if they do, they'll have to explain why."

It made sense to me but it did not help my agitated state of mind as I played the waiting game. It was a tense time and I hated not knowing what was going to happen. I felt like a piece of elastic, stretched to the limit. I had travelled so far, and now some piece of bureaucracy was stopping my journey. We had endured hardships, altitudes, hunger and death and now paperwork was the final barrier.

It was suggested that I obtained new registration papers for the horses, claiming they were Mexican, but soon that option became unrealistic. Tirso, who was initially keen on the idea, urged me in an email not to consider that course of action. It seemed that too many people knew about the *gringa* with her horses, and our illegal entrance into Mexico was now common knowledge. I was warned that I would not get past the first police control point.

"They'll confiscate your horses and you'll be deported," was the general feeling.

I dismissed the recommendation from another source that I should get two new horses.

It took a while for the seriousness of the situation to sink in. Giving up was not something that sat easy with me and I was still stuck on the idea of continuing through Mexico. Like so many other things in life, hope was not merely helpful, it was indispensable. It kept me sane.

Ultimately though, I had to come to accept the fact that this door was firmly closed. I had to recognise that and move on. Friends in Guatemala offered their insights, which frequently circled back to a common theme – my safety.

"It could be a blessing in disguise," they said. "Mexico is probably the least safe country in Latin America for a woman travelling alone, especially the way you're doing it, going off the beaten track and having to rely on people you don't know, every day and every night."

They told me not to beat myself up about it. "You gave it your all, you tried your best."

They were right. It was just not meant to be.

Dave sent a message of encouragement;

It's great that you are still committed to the project despite the difficult times that you're encountering at the moment. With your persistence and tenacity I know you'll come through these trying events. Remember Winston Churchill's words – 'If you're going through hell, keep going'.

Riki formulated a strategy to get the horses back into Guatemala once I let him know that Mexico was not going to happen. Because we had not gone into Mexico through the official border, we could not go back that way. We were also concerned that the authorities might start looking for the horses. Somebody mentioned that they could be put down if found.

He told me I could not take part in the smuggling of the horses back into Guatemala.

"You stand out too much," Riki said.

He said he had organised for somebody else to do it.

"He will approach you outside town and take the horses from you. You will take a taxi and get through the border. I will meet you on the Guatemalan side and take you to the farm where the horses will be."

I would have liked to take the horses back myself but I did not want to mess things up. I did not argue with the plan and was eternally grateful. Riki did not need to stick out his neck for me like that.

There was one funny moment when Oscar, the 'smuggler' approached me. We had a quick word.

"What would you say if an official stopped you and asked who the horses belonged to?" I quizzed him.

"I will say they are yours *señorita*," he said with an earnest face.

I gave him a wide-eyed look. "No Oscar, you can't say that. I don't exist and you don't know me. These horses are yours until we meet again."

I could only hope and pray that he understood. I could feel the butterflies and the nervous tension but I was excited too. It was so liberating to be moving again.

It was a relief to be in Guatemala once more. I thanked the gods for good friends when I saw Riki's wide smile among the sea of people at the border. Everything went according to plan. The horses were perspiring heavily and Mise walked with a slight limp but other than that, things were under control.

I contemplated long and hard how I would proceed. One idea was to get to the north of Guatemala with the horses and go by boat to the USA. I sent a few emails enquiring about the possibilities but nobody got back to me.

Whichever way I was going to get into the States, the horses had to be tested for piroplasmosis. As there was no lab in Central America that could perform the test, the blood had to be sent to the US. The samples were sent via DHL in ice-cold sealed containers, and I awaited the results with baited breath.

A week later a fax arrived back with devastating news: Tu Fein had tested positive. Even more serious was the diagnosis that he suffered from both forms of piroplasmosis caused by parasites called *babesia equi and babesia caballi,* which attack and destroy red blood cells in horses.

It was impossible to tell how and when Tu Fein was infected. I heard later that many horses in Central America carry the virus without the owners knowing, as very few have their equines tested for the disease. I spent hours on the internet trying to figure out what I could do. I sent off numerous emails to vets asking for advice. They all had the same thought – it was not worth trying to treat Tu Fein's condition given that he had it in its most severe form. According to the Unites States Department of Agriculture no cure existed for the *B. equi* infection. I was told that had he only *B. caballi,* the antibiotics to treat it would have to be given at toxic levels.

"A lot of horses suffer and die from the medicine," I was advised.

I explored whether anybody would keep Tu Fein indefinitely, apart from other livestock to prevent contamination. Nobody was prepared to do it. It was probably for the best as it would have been torture for a social animal like that to spend his days in isolation.

I was overwhelmed at the thought that yet another horse of mine would have to be put down. It felt unreal and brought back too many sad memories of Tusa's demise in Manaus. I never thought I was going to have to go through that again. This was not part of the plan. I kept on thinking if only it was just a bad dream from which I would soon wake up. I wondered about the sense of all this heartache.

But for my own sanity I knew I could not continue beating myself up. There was nothing I could have done to prevent Tu Fein falling ill to this virus. Had there been a vaccination or something within my powers to have changed the course of events I would have done it. I needed to accept what happened and deal with it. But it was not easy.

Yet again I had to separate the horses. They were confused and unhappy. It broke my heart to see them like that. I felt for Mise who I'm sure could not understand why she was losing another friend, unceremoniously and without warning. I also worried about her health. Was it just a matter of time before it was her turn? I did not think I would have the strength to cope if something were to happen to her.

I could not tolerate the idea of another long drawn-out period before Tu Fein had to be put down. I knew it had to be done and wanted it over as quickly as possible. Riki was once again my saviour and handled a painful situation with sensitivity. He took charge and knew that I did not want to be present. I had said goodbye to Tu Fein that morning. I fed him his favourite food – it was important to me that he left this earth with a full tummy.

Tears rolled down my cheeks when Riki got into his pickup to go into the field where he was. There was nothing more I could do.

"I will make sure Tu Fein is heavily tranquilized," he said sympathetically.

I was too upset to talk.

The ground was too hard to dig a hole and Tu Fein's body was cremated instead.

Riki assured me he did not suffer. I believed him. I am also content that Tu Fein knew the affection I had for him. He was in no doubt that I loved him very, very much. May he rest in peace.

For the next few weeks the house of Ana Lorena Cordova (sister of Tirso who lived in Reu) and her mother in Guatemala City became my home. I shared a room with Ana Lorena, a caring girl with a big heart and warm eyes. It was also due to her that Mise ended up staying at the luxurious stables of close friends of hers. Ana Lorena, her mom and brothers were incredibly kind to me and even though I knew I could call on them for anything I needed, they allowed me freedom to get on with things. I also met her dad while I was in Reu – a generous and jovial man with lots of stories to tell.

They were mortified when I used public transport in the city. The buses were called chicken buses, which they considered far too dangerous. I loved using them despite rumours of regular muggings. They were full of characters and I especially enjoyed the kids who jumped on at every traffic light, their hands filled with sweets which they tried to sell. I can still hear a boy of about ten belting it out in a monotone voice.

"Thank God I'm not a delinquent and not doing drugs. To stay this way you have to buy these from me. Think of your little grandmother and the smells in her kitchen... this is where these sweets were made!"

The world continued to be in turmoil while I organised to fly Mise to the USA – suicide bombings in Turkey, a revolution in Georgia in Russia, and Michael Jackson accused of child molestation. I saw snippets of the news on television but I did not really connect with it. Just as in the beginning of my journey, I felt completely removed from what was happening elsewhere and continued to be absorbed with my travels in a rather insular way. In some ways I acted selfishly. I knew the opportunity to lead a life detached from routine and the humdrum was not likely to come my way again. So I savoured what I had in my unique world for a just a bit longer.

DHL came to my assistance for a second time and it was agreed that Mise could be flown to Florida, although unfortunately not until three months later when there would be space for her in quarantine. Waiting for that length of time was not going to work for me and I set out to get to the United States as soon as possible to continue my travels. There was only one obstacle to overcome – I needed two horses to proceed.

"I do the very best I know how, the very best I can, and I mean to keep doing so until the end. If the end brings me out alright, what is said against me won't amount to anything. If the end brings me out wrong, ten angels swearing I was right would make no difference"
— *Abraham Lincoln*

Never trust a horse dealer. That piece of advice was regrettably not given to me in time, and my innocence in the matter led to quite a bit of hassle and headache.

A complete stranger called Jerry who is from Kentucky, sent me an email while I was still in Venezuela, having stumbled across news of my travels on the World Wide Web. He offered assistance whenever, wherever. I am not keen on asking favours but I needed help to get two suitable horses for the stretch through the USA until Mise could join me so I asked Jerry for a hand. He indicated that he would give me the loan of two Tennessee walking horses.

"We'll arrange how I'll get them back from you once you have reached New York," he said.

I cannot say that I felt completely comfortable with the increasingly familiar tone of his emails prior to my flying from Guatemala to the US. He mentioned once too often how he could not wait for us to meet. We had arranged to hook up and then drive, with two horses on board, down south towards Alabama from where I would start riding. I remember that I hoped he had not only a wife but that he was happily married as well.

Jerry and I met at the airport in Nashville. He was lanky with a self-conscious demeanour and an exaggerated Kentucky drawl. He drove a massive pickup truck with an oversized trailer attached, carrying not two, but three horses. The alarm bells went off that evening when I wanted to pay for my room at the motel which Jerry had booked.

"It's all looked after," the girl at reception said.

It transpired that Jerry had organised for us to be in the same room. It was a rather awkward moment as I arranged to pay for my own space for the night.

Whatever Jerry might have envisaged during our short encounter did not happen and I greeted a less friendly man the following morning. But his real self came to the fore when we discussed the horses. Of the three, only one seemed suitable for the kind of riding I was doing. I decided to call him Toto.

"He's 1500 dollars," Jerry said, rather uneasily.

I did not have the courage to tell him that he had already told me the horses were to be a loan. I could not travel with only one horse so of the other two I chose the 'quieter' one.

Pepsi was a wild thing, young and flighty and had not yet mastered the unique gait (called a 'rack'), typical of Tennessee walking horses. Even to this day, my blood boils every time I think what an inexperienced horse Jerry was willing to pawn off on me, despite the obvious dangers it would bring on the road. He had his plan worked out. He would be paid for one horse and the wild one would be tamed and worth much more by the time we reached New York. That is, *if* we reached New York.

Jerry left in a huff a day sooner than planned. He probably did not see the sense in hanging around any longer if there was not going to be any 'action'. I told him I would forward on the rest of the money I still owed for Toto. Given his attitude and that he had not been straight with me, I thought I would delay payment for a while and let him sweat a bit. He got into his truck the day of his departure without as much as a good wish for the rest of my trip. I was glad to see him go.

I have one friend in Ireland whose correspondence to me usually differed greatly from that of my other friends. When others gave sympathy, Eugene teased; when they seemed in awe of what I was doing, he mocked me for things that were going wrong. He responded to a mass email I sent after my first day's ride in the US. Like his other correspondence, this one put a smile on my face.

> So, you're finally on the home stretch, well final continent anyway, though skipping Mexico and omitting the first third of the USA is gamesmanship at its best/worst. How come you have two new Mules? I thought only one of the previous two required the trip to Elmer's factory? Or was the remaining mule just not arsed entering the States? I reckon he was denied entry when he refused to remove his shoes when instructed by Immigration Officials. And as for Pepsi and Toto? What happened to the days of Trigger or Black Beauty? Also what the Christ is a 'Tennessee Walking Horse'? Either somebody is taking the piss or you've just purchased a rejected batch of Southern Whiskey. What happens if he's required to run? Not in his job description? Most people would hope to complete the final stage of their journey ASAP, only you would want to actually go slower, and it's not as if you've being achieving warp speed to date.

Pepsi was a nightmare from the start. He jumped at everything. I reckon if he only jumped while I sat on him, I could have gotten used to it but it was worse than that. He had a tendency to charge around without warning and take off at the most unexpected moments. A stationary tractor in a field far away would make him panicky; the shape of an unusual tree would give him a fright. He even had the jitters when the wind blew. I could not relax with him and had to anticipate his every move.

Toto was no angel either and I had a handful between the two of them. On our first day's ride I realised it was impossible to steer Toto using the reins against his neck. He would only react when he felt a pull in his mouth. So, on top of having to stay safe on the US roads, I also had to train my horse. But I felt great pride when after two weeks in the saddle, I noticed he had developed a greater sensitivity in his neck and allowed me to guide him that way.

It was eighteen months since I left Argentina when I commenced the US stretch in Georgia, not far from the border with Alabama. I had nothing planned. Nobody knew about my journey or waited to meet me. I was curious how I was going to be received in this mighty land of freedom and liberty.

As we travelled through North America it was not that easy in the beginning to establish a chain of contacts and I found myself a few times managing to find a spot for the horses, but having to book into a motel myself for the night. In one place I was even given the use of a trailer complete with bed, bathroom and kitchen for a couple of nights. When people knew about our travels or were asked by a friend or acquaintance to look after us they were welcoming, but I sensed reluctance when I appeared 'out of the blue' with my two horses. I was fortunate though to have had a bed most nights in the comfortable home of some American family or other. The majority of people opened their homes and hearts with unrestrained generosity, making no secret of their excitement to be part of my adventure even for a short while.

It was curiosity and the potential for a story that made a man in Colquitt, Georgia, come after me when his daughter shouted, "Daddy, daddy, there's a girl going down the street on her horse!"

Terry was the editor of the local newspaper, the *Miller County Liberal*, established by his grandmother in 1897. Miss Zula B. Toole was the first successful female founder and owner of a weekly newspaper in the State of Georgia, well before women were allowed to vote.

Terry got more than what he bargained for. I was willing to talk to him but I needed a place for me and the horses as well. It was winter, the Christmas spirit was in the air and their house warm and inviting. The horses were kept with his 90-year-old mother-in-law and I stayed with him and Betty Jo for three days. They treated me like a daughter and tried to persuade me to stay until Christmas. They could not bear the notion of me being out on my own in the cold. I could not allow myself to become too comfortable and reluctantly announced that I would be moving on soon again.

"Leave your horses somewhere after your next day's ride and come back to stay with us for a night again," they suggested.

I was happy with that arrangement. But it turned out not to be that easy to organise a place for the horses. Going through Baker County I stopped in the late afternoon when I saw a house with a small plot of land on the left. There was nobody home and I enquired at a house on the opposite side. A man of about thirty opened the door and looked at me sceptically.

He listened to my request and said, "There is a graveyard four kilometres down the road, you can tie up your horses there."

I tried to keep my cool at the outrageous suggestion and enquired about the opposite field. It turned out that it belonged to his family, and after serious consideration, he agreed for the horses to rest there for the night.

I hitched a lift with a man and his wife who first drove past and then reversed to pick me up. They both looked quite prim and proper and for some reason I imagined they would be God-fearing people. The man, who was driving, turned his head towards me.

"You shouldn't be travelling alone through these parts. It's dangerous."

He looked at his wife and then back at me again and said in a whisper, "There are *blacks* here you know."

I nearly choked on the roll I was nibbling on.

"I'm not fifteen," I said as nicely as possible.

I told him I was from South Africa and that people of a different colour do not necessarily spell 'danger' to me.

Travelling through what is called the Bible-belt I regularly encountered people with bible under arm proclaiming their Christianity while holding racist views.

"We don't like blacks to come to our church," or "We might all join together in heaven one day but I wouldn't allow my daughter to marry a black man."

At the same time, these people showered me with kindness and I did not think it was my place to get into discussions about controversial issues.

While I was in Colquitt, Sadam Hussain was captured. The atmosphere in town was jubilant. Almost everybody felt his capture justified the war in Iraq and that it would mean the end of terrorism.

On my way to Lester I began to look out for farms for a night's stay. A woman drove past in one of those big American pickup trucks, stopped and reversed. She rolled down the window.

"Are you running away from home?" she asked in a teasing tone.

Marilyn, a woman with long brown hair and a youthful face stopped for one reason only, she was there to help. Married and the proud mother of two boys in their twenties, and a daughter who worked in the offices of the Republican Governor of Georgia, she even took a day off work to assist me with everything I needed. It was as if Marilyn was just waiting for an opportunity to show kindness. She took me to a mobile phone company where I managed to get a phone from Alltell to use for the duration of my trip. She kept in touch regularly for moral support, to share gossip or just have a laugh. It was a great feeling to know that somebody was rooting for me all the way.

She arranged that I stayed with her friend Diane, an artist, who lived down the road and who also had extra stables. Diane's husband, Joel, a humble man reluctant to talk about himself, lives the true American dream. He had started working in a company thirty years before as a steel manufacturer and was now president of this prosperous enterprise.

"We are part of your adventure from the comfort of our couches," Joel said. "You are doing the hard work and we share in that energy but we have to do nothing."

Maybe that was true in some instances but certainly not in their case. They showed tremendous generosity when they offered to pick up Mise in February when she was ready to come out of quarantine. At their own expense they took a trailer down to Florida and collected her, travelling the 7 hours back to their home in Georgia. Mise stayed with them for another few weeks to acclimatise. Diane even kept a log of the times when Mise ate, urinated, rolled over or whatever else horses do.

I met Bobby, a man in his early forties with an 'I'm here to help' attitude, when he and his daughter came along in their pickup truck after they had spotted us going past their shop. Showing true southern hospitality he offered bags of horse food and even dropped some off in different towns.

He also played a key part when the writing was on the wall with Pepsi. With Bobby and his family watching, as well as a group of about six others, Pepsi started his antics one morning as we were setting off. An accident was inevitable and everybody agreed that I needed another horse.

That evening, Todd and Maria who were friends of Bobby, pulled into the driveway with a trailer and two Appaloosas inside. Maria was a petite Spanish woman, and her husband, twice her size, used to be a professional basketball player. They had tremendous goodwill and I could not have asked to meet more genuine people. We had never met, yet they were willing to hand over two of their beloved horses, no questions asked.

"You just take them," they said, "and finish your journey. We won't hold you responsible if anything happens to them on the road."

I chose Camanchi, Maria's favourite horse, and I mentioned that I would like to continue with Toto. They offered to keep Pepsi until they arranged with Jerry to get him back to Kentucky.

Their extraordinary generosity might have saved my life. Going with Pepsi on the road was like playing Russian roulette and it was just a matter of time before something serious was going to happen.

There was no time for practice. Camanchi was saddled up the following morning and without even a spin down the garden to suss him out we were on the road again. We gelled from the very beginning and I was in love with him before the end of our first day's ride together. Maria said it could be a challenge to catch him if he was in a field but I never had that problem. I sang or whistled and kept my head down as I moved in his direction. He never ran away from me. He was lively and had great energy, never giving me a moment's hassle.

The sun and blue skies were deceptive while we travelled through Georgia. It was regularly around 0° Celsius outside and I tried to leave a little bit later in the mornings, waiting for the chilly air to warm up with the first rays of the sun. The Browne family, who looked after me while I was in Dakota, had a 13-year-old son, Matt. He was quite a big boy and asked me during dinner.

"Do you ever get hungry during your journey?"

I nodded that I did and he said, "I could never do what you're doing, I might just lose weight!"

Later that evening he stood in the doorway of my room while I organised my bags.

"I really respect what you're doing," he said with the maturity of somebody much older. "People talk about 'real life heroes', well to me you're one of them."

I was so moved by his words that I did not know what to say.

The morning of my departure, Matt asked if I could lead him around on Toto. He had never been on a horse before and this was a big deal for him. He struggled to get on to a wall not higher than half a metre, and breathing heavily he followed my instruction to put one foot into a stirrup. Perspiration was forming on his forehead as everybody looked on. His hands were shaking. Toto moved slightly and Matt lost his nerve momentarily. Friends and family continued to urge him on and finally he had one leg over and was sitting astride Toto. We all cheered and clapped. I would never forget the look of joy and pride on Matt's young face.

A few days before the 25th of December 2003, Dave sent me a message;

Just want to wish you a happy xmas. I know it is a more difficult time for you being away from family and friends. Having said that, it is important to keep the bigger picture in mind. You are now literally counting down the days until you reach your wonderful goal. You know a lot of people will be thinking about you – only geographical distance separates, not distances in the mind. Mar, enjoy xmas the best you can and realise what the new year holds for you and your horsies. Every reward it brings will be richly deserved.

I also particularly remember a young man called Justin, who was that what-you-see-is-what-you-get-type, sporting a short back and sides army-style haircut. Danny, his friend, had seen me earlier on the road and went to collect Justin to give him a bit of Dutch courage before approaching me. It was a cold day and later Justin caught up with me again, handing me a cup of hot instant soup and a few snacks. He organised for me to stay at the house of a Mennonite family that night. But his generosity did not end there. That same evening he picked me up to join in the Christmas spirit with his family and on the way back he handed me eighty dollars. I objected strongly but he would not hear about it.

"I feel in my heart that I want to give and I know that God is looking after me," he said. "I'll be rewarded not necessarily with money but in this case by being given a new friend."

My stay with Sim and Sara Yoder, head of the Mennonite family and their fourteen children, three of them adopted, was quite interesting. The girls wore long dresses and crisp white bonnets that covered their heads. The house was like an ants' nest of activity when I arrived on Christmas Eve. Everybody helped to get the house ready before they left the following morning to spend Christmas day with family. The kids were quiet and respectful but not in a spiritless way. They answered brightly when spoken to and as they warmed to the stranger in their midst, they began to ask more questions.

We all had a good laugh when the father told me how his youngest boy of seven asked that morning before my arrival, "Daddy, is this girl who is visiting with her horses going to have a baby?"

He must have heard the story of Mary, Joseph and the donkey probably one time too many and given the timing of my arrival, one could not blame him for his innocence.

Danny and his wife, Tish, caught up with me as I was riding along the following day. They tried to persuade me to go home with them.

"No person should be alone like this on Christmas day," Tish urged.

I was in two minds but they were very persuasive and I relented finally. I immediately felt at ease in their modest, yet cosy mobile home. With their 15-year-old daughter, they were a lovely almost quirky family (they also adored animals), and Tish and I got on very well.

"She doesn't like a lot of women," Danny whispered in my ear, "so you must be doing something right."

I found Tish an interesting woman and more true to herself than anybody else I knew. She was comfortable with who she was and made no fuss about the fact that her hair, which once extended down to her backside, was now short after she was diagnosed with breast cancer. Tish was a survivor and she took the health setbacks in her stride. She was adamant that nothing was going to stop her living life to the full.

Another thing that intrigued me was how Danny and Tish would discuss me and my journey among themselves while I sat with them, hearing every word.

They would look at each other with concerned faces and one would say, "She'll freeze as she goes up north, she's going to ride straight into blizzards," and in that tone they would continue to visualise all the potential hardships on my way.

One time I could not keep quiet any longer and said, half-jokingly, half-annoyed, "No wonder you tell me that you're Murphy's Law with all the bad things happening to you! You are just so pessimistic about everything."

They laughed and continued their discussion.

It was a freezing cold day as Camanchi, Toto and I made our way to Wrensville. Soon my face and toes felt numb. A man stopped to chat but I had difficulty speaking as my jaw was frozen stiff. I must have looked comical as I tried to tell him my name moving the lower part of my face left to right to left in the hope of getting some circulation going.

Tommy Lee was a thoroughbred breeder and wanted to know everything about my travels. Not only did he help put up the horses that night but for the following week he was actively involved with my travels, organising places to stay, making phone-calls and driving out to where we were on the road checking if everything was alright. On another very cold day he brought along a new windbreaker and gloves, courtesy of a shop in his hometown. He also handed me a flask.

"Put hot tea in it every morning, or better, good whiskey," he recommended with a smile.

The first day I met him, he showed me the baby wild pigs he kept in a pen on his farm.

"I give them a good life," he said, "and then I butcher them. It's better than being shot in the wild by farmers."

I nodded without commenting.

Tommy's wife, Barbara, looked typically Irish with her ginger hair and fair complexion. She had a caring demeanour and invited me to a social gathering at their fox-hunting club. I did not have the heart to tell them that I am opposed to this blood sport – it was one of those times I just knew it was better to keep quiet.

Barbara was as thrilled as her husband to be of assistance and quickly organised a small fundraiser among the other fox-hunters. She asked if I would say a few words and self-consciously I stood up and shared a couple of experiences with the captive audience. I also told them about my desire to create awareness for therapeutic riding in Ireland. The evening ended on a high with about 300 dollars in generous contributions, many good wishes and yet another warm jacket for the cold.

Barbara told me how fox-hunting in Ireland is really wild and risky. She laughed.

"A man came over from there and teased us about our little jumps. On his first outing with us he fell off his horse!"

She told me how the following day his horse ran away with him. She explained that because the surfaces in the States are harder, the horses go faster.

On our day's ride from Modock to McCormick we passed long stretches of woods on the left and I noticed a baby deer standing all alone, quite close to the road. I stopped and took a picture, went closer and still he did not move. I got off Toto and approached the little animal. To my amazement I managed to touch him. He gave a small jump and I touched him again. I reached for my pocket to hand him a carrot but my luck ran out as he hopped away between the trees without as much as a backward glance.

I noticed a strange habit in Toto. He nibbled gently on Camanchi's neck, and with a smacking of his lips, pretended he wanted to lick him and then suddenly he would strike and bite. I did not know what was up with him. Tommy, who has a lot of experience with horses, reckoned that Toto was jealous whenever I gave Camanchi attention and that he wanted me for himself.

My relationship with my horses was different from what it would have been in ordinary circumstances. I was not their master. In their minds, and probably mine too, we were quite equal and more like companions. I needed them and even though I was strict with them, I ended up giving more loving pats than raps. As we travelled through the States, some horse 'experts' warned me that I needed to keep my distance from them.

"They need to respect your personal space," was how they put it.

It was difficult to explain my relationship with them and our mutual dependency. You had to be in my shoes to know that how we travelled, only having one another, gave a different dynamic to our bond. It was unique and it was special.

Just before the town of McCormick, the road split in two and I was unsure what the shortest way was. I tried to flag down the passing cars but nobody stopped. Frustrated, I went on the tarmac after a while, hoping it would force somebody to a standstill. A black man coming from the opposite direction stopped and rolled down his window.

In an exasperated voice I said, "What does one have to do to make somebody stop?"

He was friendly and chuckled.

"No offence madam, but you look like a huge black man from behind with that chunky woolly hat on you and the dark jacket. I guess that is why nobody wanted to stop!"

After he had indicated the better way to go, I thanked him for stopping.

"Have a wonderful Sunday," were his parting words.

At a self-service kiosk outside town, I said to the woman behind the counter that I smelled 'all horse' and she kindly offered to prepare a sandwich for me. A black girl behind the till giggled when she looked at my riding gear. Further down the road I passed a number of houses and in front of one stood a black family. The man indicated for me to stop and called his children over. I gave them each a chance to go on Camanchi and there was no hiding the looks of delight on their faces.

"Now say thank you to this sweet lady and remember to tell your mama that you've been on a horse this afternoon," the man said.

Without my giving any indication of where I was heading, he mentioned the name of the people that were waiting for me that evening. Maybe he guessed or maybe word was just spreading fast in these small towns.

On the way to Saluda I had to flag down yet another car to ask for directions. Interestingly, again it was a black person that stopped, this time a woman. She asked me for my phone number and rang later to check if everything was going okay. She also invited me to her house should I be in need of a place to stay. I revelled in all the goodwill. The feeling I had that American people would be kind, hospitable and open turned out to be true.

From the time I met Tommy in the northern part of Georgia, we had a place to stay every night in every state we went through. My stay-overs were organised in advance by people who had phoned friends and acquaintances. A few times my hosts would live a few miles off our intended route and without hesitation we would be picked up and brought back the next day to continue our travels towards New York City. To have had secure accommodation arranged in advance was a great relief, especially as it meant the horses were well-fed and in a stable most nights.

On another level though I missed the adventure of Latin America, the not-knowing and anticipation of what could be around the corner. The fact that I now had a phone also restricted my freedom. In a few places, concerned hosts would ring me constantly to check up on my progress and to see when exactly I would arrive. Some of them even appeared out of the blue with trailers. Their intentions were well meant but I had to explain that I actually wanted to ride that last six or eight kilometres to their homes. Most of them understood. A few times though a trailer came in very handy, especially when the traffic was just too heavy or if I was going to be on the road in the dark.

I constantly had to be on guard with the horses when going alongside the main roads. Toto was not the most placid, although his big dewy eyes could easily mislead.

He was strong-willed and dominant and wanted his way most of the time. He was also a bit uptight and did not like surprises. Not far from Saluda we went past a deserted house, and just as we were opposite it, a door creaked loudly. Toto gave a mighty jump, straight on to the road. My heart missed a beat – we were lucky there was no traffic.

Saluda has in recent years become known as 'little Mexico' due to the large number of Mexicans working and living in the town. Some people I met there were disgruntled about their presence.

"They can work here for five years without paying taxes and they don't even make an effort to learn English," they moaned.

That evening at my hosts' house I had little time for myself. Family and friends drifted in and out and everybody had questions. There was one man however whose story I was more interested in than telling my own. His name was Joe and he looked the true cowboy with his handlebar moustache and bushy beard. He told me how for three years he lived on trains (he called it train-hopping), at other times finding shelter with the Salvation Army.

When dinner was served I tried to hide my surprise when the moment we started to eat, three men around the table lit up cigarettes. My appetite was gone. I coughed through the night and entering the living room the following morning, walked into a cloud of grey smoke hanging from the ceiling. My host sat smoking at the table.

As I was saddling up, the dog spotted a chicken salad sandwich which was to be my lunch for the day and which I yet had to put into a saddle bag. He was polite enough to leave me the tomato and pickle. Leaving the town of Saluda we had to cross a narrow bridge. There was a pickup truck and another truck behind us but neither would wait until we reached the other side. A car approached from the opposite direction and we got sandwiched when we got to the middle of the bridge. The horses nervously jumped and twisted around. I cursed out loud and shook my head angrily at the two ignorant drivers.

At my next stop, while staying with the hospitable Irma who put her horses out so that mine could be stabled, I received a phone-call from a woman who was interested in buying Pepsi. Jerry, the horse dealer told her to ring me. She enquired about what kind of horse he was, his disposition and faults. I tried to be as honest as possible.

"He's a sweet horse with potential but he is young and needs time and good training before he would be safe for riding."

I felt proud of myself, speaking with authority about the suitability of a horse. As it turned out, the woman decided not to travel the four hours to look at Pepsi where he was still residing with Todd and Maria. A few weeks later a plan was organised to get Pepsi back to Jerry in Kentucky.

The day's ride to Newberry was an exciting one. A film crew was commissioned by ABC television to get footage of me and the horses, to be broadcast later in the weekly 'person of the week' programme presented by Peter Jennings. I was still not entirely comfortable with being in the spotlight although I knew that publicity on that scale would serve my cause well. I knew it would also make people more inclined to help.

The day, a pleasant diversion from the usual routine, turned out to be most enjoyable while Kip and his crew, friendly, undemanding and jovial, seemed to enjoy themselves too. The hours passed without us noticing and the last bit of footage was shot under a fading light while I (reluctantly) played a few notes of "*Nancy Spain*" on my Irish tin whistle.

The following morning my hosts in Newberry offered to take us a few kilometres up the road to make the route shorter but I declined. It was 32 kilometres to Salem Corner and leaving at 10 a.m. I knew we would still arrive in daylight. On the way, quite a few men attempted to make conversation but I kept the communications short. Before a crossroads I saw three Shetland ponies and a donkey in a field running towards us and making a lot of noise. Toto jumped so vigorously that he slipped and fell on his side. I do not think they had ever seen a horse as small as the Shetland pony and must have thought it was some kind of wild creature.

I enjoyed very much meeting a couple of fellow adventurers when I stayed with the Colemans for one night in South Carolina. Christians, they were Harley Davidson enthusiasts and regularly took trips across the States, covering thousands of miles with each journey. Soon after my arrival at their house I was kitted out in a thick leather suit, jacket and gloves, and as the sun was setting David took me for an exhilarating spin through curvy country roads.

The following evening at their friends' house we watched the ABC program over tasty seafood take-away.

The interviewer asked whether I was afraid and I replied, "If you're going to be afraid when travelling, you should stay at home."

My remark was met by enthusiastic 'Amens' by all the Harley riders.

A funeral procession was in full swing as we entered Great Falls.

We walked past three black girls and one of them asked, "Are you the one that was on TV?"

I said yes and she replied, "Thought so. Whadya do when it rains?"

While I waited for Dalford Wilson my host that night to pick us up, a woman and her two daughters came over for a chat. They handed me a sandwich and a drink. I was extremely grateful. Another man stopped, indicated that he knew Tommy Lee and asked if I needed help. Dalford was the type that could be affectionately described as a rough diamond but he had a heart of gold.

"You can stay with me for as long as you want," he offered sincerely.

I spent an enjoyable although hectic two days at his house and we were bombarded by curious neighbours, friends and journalists who dropped in at all hours of the day. My only complaint was his oversized mule that drove me up the wall. Apparently a cross with a Morgan horse, he was a bully and immune to discipline. He even managed to break open the door to Camanchi's stable, forced him outside and then stole all his food. My arm-swinging and roars to frighten him off had no effect at all. In fact, he frightened the life out of *me*.

It was only months later that I got to see the newspaper articles that appeared during the three months we went through the States. They were all sent by my hosts to Marilyn in Georgia who at the end of my journey sent them on to Ireland. I was tickled to go through them, not least because of the discrepancies and wrong information.

One journalist claimed completely inaccurately that I had already raised 800,000 dollars for the planned riding centre and that this amount would be matched by sponsors back home. She was also the one that 'quoted' me as saying that a 'movie' would be in the pipeline. I cringed when I read that, it could not have been further from the truth.

I told a journalist how I sometimes got the opportunity to send on my pack with somebody who would drop it off at our next destination, giving the horses respite. Instead, the article reported how I sent a *horse* ahead in a trailer many days. I read in another piece that I had sold my two horses in Guatemala before flying to the States and that Mise would be flown from Ireland to join me for the last stretch. All these reportings were wrong but fortunately they were not malicious and did not cause any harm. It was however the line that said I was fluent in six languages that really had me in stitches. I guess it looked good on paper.

A woman watched with beady eyes and a sour look on her face while I saddled up the horses in Lancaster.

"Are you afraid?" she asked.

"What of?" I said as I tightened the girth.

"Well, you might be in the woods and the horses might spook or you might get attacked or raped or murdered."

I did not answer and went to collect Toto from his stable. I took out a grooming brush from a plastic bag.

"A bag like that broke my husband's arm," the woman continued. "The horse spooked... two weeks later he broke another arm!"

I felt like bursting out in hysterical laughter.

Ten minutes later I was on the road and heard a honk behind.

"You're on the wrong side of the road," the same woman roared. "You'll get killed!"

I was beginning to lose my patience with her. I shouted back.

93. Camanchi and Toto happy for a stop in the woods.
94. With Pepsi on the leading rope, a camera man with a local US tv station tempts fate.
95. Definitely a faster way of getting there.

96. Fred and Nancy Rojo and Tom Simmons (right) the horse trainer near Roxboro.
97. Snow in North Carolina.
98. Todd and Maria collect Camanchi.

99. Two young boys eager to have their picture taken.
100. The Holland Family.
101. Yoga on horseback.
102. Endless stories to be told.

103. Keeping in touch.
104. A girl with special needs rides an imaginary horse.
105. Peter and Barbara Pegg at Gypsy Stables, Middleburg.

106. Joy hooks up with me in Maryland.
107. Giving the horses a break and my legs a stretch.
108. Finally getting the hang of it.

109. Kathleen Crompton and family.
110. Keeping on the right side of the road.
111. Carlos and Madilyn Du Toit — my organiser in New York City.
112. My mom surprises me in Central Park.

113. The welcoming committee.
114. Turlough, my mom, Sean and Deirdre.

115. Thanks to my American companions.
116. Through a snowy Central Park on the way to the parade.
117. The Saint Patrick's Day Parade in full swing.

"I'm fine! I've been going on this side for eighteen months and it's worked so far!"

A man who introduced himself as Cecil stopped me on the road to chat.

"I'm single," he said, "and I have the day off. Can I get on one of your horses and ride with you?"

I already knew what my answer would be but pretended to think about it.

"Hmm, I don't think it's a good idea," I said after a while. "I don't have a spare set of reins and anyway, I walk a lot with the horses."

About 30 kilometres before Monroe, I was met by a very gentle man called Boyce. His mobile home was simple but clean and tastefully decorated. A hearty dinner that he had prepared himself awaited me. I heard that he took the day off work to organise and get ready for my stay. I was also taken by his son Mark and daughter-in-law Geena. They asked a lot of questions but I did not mind, they did it in such a lovely way.

The mobile home was soon filled with lots of people wanting to hear my stories. One woman even video-recorded my answers to the questions and I had to make a real effort to keep a straight face. But soon I felt mentally exhausted, and by 9 p.m. I found it impossible to answer another question. Boyce had given up his bed and I gasped when after my shower I crawled in-between the sheets to find the warm blanket turned on. It was pure luxury. I drifted off feeling cosy and comfortable, my eyes fixed on the colourful fish in the tank next to the bed. It was almost a hypnotic sensation and the following day's ride felt a lifetime away.

It was time to make arrangements for Mise's departure from Guatemala to Florida where she would stay for seven days in quarantine. I was worried about broker costs and thus far had not been able to secure sponsorship for that. The quote I received for the quarantine costs also gave me a few sleepless nights. Both expenses would run into thousands of dollars. I found the contact details of Lazcar International on the web and spoke to its president, Celia Alessandrini, to see if she was willing to help get Mise into the US without charging the full broker's fees. What happened next was truly a miracle. After a ten-minute conversation with Celia, she agreed to assist me free of charge and her next line almost blew me away.

"I'll pay for the quarantine as well," she said in her warm Spanish accent.

I was overwhelmed and did not know what to say. I knew one thing – this was a remarkable woman with an extraordinary giving spirit. It still amazes me every time I think about it.

The ride from Lancaster was awkward. Toto tripped over constantly, it was cold and the route was confusing. On advice we took backroads which were maybe a bit too isolated. There were a lot of open fields and then suddenly woodlands. Only one car passed over a four-hour period. The driver was dressed in camouflage gear and I had no doubt he had a gun. I was not afraid but definitely on the alert and monitored his movements intensely. I became somewhat anxious when I saw his brake lights come on but it was only momentarily and thankfully he continued. I imagined he was only looking for a good spot to shoot deer.

The traffic before Monroe was thick. I stopped at a cemetery and picked out the horses' feet. Mark came along and told me he had organised with the police to get me across Highway 74. They were delighted to help and I did not have the heart to say that I would be okay, that I had gone through worse than that.

I could not complain of being hungry too often while riding through the States. I got fed breakfast every morning but not always on a diet that would win awards for its nutritional value. Sometimes when the woman of the house was not in the mood for cooking, something like an egg-and-bacon 'biscuit' was purchased at a fast-food outlet. I met a few families who on most days had all three of their meals from there. All that mattered to them was that it filled them up. I could not help but wonder from where their children would get the necessary brain-power on a diet like that. Interestingly, the question most frequently asked of me by children in the USA, was if I had taken the horses to the "drive-thru" at McDonalds!

Travelling through the United States was so different from Latin America. The emphasis had shifted noticeably. Now, my experiences revolved much more on the people I met, the interactions, the responses and the assistance I received. When going through South and Central America the focus was mostly on the places, nature, the newness, the cultural differences, surviving.

Here in America there was more of a uniformity of experiences. I smelled the roses less, I was not as conscious of my environment, nor the impact it had on me. I was almost on automatic pilot. The people urged me on to my destination. Everybody so badly wanted me to get there. The lingering was over. The end was in sight.

The weather turned frosty towards the end of January and I heard warnings of prolonged snow. I was lucky to end up at the house of the effervescent Annette, who had the most infectious laugh, ever. She had built herself a luxurious home overlooking large grounds, paddocks and stables. My stay with her was a highlight. We liked each other instantly and over glasses of red wine, we shared in many chats and laughter, while outside it turned whiter and whiter. We discussed her life, my life, our dreams and matters of the world. I stayed for five days and felt so sad when the snow began to melt and the time came to say goodbye.

Toto continued to trip over and a farrier suggested that his shoes be taken off. So Toto became the proud owner of brand-new 'clip-on' plastic shoes. They sounded great in theory but after just a short while on the road I found out how impractical they were. One shoe kept falling off and going through mud was a real problem.

Reaching Highway 49 we were confronted by a line of cars coming from both directions. The road was busy, actually too busy, and no place for riding. We reached a spot where I had to go briefly on the tarmac but a truck behind me could not wait and literally pushed us off the road as it rushed past.

"Sonofabitch!" I shouted loudly.

The surface on the side of the road was still icy so I walked with the horses. Toto spooked when a car with a peculiar engine-noise passed but nothing serious happened. Half an hour later Toto spooked yet again and started to run, kicking and bucking. Camanchi, who was on the leading rope, pulled in the opposite direction and to my horror, my saddle was torn in two pieces right in front of my eyes. The heavy traffic came to a standstill as everybody observed the spectacle. Toto ran a bit further down the road, crossed to the other side and snorted. A man got out of his car to help. My belongings were scattered all over the road and in the snow.

"Thank God for good friends," I whispered to myself when Annette came to my rescue a few minutes after I rung her. She transported us to a cottage near Asheboro that Missy, an acquaintance of hers, kindly offered. There were also stables with a paddock in front, which the horses shared with Dolly, their pet sheep. Missy was concerned that Dolly might suffer a heart attack from being too close to the horses but the cute tamed sheep seemed to cope fine with the new company. My saddle was beyond repair and the following day Annette brought me a cowboy saddle to use until I managed to find a lighter one.

Arriving near Snowcamp I had nowhere lined up for the night. Passing a few houses I heard someone calling, and my eye caught an overweight black boy of about nine, waving from the front garden. He obviously had a mental disability. He came over and excitedly patted the horses, a big grin on his face as saliva dripped down his chin. His mother told me he frequented a therapeutic riding centre in Greensboro.

"That explains his ease around the horses," I said.

She beamed proudly.

Down the road was another house surrounded by fields. The owner, whose son savaged my packet of nuts, wondered whether the horses might injure his cows. As it turned out, it was poor old Camanchi that was harassed. About ten cows formed a circle around him, then followed him and sniffed his backside. True to his nature, this did not faze Camanchi one bit and he could not have cared less about the unwanted attention.

I slept in the cottage in Asheboro that night again and during a lovely dinner at Missy's house, I met a woman who worked for the *Washington Post*.

"Have you got an agent?" she asked.

I told her that I travelled alone, no agent, no publicist and no backup team. She studied me for a moment, her head tilted.

"Hmm, I wonder if we did an article on you if it should be in the *style* or *travel* section," she said in all sincerity.

The two glasses of wine had already gone to my head and full of giggles I answered that it was a dilemma indeed.

I was leading the horses as we were coming to the suburbs of the small town of Roxboro. Without warning Toto got a fright and began to run. I tried to hold on to the leading rope, pulling him back and shouting, but he was too strong and took off. Camanchi was attached to the saddle and as the rope did not break, he was forced to run alongside the frantic Toto. My belongings were scattered bit by bit and I scooped up my stuff as I ran behind them. Nobody stopped to help. I found the horses in a field behind houses quite a distance up the road. They were breathing heavily and Camanchi had a gash above his eye. Disheartened I sat myself down on the ground, looking at the torn ropes, bags and a trail of destruction around me.

Tommy Lee had given me a directory of other Saddlebred breeders in the US. I randomly selected a number of somebody near Roxboro, left a message on their answering machine, picked up my things and knocked at a house on the other side of the road. The man who answered the door had to go out but agreed for the horses to be tied to a tree and for me to wait there until my 'contacts' had been in touch. The garden still had patches of snow on the lawn and while I waited I made figures and wrote with my shoe in the ice. It was cold.

Nancy and her neighbour, a black man called Tom, arrived. They were intrigued by my urgent message asking for assistance.

"We just had to come out and see what this was about," they said.

Both had a calm demeanour, and Nancy's husband Fred, had the same kind of aristocratic, regal air about him. I felt very lucky to have such good people helping me. They spoiled me no end. We had only just met and yet it felt like I had known them for years.

Tom was an expert with equines and strongly believed that they should be outside in their natural habitat as much as possible and allowed to be horses. He was well-known in the area, as well as in California, for his direct and intuitive approach with these animals.

"Toto wants to be the leader," he said, "and as long as you allow him to be that, you'll have these problems and outbursts."

He told me that Toto did not get enough leadership from me and that I hadn't yet established my authority over him. I told him how I was more a friend to the horses than a disciplinarian but that I recognised the importance of being in control.

He also reckoned that while we rested at Annette's for the five days, the daily *alfalfa* and sweet feed combination could have made him particularly hyper.

He took Toto in a ring for a bit of training and to get him to become more submissive without hurting him. Afterwards Toto was like putty in my hands. I took him on the leading rope and walked with him. When I stopped, he stopped, when I retreated, he did the same. You could see that he was now respecting me as the boss. I had a feeling Toto would always have his dominant personality, and I would not have wanted to break his spirit, but at least it was clearer to him now as to who was in charge.

Tom said that Toto needed to feel safe with me and that he needed a lot of reassurance when something frightened him. I tried to apply all the tips and advice and the improvement was noticeable immediately.

I was given the name of the owners of Rollinghills farm near Clarkesville as a potential place to stay. I left them messages but no one came back to me. I arrived at their house, a perfect set-up with stables and outside paddocks, and waited. A neighbour came over and asked what I was doing there. He said he would ring the people on their mobile from his house. He returned shortly after and informed me in a dismissive way that they could not accommodate me. It was late in the day and I had nowhere else to go so I asked him again if he was sure about this. He looked annoyed and irritable.

"I told you lady, they said *no!*" he said angrily.

Three phone-calls later I managed to secure another place. But I was not convinced if the woman of the house wanted me there. She did greet me but despite my hints that I was starving, it did not cross her mind to offer me a second helping of spaghetti bolognese. I was given the couch in a little wooden Wendy house next to the main residence. It was good to have the privacy.

There was a stove inside and the man said to me, "It will be warm in here as long as you feed it wood."

I nodded my head but felt like asking what would happen when I was asleep.

I knew the answer when I woke the following morning with chattering teeth. The stove was long dead and it was freezing cold inside. I hopped over to the house for a hot shower, passed a tiny puppy tied by a chain and exposed to the elements. An elderly dog walking with an arthritic limp also had no shelter. The house smelled deliciously of breakfast and I greeted the family sitting cosily around the kitchen table. When I came out of the bathroom nothing was offered to me. Later when everybody was outside I grabbed a cup of coffee and dry bread. The man noticed and offered me butter.

On the way to Chase city in the state of Virginia, we encountered heavy traffic and little space on the side of the road. The yellow school buses were particularly menacing. After a few hours, heavy fog appeared and I found the mist literally hanging over us, making visibility almost non-existent. It was quite surreal. The rain came and I found shelter under an outbuilding on a farm. A hillbilly with crooked teeth appeared. He told me about a couple who took a horse and wagon from there to South America.

"They were first hit by a hurricane and then got killed by an automobile," he swore as the truth.

I said a silent prayer for their souls, just in case the story was true.

My fingers and toes were numb from the cold for most of the day. We went on quiet roads where houses were neglected and gardens served as rubbish dumps. More often than not there was not a soul in sight. The few I did spot seemed as if all they lived for was their next welfare cheque. A man standing on his dilapidated porch fondled his private parts as we passed. I pretended not to notice.

A farrier and his young wife had agreed to host me for the night. Megan, who was no older than seventeen, met me on the road in high spirits.

As she fed me in their warm kitchen she remarked, "My husband said that you can sleep in the tack room but I said no, there were rats and mice there. He said it did not matter, you are probably used to much worse than that."

I managed a smile. Megan then informed me that I would be sleeping in their trailer instead, but her husband's parents intervened and offered their luxury mobile home.

I ended up staying for two nights and Megan and I visited one of the places where her husband regularly did farrier work. What I saw there was just horrendous. At least twelve Tennessee Walking Horses stood on six-inch blocks attached to the bottom of all four feet, some with heavy chains around them. I was told that they are never allowed out and because of the height of the blocks, most of them could not lie down.

"It's too difficult for them to get up again," Megan said.

I asked her why there were white cloths wrapped around the horses' legs. She told me in a matter of fact way how the legs of the horses were burned with a mixture of kerosene and mustard, a practice known as 'soring'. In short, it is hurting the horse in order to alter his gait.

"The bandages are there to cover the blisters," she said.

I was shocked.

"Stop showing your disapproval so openly," she reprimanded as I shook my head in disgust.

I was repulsed by what I saw. The horses looked more depressed than any I had ever seen, anywhere. I noticed one in particular – his eyes were lifeless, his head hung low.

According to the USDA, the application of any chemical or mechanical agent to the lower leg or hoof of any horse that causes pain, or, can be expected to cause pain, for the purpose of 'enhancing' the horse's gait for show purposes, is strictly prohibited under The Horse Protection Act.

Rhonda Hart Poe, the editor of *The Gaited Horse*, was quoted as saying;

> The vast majority of gaited horses are trained, shown and owned by people who would never stoop to soring. But when they compete, they never know when they might be up against those who don't mind taking the low road when it comes to getting a competitive edge. Soring is cheating. But it is also inhumane and illegal.

A week or so after I had seen the practice of 'soring', I rang the local police and asked to speak to somebody in the animal welfare department. The woman was most uncooperative and demanded to know my name. I explained that I would like to keep my complaint of animal abuse anonymous as I feared there might be retaliation if those people knew I was responsible. She was unsympathetic to what I told her and I knew no action would be taken.

Because of my appearance on ABC television, I received numerous invitations via my website. People left enthusiastic messages indicating their eagerness for me to stay with them. It was difficult to choose who to stay with and sometimes it was a toss of a coin to come to a decision. Often, I simply did not even find the time to let people know I would not be accepting their offers of help. It continued to be a challenge, riding everyday, staying safe, being nice to people, answering questions, writing my diaries, resting and still getting in touch with everybody who contacted me. It was impossible at times to keep all the ends together by myself.

The media interest continued and a few times the cameras would already be waiting as we trotted into a farm, neighbours and friends waving and wanting to be part of the action. I learned to take all the attention in my stride even though it was exhausting at the best of times.

I had an unusual moment in a small town in Virginia when a contact said I could not stay. Although they had agreed to accommodate me, they indicated they were consumed with family issues and that it actually did not suit them to have a guest. Having already unsaddled (they were not home when I arrived), I asked where I would go at that time of the afternoon with dusk looming.

They gradually warmed towards me however and after some soul-searching agreed to give me a bed. A pleasant dinner with easy-flowing conversation was followed by an obligatory taste of their melon and strawberry alcoholic beverages, which Mackey, the man of the house, claimed was much superior to wine. He said his sister offered him bottles of wine to give him more culture.

He initially thought I was a spoilt girl whose rich daddy was funding the trip and asked if I was from 'old money'.

When I put him right he observed, "I'm impressed that you're able to do a journey like this."

The following day, the police approached me on the far side of Victoria.

"We've had a complaint that you are holding up the traffic," they said.

I told them it was not true. Only about seven cars had passed me so far and they could see that there was no traffic behind me.

Later in the day I had to cross a very busy road that was partially under construction and Mackey, who was also bringing on my bags, was there to help. He blocked the traffic and I was surprised not to have heard a single honk. We navigated our way through town and on the other side had to go over by-passes and highways. Some motorists were more patient than others at the delay.

In Burkeville I met a woman farrier for the first time. Kelly was obviously worth her salt as I watched her change my horses' shoes expertly and without fuss. She and her husband Rick were fierce animal lovers and many dogs and cats who had been rescued occupied the house. Kelly told me how some people who are involved in fox-hunting in that area leave the dogs on the side of the roads or in woods at the end of the season.

"That way they don't have to look after the animals and feed them when it is not hunting season," she said.

She showed me two dogs that they had adopted.

"They used to hunt but were abandoned," she said.

The Wigwam Inn, a spectacular historical farm with 250-year-old oaks lining the driveway, was my home for two days. Originally belonging to the Virginia Governor William Branch Giles, it was owned by Walter Cart Jr. since early 1990 when he began a four-year restoration project, designed to return The Wigwam to its original grandeur in a historically accurate manner. With its seven fireplaces, this was no ordinary home. The stables were as luxurious as my own room.

I did not quite know what to say when Walter showed me the variety of horse feed and asked, "Which one would your horses prefer?"

I laughed and indicated that my horses would not be exactly fussy.

An overnight in Virginia with a 'know-all' yet very hospitable horsewoman (her husband was an excellent cook), was quite amusing. From the moment I arrived, she scrutinised my every movement and was not shy to dish out comments and criticism.

"How long exactly have you been involved with horses?" she asked with a dubious look on her face.

She told me I picked up the horses' feet incorrectly, that the side-ropes were tied up in the wrong place, that my horses were not fat enough and that I should put baby oil on their manes to make them shinier. The cherry on the cake was when Toto refused to open his mouth when I tried to put the bit in. He had never done that before and ditto for all my other horses and not having had much experience in that field, I struggled.

The woman noticed, stepped forward and to my embarrassment said loudly in front of three kids standing around, "Let me show you how to do this," like you would to a child using a knife and fork for the first time.

I could already hear the children rushing back home excitedly.

"Mummy, mummy, we saw this girl that says she's been riding for twenty months but she can't even put on a bridle and reins!"

I had to laugh to myself at the absurdity of the situation and listened attentively to the 'how-to-do-it-properly' lecture.

Melissa, an energetic larger-than-life personality, was my host near Cuckoo. She and her family received me warmly and no request was too much.

I continued to walk regularly with the horses and in the US it was mostly to get warm in the sub-zero temperatures. Often a car would stop and somebody would enquire if I was alright. It seemed the general consensus was that something was wrong if you were not riding your horse.

In Rhodesville, a woman my age, called Kim, cared for my horses.

"It's great that you're here," she said. "We don't have many fun things happening."

She loved Toto and said he was very clean.

"Look at him. He only poops in the corner of his stable."

She reckoned Camanchi looked like a grumpy old man but thought he was lovely in spite of that.

Kim introduced me to her friend Patrece, a charming woman. Driving her big Cadillac, she looked me up the following day as we made our way towards Culpeper, the Blue Ridge Mountains hovering far away in the distance. I was terribly hungry and she arrived like an angel sent from heaven, with a bag full of snacks. She also gave me more warm clothes.

Once we were on the road again, a man from Pet Control stopped to talk. He told me he had received a report of an 'older woman' with two horses on the side of the road.

"Well, that can only be me, sir," I said.

I tried to sound joyful but suddenly was conscious of how weather-beaten I must have looked. He said he would escort me until the Sheriff's department arrived.

His presence was invaluable and cars from both directions suddenly drove much more slowly.

When a policeman arrived, he said, "We'll have to get you off this road. It's far too busy."

I answered that unfortunately I would have to be back on it again, the following day.

Patrece caught up with me later again and escorted me in her car, directing the traffic. When I stopped for a rest she told me how she thought my horses had great confidence and trust in me.

"I could see it in the way that they walked so closely with you," she said.

It was good to hear.

The town of Warrenton, about 35 miles from Washington DC, is not so large as to be faceless but big enough to retain a sophisticated small-town charm to support a delightful coffee house, a book store and summer music in the streets. The quaintness, tradition and charm of bygone eras are also apparent along Old Town Warrenton streets lined with historic houses with brick sidewalks and painted in beautiful pastel shades. I found it was a place where people still smiled at strangers. My stay was short but sweet. I spent a comfortable night with Glenn and Amy, a delightful couple who made me feel so much at home. They did not feel like strangers at all and I was convinced we knew each from another life. The evening was spent in Molly's Irish pub with friends of theirs, everybody showing tremendous humour and goodwill.

Day 613. Still in great form from my stay in Warrenton, we were now trotting through real horse country on our way to Middleburg, the heart of the equine world in Virginia, set among rolling hills and twisting country roads. It is an affluent area dotted with the most beautifully manicured plots, farms with well-designed stables and barns, and expansive paddocks where high-pedigree horses roam. And then there were the enormous gates leading the eye along a broad and tidy pathway to the inevitable sizable mansion.

Four weeks before journey's end, some unexpected criticism came from an individual who deliberately tried to make things difficult for me. Of course it was upsetting at the time, but curiously this setback also opened so many doors and hearts that I am almost grateful for the fuss that was caused. It is strange how one person's animosity can affect your spirits when you are thousands of miles from home but conversely it also highlighted the warmth and support from loved ones, even from strangers. With the encouragement of those who knew the truth, I could continue my journey with my head held high. I just accepted that sadly this person did not make an effort to understand the scope and passion of my journey.

Glenn, with whom I stayed in Warrington, and who is also Executive Director of the Virginia Thoroughbred Association, was one of those friends who helped and stood by me. He also took the time to write a long letter to this individual, explaining the tax situation in the USA and emphasising that a private conversation with me would have provided the best opportunity to resolve matters and establish the facts. I quote the last part of his 2-page letter;

Simply put, I believe your interpretation of the US tax code as it relates to Du Toit's representations is incorrect, and your perception that wealthy donors have been solicited and duped unfounded. The fact that these errors have been shared with the media (which in many cases also lacks expertise in tax code matters) is equally troubling and unfairly detrimental to Du Toit's extraordinary efforts.

This personal disappointment however also had an upside – I ended up getting to know Peter and Barbara in Middleburg, who took me under their wing. They showed me true friendship and showered me with warmth and kindness during my week's stay with them. We also had a common bond; Africa. Barb was born in Kenya and Peter first worked as scientific officer and warden in Uganda and later as safari guide. Peter had read *Tschiffely's Ride* and was absolutely fascinated by it. He kept on saying how much he was looking forward to reading about my own experiences one day.

The horses could not have been better cared for by Patsy at her establishment on the outskirts of town, known as Gypsy stables. There was no need to check up on them and she treated them as if they were her own. I got the distinct impression that Patsy rather liked having my horses there and I noticed how she spoilt them with little treats.

In Poolesville, Maryland, I was 'mobbed' by a group of women as I rode into town. Questions were thrown at me from all directions and I was forced to end a phone conversation to a friend in Ireland when he ceased to hear me over the shrieks, shouts and laughter.

It was also here that my path crossed for the second time with polo people when I stayed with Mary and her fiancé, Dante. This time however the welcome was warm and enthusiastic and I revelled in the positive vibes and good feelings about my trip. What a stark comparison to my arrival at Zavaletta's house, now almost twenty-one months ago.

It felt like a life-time when I stopped to think how far we had come and what we had been through. I could not quite get my head round the fact that in three week's time, I would be riding into New York City. It felt too good to be true.

Mary's stepmom Alyse, a quietly spoken woman with a soft touch, fell in love with Toto the moment she looked into his brown eyes and asked if I would consider selling him when finished with my trip. I took her card and told her I would be in touch. To me there was no doubt that Mise would follow me eventually to Ireland but I did not have the finances nor the facilities back home to accommodate two horses. Well truthfully I did not even have a place for one horse so selling Toto was the logical thing to do. Most important was that he went to a loving home.

My horse education did not stop with the basics I learnt along the way. I also had the 'privilege' to watch an artificial insemination procedure first-hand. Shamrock Farms consists of 640 acres, and along with Thoroughbred and Standardbred breeding they offer racehorse lay-ups, sales preparation and stallion station facilities for collection of stallions and shipment of semen. They foal out 50 to 70 mares per year.

I could not decline an invitation to witness what the farm was really about. So the morning of my departure I got up earlier than usual and, with camera in hand, stood where the mare was waiting in anticipation for the stallion to make his entrance.

"She actually loves all of this," one of the workers told me with a cheeky grin.

I heard a commotion outside and next a fired-up horse came in, excitable and jumpy. He made the most awful noises as he pranced about. Mesmerised, I forgot to take a picture. I would like to spare the reader the rest, but let's just say I found it 'gruesome' to watch as two men 'guided' him to his target. Just for the record – there's no way that poor mare enjoyed *that*!

After breakfast, Christie, who managed Shamrock Farms with her husband, loaded the horses and took us a bit up the road so that I could make it to my next organised destination before darkness fell that evening. She was chatty with an endearing way about her and completely in awe of my pack and how I tied everything together. I kept the conversation light and did not burden her with the epic saga of lopsided saddlepacks throughout my travels.

It was a pleasant day's ride to Monkton as the horses and I went on winding roads past beautifully maintained farms. We needed to cross a few small bridges that would intimidate most horses but Camanchi and Toto followed me without hesitation. I was delighted at how little traffic we encountered, although a lot of people approached when they heard the horses passing their houses.

A few kilometres away from our destination the traffic picked up and a woman came along in her car, gave me a scarf as a present and volunteered to go slowly behind me to force other motorists to reduce their speed. We caused a huge backlog of cars and trucks but I was in great form and could not care less about the hold-up. I waved at everybody that eventually managed to pass and received either open-mouthed stares or similarly friendly responses. When the police came to investigate, my 'helper' told them that I needed all the assistance I could get.

"She's travelling all over the world!" she said to the officer.

I smiled to myself but allowed her to do the talking on my behalf.

Late afternoon we entered a fancy driveway with mature trees on both sides. In the distance I could see a mansion surrounded by acres of land. My hostess, Ms Ellie Shapiro, was a most sophisticated woman, with lots of energy and style. Her vibrant appearance belied her seventy-two years and I was told she still hunted regularly. The horses' stables were cosy and inviting and their bedding so soft, I would have been very happy if she told me I needed to share accommodation with my two equine pals.

My room was equally plush and the evening passed in refined fashion – drinks in the drawing room, her grandson entertaining us on the grand piano and later a friend, with her own quota of energy joined us. They told interesting stories and exchanged harmless gossip. I was also informed that Ms Shapiro's friend was once married to the actor Peter O'Toole.

"He was such a darling," the friend said in a dramatic voice.

Later that evening I lay in bed, warm and comfortable after a long shower. I could not help but think about our days going through Latin America, sleeping in the tent, the discomfort, aching bones in the morning, lack of food, high altitudes and the struggle to find a safe place every night. I felt grateful and happy for where I was at that moment. It was so much easier to appreciate the good when there were uphill battles and headache as well.

Ms Shapiro scolded me the following morning when she saw Camanchi's tail.

"It's so dirty!" she said.

I laughed and told her that a clean sparkling tail was not quite a priority when you travelled the way I did. She would not hear of it and ordered a girl to wash Camanchi's tail with soap and water until it was pure white again. Ms Shapiro handed me an envelope as I mounted Toto. It was a cheque for 500 dollars. I had told her what happened in Middleburg and her belief in me warmed my heart greatly.

The road to Darlington was insanely busy. It is worth mentioning that in 1927, Tschiffely finished his journey prematurely in Washington and not New York City as originally planned, due to ignorant drivers and a near fatal accident on the US roads.

An uninterrupted line of traffic came from both sides giving us no respite from the fumes, metal and wheels that brushed past us. The wind was chilly and I changed jackets. Both horses were jumpy. They must have found the constant flow of cars and trucks nerve-racking.

A woman stopped, did not even greet me and asked in a brisk manner, "What are you doing?"

I was irritable and felt like saying, "I'm riding a buffalo, can't you see for yourself?"

But I chose to remain dignified and gave her only a short answer.

"I'm heading to Bonita farm mam."

My host for that night rang and Bill suggested he come and pick me up. Despite my better judgement I told him I would prefer to go on for another while. Not far from his farm, a pickup truck with trailer pulled up.

"I decided to come and get you," Bill said. "You shouldn't be on this road with horses."

His 'intervention' was most timely. My concentration was waning and I was fed up with the traffic and impatient motorists.

Bonita Farm was spectacular. I noticed how tidy and organised the place was as we drove past many open paddocks, an indoor track and turf course. The stables were equally impressive and perfectly maintained. As a breeding, training and racing facility, it was developed to the highest standards. Bill believed that having a horse was a life-long commitment. To him it was important that it was well looked after, whether it was racing and bringing in money, or not. He summed up the operation at Bonita Farm and said;

I've always had the concept of a one-stop facility. A place where a horseman can board a mare, have a yearling broken, train that yearling to be a race horse, and then retire the horse after his or her racing career is over.

While Toto and Camanchi were unloaded, I walked round the pickup and straight into the top swing-door of the trailer that was open. It knocked me to the ground and I saw stars for a moment. Bill was concerned but thankfully did not give me too much sympathy. Just as well as I might have burst into tears otherwise. I was feeling somewhat fragile – the constant demands of the road and hectic traffic were wearisome. I rubbed my head hard, already feeling a lump growing.

At the house Joan his wife told me to use the closets in my room to hang up my clothes. I said thank you but mentioned that she should have a peek into the bags and see what was inside. The contents of my saddlebags had remained painfully basic. After twenty months on the road I still had only one pair of jeans and one top for special occasions. My faithful flip-flops continued to count as my primary 'going out' shoes.

Bill looked dashing in a sports jacket with his grey-white hair combed back smoothly when we all had gin and tonics in the drawing room later. A few of his sons and their partners joined us.

"There are two things in this world that give me a good feeling," Bill said, "horses eating contentedly at the end of a day and the sound of ice in a glass."

A superb cook, Joan pulled out all the stops for that evening's dinner.

With plenty of wine and Bill quoting from *"If"* by Kipling, it was a most memorable night.

> If you can keep your head when all about you
> Are losing theirs and blaming it on you;
> If you can trust yourself when all men doubt you,
> But make allowance for their doubting too:
> If you can wait and not be tired by waiting,
> Or, being lied about, don't deal in lies,
> Or being hated don't give way to hating,
> And yet don't look too good, nor talk too wise;
>
> If you can dream and not make dreams your master;
> If you can think and not make thoughts your aim,
> If you can meet with Triumph and Disaster
> And treat those two impostors just the same.

I got up early the following morning to watch the procedure at the stables before the horses were taken to the race track for exercise. To me it looked like a military operation. Everybody was focused and rushed around as stables were cleaned out with intense concentration and horses expertly tacked up. I said 'no' nicely when somebody asked if I would like to take a horse around the track.

With saddlebags bursting at the seams from all the food and snacks Joan packed for the road, I continued on to Fair Hill. The traffic remained heavy. At one stage I took up a whole lane and surprisingly only received stares and no honks. Many people stopped to chat. One woman gave me ten dollars although she admitted not knowing what I was doing while another man brought me apples. When we took a lunch break in a field someone else came along and mentioned pesticides that might be harmful to the horses. A large number of people wanted to know if they could trailer me to my next destination. I had to tell each one that I walked a lot with the horses. There was nothing wrong. A man stopped and told me there were many 'rednecks' on the road.

"You have to be very careful," he said.

Not far from Fair Hill we officially crossed the Mason Dixon line, which is part of the borders of Pennsylvania, Delaware and Maryland, surveyed when they were still British colonies. Symbolically the Mason-Dixon is seen as a cultural boundary between the free and slave states, North and South.

While I was travelling through the southern states, people would often remark, "Just wait until you cross that Mason Dixon line. You will see the difference. The people there are not very helpful."

I remembered this piece of 'advice' but was pleased that I did not find it to be the case. I continued to receive assistance and people kept on being warm and welcoming.

In the late afternoon, on the outskirts of Fair Hill, a Mexican man and his young son stopped. Carbon copies of each other, they both wore jeans, red shirts and white cowboy hats. We conversed in Spanish.

"Can I put my son on your horse?" he asked.

I agreed and the next moment they both sat on Toto. I led them down the busy road. The man's feet could not reach the stirrups. We stopped when the little boy began to cry. Later the Mexican man, this time with his wife, looked me up again with an invitation to his house. I would have gone had I not got somewhere else lined up.

Joy, a lady in her early sixties, living in Ohio, made contact with me after she saw my ABC television appearance. In an email she asked if she could come to meet me. I felt honoured that a stranger would want to travel for so many hours (she slept over half-way between Ohio and Maryland) just to do that.

She caught up with me as I was heading for the house of the easy-going Louisa, who kindly accepted me (as well as Joy) into her house at short notice. Joy, a warm, engaging and serene lady, told me tales of many adventurous trail rides she had done over the years. Driving her pickup she travelled with me for two days, taking pictures and keeping us company. It was a special experience to have shared part of my travels with her.

A very perceptive woman, she noticed my relationship with the horses and commented that I was relaxed and confident with them rather than a perfectionist and anxious to control.

"Like Tschiffely," she said, "you have real love and affection for your horses."

On the day of her departure she presented me with a silver ring, a horse's profile engraved on top, and a kind note;

Thank you Marianne for allowing me to participate in a small section of your incredible journey on leap-year day 2004. You are the 'ring-bearer' of all those who yearn for adventure, but for one reason or another cannot completely fulfil their dreams.

Going through the US I was overwhelmed (and I mean this in the best sense of the word) by people, every day and almost every moment. There was a constant flow of interest in what I was doing. I never got the time nor had I the energy to stop for a moment and think. No time to think where I was, how I felt, reflect on my experiences or contemplate the future. This was survival of a different kind. It made my head spin at times. I so badly craved solitude, no traffic, no probing questions, no media presence. But despite the feelings of increasing mental exhaustion, I forced myself to act bright and cheery. I thought I owed it to all the incredible people who showered me with enthusiasm for my journey, who helped and supported me unconditionally. I told myself to stay strong and focused. We were nearly there.

Late January 2003, my friend Dave shared these lines with me. He understood.

Great to hear that you are still bounding on and that public enthusiasm is still alive. I'd say at times you get tired meeting new people, but for them it is only the first time to meet you. You are the newness and inspiration in their life for at least the time you are with them, and most likely for some time after. The finishing post wants you in its sights now and has already starting engraving a sign, reading 'what an achievement'. Keep happy and enthusiastic — after all it is pissing rain here in Dublin!

I met another very interesting woman near a town called Unionville on my first stop in the state of Pennsylvania. Kathleen, who was a contact of Peter in Middleburg, received me with open arms. She struck me as straightforward and genuine with no airs and graces. I liked her instantly.

She invited friends and acquaintances to her home on my first night for a social evening. The next day Kathleen shared snippets of her life with me. A keen traveller, she also looked for adventure and the exotic whenever she could. The day I left her home, she gave me a book by Beryl Markham called *West with the Night*. One paragraph in this book stuck with me. Maybe because it was a sentiment that could be applicable to nature and the physical world we all are living in, maybe because it was a reminder of how I felt about my journey.

We fly, but we have not 'conquered' the air. Nature presides in all her dignity, permitting us the study and the use of such of her forces as we may understand. It is when we presume to intimacy, having been granted only tolerance, that the harsh stick falls across our impudent knuckles and we rub the pain, staring upward, startled by our ignorance.

Visiting with Charlie (Kathleen's partner) the Pennsylvania School of Veterinary Medicine, a teaching hospital and also one of the busiest veterinary clinics in the US for large animals, was fascinating. It is an impressive, expansive facility offering 24-hour emergency service, an orthopaedic and rehabilitation centre, an intensive care unit, nuclear medicine and a research centre for animal reproduction amongst others. The latter group also includes an internationally known large animal behaviourist who specialises in sexual dysfunction in horses and farm animals.

I was impressed with the orthopaedic surgery suite which consisted of a pool and monorail system (exactly what I needed to get my horses into that *lancha* in Potosí) to assist in safe recovery from anaesthesia and transport, to after care.

From Kathleen's house the road was initially calm and tranquil with few cars, but this changed once we entered West Chester and got on to what is called the Pioli Pike. Despite the manic traffic, two men stopped to chat. One in particular was quite animated and seemed amazed that I would actually talk to them.

"This is incredible," he said, shaking his head. "You are doing this and all that our girlfriends are interested in is going to the salon and having their nails done."

He gave me fifteen dollars that he suggested I use to buy water for the horses. He shook my hand and congratulated me on coming this far. Half an hour later he pulled up again.

"I know everybody in town," he said as he handed me his business card. "If you need anything between here and New York City, just call me. I mean absolutely anything."

I could not help but enjoy his good energy and enthusiasm. His kind of character was what made this journey worthwhile. No agenda or bullshit. Just real good vibes and goodwill.

While on the topic of good energy, it is most appropriate to mention my next stop later that day. Sallie and Saunders run a successful therapeutic riding centre called Thorncroft. They invited me to stay, 'for as long as you wish', to use Sallie's words, via a message they sent to my website. I relished the good atmosphere. Saunders, who is twenty years older than Sallie, looked like a modern-day Moses with his long white hair and grey beard. He had the serenity you would expect from a spiritual icon and just being in the same room as him had a calming effect. Sallie was sweet, bubbly and just her own person. I loved my stay with them in their wooden-floored house full of character and memorabilia. If New York was not calling I might still be there.

On Sally and Saunders' recommendation, I allowed them to trailer us around the busiest parts of the road going to New Hope. With heavy fog reducing visibility to only a couple of metres it would have been too dangerous to do it on horseback. It was a very pretty ride though once I got into the saddle again. I enjoyed being out and about surrounded by low-hanging mist and atmospheric mountains.

Tiffany (who was a friend of Kathleen's), a pleasant and assertive woman, caught up with us before we were due to cross a very busy, long bridge. Two policemen were already waiting to escort us across. I had to tighten the pack on Toto and asked one of them to hold Camanchi. He appeared shocked at my request and nervously held the rope, standing a safe distance away.

A long winding road surrounded by winter trees and yellow, brown and orange leaves on the ground, led to the picturesque farm of Tifanny and Jim. In the distance I could see the stone cottage sitting mystically on acres of spectacular natural scenery. They were a warm, friendly couple, and over dinner at a cosy restaurant that evening, they told me of their regular visits to Ireland where they own a racehorse.

My last official day's ride, given the traffic, was going to be to the house of Mrs Bunny Murdock who lives in New Jersey, about 50 kilometres from New York City. I stayed a week with Mrs Murdock in her tastefully decorated home. It was the perfect place to plan my entry into New York.

She was a strong and opinionated character with a dry, wicked sense of humour. I was slightly scared of her but she also made me laugh often with her sarcastic, pin-sharp anecdotes. Despite being in remission from throat cancer, every morning she stepped into the kitchen, beautifully turned out, made-up and a pretty scarf around her head.

Mrs Murdock was very good to me. She must have been mortified at my lack of clothes and discreetly handed me a few items, amongst them a snug winter coat. I was also lucky to have had the use of her car although I found driving on the US motorways more terrifying than being on horseback. One day she gave me directions to her local beauty salon. Great was my surprise when on arrival I was informed that it was arranged for me to have a hair cut, facial and manicure, courtesy of Bunny.

She was well-known in the area. Her deceased husband was senior vice-president at Citibank in New York when he retired, and then became Master of the Essex Fox Hounds in New Jersey. Bunny herself was an avid steeplechase supporter and had several horses in training with Burly Cocks. The best was a horse named Zaccio – Champion Steeplechaser in the United States for several years.

While at Mrs Murdock's, I received a last email from Dave. I had a feeling of melancholia while reading it. The thought of finishing in a few day's time was bittersweet.

I'm sure you are counting the days now and often cast your mind back to the days in the mountains in Bolivia... how far you have come on your wonderful adventure. You managed to stay focused, live in the present and accept change, hardship, and moments of sheer pleasure as part of the natural cycle of your daily life. Not many in this life can claim that.

It was also during this time that I had to say goodbye to Camanchi. His owners, Todd and Maria, had offered to bring Mise (who was already out of quarantine in Florida) up to New Jersey. Mise had started this trek with me and she simply had to be there at the end. Camanchi was outstanding and I regretted that he could not be part of our last day.

It was a long drive for Todd and Maria but they saw it as one big adventure.

Arriving late into the night having spent about eighteen hours on the road, Mrs Murdock kindly offered them a bed.

With great sadness I helped them to load Camanchi into the trailer the following morning. I was so sorry to see him go. He was the perfect companion – consistent, sensitive and funny. Todd and Maria refused to take money for petrol and I had to hide a token one hundred dollar bill in their pickup.

A couple of days later, Andy arrived. A documentary producer from London, he had expressed interest in getting footage of myself and Mise to use as part of a programme about the Criollo horse, which was to be aired later that year on the History Channel. The day was delightfully pleasant. Not only did we have fantastic weather with clear blue skies, but I found Andy a joy to work with as well. He was laid-back and unobtrusive, making suggestions for shots and asking questions in an interested and professional manner. Not once did I feel uncomfortable under the glare of his camera.

I was relaxed in the knowledge that everything was in place for our last day's ride, less than a week away. It was all due to a special South African woman called Madelyn, living in the Big Apple and who unwittingly became a part of this story. Sharing the same surname and having heard from her boyfriend about my ABC appearance, she decided to make contact. Our link became a crucial one. Madelyn was a woman who got things done. Not only did she manage to get permission for me to enter NY City with two horses assisted by police escort, she also sorted free stabling (not an easy feat) and managed to persuade the organisers of the St. Patrick's Day Parade (with the help of Albert Reynolds, former PM in Ireland) to let me participate. She did all of this with quiet and efficient grace. Her help took a huge weight off my shoulders. It meant I could concentrate on the road and enjoy the last few weeks of riding while she worked tirelessly behind the scenes.

The horses needed their final set of shoes. It felt incredible to think that the agony and headache of finding expert farriers and quality shoes were over. A significant part of the journey, it always caused worry and anxiety. The well-known 'no foot, no horse', expression was so true. I felt blessed to have managed throughout my trip. Sometimes it was touch and go. Too many 'cowboy farriers' tried to chance their arm, hoping that a *gringa* would not know any better. But with time I did and I did not hesitate to speak up if I thought we were heading for disaster. Shoeing a horse is an art, a talent that not everyone that possesses a clincher, hammer and rasp, necessarily has. After twenty-one months on the road I never became confident enough to attempt this difficult job, especially if one was to do it well. A skilful farrier just makes it *look* easy. Constantly looking for the perfect shoeing solution during my journey, I was open to all suggestions.

While I was in Central America, a company in the UK sent vibrantly coloured yellow and green plastic shoes which I believed could minimise the impact on the horses' feet and joints when we had to go on tarmac. Unfortunately I never found out how well they worked as I could not find a farrier that had experience putting on this type of shoe. In Mexico, I visited a company that sold a product called Superfast which works as follows:

1. Prepare the hoof by rasping off all the uneven edges
2. Apply a white paste from a large syringe-like tube all over the hoof
3. Keeping the hoof still in the air, use a hair-dryer to set the paste
4. Once dry, rasp again and *voila*! the horse is wearing shoes with no nails

When I first heard about this product I thought it sounded perfect and the solution to my problems. However, I was advised that it was not ideal for going on tarmac but used much more successfully in trail rides. Also, I wondered where I would fit the hairdryer in.

In January I received a message on my website from Matthew Gillis, President of the Indiana Farrier's Association. He generously offered free shoeing by any of their members (the American Farriers Association) for the remainder of my journey. I took up this offer when in Virginia and Pennsylvania. Now in New Jersey, a farrier in the area was called out again, two days before my departure from Mrs Murdock's.

Andy continued to film this last ritual of hammers on nails, a cloud of smoke accompanied by sizzling sounds, and the smell of burnt hoof when the hot shoe was put on Mise. I was told it did not hurt. I hung around, trying to be useful by handing tools to the farrier but probably making more of a nuisance of myself than anything else. Unfortunately nobody alerted me to the black streaks of dirt under my nose when I spoke into the camera.

15 March 2004. Journey's end.

Mrs Murdock arranged with Lisa, her right-hand woman at the stables, to transport us into New York City. As we got ready, Lisa asked why I kept on shaking my head and smiling to myself. I told her I felt a bit strange. I could not quite believe that this was it. This was our last day. This journey was over.

The day was bright and sunny and even though it was winter we were blessed with wide open blue skies. A perfect day to celebrate the final moments of an imperfect journey, flawed with many hardships, tears and pain but enriched beyond my wildest expectations by so many extraordinary experiences and encounters. I felt so lucky. I could not wait to see the familiar faces of friends from Ireland, sharing in my last special day.

Due to the volume of traffic I did not get permission to ride across the George Washington Bridge, so after the 30 mile journey into the city, Lisa dropped us off not too far from Central Park. Soon after, I was met by my escorts, Captain Chris Acerbo and Officer John O'Reilly, both of them attached to the mounted patrol unit of the New York Police Department. They were cheery, good-humoured and friendly and obviously delighted that they were the 'chosen ones'.

On our way to Central Park, Officer John gave a live commentary on sights that we passed, pointing out John Lennon and Yoko Ono's one-time love nest and the famous café used in the popular US sitcom, *Seinfeld*. Amidst the cyclists, strollers and joggers, we made our way through Central Park. I was wearing my Saltanian red Argentine poncho, a cowboy hat (courtesy of Peter in Middleburg) and brand new half-chaps. The vibes were good. I was riding Toto and Mise was carrying the pack. I chose to do it this way having less faith in Toto, and knowing I would be able to control the riding horse better should they become too nervous with the city noises and chaos. For old time's sake, Mise, in typical female fashion trying to have the last word, had one more spook reaction when the pack slid to the side. My escorts watched wide-eyed while I calmed her down with little fuss and a 'been there, done that' attitude.

"You don't want to know," I said laughing to the two men, once everything was under control again. "I could do this with closed eyes by now."

As we trotted slowly through the park, I decided to ring my mom in South Africa but not finding her home, left a message saying how I wished she could have been there too. The only dark cloud on the day – my parents and brothers could not be there. (Only later did I find out that problems with visas prevented this).

Three quarters way through the park we were met by broadly smiling and excited friends from Ireland. Turlough, Deirdre, Sean and Cathal were in great spirits, soaking up the electric atmosphere. I was reluctant when Turlough suggested I got off to meet a lady that was keen to say hello to me.

"I am not done yet," I said. "We still have to go down Fifth Avenue."

I got off however when he told me she had been waiting since early that morning just to catch me. Walking up a little lane surrounded by trees, I spotted a woman in a wheelchair. Turlough indicated it was not her but the woman lying on a bench under a large coat, clutching a bottle of wine.

"Surely we won't be able to have a conversation," I whispered. "She looks pissed."

He urged me on nevertheless and before I knew what was happening, the woman jumped up and ran towards me. It was my mom! Our jubilant shrieks and laughter echoed through the park while we hugged and danced around. Curious onlookers smiled warmly at the joyous commotion.

Chris, John and I continued with the horses through the last bit of the park and then down towards Time Square. Without warning, two people jumped out in front of us. It was my friend Dave, author of all those inspirational emails, and his girlfriend Jennifer. A complete surprise. The day was getting better and better. Also part of the welcoming group was Mary (David's sister) and her two friends Noreen and Aileen. None of us could stop grinning, beaming and laughing.

Andy was also there, capturing the ride on his video camera as we trotted through concrete jungle, traffic and fire brigade sirens. In stark contrast to the perils of the jungle, high mountains and open grasslands that had become synonymous with our travels, I marvelled at how well the horses were behaving. Andy asked how I felt. This is what I said;

> I don't really know what to feel and what to think. I'm exhilarated, I'm happy, I'm a little bit nervous. Great excitement but I'm sad too that my journey has come to an end. Mise is here with me, my beloved Criollo. She has been extraordinary. She kept going no matter what happened. This is the end.

Having done a loop coming back up Ninth Avenue, the final stop was Central Park again. Surrounded by curious bystanders, tourists taking pictures but most importantly, dear friends and my mom, added to a truly memorable moment. I said a silent heartfelt thank-you to every single person who played a part in getting us there. I thanked Camanchi for his loyal companionship but felt special gratitude and a wave of sudden sadness when I thought of Tusa and Tu Fein. The presence of those horses, friends, and family who could not physically share in the moment was nevertheless tangible in spirit. It was as if Jo was there too, floating through the winter trees, weightless and devoid of any burden. Her face was happy.

Champagne was popped and glasses were raised. Sitting on Toto, sipping bubbly and looking at the faces in front of me, I could not have been happier. I leaned over to kiss Mise who stood serene, almost as conscious of the significance of the moment. Tears burned behind my eyes. We made it. We were safe.

Two days later, in blizzard and snow, I participated in the St. Patrick's Day Parade. I so much looked forward to it and could hardly sleep the night before. I heard there would be marching bands, various Irish societies, police, firefighters, and scores of others (including myself!) to make up the near 200,000 marchers who will follow the course from St. Patrick's Cathedral up Fifth Avenue to 86th Street. Hundreds of thousands of spectators were expected to line the sidewalks, watching and cheering. To me it was such an honour to be part of something so important.

It was arranged that I would ride with an equestrian group that kept their horses stabled in the city. Scrutinising me up and down when I arrived with two mounted patrol men, the woman at reception turned up her nose.

"Are you riding in *that?*" she asked, pointing at the attire that I wore a couple of days before. "All our riders are in uniform," she said. "Make sure you don't ride too close to them."

I declined to reply to a remark dripping with snobbery.

One of the policeman stepped in.

"We would be honoured if you rode between us," he said warmly.

I gave him a grateful look.

The man leading the equestrian group was hyper. On our way to the pre-arranged spot where we would be waiting in a side-lane before getting the green light to join the parade, he roared and shouted at passing cars, creating tension and making everybody nervous.

A woman in her early sixties riding next to me sipped constantly from a little flask she kept in her jacket. She also offered me a few gulps, the strong liqueur warming up my chilly bones immediately. Soon I noticed that she began to sit rather unevenly on her horse, drooping over to the one side. I struggled to keep a straight face, hoping for her sake she would not make a spectacle of herself during the parade.

Finally, joining the numerous brass bands and other groups, we waved and smiled at the crowds on the side who huddled together trying to find warmth in the freezing weather. Behind us were a number of 'pooper scoopers', men and women dragging large plastic trolleys and with plastic shovels in hand, making sure the city remained manure-free. The 'leader' of our group reprimanded me when I overtook him by accident (he kept on going to the side to allow people to touch his horse, slowing everybody down).

"Get back," he hissed. "I am leading this."

I was tempted to point out to him that he was far from leading anything, there were thousands of other participants in front of us, but I bit my tongue. Shortly after, I was in the dog house again when spotting my mom and Turlough in the crowd, I steered Mise over to where they were, going in front of another rider in the process. It was nothing major but judging by his sour face and heavy sighs you would have thought I had climbed over him. This time I could not keep quiet.

"Chill out," I said. "This is supposed to be fun."

For a moment I had the desire to use my crop and give his horse a good whack on the bum, giving the man really something to get uptight about.

But I soon forgot about the grumpy men and simply enjoyed the vibrant atmosphere with Mise. This was a once in a lifetime moment and I would not allow anybody to spoil it for me.

A bachelor's apartment in Greenwich Village was my home for two weeks, courtesy of Robert Hunker. During a visit to South Africa when he met my mom, he kindly offered his pad for as long as I wished. I was on my own yet again, still on a high from all the good energy of the past week, but also conscious that I needed to get practical and sort out a few things.

Captain Chris, the ultimate host for the duration of my stay in the city, had indicated that the mounted patrol unit might be interested in purchasing Toto, offering double what I had paid. I remembered Alyse who also mentioned that she would love to buy Toto at the end of my trip. From our conversations I knew she could pay the amount that I did – 1500 dollars. Although I saw first-hand how well horses were treated at the mounted patrol unit, I envisaged a different sort of life for Toto. It was important to me that he had space and fields to roam in and that he was not cooped up in a stable for long periods. For some reason I also wanted his owner to be female. Toto was a sensitive soul and I believed he needed a soft and understanding touch. I was convinced he would not cope in a pressurised environment.

Alyse and Jo her husband, travelled the ten-hour journey from Maryland to pick up Toto in New York. It was organised that Mise would travel with them, as far as Pennsylvania, where she would be dropped off to reside with Tiffany and Jim until she could be flown to Ireland. Once again, all the goodwill and offers of help had me gobsmacked.

Two months after I had left New York, it was time for Mise to come home. Joy and her husband Don suggested travelling all the way from Ohio to Pennsylvania (despite Don being diagnosed with cancer a few days before) to pick up Mise, and then drop her off in Chicago from where she would be flown. All in all, they covered more than 3,000 kilometres. I do not know too many who would have been prepared to do the same. It was simply a true testament to Joy and Don's extraordinary generous spirits.

I can now say that nothing about my journey really worked out as I had anticipated. But maybe, looking back, that was part of the appeal and excitement it held as each day brought with it many wonderful surprises.

What made my journey unique for me was how I, a novice rider and two horses, eventually managed to travel from Argentina, arriving almost two years later in New York with saddlebags full of mostly feel-good stories and adventures to tell.

My horses played the most important part in travelling through these countries but there were boats too, planes and also the occasional truck when there was a major problem, lunatic traffic, a particularly risky area I was strongly advised to avoid, or a horse that was not well. Whichever way we travelled, each proved to be as important and crucial as the other. Collectively, they made my journey what it was. I do not think

I would have wanted to change a thing. Nancy in Roxboro summed it up. She said I would always draw from every experience along the way, and that every action I took, every decision I made, required problem solving skills, lateral thinking and the ability to figure out what to do.

Disappointingly, I did not get to travel through all the countries I intended to but it was not for lack of trying. Having had to rely on my judgement constantly, I made choices that I believed were best, first and foremost for my horses, and then for me. Other times, those choices were made *for* me and I had no power to change that. In the beginning it was so important to say, 'I've done a thousand miles' or 'last week I travelled from here to there'. But as the journey progressed, that became more and more irrelevant. I stopped counting distances. It became much more personal than that.

I got the opportunity to experience parts of the world unknown to me, in an exceptional and interesting fashion. Not to mention the slow pace of it all. Having the opportunity to share it with so many wonderful people on the way made it that extra bit special. To share it with my faithful horses made it a privilege.

The note below from Marilyn, my good friend in Georgia, gave me the hope that my journey was indeed worthwhile. I know that my travels offered *me* so much, giving me abundant experiences and remarkable moments beyond my wildest dreams. They made me grateful for every day that I have, to live and breathe this world. Only when we see how others live and what they have to cope with do we truly appreciate what we have. Only then do we fully understand that we are so fortunate. I came to believe that I was indeed a lucky girl. To know that others gained too for having been part of my journey and to have known me is something that warmed my heart tremendously.

Carpe Diem.

Marianne, while you were on your journey you touched and made such a strong impression on so many lives. I hope I can word this right... Even though part of your journey's aim was to create awareness for therapeutic riding for disabled people in Ireland, you reached out to so many disabled individuals on your journey... not disabled mentally or physically, but emotionally. Whether it was through troubles of daily living, life, family, financial problems or depression. You caused people to become more aware of the true meaning of life, giving, sharing, caring, being thoughtful and considerate, and you helped people to feel better about themselves without even being aware that you were doing that!

Letting go of a book one has written is the hardest thing in the world. It is truly a leap of faith and there is no guarantee of its success. It is a complete gamble. The uncertainty of who might read it, but also more importantly who might like it, can be mental agony. But to me, the ultimate satisfaction lies not in who praises my book, but knowing I managed to do it and that somebody could benefit from reading it. Writing about a journey that meant so much to me has been an extremely gratifying pursuit.

I cannot help but be amazed by how things have a way of working out. Often, our dreams and aspirations fall perfectly into place without our pushing too hard. It's as if a force greater than ourselves takes over and completes the puzzle, expertly and with little effort. It can be mind boggling yet also incredibly reassuring.

Henry David Thoreau said;

> If you have built castles in the air, your work need not be lost, that is
> where they should be. Now put foundations under them.

I knew in my heart that my idea of creating awareness for therapeutic riding in Ireland would happen in the right way. It did, and I am pleased no end to have become involved with Tina Schmill, founder of Pegasus, a small riding centre for adults and children with disability near Sligo. To know that my help makes a difference is a wonderful feeling. To share my vision and energy with someone on the same wavelength, who dreams big and who is so totally committed, is more than I ever expected.

Tina and I both know what needs to be done and being positive helps us not to forget the big picture and our ultimate aim. We are both aware of all the hard work that is still required, the joys and agonies of having to raise funds, begging and hoping and getting others excited about our plans... But we believe it will happen. There have been many magical coincidences, surprising happenings and moments of fate to convince us that we are on the right track.

The ethical treatment of animals is something very close to my heart. Although not a devoted vegetarian and occasionally eating meat, I do believe that all creatures should be treated with dignity and compassion, even those that are reared to be slaughtered.

Whenever I read or hear about cruelty towards animals, I am enraged. What does it say about an individual or society when helpless animals are abused, mistreated and tortured? What does it say about us that we do not speak out, show our rage and demand change, instead of just turning a blind eye, thinking there is nothing that can be done?

I believe the answer lies in education. Each of us has a responsibility to educate, inform and teach by example, those who do not know any better. I do believe it is our moral obligation. By teaching, especially children, compassion and to have a caring attitude to all living things, we are making this world a better place. Moreover, it is my belief that children who develop this empathy are less likely to become involved in violence and other anti-social behaviour when outside the house. Teaching a child to treat a pet or animal with respect and humanity, will without doubt have a positive effect on other parts of his or her life.

A practice I have recently become interested in is the idea of riding a horse with a bitless bridle. I heard about Dr Robert Cook, a veterinarian with many publications in both scientific journals and horsemen's journals, who has advocated the advantages of riding a horse without a bit.

Dr. Cook believes that the work he has done since 1997 to investigate the bit method of communication in the horse and to validate the bitless bridle, is now doing more for the welfare of both horse and rider than anything he has done previously. It is helping horsemen in all disciplines of equitation to achieve improved performance.

The horse's mouth is one of the most sensitive parts of its anatomy. According to Dr Cook, the application of pressure to a steel rod inserted in this cavity inflicts unnecessary pain and frightens a horse. Fear initiates a flight or fight response (bolting or countless forms of resistance). In addition, putting a bit in the mouth of a horse that is about to run is akin to putting a muzzle on a horse that is about to eat. A bit is contraindicated, counterproductive and, in the wrong hands, potentially cruel. His research has shown that the bit is responsible for over a hundred behavioural problems.

The bitless bridle designed by Dr Cook provides a method of communication that is safer, more humane, and more effective than the bit. It does not depend on the application of pain or the threat of pain. The bitless bridle provides the rider with effective communication through the ability to apply gentle and painless pressure to either the whole of the head (slowing and stopping) or half the head (steering).

And where the head goes, the horse follows.

USEFUL WEBSITES

tatachallenge.com	Stories and pictures from my journey
pegasuscentre.org	The first theraputic riding school in Ireland
thorncroft.org	A theraputic riding haven in Pennsylvania
highhopestr.org	High Hopes therapeutic riding centre in Connecticut
lazcar.com	Professional livestock and horse shipping in Florida
watersongwoods.com	Vacation cabin getaways in the Hocking Hills of Logan, Ohio
redeagleranch.com	A full-featured polo and equestrian sports facility in Maryland
millercountyliberal.com	Newspaper of Terry Toole in Colquitt, Georgia
studiodj.net	True to life portraits of pets, still lifes and more
ecolodgecarazo.com	An eco lodge and tropical garden near Diriamba, Nicaragua
hotelbalcones.com	The best hotel in León, Nicaragua
cayara.com.bo/cayaranet	Information on Hacienda Cayara near Potosí, Bolivia
dspca.ie	The Dublin Society for the Prevention of Cruelty to Animals
farmsanctuary.org	20 years of rescue, education and advocacy for farm animals
paws.org	Care for injured or orphaned wildlife and homeless dogs & cats
bitlessbridle.com	Information on the benefits of the bitless bridle
horsemanship.com.au	Same as above
worldanimal.net/fur-index.html	A worthy anti-fur information and campaign site
stopforcefeeding.com	Foie gras, the French term for 'fatty liver', is the product of extreme animal cruelty. It is the swollen, diseased liver of ducks and geese that are force-fed just up until the point of death before being slaughtered. Birds suffer tremendously, both during and after the force-feeding process (which involves a metal pipe being thrust down their throats), as their physical condition rapidly deteriorates. In just a few weeks, their livers swell up to ten times their normal size, and the birds can scarcely stand, walk, or even breathe. At this point, they are slaughtered, and their (sick) livers are peddled as a 'gourmet' delicacy. I would like to urge all socially-minded people to whom it matters where their food comes from, to object when they see this product on the menus of the restaurants they frequent. Ideally, I would like restauranteurs and chefs to come to the compassionate understanding that to produce good ethical food, an animal need not have been subjected to prolonged torture, and that they would review serving this product.

alfalfa	herb widely cultivated as a pasture and hay crop
alforjas	saddlebags
alojamiento	basic room to rent in Latin America, no breakfast included
alpaca	related to the llama and having fine, long wool
altiplano	high plain, mostly in Bolivia
amigo	friend
angelito	little angel
apache	indigenous inhabitants of North America, who speak an Apachean language
armadillo	small armoured desert animal
avena	A genus of grasses, including the common oat
aymara	Indian tribe and frequently used Andean language
boliviano	local currency in Bolivia
bombachas	thick, wide cotton trousers
bombilla	thin tube that is used to suck the maté
caballos	horses
camioneta	pickup truck
campo	the country-side
catalina	dry, sweet bread
cebada	hay for cattle or horses
cerquita	close-by
cerveza	beer
chica	girl
chicha	an alcoholic drink made from maize
chirimoya	heart-shaped, edible fruit with green skin and white aromatic flesh
coca	plant from which cocaine is derived
corral	an enclosure for confining livestock
criollo	native horses originally from the Argentine pampas
demasiado	too much
dulce de leche	caramelised milk paste
empanada	a pastry pocket filled with a spicy or sweet filling
entiendo	understand
estancia	estate, usually quite large
finca	farm
frijole	black beans
garrapata	tick
gaucho	a cowboy or horseman

gringo	used as a disparaging term for a foreigner in Latin America, especially a North American or European white person
hacienda	farm
llama	a domesticated South American mammal related to the camel
loco	crazy
locro	a hot, thick soup based on maize, pumpkin and pigs' trotters
machete	cleaver-like tool that looks like a very large knife
mas o menos	more or less
mate	a herbal tea which is drunk from a gourd and through a metal straw
moto	motorbike
no hay	there is none
nunca	never
pampas	fertile South American lowlands (from Quechua, meaning 'plain')
pechos	breasts
pensión	boarding house
perro	dog
piquetero	an unemployed person in Argentina, who blocks roads to demand subsidies for the jobless
porteños	local inhabitants of Buenos Aires
puente	bridge
quechua	the Quechuan language of the Inca empire, widely spoken throughout the Andes highlands
solita	alone
sombrero	hat
suerte	good luck
tortilla	a kind of unleavened bread, generally made from corn and lime water
una amazona	a horsewoman
vamos	let's go

Impossible is just a big word thrown around by small men who find it easier to live in the world they've been given than to explore the power they have to change it.
Impossible is not a fact. It's an opinion.
Impossible is not a declaration. It's a dare.
Impossible is potential. Impossible is temporary.
Impossible is nothing.

ADIDAS advertisement in NY city